Russian
Culture
at the
Crossroads

(

Russian Culture at the Crossroads

*Paradoxes
of Postcommunist
Consciousness*

EDITED BY
DMITRI N. SHALIN

University of Nevada–Las Vegas

WestviewPress
A Division of HarperCollinsPublishers

Published in 1996 in the United States of America by Westview Press, Inc., 5500 Central Avenue, Boulder, Colorado 80301-2877, and in the United Kingdom by Westview Press, 12 Hid's Copse Road, Cumnor Hill, Oxford OX2 9JJ

Library of Congress Cataloging-in-Publication Data
Russian culture at the crossroads : paradoxes of postcommunist
    consciousness / edited by Dmitiri N. Shalin
        p. cm.
    Includes bibliographical references and index.
    ISBN 0-8133-2713-X. — ISBN 0-8133-2714-8 (pbk.)
    1. Russia (Federation)—Civilization—20th century.   2. Post-
    communism—Russia (Federation)   I. Shalin, Dmitri N.
DK510.762.R87   1996
306'.0947—dc20
                                                        95-46271
                                                        CIP

The paper used in this publication meets the requirements of the American National Standard for Permanence of Paper for Printed Library Materials Z39.48-1984.

10   9   8   7   6   5   4   3   2   1

To My
Russian Colleagues
and Friends

Contents

Acknowledgments

A few words about those who helped make this study possible are in order here. I wish to thank the Harvard University Russian Research Center for a research fellowship that allowed me to spend my 1989–90 sabbatical year at the Center and afforded many a fruitful encounter with its members, whose advice and friendly criticism helped get this project off the ground. Special thanks are extended to the MacArthur Foundation for a grant that made the Russian participants' visit to the United States possible. We owe a debt of gratitude to the International Research and Exchanges Board, the George Soros Foundation, the Nevada Humanities Committee, the UNLV Foundation, UNLV College of Business and Administration, and the Jewish Federation of Las Vegas, which provided partial support for the Nevada Conference on Soviet Culture. Several Las Vegas businesses—the Tropicana Hotel, the Vista Group, Nevada Gaming, Inc., Aztec Gas and Oil, United Gaming, Inc., and First Interstate Bank—pitched in with local accommodations for conference participants. The contribution of Lonnie Hammargren, who graciously greeted the conference participants at his home, is also gratefully acknowledged. The help from the business community for a strictly academic enterprise is highly appreciated, particularly at a time when federal funding sources for such international projects have dwindled.

Dr. Yuri Levada, director of the National Center for Public Opinion Research in Russia, and Dr. Vladimir Yadov, director of the Russian Academy of Sciences Institute of Sociology, helped facilitate the project on the Russian side and accommodated American participants visiting Russia. I thank Vladimir Magun, Daniil Dondurei, Zara Abdullaeva, Alexander Etkind, and Igor Kon, who helped me personally to navigate through the Russian bureaucracy and engaged me in numerous conversations that gave the project its present shape.

Finally, I wish to thank my wife, Dr. Janet S. Belcove-Shalin, for selflessly aiding in the work and putting up with the temporary insanity that several years of writing proposals, organizing conferences, translating Russian texts, and editing the manuscript in its numerous incarnations might have induced in her husband. I owe her a debt that could never be repaid in any coin.

Dmitri N. Shalin

Introduction: Continuity and Change in Russian Culture

DMITRI N. SHALIN

This project on Russian culture goes back to the spring of 1990, when several American and Russian scholars met at the Russian Research Center at Harvard University and decided to join forces in a study of the changes sweeping the Soviet Union. From the start, the participants agreed that they would not try to chase fast breaking news from Russia—a hopeless task, given the pace of recent changes—but rather would focus on the continuity and change in Russian culture, on the long-term social forces that compel the Russian people to reexamine their values and reevaluate old ways.

We divided the labor so that each participant could explore a single cultural domain—religious, artistic, intellectual, political, economic, and so on. The borders demarcating each domain are not sharp, and the map of Russian culture we have drawn is admittedly arbitrary; but our survey is comprehensive enough to give the reader some insight into Russian culture, the key junctures in its historical development, and the momentous transformations it has been undergoing in recent years.

Our interdisciplinary project drew on the resources of both the humanities and the social sciences, which allowed for a cross-pollination of ideas. Our team of authors included historians, philosophers, psychologists, sociologists, political scientists, and literary and film critics. The participants used a wide range of methods to explore their subjects, including personal interviews, analysis of Soviet literature, film, and fine arts, and opinion surveys. We proceeded on the assumptions that humanists and social scientists can learn much from each other, that sociological surveys illuminate relationships crying out for fresh interpretations, and that humanistic insights open new vistas inviting further sociological probing.

Scholars working on this project met in Las Vegas, Nevada, on November 19–20, 1992, for the Nevada Conference on Soviet Culture. Here, intellectuals raised in vastly different cultures reflected on their biases, enriched each other's perspectives, and set up a framework for future collaboration. We plan to follow up this study with three more conferences and volumes, which will explore in greater depth the artistic, political, and economic realms in Russian culture. Meanwhile, we offer the first results of our joint efforts to our colleagues, students, and the general public with an interest in Russia's past, present, and future.

The remainder of this introductory chapter focuses on several sticky methodological issues and substantive difficulties facing students of culture in general and Russian culture in particular. This is not an attempt to settle the problems vexing cultural studies but rather an effort to spell out assumptions undergirding our collective undertaking.

* * *

The vast literature on Russia has numerous references to culture. Each time this term is invoked, it acquires a somewhat different meaning, depending on whether the researcher is dealing with Russian culture, Bolshevik culture, Soviet culture, post-Soviet culture, and so on.[1] In the broadest sense, the term refers to an enduring configuration of thoughts, actions, and institutions that distinguishes people inhabiting a given sociohistorical niche. Yet, there is always some ambiguity involved in the rhetoric of culture as to how enduring the pattern in question is, how much local diversity it allows, and how far a given variation has to stray from the main theme before it becomes a cultural theme in its own right. There is also a nagging concern that the values and beliefs people express verbally do not always match the preferences and commitments they reveal in their conduct. Finally, it is not altogether clear whether high culture—literature, theology, political critique, philosophical treatises, and other highly stylized forms of public discourse—give us a reliable insight into the behaviors and lifestyles of society at large, especially when it comes to groups that do not consume high culture and are more attuned to popular culture.

In its extreme form, cultural determinism encourages one to string vastly diverse social facts on a single conceptual cord and to look for a cultural continuity impervious to historical change. Thus, Nikolai Berdiaev discerns in Russian history "spiritual ailments that could not be cured by any external social reforms and revolutions," personality traits that "belong to the metaphysical character of the Russian people and manifest themselves in the Russian revolution." The grotesque characters that Nikolai Gogol pictured in his famous stories, Berdiaev is convinced, "are not phenomena generated by the old regime, by certain social and political causes; quite to the contrary—[these characters] have informed the regime's political and social forms, determined all that was bad in this regime."[2]

Where Berdiaev sees a seamless line between pre- and postrevolutionary Russia, Aleksandr Solzhenitsyn envisions a dramatic break: "[T]he transition from pre-October Russia to the USSR is no continuation but a deadly break of the spinal cord that nearly resulted in the nation's death. Soviet history does not continue the Russian evolution but perverts the latter, pushing the country in a new, unnatural direction inimical to the nation's past. . . . The terms 'Russian' and 'Soviet,' 'Russia' and 'the USSR,' are neither interchangeable nor compatible—these are polar notions which completely exclude one another."[3]

These extreme views have one thing in common—a cultural determinism that hampers inquiry and forestalls efforts to understand how the interplay between tradition and structural transformation has been shaping Russian culture. Such an overdetermined view often results in attempts to decipher an immutable code enciphered into the national character and informing the nation's past, present, and future. Witness the research tradition that sought to articulate a "modal personality," "attitude set," "national character," and other transhistorical cultural formations designed to explain every turn in a particular nation's history.[4]

The same logic fueled the debate about Russia's relationship to the West and the East. Recall the longstanding dispute between Slavophiles and Westernizers, which has yet failed to settle the question of whether Russian culture belongs to the European civilization or embodies Byzantine values. The same issues dominated Eurasionist theories about the link between the Russians and people populating Far Eastern and Central Asian regions. This controversy was echoed in Bolshevik writings and is evident in Anatoly Lunacharsky's contention that "we, communists, even back then when we were called social democrats, to say nothing of our predecessors like Nikolai Chernyshevsky and his spiritual brethren, always were Westernizers . . . you've got to understand that our communism is an offspring of the West."[5] This interminable discourse on whether Russia is the westernmost frontier of Asian civilization or the easternmost flank of Occidental culture glosses over the complexities of lived history and seems particularly dated now, when the excommunists have forged an alliance with ultranationalists in post-Soviet Russia.

Let us not forget, however, that some Russian thinkers have spurned sweeping generalizations about their country's cultural patterns. As Fyodor Dostoevsky put it, "All our Slavophilism and Westernism is but one great confusion, albeit a necessary one."[6] "Should we blame our national character?" queried Nikolai Dobrolyubov. "This invocation hardly resolves the issue, it only pushes it further back: How did our national character, passive and weak as it is, evolve? We are simply forced to move the deliberation from the present onto a historical plane."[7] There is ample evidence, also, that Russian thinkers could rise above their partisan divisions, show respect for their opponents, and affirm their common intellectual grounds. Thus, when Timofei Granovsky, an avowed Westernizer, delivered his series of public lectures on Europe and the Middle Ages in 1844, the occasion was celebrated by both Slavophiles and Westernizers, while *Moskvitianin*, a Slavophile publication, gave this paean to Granovsky:

> The main feature of Granovsky's public lectures is his extraordinary humanism, a sympathy for everything that is alive, thriving, and poetic, a sympathy that is ever ready to respond; a love that knows no boundaries, a love for whatever is nascent, and fledgling, as well for everything passing and dying, which he buries with tears in his eyes. Not a word of hatred toward a historical event escaped his lips; passing the tombs, he would peek inside but never dishonor the deceased. . . . Love and sympathy for the vanquished is the highest victory.[8]

The search for the Russianness supposedly residing in all Russians is bound to lead us astray. For every Vissarion Belinsky there will be a Nikolai Stankevich, for every Nikolai Chernyshevsky we can find an Anton Chekhov, and for every Andrei Zhdanov one could always point to an Olga Fridenberg.

In this spirit, we have resisted the temptation to collapse unwieldy historical particulars into an overarching theoretical scheme. At the same time, we did not rule out a judicious look into transhistorical patterns informing Russian culture. To discern the contours of Russia's future, we must try to disentangle the forms indigenous to Soviet culture from those going back to prerevolutionary times and the fledgling patterns coming into being right now.

We share our starting premise with those students of Soviet society who believe that a "genuine understanding of events in the Soviet Union must incorporate both density of detail and a historical perspective."[9] Our volume opens with chapters focusing on the historical forces that shaped Soviet culture, the evolution of beliefs, values, and action patterns in key cultural spheres, and the internal contradictions peculiar to each cultural area. Then, the authors move to the transformation that various cultural spheres underwent during the perestroika years and beyond. In each of these domains we have witnessed a far-reaching reconstruction punctuated by the conflict between old values and the new, often confusing precepts brought forth by reform. We proceed on the assumption that reforming society is impossible without reforming its members' consciousness, that macro-institutional changes must be translated into the ways people think, feel, and act if these changes are to endure. Our emphasis, therefore, is on the beliefs, attitudes, and values behind new ways of doing things, on the changes in personal and group orientations insofar as these are reflected in mass consciousness and elite cultures, which find expression in opinion polls, the popular press, literary magazines, and personal conversations.

In theoretical terms, we take our inspiration from an interpretive tradition that gives the human spirit a central place in scholarly narrative.[10] Our outlook on culture owes much to Max Weber, who, in Clifford Geertz's words, taught us that "man is the animal suspended in the webs of significance he himself has spun."[11] This precept calls for special attention to the sense that people make of their own life situation, their professed beliefs, values, and meaningful actions. We view humans as self-conscious beings, "as characters in enacted narratives,"[12] or individuals bent on choosing their own narrative system and narrating their own lives. Starting with discourse, we move beyond it and try to discern the voice behind discourse; exploring a given narrative sequence, we want to be sensitive to individual intonation and emergent meanings, which sometimes subvert the very intent of institutionalized narrative. Bukharin might have been a faithful communist, but his unorthodox pronouncements—his individual voice—repeatedly broke through the stifling political discourse of his time. Time and place may severely constrain individual choice and personal voice, but structural constraints cannot extinguish the quest for a different, more satisfying system of values and a better lifestyle.

Although human understandings form a system, the latter is never devoid of inconsistencies and contradictions. In cultural domains, "pluralism is common, inconsistency is pervasive and syncretism is general practice."[13] For students of Soviet culture, this insight is signally important, for it highlights conflicts endemic to the system of values supported by official Soviet culture. In the decades before perestroika, these conflicts were submerged. As time went by, they grew more visible, the gap between official values and everyday reality became more tangible, and the double life—one for official consumption and another for an inner circle of trusted friends—increasingly intolerable. We fully appreciate what Ernest Gellner calls "the social role of absurdity."[14] In the years immediately preceding Gorbachev's reforms, this absurdity manifested itself in pervasive disenchantment, ironic detachment, mockery of official cultural norms, and other nonconformist gestures that exposed official hypocrisy and hinted at an autonomous agent behind the official role, an irrepressible private self ready to burst out and subvert the official grand narrative.[15]

We take issue with those who believe that there is "no 'usable past' in Russian thought,"[16] who are inclined to view the Soviet era as Russian culture's Dark Ages. A similar attitude prevailed among Enlightenment philosophers, who harshly judged the European Middle Ages a period hopelessly marred by human waste and spiritual stagnation. The Romantic successors to the Enlightenment cast a more ambivalent glance at the period; the new perception was colored in part by the growing awareness that capitalism and modernity brought in their wake deprivations and horrors all their own. To judge Soviet civilization fairly, then, one cannot only stigmatize its many failures but must also highlight its occasional graces.

We must try to understand why so many talented painters, writers, and poets placed their names on the revolutionary masthead; how Aleksandr Blok, Kazimir Malevich, Vladimir Mayakovsky, Sergei Eizenshtein, and scores of other artists managed nonetheless to remain true to their talent. What is there in the totalitarian environment that nourishes friendship and creativity, which are this era's undeniable, even if perverted, gains— gains that might disappear in a democratic, market-oriented society of the future? Yes, Soviet art helped to prop up the Bolshevik regime, but it also engendered works that through their very aesthetic qualities undermined the legitimacy of Soviet power. Why else would Soviet artists face such relentless persecution from the authorities? After all, Soviet society produced not only Andrei Zhdanov, Anton Makarenko, Trofim Lysenko, Vadim Kozhevnikov, and Georgy Markov but also Aleksei Losev, Dmitry Shostakovich, Andrei Sakharov, Yury Lyubimov, Sergei Averintsev, and many other cultural figures whose personal courage and creative accomplishments cannot be denied. Whatever lofty aspirations and momentous transcendence existed in Soviet society and culture deserve to be salvaged for posterity.

We also want to stress that the recent reforms in Russia by no means embody a uniform progress. Perestroika did not free cultural life in the Soviet Union from contradiction. "Societies do not necessarily move from one type or stage to another in an 'upward ever, backward never fashion.'"[17] Far from it, Soviet reforms set in motion fresh conflicts and bred new ironies. As one observer wrote, "Glasnost may be vital to perestroika; but it may also be its undoing."[18] The same goes for many hardwon freedoms in Russia today. Soviet artists may be free now to follow their creative instincts, but they are also relieved from the state subsidies that used to support their art. Soviet entrepreneurs can now set up their own businesses, but they must also deal with ambiguous laws, face hostile customers, and fight ruthless racketeers. Dissidents, who used to be outside critics, find themselves in a position of authority where they are expected to make good on their earlier promises. Contradictions and ironies are the stuff of which social change is made, and we have tried to give them full treatment in this book.

Nor should our premises be taken to mean that culture exists in a vacuum, that it informs without being informed. All cultures are embedded in historical contexts and are constrained by social, economic, and political structures that inhibit or facilitate social change. The point is rather that cultural rhetoric matters, that each culture has a logic of its own, that any attempt to manipulate values and subject culture to legislative dictate are bound to misfire, as many revolutionary regimes have discovered. The line separating substance and style, rhetoric and reality, attitudes and behavior, meaning and structure is never very sharp in matters of cultural politics. Style is not some sort of wrapping that can be readily replaced, nor is substance a wine that can be poured into a new container and retain its properties intact. There is no such thing as styleless substance any more than there is substanceless style. When people forgo old rhetoric and switch to a new cultural narrative, they undermine the status quo and weaken established structures. Gorbachev learned that the hard way, when his rhetoric of glasnost went far beyond his original plan to update the cumbersome Soviet system. The same goes for Solzhenitsyn: Once he declared that "ugly methods multiply in ugly results,"[19] he had little choice but to disavow Vladimir Zhirinovsky and the ultranationalists, whose venomous rhetoric and hatred toward "alien elements" are sabotaging serious efforts at social reconstruction in Russia.

In interpreting cultural discourse, however, we do not conflate it with social life in its totality, nor do we cast verbal culture as a primary causative factor in social evolution; rather, we contend that public discourse, in both its high and popular cultural forms, feeds into reality just as it takes into itself and continuously articulates the ongoing social transformation.

In sum, we view culture as action steeped in personal narrative, drenched in emotions, grounded in common needs, and informed by institutional discourse that serves to legitimize our public conduct and justify our action to ourselves and to others.[20] Attitudes and conduct belong to one continuum, and values are to be understood as verbal behavior, action at a slice, while conduct is to be seen as a succession of attitudes displayed for the purpose of legitimizing oneself to others and to one's own self. Thus, we define national character here not as a psychological structure formed at some early point in a nation's history and determining immutable personality traits but as a semiotic or narrative structure comprised of roles, scenarios, behavioral strategies, and emotional attitudes that might be deployed on a particular occasion to legitimize the chosen course of action but that do not preclude the situational and historical transcendence of the established cultural forms. Far from being a set of hidden values, sacred texts, socialization practices, and behavioral patterns enciphered in a code that foreordains the historical process, a nation's culture is multitextual, polyvocal, and inherently contradictory, leaving ample room for choice and creativity, personal commitment and responsibility.

Throughout this volume, we have tried to demonstrate that there is a choice to be made and a responsibility to be claimed by those who have to grapple with Russian culture at this critical historical juncture. Russian culture is at a crossroads; its future depends in large measure on the choices that its agents make at present and in years to come. To be sure, the cataclysmic break with the past we have witnessed in Russia in the last decade cannot be directed and controlled from above. This break produces unanticipated consequences, stirs conflicts, and breeds deviant conduct—a pattern well known to students of social change. Underlying this pattern is what Emile Durkheim called anomie,[21] when old norms no longer apply but new ones are too vague and problematic to command universal assent. As numerous accounts attest,[22] behavioral changes in revolutionary times are accompanied by a cognitive restructuring that sets new standards of valuation and breeds a sense of moral malaise. What people in Russia are discovering is that the system is encrypted in their selves, that it cannot be turned on and off at will. Bred into people's bones for seventy-odd years, Soviet culture is bound to persist for some time after the coercive structures supporting it have crumbled. It would be naive to believe that our efforts to illuminate Russian culture could have any discernable impact on its course. But to the extent that our study facilitates Russian people's efforts to come to grips with their past traumatic experiences, it might make cultural change in Russia less painful for those who have to live through it.

Although our project attends to an unfinished revolution and deals with history in the making, it has something to offer to the timeless mission of the humanities and social sciences. Perestroika is a story of the human spirit in distress. It tells us about peoples trapped in history, sucked into a system they despise, yet unsure of the way out. If progress to date has been disappointing, that is not necessarily because the reformers have charted a wrong course. It took one day for the Israelites to exit Egypt and forty years to reach the promised land. An entirely new generation had to come into its own, one unschooled in the old ways and raised in a new culture, before the Israelites managed to leave their gloomy past behind. Russian reforms represent the quest for a new culture that several generations take part in but will bear fruit for generations to come. This may be a local history, but its lessons are universal. Its significance reaches far beyond Russia, and it can teach us about our own values and cultures, and the human predicament in general.

Notes

1. E.g. Sheila Fitzpatrick, ed., *Cultural Revolution in Russia, 1928–1931* (Bloomington: Indiana University Press, 1978); Maurice Friedberg, *Russian Culture in the 1980's* (Washington, D.C.: Center for Strategic and International Studies, 1985); Abbott Gleason, Peter Kenez, and Richard Stites, eds., *Bolshevik Culture: Experiment and Order in Russian Revolution* (Bloomington: Indiana University Press, 1985); Nils Ake Nilsson, ed., *Art, Society, Revolution: Russia, 1917–1921* (Stockholm: Almqvist & Wiksell International, 1979).

2. Nikolai Berdiaev, "Dukhi Russkoi revoliutsii," in *Puti Evrazii: Russkaia intelligentsiia i sudby Rossii* (Moscow: Russkaia Kniga, [1922] 1992), p. 7. Unless otherwise indicated, here and elsewhere in the Introduction, the translation from the Russian is by Dmitri Shalin.

3. Aleksandr Solzhenitsyn, *Publitsistika: Stati i rechi* (Paris: YMCA Press, 1981), p. 273.

4. See Margaret Mead, *Soviet Attitudes to Authority* (New York: William Morrow, 1951); and Geoffrey Gorer and John Rickman, *The People of Great Russia* (London: Norton Library, 1949).

5. Anatoly Lunacharsky, "Nashe zapadnichestvo," *Ogónek,* no. 5 (1929): 4.

6. Fyodor M. Dostoevsky, *Polnoe sobranie sochinenii v tridtsati tomakh,* vol. 26 (Moscow: Nauka, [1880] 1984), p. 147.

7. Nikolai A. Dobrolyubov, *Izbrannoe* (Moscow: Sovremennik, 1984), p. 458.

8. Quoted in A. Stankevich, *T. N. Granovsky i ego perepiska,* vol. 1 (Moscow: Tovarishchestvo Tipografii A. N. Mamontova), pp. 127–28.

9. Ben Eklof, *Soviet Briefing: Gorbachev and the Reform Period* (Boulder: Westview Press, 1989), p. 7. See also Timothy Colton, *The Dilemma of Reform in the Soviet Union* (New York: Council on Foreign Relations, 1986); Robert O. Crummey, ed., *Reform in Russia and the U.S.S.R: Past and Prospects* (Urbana: University of Illinois Press, 1989); Frederick S. Starr, "Soviet Union: A Civil Society," *Foreign Policy* 70 (1988): 26–41; Robert Tucker, *Political Culture and Leadership in Soviet Russia* (New York: Norton, 1987).

10. See Max Weber, *The Methodology of the Social Sciences* (New York: Free Press, 1949); Dmitri N. Shalin, "Behavioral and Post-behavioral Methodologies in Communist Studies," *Soviet Union* 8 (1981): 186–222.

11. Clifford Geertz, *The Interpretation of Cultures* (New York: Basic Books, 1973), p. 5.

12. Alasdair MacIntyre, *After Virtue* (Notre Dame: University of Notre Dame Press, 1981), p. 202.

13. Margaret S. Archer, *Culture and Agency* (Cambridge: Cambridge University Press, 1988), p. 9. See also Myron J. Aronoff, *Culture and Political Change* (New Brunswick, N.J.: Transaction Books, 1983); Ernest Gellner, *Legitimation of Belief* (Cambridge: Cambridge University Press, 1974); Feliks Gross, *Ideologies, Goals, and Values* (Westport: Greenwood Press, 1985); Lynn R. Kahle, ed., *Social Values and Social Change* (New York: Praeger, 1983).

14. Gellner, *Legitimation of Belief,* p. 36.

15. Various dissimulation schemes employed by Soviet scholars are discussed in Dmitri N. Shalin, "The Development of Soviet Sociology, 1956–1976," *Annual*

Review of Sociology 4 (1978): 171–91; "Marxist Paradigm and Academic Freedom," *Social Research* 47 (1980): 361–82; and "Sociology for the Glasnost Era: Institutional and Substantive Changes in Recent Soviet Sociology," *Social Forces* 68 (1990): 1–21.

16. Marshall S. Shatz, *The Soviet Dissident in Historical Perspective* (Cambridge: Cambridge University Press, 1980), p. 38.

17. Myron J. Aronoff, *Culture and Political Change* (New Brunswick, N.J.: Transaction Books, 1983), p. 7.

18. Eklof, *Soviet Briefing,* p. 183.

19. Solzhenitsyn, *Publitsistika,* p. 169.

20. For further discussion of some of the theoretical issues raised in this introduction, see Shalin, "Behavioral and Post-behavioral Methodologies in Communist Studies"; "Pragmatism and Social Interactionism," *American Sociological Review,* no. 1 (1986): 9–30; "Romanticism and the Rise of Sociological Hermeneutics," *Social Research* 53 (1986): 77–123; "Introduction: Habermas, Pragmatism, Interactionism," in Dmitri N. Shalin, ed., *Habermas, Pragmatism, and Critical Theory, Symbolic Interaction* (special issue), no. 4 (1992): 251–59; "Critical Theory and the Pragmatist Challenge," *American Journal of Sociology* 96 (1992): 237–79; and "Modernity, Postmodernism, and Pragmatist Inquiry," in Dmitri N. Shalin, ed., *Self in Crisis: Identity and the Postmodern Condition, Symbolic Interaction* (special issue), no. 4 (1993): 303–32.

21. Emile Durkheim, *Suicide: A Study in Sociology* (New York: Free Press, 1951).

22. Roy Medvedev and Giulietto Chiesa, *Time of Change* (New York: Pantheon Books, 1989); Milton Rokeach, *The Nature of Human Values* (New York: Free Press, 1973); George Stocking, *Romantic Motives* (Madison: University of Wisconsin Press, 1989); Nancy Eisenberg, Janusz Reykowski, and Ervin Staub, *Social and Moral Values* (Hillsdale, N.J.: Lawrence Erlbaum, 1989); Melford Spiro, *Culture and Human Nature* (Chicago: University of Chicago Press, 1987); Michael Thompson, Richard Ellis, and Aaron Wildavsky, *Cultural Theory* (Boulder: Westview Press, 1990).

1

Historical Culture

BORIS M. PARAMONOV

Russia's nearly seventy-five-year-long experiment with communism is over, but it remains to be seen whether the Soviet regime was a historical aberration or an expression of the country's destiny. This question is as old as the Bolshevik revolution. It has produced a voluminous literature and will no doubt continue to attract attention in the near future. Unfortunately, it cannot be answered conclusively, for it is grounded in the questioner's ideological a priori and tells us more about the historian's biases than about Russian history.

Still, it would be wrong to dismiss this question as purely theoretical. The point is not so much to fathom some impersonal logic determining Russia's fate as to understand how Russia's history has been construed by those caught in its web and how this self-understanding has shaped the nation's historical landscapes. We can talk in this regard about "historical culture" or a set of beliefs about the nation's destiny entertained by its subjects in a particular era. Tradition informs the ways people think and act, but concrete individuals reproduce their tradition at various points in history according to their personal knowledge about its hidden logic, ultimate meaning, and final destination. A historical culture is rarely uniform; it contains diverse, even contradictory, precepts that could gain prominence for a time and leave their mark on the course of national development. There is a choice to be made, a legacy to be claimed, and it is up to concrete historical subjects to grasp the alternatives and realize them in their historical practice.

Our task here is to understand Russian historical culture in its internal contradictions, to delineate the guideposts it offers to historical actors, and to assess the impact these broad orientations might have on the development of postcommunist Russia. I start with the main themes and symbols informing Russian historical culture, show how these key insights have been appropriated in Soviet and post-Soviet Russian history, and conclude with some speculations about Russia's future.

Images of the National History
in Prerevolutionary Russia

Central to Russian historical culture is the issue of Russia's relation to the West. Westernizers believe that Russia is fundamentally a European country, that it shares with the West basic values and institutions, and that in spite of unfortunate historical detours, it evolves according to Western historical blueprints. Slavophiles, in contrast, are convinced that Russia's historical path is unique, that its spiritual values are at odds with the Occidental tradition, and that its historical destiny is loftier than the fate ordained for Western countries. The conflict between Westernizers and Slavophiles was fully articulated in the nineteenth century. In many ways, it reflected the spirit of the time, notably the Romantic reaction to the French revolution and the Enlightenment. But the political fissures on which this division was based go back to the origins of the Russian state.

The oldest Russian chronicle narrates a story about the Slavs calling on the Normans to come to Russia and reign over its unruly subjects. The debates about the veracity of this account are as interminable as those about the origins of Russian communism. We have nothing to add to this controversy except to point out how profoundly ingrained it is in the nation's psyche. If it is a myth, it is a productive one, and we should grasp it in the Jungian sense, that is, not as a legend or fable but as a formative element of the collective subconscious, where many features determining the nation's character and spiritual potential take shape. The story about the Scandinavian warriors invited to bring order to Russia hints at the Western roots of Russian statehood. In the Westernists' reading, it is primarily a story about the relationship between the leaders and the populace, in which the dominant role is accorded to the state and state power.

According to Sergei M. Solovyov, a nineteenth-century Russian historian, the Russian knights from the house of Rurik, founded by the Normans, were originally collective owners of Russian land.[1] Each knight was assigned a particular estate or domain according to his seniority in the ranks of the nobility in the patrimonial hierarchy. The relationship between the knight and his abode was a tenuous one. Knights frequently moved to new locations according to their seniority. The older the knight and the greater his prominence, the more central and desirable his domain. With such a pattern of mobility, no strong relationship could form between the entrusted territory and a particular knight and his family. It was certainly not the relationship of ownership, insofar as the nobleman owed his fortunes to the state and had to be prepared to move on to a new location at a moment's notice. You can discern in this social order a vague prototype of the communist *nomenklatura*, with its lifelong security and requisite perks: dedicated servants of the ruling house were sent to represent the central powers in a region where they wielded power over a given domain and its people for as long as they retained the ruler's trust. It was not until the twelfth century, when Andrei Bogolyubsky, the most senior nobleman at the time, refused to move to the central principality of Kiev and announced his decision to stay in his old Vladimir-Suzdal domain, that a more enduring bond began to form between the knight and his estate.

This train of thought was further developed by another nineteenth-century historian, Boris N. Chicherin, who argued that the state dominated civil society in Russia: the state used its power to elevate or downgrade individuals' social status and to institutionalize certain social processes that might be alien to popular impulses. Thus, the Russian gentry first appeared not as a class of warriors spontaneously settling the land but as a special service stratum whose members were summoned to fulfill certain state-appointed duties. The same was the case with the Russian peasantry, which was assigned to work for the gentry in lieu of payment from the state to its noble servants. By the mid-seventeenth century, most peasants had been pressed into bondage to the gentry, which in turn was rewarded for military service with bigger and more populous estates. As time went by, the state again took the initiative in creating new social estates and groups. In 1762, a state decree freed the nobility from the obligation to serve in state institutions, turning it into a landed gentry proper. Next, urban craftsmen and merchants were pressed into a kind of third estate and encouraged to evolve into a Russian bourgeoisie. Finally, in 1861, the serfs were freed from bondage and permitted to function as free peasants tilling the land.[2]

Both Chicherin and Solovyov were Westernizers by nineteenth-century standards, their ideas inspired by Friedrich Hegel's teaching about the state as a pinnacle of sociohistorical development. Their message to the authorities and the educated Russian class was that all historical states, including Russia, evolve according to the same blueprint, pass through similar stages, and end up in a legal, rational, ideologically neutral state that embodies world-historical wisdom. Note that this Westernizing mentality was largely secular. Westernizers refused to acknowledge the propriety of the special relationship that had formed between state and church in Russia. And this is where the Slavophiles took them to task.

The Russian state was never ideologically neutral. From the start, the paternalistic powers of the tsars were inextricably linked with the religious authority of the Russian Orthodox Church. The latter comprised a crucial element in the triangular structure of power in Russia, captured in the official motto, "Orthodoxy, Autocracy, Populism" [*pravoslavie, samoderzhavie, narodnost*]. Until the seventeenth century, the state power retained the unmistakably sacred character conferred on it by Russian

Orthodoxy. The desacralization of the Russian state began in the middle of the seventeenth century, under Tsar Alexander Mikhailovich, when the Russian Orthodox Church split into the "Old Believers," who advocated the autonomy of the Russian Church, and the proponents of the Patriarch Nikon, who pressed for changes in the traditional Orthodox liturgy and bowed to the state as a supreme authority in spiritual matters.[3] The schism within the Church marked the beginning of secularization, during which the state increasingly emancipated itself from religious influence and eventually subordinated Eastern Orthodox Christianity to its needs. The secular reforms undertaken by Tsar Alexander Mikhailovich were further enhanced in the early eighteenth century by Peter the Great, who did more than any other tsar to contain clerical influence and establish the Russian state as a secular entity similar to the absolute states found in European countries at the time. However, the secularization of state power was never completed, nor was it as auspicious a development in Russian history as Westernizers thought.

If Westernizers saw the state as a conduit for the Western spirit and credited it with civilizing Russia, Slavophiles considered it a necessary evil, a legal-rational political form alien to the people's ethical sensibilities and inimical to the nation's historical destiny. Nineteenth-century Slavophilism is reminiscent of Jean-Jacques Rousseau's deep mistrust of science, technology, and progress. The place of the noble savage in the Slavophile teaching was assigned to the Russian peasant, whose simplicity, endurance, and faith defeated the "enlightened" emperor Napoleon. Lev Tolstoi's novel *War and Peace* was perhaps the best literary rendering of Slavophilism.[4]

It was an article of faith with Slavophiles that the form of political and spiritual life endogenous to Russia was the peasant commune (*obshchina*): "A commune is a union of people who have shed their egoism and renounced their personality; it is an expression of collective consensus, a high Christian act of love," wrote Konstantin Aksakov, a prominent Slavophile. "Thus, the commune is a moral chorus . . . a chorale celebrating the soil, while the individual is like a false note in a choir."[5] Slavophiles liked to dwell on the fact that "peasant" and "Christian" in the Russian language were kindred words (*krestianin* and *khristianin*). "Commune" was for them not so much a social as a religious category. A repository of nonsecular consciousness, the commune embodied the pristine qualities of sacred Russia, the qualities preserved by the Old Believers rather than by the established, state-controlled church. Aksakov deepened the schism by juxtaposing the folk (*narod*) to the state and the public (the educated, Westernized class). "State" and "land" likewise were radical opposites in Aksakov's interpretation, with "land" symbolizing folkways, heaven, truth, virtue, and beauty, while "state" connoted everything secular, mundane, willful, and immoral. The history of the state was intricately tied in Aksakov's thought to the story of original sin. Both represented the fall from grace and pointed to the inevitability of suffering and redemption in post-Edenic history. However, people were believed to be loftier than the state, for they were closer to the pristine condition of paradise lost. Although people must submit to the state power, they also have to stay aloof from it and resist its contaminating influence. No formal legal category could do justice to folkways—the very notion of law was deemed beneath the dignity of the Russian people. "Render unto the State the unlimited right to act and set laws; give to the Land the right to free opinion and speech . . . Formal truth belongs to the State, inner truth to the Land; give unlimited power to the Tsar but full freedom of spirit to the people; the freedom of law and legal action goes to the Tsar, the freedom of opinion and word to the people."[6]

Under the mask of resignation, we find here a rejection of formal legal institutions represented by the state, which was denied any moral sanction. This mistrust of the state and the rejection of legal institutions would profoundly influence Russian consciousness. It accounts for the strong inclination on the part of Russian intellectuals to define concrete sociopolitical problems in ideological and quasi-religious terms.

The authorities were aware of this deep-seated resentment that Slavophiles harbored toward the state and paid it back with suspicion. Under Nicholas I, Slavophiles were treated rather harshly. His successor, Alexander II, tried a different tactic: he incorporated some of the Slavophile premises into his political program. The Slavophile influence could be seen in the 1861 reform, which freed the Russian peasants from bondage but preserved intact the commune as a social unit around which village life would evolve after the emancipation.[7] By making a concession to Slavophilism, state authorities sought to preserve and strengthen their paternal image. As a result, the great masses of Russian people, most notably the peasantry, were not exposed to a Westernizing influence.

The state's concern for its image among the Russian people was due in part to the authorities' fear of a new social force emerging in the Russian political arena—the intelligentsia. In the pre-Soviet Russian context, the intelligentsia were not a professional class or an intellectual elite but a radical group of ideologues and self-styled guardians of the common people against the tyranny of the state and exploitation by the ruling classes. At first, the intelligentsia's members came mainly from the ruling strata. These were the so-called repentant noblemen, who were troubled by a sense of guilt about serfdom. Later, a socially more diverse group of educated individuals joined the ranks of the intelligentsia and carried the torch of struggle against oppression. The group's outlook was distinguished by an ideologically supercharged, quasi-religious perception of the Russian people as the embodiment of everything good and by a rejection of the godless state as a callous institution unsympathetic to the plight of its meek subjects and willing to use naked power to assert its will. The Russian intelligentsia was the first group to embrace socialist teachings and make a strenuous attempt to bring socialism to Russia. Although they were more pragmatic and sociologically minded than the nineteenth-century intelligentsia, the Bolsheviks later inherited and perpetuated this lofty, paternalistic vision of the people as a toiling mass that would be led to freedom and happiness by the revolutionary intelligentsia.

In sum, the historical culture in prerevolutionary Russia was informed by the ongoing debate about Russia's relation to the West. Whereas Westernizers saw nation-building in their country as part of global historical evolution, Slavophiles drew attention to the unique properties of Russian history manifest in the sharp split between the power-wielding, law-giving, secular state and the pristine, religious, communally minded people. Both readings reflected some historical realities, yet both were highly selective in what their proponents chose to highlight or ignore. Westernizers tended to forget that the Russian state did not completely sever its ties with the Church, that it never became a genuinely secular institution, that it paid more than lip service to Slavophile sentiments, and that it often carried out pro-Western reforms in a brutal fashion that undermined their liberal spirit and reflected the heritage of native despotism. By the same token, Slavophile intellectuals conveniently overlooked the fact that state authorities made genuine strides in building a civil society in Russia and relieving the plight of its people. Indeed, it was the Russian state that freed Russian peasants from bondage in 1861 and was behind the 1909 Stolypin reforms, which were designed to create strong farmers tilling their own land. Again, it was the state that initiated liberal reforms in the communist era, such as Vladimir Lenin's New Economic Policy in the 1920s, Nikita Khrushchev's anti-Stalinist campaign in 1956, and Mikhail Gorbachev's perestroika in the late 1980s. The question about the role of state and commune in Russian history was not settled in the nineteenth century, and it reemerged with renewed force after the revolution of October 1917.

Early Images of Communism and Its Place in Russian History

Did the Bolshevik-led uprising move Russia into or away from mainstream European history? According to Lenin and other Marxists who embraced Bolshevik premises, the Russian revolution was firmly grounded in the world-historical (read "Western") process. The fact that the first "proletarian revolution" occurred in a largely peasant country where capitalism was still in the nascent stage did not bother Bolsheviks. They expected the Russian revolution to be followed by an uprising in the more economically developed Western countries, which could help solidify the revolutionary gains in Russia.

But there were other commentators, including some Marxists, who rejected this interpretation of the Bolshevik revolution. Perhaps the most remarkable among the doubters on the left was Pyotr Struve. A prominent Russian intellectual who came under the spell of Marx's teaching in his youth, he formulated a far-reaching critique of Bolshevism from the standpoint of "scientific Marxism."[8] Struve pointed out that Marxism gave its seal of approval to capitalism and bourgeois institutions as historically superior to the relatively undifferentiated precapitalist conditions. In contrast to the Bolsheviks, Struve interpreted Marxism as a paean to Western bourgeois values and not to primitive communism, which Marx had explicitly denounced in his writings. Yet, it was precisely this primitive communism, willed into being by the toiling masses under the guidance of the communist party, that Lenin and his followers distilled as the essence of Marxism. In giving priority to political expedience over economic necessity and to the party's will over evolutionary gradualism, Lenin unwittingly succumbed to the old Russian tradition wherein individual rights were sacrificed to state imperatives and force routinely used to accomplish state goals. Lenin's emphasis on the cleansing role that the wholesome proletariat played in society, enabling it to achieve revolutionary transcendence, also dovetailed more closely with nineteenth-century Slavophile sensibilities than with twentieth-century Western political dynamics.

We should note here that Marx's teaching partially justified this "romantic" interpretation of revolution. There was a strong utopian component in Marx, which he never fully overcame and which was embedded in his notion of the proletariat as the class-messiah called upon to cleanse the world from the original sin of alienation, to which humans succumbed when they embraced the culture of science and technology. This Rousseauistic element in Marx reinforced the crypto-Slavophile leanings of Russian Marxists. We can see it in the case of Nikolai Berdiaev, an outstanding Russian philosopher who read Marx in a romantic, if not messianic, fashion. Many years after he lost his youthful enthusiasm for Marxism, Berdiaev recollected in his autobiography his early infatuation with the Marxist notion of the proletariat:

> Class truth is indeed a non sequitur. But [back then I thought that] there
> could be a class lie, which is evident in the bourgeois classes, who
> sinned by exploiting other human beings. The proletariat is free from
> the sin of exploitation; it is socio-psychologically ripe for the message of

truth and justice determined by transcendental consciousness. That is to say, both psychological predisposition and transcendental necessity are intimately intertwined in the working class.[9]

This testimony suggests that at least some Russian communists took "proletariat" to be a Marxist code word for the Slavophile communal man, that is, a holistic, natural being who transcends the alienated conditions of the times. The toiling people were cast here as a transhistorical force destined to redeem Russia's—and, by implication, humanity's—sins. Western rhetoric masked peculiarly Russian sensibilities, which were incompatible with the positivistic reading that Marxism would be given in much of Western Europe.

If we turn to the Slavophile-inspired response to the revolutionary movement in Russia, we can see that it was far more reserved than that of the Marxists, although not entirely unsympathetic. Slavophiles, you may recall, harbored a deep suspicion about the state as a foreign entity on the native Russian soil. They also shunned liberalism because they feared it could breed violence. (Dostoevsky expressed this fear in his famous novel *The Possessed,* in which he depicted a liberal idealist father and his radical nihilist son.) From this vantage point, Slavophile intellectuals could not possibly be enamored of orthodox Marxism and its Westernizing influence in Russia. But Marxism's egalitarian spirit appealed to Slavophiles. They also entertained a mystic belief in the sacred calling of the Russian people and the special role of the native commune, which could be construed as an analogue of the liberating class and the authentic harmonious community envisioned by the communists. Aleksandr Blok, a talented poet particularly sensitive to the Slavophile ethos, hailed the revolutionary movement in Russia as a spontaneous popular uprising guided by primeval instincts and yearnings for justice. He transformed the familiar Slavophile polarity of state and land into a titanic struggle between culture and nature, civilization and organic historical elements, with the revolution signifying the ultimate triumph of the natural man over flabby, civilized humanity. "The Folk could not be base," intoned Blok, "this elemental force, which cannot and should not become aware of itself, will never deserve a bad word from the poet. You do not call people 'rabble' who sprang from the soil they till, who resemble the morning fog out of which they have crystallized, the beast which they hunt."[10] Blok's musings about the Folk as an elemental force sweeping artificial political institutions away would provide a basis for an account of the revolution as the victory of nature over culture. The uncontrollable torrent engulfing the islands of civilization in the vast Russian sea—this is how the Bolshevik revolt appeared to Slavophile-minded Russian intellectuals in the early revolutionary era. Westernizer Pyotr Struve saw the revolution along similar lines, even though his assessment of it was negative: "The Bolshevik uprising and the Bolshevik reign represent the social and political reaction of egalitarian masses against centuries-old efforts to Europeanize Russia, both socially and economically."[11] Russian philosopher Semyon Frank stated: "In its sociopolitical essence, the Russian revolution is nothing other than a painful crisis of rapid democratization in Russia."[12] This accelerated democratization had little to do with democracy as the term is understood today. Rather, the term meant the revolt of the elements against the encroachment of social engineering. But what Aleksandr Pushkin decried as the "Russian insurrection, senseless and merciless," acquired in the early twentieth century a new and higher cultural value. Again, Aleksandr Blok led the way here (though not without the influence of Nietzsche) by sharply contrasting culture and natural force to "civilization."

Highly symptomatic in this respect is a group that named itself after the ancient nomadic tribes of the southern steppes—the Scythians. This artistic/political current dates back to the first days of the Bolshevik uprising and included—in addition to its spiritual leader, Aleksandr Blok—two Russian "peasant" poets of the first rank, Nikolai Klyuev and Sergei Esenin. This connection is significant because it points to the missing link between Bolshevism (or at least the way it was perceived by some cultured Russians immediately following the revolution) and the Slavophile tradition. The group's chief ideologist, R. V. Ivanov-Razumnik, belonged to the party of left Social Revolutionaries, who formed a coalition with the Bolsheviks in the period between November 1917 and July 1918. The Social Revolutionaries, in turn, traced their origins to the Populists—a powerful intellectual/political movement that came into being in the last third of the nineteenth century and that advocated a kind of "peasant socialism" to be built around the familiar Slavophile "commune." The Scythians could be best understood as a movement that gave artistic and intellectual sanctity to the populist sentiments expressed in the twentieth century by extreme Social Revolutionaries. They thought—quite mistakenly—that the Bolshevik crowd was part of this primeval revolt of Russia's peasants against their ancient oppressors. The "nativist" October revolution that brought Bolsheviks to power appeared to them as an antithesis to the "Westernizing" February revolution, that replaced the tsarist government with a "bourgeois-democratic" regime. The fact that Lenin and his followers subscribed to the Western doctrine did not bother Slavophiles at the time: Social Revolutionaries and their intellectual allies saw Bolshevik Marxism as something superficial and accidental. Whether knowingly or unwittingly, the Scythians helped create a certain peasant mythology that contrasted "Bolshevism" as a native Russian phenomenon to "communism" as an unworthy doctrine imported from the West.

The Scythians did not exist as a coherent ideological current for long. They disbanded after the left Social Revolutionaries staged their unsuccessful revolt against the Bolsheviks. But their ideas continued to resonate for quite some time. Unmistakably "Scythian" was the immensely popular novel *Naked Year* by Boris Pilnyak, published soon after the October revolution. Pilnyak depicted Bolsheviks as a native force stirring the insurrection against the Western influence in Russia. The October revolution was glorified here as the break with Westernizing reforms initiated by Peter the Great, as a return to pre-Petrine and even pre-Christian, pagan Russia. Lev Trotsky, the number-two Bolshevik at the time, took notice of Pilnyak's book and chose to counter it with a memorable quip. Commenting on the Bolshevik Arkhipov, the hero depicted in the novel as a pre-Petrine, unshaven bear of a man, Trotsky said that he knew many comrades like Arkhipov but that, contrary to Pilnyak, all of them shaved. (Forced shaving was a common practice in Peter the Great's Russia and much reviled by conservative Russians.) As subsequent developments showed, Trotsky was far too hasty in dismissing the link between Bolshevism and anti-Western nativism in Russia. The "populist," "nativist," and "fundamentalist" reinterpretation of Bolshevism would become a major theme in pre- and post-perestroika debates about the meaning and destination of Russian history.

Yet another influential perspective on Russian communism emerged soon after the October revolution. "Eurasianism," as this intellectual current became known, could be seen as an attempt to reconcile the Slavophile premise about Russia's unique historical destiny with the Bolsheviks' emphasis on a strong state. This influential school was founded in the 1920s by Russian emigrés Nikolai Trubetskoi, Lev Karsavin, Georgy Florovsky, Pavel Suvchinsky, Pyotr Savitsky, and Georgy Vernadsky. Eurasianists interpreted the Bolshevik revolution as the triumph of the Eurasian principle over European reforms in Russian history. According to Nikolai Trubetskoi,[13] the most influential figure among Eurasianists, Russians shared their mentality and political sensibilities not with other Slavs but with the Turkic peoples inhabiting the Eurasian steppes. Like Turks, Russians could not work out a worldview of their own, but easily adopted coherent, schematically simple beliefs. Turks accepted Islam, Russians borrowed their Christianity from Byzantium. In its emphasis on "ritual piety," Trubetskoi implied, Orthodox Christianity was not so different from Islam. Similarly, Russian culture lacked the characteristic Western emphasis on the individual and legal rights—another trait that hinted at its non-Western origins. Like other Eurasianists, Trubetskoi praised the Mongol-Tatar domination over Russia as a positive chapter in Russian history. For some two and a half centuries under Mongol rule, Russians developed their political tradition, which was marked first and foremost by powerful state institutions. The fabric of Russian statehood, said Trubetskoi, might have been "poorly designed but deftly sewn together." If the tsarist state was largely a creation of the Mongol yoke, the Bolshevik state owed its being to Germanic influence. Under the veneer of Western phraseology, however, communist Russia preserved and even strengthened its imperial Eurasian heritage. From this fact, Eurasianists optimistically inferred that the nation's future was bright: in due course, Russia would reclaim its cultural archetype marked by strong state power and the subordination of the individual to the social whole.

Eurasianist writings bore more than a fleeting resemblance to Oswald Spengler's famous thesis about Europe's imminent demise. Just like Spengler, Eurasianists tried to isolate "sociocultural types" supposedly governed by historical fate and not by choices made by conscious historical agents. Members of this school also studiously avoided value judgments. The fact that in the Turkic sociocultural type the individual bowed to the state was neither good nor bad, according to Eurasianists. It should not be taken as a mark of "Russian servility" but as the sign of a genuine respect for power indispensable to a strong state. Although no judgment was explicitly passed, it was quite clear that Eurasianists saw the Russian mentality as a viable alternative to the Western political tradition, if not the way of the future for the entire world.

In sum, then, the October revolution evoked conflicting interpretations from those who lived through it. To Lenin's followers, the proletarian revolution was an episode in the universal drama of history, the first step toward the kingdom of freedom where all nations were heading at their own pace. The revolution that crushed capitalism turned Russia into the vanguard of world-historical emancipation. This sanguine interpretation was countered by liberal intellectuals like Pyotr Struve, who were appalled by Lenin's disregard for civil rights and democratic procedures and saw Russia's failure to develop a Western-style state based on law as an indictment against the revolution. Slavophile-inspired writers, also known as Scythians, felt a certain affinity for the revolution's egalitarian and communal ethos but were concerned about the communists' modernizing propensities and their reliance on the powerful state. And Eurasianists labored to reconcile Bolshevik statism with Slavophile nativism.

All these perspectives on the place of communism in Russian history resurfaced in the Soviet era and were further elaborated by the critics and advocates of communism.

Westernizing Dissidents and Their Critique of Soviet Communism

Although in its formative years the communist regime allowed some ideological diversity, Joseph Stalin put an end to serious debate about the country's destiny and its relation to the West. Any view that did not accord with Stalin's latest pronouncements placed the nonconformist in mortal danger. After Stalin's death, however, the debates resumed—subdued and muted at first, but increasingly open and vociferous with the passage of time. The dissident circles that sprang up in urban centers following Khrushchev's "thaw" contributed heavily to this resurgent interest in the nation's past and the willingness to reconsider its future. Among the first to take up the issue once more were liberal dissidents, who sought to pry open the Bolshevik tradition with liberal Marxist schemes.

The first instinctive reaction of Russian crypto-liberals emerging from their decades-long hibernation was the campaign to cleanse Marxism-Leninism of "Stalinist perversion." This liberal line was all the more convenient in that it harmonized with the official line proclaimed by Khrushchev at the Twentieth Congress of the Communist party. The critique of Stalin was carried out under the banner of "restoring Leninist principles," the latter being presented by official propaganda as the historically approved guidelines for building humane socialism. Outside party officialdom, the historian Roy Medvedev was the movement's most vocal proponent. He tried to prove the unprovable, namely, that the locomotive of Soviet history was derailed by the evil genius of one man—Joseph Stalin. That something might have been wrong with the communist project itself did not seem to cross Medvedev's mind. In time, a modified version of this intellectual/political current branched out that condemned "true Leninism" as a peculiarly Russian perversion of Marxism. It was no longer Stalin vs. Lenin but Lenin vs. Marx. The old controversy between Westernizers and Slavophiles reappeared in a new form. This debate smoldered for a while without attracting much attention in the West, but it was implicit in the early samizdat (self-published and clandestinely circulated) publications, and it began to influence the writings of Soviet emigrés of the early 1970s.

Alongside but somewhat apart from this thorny issue, a new kind of Westernizing current found a foothold in Russia that transformed this theoretical question into an explicit political program: the human rights movement, which made itself known in Russia and the West in the early 1960s. Its adherents derived their inspiration from the liberal Western precept that a law-abiding state respecting inalienable human rights is indispensable to a civilized, democratic society. Dr. Andrei Sakharov, the widely recognized leader of Soviet liberal Westernizers, spearheaded this movement with carefully worded, yet daring leaflets that first appeared in Soviet samizdat and were later reprinted in the West. Dissidence grew in prominence after 1963, when Khrushchev was deposed from his position as party leader, becoming a highly visible form of resistance to official communist dogma after the Soviet-led invasion that crushed the Prague Spring in 1968.

The dissident movement of the 1970s was a heterogeneous phenomenon. It harbored intellectuals supporting the Western-liberal program of Russian renewal as well as the critics of Soviet power with undisguised

Slavophile leanings. The latter included a highly influential group of "village prose" writers, or so-called *derevenshchiki,* who focused their critique on the devastating impact that communist policies had had on the nation's physical environment and its rural population. Sympathetic to these writers was Aleksandr Solzhenitsyn. Too complex a figure to be subsumed under a neat political label, Solzhenitsyn was a writer and political essayist highly respected in dissident circles for his personal courage and literary gift. His "stylistic integrity" prevented him from embracing extreme ideological claims, whether coming from the political left or right, but his politics had a pronounced anti-Western bias. In particular, Solzhenitsyn harbored a deep suspicion of Russian and Soviet liberals. In his famous literary memoir, *The Calf and the Oak Tree,* he ridiculed liberals' reliance on legalistic concepts like "human rights" and "law-based state" and scorned Valery Chalidze, a leader of the human rights movement, who had been allowed to go to the West on a "lecture tour"— a decision that could not have been made without KGB approval, as Solzhenitsyn sarcastically pointed out.[14] Personal animosities aside, the reemerging ideological split between the neo-Westernizers and neo-Slavophiles (if we are to stick with an old taxonomy) marked an important development in Soviet historical culture, which reignited an interest among Russian intellectuals in the centuries-old discourse about Russia's destiny. While the neo-Westernizers continued to blame Russia's historical tradition for the nation's misfortunes and saw the best hope for the future in the country's rejoining the West, the neo-Slavophiles decried the foreign influence in Russia and urged a "return to roots" as the only solution to the country's problems. Intellectuals sympathetic to the Slavophile tradition framed the question even more broadly. The entire modern culture is mortally ill, they insisted; Russia is but the first victim of Western liberalism; unless forced to retreat, the Occidental model would continue to self-destruct, dragging other, more viable cultural forms down with it.

Neo-Slavophile Ambivalence Toward Communism

Whereas liberal intellectuals in the post-Stalin era tended to gloss over the difficulties facing the capitalist West, the conservative opponents of Bolshevism idealized the native cultural tradition. A prominent place among Soviet conservatives belonged to village prose writers, of whom Valentin Rasputin, Vasily Belov, and Viktor Astafiev are perhaps the most prominent, but it was undoubtedly Aleksandr Solzhenitsyn who galvanized this powerful political-literary current. Particularly instructive in this respect are Solzhenitsyn's attacks on Bolshevik-Westernizers, with their unabashedly technocratic ethos.

Technocratic Westernism was quite popular among the Russian artistic intelligentsia and had its adherents among Bolsheviks as well. Nikolai Bukharin's pro-Western and anti-Slavophile sentiments came to the fore in an article on the occasion of Esenin's death, in which he wrote that the poet's suicide marked the passing of the old, peasant, patriarchal Russia and the emergence of the new—industrial and socialist—Soviet Union.[15] Another prominent technocratic Westernizer who earned scorn from Solzhenitsyn and other neo-Slavophiles was Maksim Gorky. This prominent writer cum Soviet bureaucrat edited a volume about an early Soviet era construction project—Belomorkanal—the channel between the White and Baltic seas that was to be built on Stalin's order. For Gorky, the project exemplified the grand battle between culture and nature, with Bolshevism carrying out the rationalizing, Europeanizing mission that promised to bring industrialization and the rational organization of labor to Russia. For Solzhenitsyn and his followers, the project symbolized the reckless disregard for nature, environment, and human life typical of communist rule: the project had little or no economic significance, adversely affected the natural environment, and claimed numerous casualties among political prisoners, who were forced to labor in degrading conditions.

The anti-state, anticommunist agenda advanced by village prose writers marked the resurgence of Slavophilism in Soviet Russia. We find in this neo-Slavophile current a powerful strand of Rousseauist rhetoric celebrating a back-to-nature lifestyle and waxing nostalgic about patriarchal values once found in the peasant commune. According to *derevenshchiki*, these simple values were systematically destroyed by the communist policies of forced collectivization and the mechanization of village life. The tractor—the machine touted by Bolsheviks as a chief tool of peasant emancipation—was denounced by village prose writers as an instrument of "Americanization" destroying traditional Russia. Village prose was the revolt of the swamp against land reclamation, a stirring cry for help on behalf of a starving, exploited, demoralized, and gradually disappearing Russian peasantry that was being sacrificed to the communists' ambitious industrialization plans. After Gorbachev unleashed his perestroika, village prose writers quickly moved to political center stage, mounting a strong campaign against government-sponsored plans to divert water from Siberian rivers to Central Asia. This widely publicized political initiative, which in the end led the government to drop its ecologically disastrous plans, earned village prose writers public sympathy. This was the first successful campaign in the Soviet Union's history in which public opinion prevailed on a vital policy matter.

The considerable public capital that village prose writers earned with their talented fiction and civic courage tended to obscure another, far less benign aspect of their political agenda—their nativist, anti-Western proclivities. Ecological catastrophes, like the Chernobyl nuclear plant explosion, evolved in their writings into a broad antiprogressivist metaphor. The writers of this school blamed the West for all the suffering the country went through under Bolshevik rule. As long as Russia remained preoccupied with world politics and allowed itself to be dragged into conflicts on the other side of the globe, it would continue to neglect its own people. Worse, it would serve as a dump for Western waste—industrial, political, and social. *Derevenshchiki* saw communism as just another discarded Western project carried out on Russian soil against the wishes of the Russian people. For Soviet intellectuals embracing Slavophilism, this was more than a literary trope: it was an indubitable, pernicious reality that required urgent action.

There is much that is sound in the village prose writers' critique of Soviet communism. One cannot read their works, especially their literary accounts, without feeling sympathy for the plight of the Russian peasantry. It is also widely acknowledged today that industrial civilization has left in its wake appalling ecological and spiritual wreckage. But in their attacks on science and technology, *derevenshchiki* went far beyond like-minded Western counterparts. In the postcommunist period, village prose writers' polemics have fed into a full-blown anti-Western program that equates European civilization with technocratic extremism. This program has a strong nativist flavor, most evident in Igor Shafarevich's book *Rusofobia*,[16] in which the author offers a quasi-theoretical analysis that decries Jews as a conduit for Western ideas in Russia. The author discerns two contradictory currents operating in nature: an organic movement of life itself (something akin to Henri Bergson's "creative evolution") and a theoretical force of "pure reason" exploited by those who, in the name of abstract reforms, distort nature's own inimitable, mystic ways. According to Shafarevich, Jews are notorious villains determined to force their abstract ideological schemes on reality and in the process destroy the organic foundations of nature and society. In this paranoid theory, Jews, whom the biblical tradition treats as the "salt of the earth," are cast as an embodiment of evil, a people collectively responsible for past and present crimes against humanity. The nativist tendencies already present in Slavophilism are pushed to the extreme in this neo-Slavophile diatribe, which renounces every political and social innovation as a regression or a perversion. This stance is not "cultural conservatism" but "hysterical conservatism," for it anathemizes any literary or political criticism directed at Russia as blasphemy and treason.[17]

As we pass judgment on contemporary Slavophilism, we should bear in mind the paradoxical metamorphosis that has marked this intellectual current. There is no reason to doubt the *derevenshchiki*'s sincere concern for the plight of Russia under communist rule, and after. Neo-Slavophiles opposed communism, sometimes openly, long before doing so became a safe and popular pastime in Russia.[18] What neo-Slavophiles refuse to see, however, is that Russia was not just a hapless victim raped by historical forces imposed from without, as neo-Slavophiles like to picture it, but a determined aggressor carrying a considerable destructive and self-destructive potential. In Bolshevism, Russia—this "mystical harridan" (to use an expression that Nikolai Berdiaev coined about Vasily Rozanov, an archetypical Russian Slavophile)—mutated from a "meek" into a "predatory" type, as an early twentieth-century literary critic, Appollon Grigoriev, would have put it. This transformation is echoed today in the paradoxical alliance that neo-Slavophiles have formed with communists in the post-Gorbachev era. When called upon to assess Bolshevism on the seventy-fifth anniversary of its ascension to power, anticommunist Shafarevich declined to indict it on the grounds that settling old accounts now could only sow disunity among the true patriots, whose urgent task was to confront their common enemy: liberals preying on Mother Russia. Valentin Rasputin, the most talented writer in the village prose group, and a patent anticommunist, has experienced a similar change of heart. During the first Congress of People's Deputies, he voiced his opposition to the anti-army stance taken by the glasnost-emboldened press. Later on, he joined the National Salvation Front, which united communists and nationalists into a "red-brown" faction and defended the very communism that killed the Russian village and despoiled his beloved Lake Baikal. Now Rasputin is saying that Western communism lost its internationalist agenda after being transplanted onto Slavic soil and, with the passage of time, evolved into a benign, genuinely national cultural form dovetailing with the Russian political tradition. The same shamelessly procommunist sentiments can be found in such Slavophile publications as *Nash sovremennik* and *Den*. One could hardly think of a greater irony: The very neo-Slavophiles who started out by denouncing communism as the planned destruction of Russia became the communists' allies in post-Soviet Russia.

The possible reasons for this miraculous transformation are many. The most important among these is the warped consciousness bred by Soviet Russia's isolation from world civilization. This isolation is at the heart of the neo-Slavophile belief that Russia and the West are antithetical historical entities, that the two oppose each other as the masculine and the feminine, form and matter, executioner and victim. The neo-Slavophile philosophy of history reveals a deep-seated fear of historical change and critical reason that goes back to prerevolutionary times (remember Lev Tolstoi's *War and Peace*). This philosophy also shows its proponents' failure to appreciate both the historical and metaphysical role of human rights and the individual. In place of the concrete historical individual, neo-Slavophiles put the "people," a collective national body endowed with natural wisdom and superhuman capacity to discern the unvarnished truth. Individuality, by contrast, is dismissed as an aberration, a product of critical reason that willfully encroaches on nature's eminent domain. In their juxtaposition of Russia (standing for the natural, organic form of historical being) to the West (representing the evolutionary hypertrophy of abstract reason), neo-Slavophiles suppress all evidence that points to the historical cross-fertilization between Russia and the West. As a result, they fail to complete their critique of the communist utopia, which continues to attract neo-Slavophiles as a teaching that elevates nature over culture, society over the individual, communal imperatives over human rights. The communism favored by neo-Slavophiles is not only a native but also a nativist phenomenon, it is a Slavic "Land communism" juxtaposed to the Occidental "State communism." If one is looking for proof that communism is in some way endemic to Russian mentality, such proof could be gleaned from the persistent strand of Slavophile nativism in Soviet and post-Soviet Russian political thought. Isolationism, nativism, and obstinate anti-Westernism continue to define the limits of Slavophilism as both an intellectual and a political phenomenon.

The Resurgence of Eurasianism

Slavophiles and Eurasianists alike have sought to drive a wedge between Russia and the West. But where Slavophilism stresses the uniquely Slavic path toward nation-building that eschews statism and relies on the native commune, Eurasianism affirms the common destiny of the Russians and the Asian peoples and seeks the restoration of imperial Russia.

Lev Gumilyov and his prodigious writings form a vital link between the original Eurasianism, which emerged as a coherent intellectual-political current in the Russian emigré community, and the renascent Eurasianist movement in post-Soviet Russia. Gumilyov's pedigree (he was the son of Anna Akhmatova and Nikolai Gumilyov, two great Russian poets victimized by the communists) lent his ideas a special significance in the eyes of his contemporaries. Gumilyov spent his youth in Stalin's prison camps, where he first learned about Eurasianism from Pyotr Savitsky, a member of the original Prague group arrested by the Soviets during World War II. It is said that people subjected to prolonged isolation in prison sometimes become monomaniacs. Gumilyov's case supports this view. Otherwise, it would be hard to understand why an offspring of an extraordinarily cultured Russian family embraced without apparent reservations this reactionary political doctrine.

Even before Gorbachev, Gumilyov managed to publish in the official press his work on "the great steppe" and its role in the history of Turkic people, with whom, Gumilyov implied, the Russians shared some social-psychological traits. He radicalized the old metaphor of "land," which was for him not just a symbol but a biogeographical ground for the folk's habits, a physiological source of national uniqueness. According to Gumilyov, the laws of history are similar to the laws that propel swarms of locusts to advance and recede. The border that separates Russia from the West is comparable to the negative isotherm for the month of January. In other words, nature itself sets the two cultural entities apart. One of his followers, Dmitry Balashov, paraphrased Gumilyov in this way: The iron plow that destroys the soil's organic structure destroys Russia as well. In Gumilyov's programmatic article "The Last Eurasianist," he openly declared himself an heir to the Eurasianist legacy:

> All Eurasian ethnoses managed to live and prosper as long as they stayed on their native territory. However, they perished . . . when intermingled with alien worlds. All contacts on the superethnic level yielded negative results. . . . The Eurasian concept of ethnocultural regions . . . applies to the world-historical process as well. Wherever emulation [mimesis] prevails, it runs contrary to originality and violates the principle "know thyself" and "be your own self."[19]

As an intellectual movement, the original Eurasianism encountered strong criticism in the emigré community. No less a luminary than Nikolai Berdiaev voiced his opposition, pointing out a striking resemblance between Marxism and Eurasianism: both hail necessity and scorn choice and freedom as factors in history. It is this deterministic and monistic metaphysics, rather than any shared political sympathies, that explains the Eurasianists' willingness to cooperate with Bolsheviks and their endorsement of the Soviet state as the continuation of the Russian ethnos's historical mission. Father Georgy Florovsky, a member of the original Eurasianist group, later dissociated himself from the movement and mounted an influential theological critique of Eurasianism. In "Metaphysical Underpinnings of Utopianism," he wrote:

> A utopianist is bound to read history in teleological categories, as a development, an unfolding of innate traits, the growth of a seed. . . . What is justified here is the world and history as a whole rather than man and private life. This historical teleology rationalizes the anti-individualistic bias of utopian consciousness. Human being—species being—is tied in with nature here, while societal good is magnified to cosmic proportions. . . . Herein lies the commandment to obey. Since it is madness to struggle with reality itself, just grasp the "natural evolutionary trends"

and adapt yourself to them. Historical automatism alleviates the risk of
failure and along the way kills the very possibility of creativity.[20]

This critique is targeted not only against Eurasianism but also against
Marxist historical metaphysics, Spengler's organic determinism, and certain strands in Russian theological thought that advocated various forms of
Christian Platonism (Sergei Bulgakov, Pavel Florensky, Lev Karsavin), with
its emphasis on a preordained, divine plan for historical development that
rules out unpredictable, genuinely novel developments. This line of criticism is very timely, for it exposes the fatalism and antihumanism deeply
rooted in Russian consciousness and palpably present in several powerful
currents in today's political thought. Calls to restore the Russian empire to
its past glory are coming from such diverse personages as the neo-
Slavophile Rasputin, the communist Gennady Zyuganov, and the statist
(*derzhavniki*) Aleksandr Prokhanov, and it is highly indicative that these diverse thinkers and groups invoke Eurasianist arguments to justify their demands. Radical nationalists and etatists conceive the future Russia as a
great Eurasian empire uniting Orthodoxy and Islam on the basis of shared
physical territory, kindred psychological traits, and common stress on ritual piety. Perhaps Sergei Trubetskoi and Gumilyov were right and Islam is
Russian Orthodox Christianity minus Christ. There certainly was a historical precedent for the Great Eastern Orthodox Christian state converting to
Islam—in Byzantium. But as the nineteenth-century philosopher Vladimir
Solovyov pointed out, Byzantium fell not so much because of the irre-
sistible force of Muslim arms but because it exhausted its potential for inner
growth, for a spiritual resistance to Islam: Eastern Christianity surrendered
the Christian spirit of freedom. It seems that today's imperial *derzhavniki*
are ready for a similar surrender. This is just another paradox of Russian
history: If neo-Slavophile *derevenshchiki* feel nostalgic about the communism that defiled the country's environment, then neo-Eurasianist
derzhavniki are sizing up the political yoke that Russians shook off back in
the fifteenth century. They are willing to be slaves, as long as they are subjects of a great empire. The question is whether this is the last gasp of the
imperial Russian idea or the beginning of the new cycle in the geopolitical
struggle for Eurasian supremacy.

Russian Communism as a Spiritual Phenomenon

The breakdown of the Soviet regime brought in its wake a heightened interest in long-suppressed Russian thought. Many readers saw in
Slavophilism, religious philosophy, and great Russian literature an anti-

dote to communism. Some hoped to find therein a special path that could save Russia from the extremes of Western rationalism and capitalism. However, the "Russian idea" proved to be exceedingly muddled, and the blueprint for the future it offered its adherents seemed tainted by the very communist spirit to which the Russian idea was supposed to be immune. Nothing illustrates this point better than the plight of the Orthodox Church in postcommunist Russia.

The renaissance of Russian Orthodoxy began long before perestroika. Many dissidents saw religion as a natural bulwark against godless communism and actively sought to establish ties with the Russian Orthodox Church. The passing of communism spurred a religious revival. In the early perestroika years, the Church visibly strengthened its position; for a while, it wielded considerable moral authority, and its blessing was central to settling political disputes. Politicians of different stripes made a point to be observed attending church ceremonies and actively sought audiences with the Patriarch of All Russia. This revival proved surprisingly short-lived, however. Once a dissident and now a radical nationalist, Vladimir Osipov recently lamented that the Russian Church was once again treated as a nuisance, its priests singled out for ridicule. This loss of authority has much to do with the fact that, freed from the patronage, the Church showed little stomach for administrative independence and creative spiritual leadership. Church leaders seem to desire little more than a new alliance with the state that would restore the Church to its pre-Bolshevik role as an official state religion. For centuries, Russian Orthodoxy operated under state patronage, and its servile attitude toward state power apparently became an ingrained habit. The open support that some Church leaders showed to the communist nationalists further discredited the Church as a political force (the most insidious case of this kind is that of Metropolitan Ioan of St. Petersburg, whose ultranationalist and crypto-anti-Semitic sentiments had been disavowed, albeit only tacitly, by the patriarch of the Russian Orthodox Church). All the proud talk about Eastern Christianity as the core of Russian culture, supported by such giants of the Russian spirit as Fyodor Dostoevsky, proved groundless. The Church's equivocal pronouncements and less than forthright actions dealt a devastating blow to many Christians who had pinned their hopes for national renewal on Russian Orthodoxy as a guardian of national values.

Without dwelling on the metaphysics of Eastern Orthodoxy, we can point out that its diminishing stature in public opinion has much to do with its ritualism, its conservative organizational forms, and the fact that it never underwent a genuine Reformation. Official Russian Orthodoxy sanctified the quasi-spiritual forms of patriarchal life inimical to the individual, human rights, individual initiative—all those cultural forms that are central to modernity. The Church opposed not only political but also spiritual creativity, which made it suspicious of any new departure. The excommunication of Lev Tolstoi—a Russian Luther of sorts, who protested the Church's corrupt ways and called for church reforms—is highly emblematic in this context. An even stronger indictment against Russian Orthodoxy was the persecution of the Old Believers, a powerful movement that came out of a schism in the established church in the seventeenth century. This episode in the history of Eastern Christianity is particularly pertinent today, when the country is striving to build a market economy. It is well known that early capitalist entrepreneurs in Russia came in disproportionate numbers from the ranks of the Old Believers, who formed the proto-bourgeois stratum in Russia. Their marginal status as a persecuted minority and their strong religious convictions emphasizing personal responsibility and the need for constant self-improvement call to mind Weberian puritans engendering the "spirit of capitalism" in the Western world. Sergei Bulgakov noted this fact in his 1909 review of Max Weber's famous book, *The Protestant Ethics and the Spirit of Capitalism*.[21] Official Orthodoxy, by contrast, frowned upon entrepreneurial activity, as it still does, remaining more or less aloof from efforts to develop a market economy in Russia. The Church's indifference is evident not so much in any open opposition to capitalism as in the official stamp of approval that it has bestowed on the collectivist psychology endemic to patriarchal economic and political forms. Until the Russian Orthodox Church finds a way to sanctify the spiritual foundations on which human rights and entrepreneurship can thrive, its contribution to political and economic reforms in postcommunist Russia will remain very limited and inconsistent.

Religion is not the only institution that failed to manifest itself as a cultural form resistant to communism. The same could be said about another cultural resource that for a long time enjoyed considerable authority in the country—Russian literature. "What would Russians do after the collapse of communism?," a Russian luminary was asked in the heyday of perestroika. "Read literary magazines," came the answer. The answer did not raise many eyebrows at the time. This conclusion seemed to have been borne out by the astounding explosion of publishing activity in Gorbachev's Russia. The country reveled in its newly found freedom to read, write, and criticize. Between 1987 and 1990, long-suppressed books reached the reading public, everything from Dr. Zhivago to Dr. Freud. But this literary orgy did not last. By the end of perestroika, the demand for serious literature in Russia had dropped precipitously. The "thick" literary magazines that were once obligatory reading for every intellectual saw their circulations cut from millions to a few thousands. The nation's attention turned elsewhere, leaving Russian writers, poets, and filmmakers to fend for themselves.

That great Russian literature could not survive communism does not seem strange now. In retrospect, Russian communism was in large measure a literary phenomenon, a popular book that enthralled its readers and kept them from other, more mundane, pursuits. Thrust into the public eye by idealists and ideological visionaries, communism represented a species of gnostic consciousness that longed for a cosmic revolution, a resplendent society that would meet all human needs and pursue universal happiness as its highest goal. But for those who believe in it, the ideal of such a society is ultimately more important than the society itself. The real is sacrificed to the ideal, illusion wins out over fact, and the laws of beauty gloss over the messy currents of everyday life—which is what literature has always been about, certainly the great literature that flourished in Russia in the nineteenth century and survived into the twentieth through the heroic efforts of writers like Aleksandr Solzhenitsyn. Communism was a literary project par excellence, an aesthetics embraced by a people who had created a great literature.

Far from being merely formal, this continuity extends to substantive issues as well. Epic in its scope, Russian literature expressed the holistic consciousness endemic to primitive communism and codified by the nation's leading writers, who sought to impart a collectivist mind set to elites and commoners alike. Great Russian literature flourished in a traditional patriarchal society; its preoccupation with the people and their terrible plight was fed in part by the guilt and personal responsibility felt by educated noblemen toward their subjects. With the notable exception of Dostoevsky, Russian literature deliberately pushed Russians toward primeval, collective ("swarming" as Tolstoi would have said) existence; it represented a discursive form that roughly corresponded to the cosmological period in ancient Greek thought associated with pre-Socratic philosophers. Dostoevsky had moments of genuine "anthropological revelation," as Berdiaev used to say, but ultimately he called for a return to the pristine, wholesome "land," just as his great contemporaries did. It is a sad fact that Russian literature failed to inoculate its readers against communist temptations, and it failed to do so because it was antibourgeois and antipersonalistic to the very core. This important precept was first powerfully enunciated by writer Varlam Shalamov, once a prisoner of the Gulag, and then popularized by several commentators, most recently Aleksandr Ageev:

> Russian literature of the nineteenth—"golden"—century was the last epic, titanic literature in European history. It flourished in a short and very peculiar time span [when] writers, already familiar with the European, personality-conscious literary culture . . . still felt behind them the biblical presence of organic folk life in all its enormous biologi-

cal might. This fact gave writers the right to speak on behalf of this dormant elemental force; it encouraged them to undertake monumental literary projects and assured the psychological veracity of their writings.
Surveying Russia's endless territory, [Russian artists] felt that "eternity
was on their side." But time refused to succumb to space. What seemed
like biblical eternity exploded into a series of extraordinary dynamic
events. Judged against the backdrop of real history, the "golden era" of
literature, although brief indeed, exerted an inordinate influence on
spell-bound Russian literature, which ever since has moved crabwise
into the future, its eyes glued to its illustrious predecessors whose accomplishments Russian writers are still trying to emulate.[22]

The main target of this criticism is no doubt Aleksandr Solzhenitsyn, who
likes to rail against younger writers preoccupied with self-expression and
indifferent to the great Russian literary tradition. What Solzhenitsyn fails
to realize is that this shift is not just an aesthetic but a cultural historical
phenomenon heralding the emergence of a new mentality in Russia—individualistic, bourgeois consciousness. This shift marks a genuine historical
change and presages the final demise of communism. The new Russian literature tends to be either purely commercial or aesthetically elitist, but this
fact should be greeted as a sign that this historical transformation is becoming irreversible. As a novelist, Solzhenitsyn may have little to offer to
the literature of the future, but as the author of *The Gulag Archipelago*, he
should rejoice in this development, for along with the gruesome gulags, so
too expired "great" literature—literature as "communism."
  All these heady developments were duly noted by well-known critic
Georgy Gachev. In his essay, programmatically titled "Honest Private Life
as an Alternative to Russian Literature," Gachev drew attention to the literary memoirs of an eighteenth-century Russian, Andrei Bolotov. Bolotov
exemplified a relatively rare type in the Russian context, a cultured
landowner who spent considerable time improving the agricultural yield
on his estate. For Gachev, this is an astounding example of a self-made
man whose down-to-earth rational undertakings contrast sharply to the
idealistic castle-building so common among the Russian gentry and intelligentsia. Here is an excerpt from the paean to Bolotov that Gachev wrote
to dramatize this man's accomplishments and to juxtapose them to the
Russian literary canon:

> An enlightened owner! An autonomous human being—what
> Englishmen call a "self-made man"—who comes to terms with his envi-
> ronment and his own self and creates the conditions for decent exis-
> tence. As *causa sui* (an attribute of the Absolute, of God), he is a cause
> unto himself. Under Russian autocracy, such a free private autocrat was

little appreciated as a subject of history or source of creativity. . . . But much scorned common sense seems to work just fine when practiced by this man: instead of a generous Russian soul, he displays German "moderation and reliability"—he is a veritable antihero of Russian literature! . . . What we witness is the ethos and eros of private honest life miraculously unfolding outside mainstream history.[23]

For all its exalted tone, Gachev's "antiliterature" article, ironically published in *Literaturnaia ucheba* (*Literary Training*), is highly symptomatic of the subterranean currents in contemporary Russian consciousness, which is reevaluating old values and experimenting with new attitudes. The latter goad Russians to leave behind their utopian literary projects and embrace real life with all its complexities. Russian critics have spotted unrecognized heros in the literary past—private owners, hard workers, businessmen—and now seek to imprint their images upon mass consciousness as models worthy of emulation. Once again, the past has proved as unpredictable as the future, and herein lies the best hope for Russia in the decades to come.

Back to the Future: Concluding Remarks on Russian Historical Culture

As I have tried to show above, Russian communism has been nourished by communalism, nativism, and anti-Westernism—a set of beliefs and practices that elevate the species' life over individuality and sacrifice individual freedom to collective imperatives. There is more to the Russian tradition than its dominant historical culture would make you believe, however, and the search is now on for alternative values that could help the nation break free of its communist fetters.

The official memory embodied in the Russian cultural canon is very selective: it brings to the fore certain historical events and downgrades or completely ignores others. As the case of Andrei Bolotov suggests, this unclaimed historical heritage is finally beginning to attract serious attention in Russia. An enlightened owner, a self-made man, Bolotov is transformed from a cultural villain into a hero, and with him thousands of other Russian men and women once denounced for their personal initiative as hopelessly individualist are being restored to their proper place in the nation's cultural memory. This belated rehabilitation is not confined to archaic figures like Bolotov but extends to more recent personalities and their undertakings, which are being reappraised as valuable cultural resources. The names of Russian entrepreneurs—Aleksei Putilov, Pavel

Obukhov, and Savva Morozov—are now frequently mentioned in Russia, their products praised for their quality, their factory buildings, still in use, noted for their durability and workmanship. The Russian kulak, a much maligned family farmer hounded by Stalin's henchmen during the forced collectivization campaign, is celebrated today for his initiative and hard work, as well as his spiritual strength in the face of endless political repressions. Equally portentous are recent attempts to reinterpret the old literary canon, such as the novel by Mikhail Sholokhov—*Virgin Soil Upturned*. For decades, Soviet pupils studied this novel as a literary paean to the battle against the kulaks. Now revisionist critics argue that the novel could be read as a satire on communists and their never-do-good helpers among the local peasants, who enforced the Communist party's ruthless policies among the rural population. Hidden historical resources are discovered everywhere and brought back into wide cultural circulation. Old Believers cum entrepreneurs, Russian landowners devoted to their land and people, even greedy profiteers—the antiheroes of Russian literature—are recast as bourgeois entrepreneurs courageously defying ancient customs and asserting their will against the spineless traditionalism of their time. Practicality, efficiency, and businesslike attitudes are seen in today's Russia not only as economic virtues but also as values indispensable for the rejuvenation of the entire spiritual/cultural domain. What Soviet ideologists denounced as arch-heresy—the "bourgeois mentality"—is redefined as essential to current reforms.

To be sure, these changes have been slow in coming; there are social strata and individuals who fervently resist attempts to reevaluate old values and continue to extol the values of nativism. The results of the December 1993 elections to the Russian Parliament, which showed considerable popular support for communists and ultranationalists, are more than a bit discouraging. But it would be wrong to view efforts to redefine Russian historical culture as inconsequential or to relegate them exclusively to the cultural domain. Witness the emergence of "nomenklatura capitalism," a powerful trend that has been revamping the nation's economic and political scene in post-Soviet Russia. At the heart of this movement is the transformation of ex-party apparatchiks, administrators, and industrial managers into a new class of property owners. Far from being ideological watchdogs determined to reverse the course of history (they are largely extinct today as a viable political species), these remnants of the past political and economic elites strongly support privatization and market reforms, if for no other reason than because they stand to benefit personally from these changes. The confrontation between President Boris Yeltsin and Ruslan Khasbulatov's Parliament was precipitated primarily by the tension between the central and local elites after the latter endeavored to shed their suzerainty to their old bosses. The haste with which the old nomenklatura began to transform itself into a new class of property owners was scandalous indeed, but the political-economic thrust of this process was undoubtedly positive. It marked the dispersion of power in Russia, its gradual metamorphosis from a political form of totalitarian control into an economically based and hard-won authority. This process is the best guarantee that the difficult transition to a market economy would be a nonviolent, even if unseemly, process. No need to "liquidate the nomenklatura as a class" (to use the Bolsheviks' favorite expression); the mutation would be gradual and voluntary. This transformation of yesterday's nomenklatura workers into today's bourgeois property owners might be even more significant than sputtering democratic political reforms. The latter could be reversed under the emergency powers granted to the Russian president, but the former are far less likely to be dismantled by any presidential decree or legislative action.

Today's situation brings to mind the previously mentioned historical precedent—Andrei Bogolyubsky's refusal to move to the Kievan principality as mandated by the nomenklatura system. This pioneering attempt at privatization was restarted after the collapse of the Communist party nomenklatura, and there is reason to believe that this time the process will go far enough to become irreversible. Nomenklatura functionaries are eager to trade off their coveted positions in the state/party hierarchy for a place in the emerging economic order, to exchange their political status for the promise of economic riches. The decentralization of political power, the regionalization of economic activity, the fusion of economic and political authority, the sanctification of private property—these developments might seem like the return to "feudalism," but in Russian history they count as progress. The new trends have been slowed down by the executive power's struggle against legislative independence and by presidential decrees stifling regional autonomy, but they can hardly be reversed. It is highly unlikely that Russia will ever return to a unitary, nomenklatura state.[24]

If post-Soviet Russia offers any historical lesson, it is that the past is a valuable national resource, that it is as problematic as the future, and that alternative scenarios for the future are inextricably linked to the discovery of an alternative past. It is time for Russian thinkers to reexamine those periods in their history when the nation enjoyed close relations with the West, most notably the St. Petersburg era and the empire built by Peter the Great. Moving further back into Russian history, one could ponder what the historian Georgy P. Fedotov hailed as a "Moscow serviceman" and what Dostoevsky described as a "state servant"—a shrewd man who repeatedly demonstrated his flexibility, resourcefulness, and capacity to adapt to extreme circumstances and find ingenious solutions to knotty practical problems.[25] Today's industrial managers keeping their enterprises afloat under the most trying conditions are the latest incarnation of this historical type. Ex-nomenklatura functionaries, or at least the most productive of them, show the will to become capitalist entrepreneurs and turn Russia into a viable market economy. This servant of the state who used to do its bidding has shown that he has a mind of his own. Like the "slave" transcending his bondage and mastering his "master" in the Hegelian dialectical scheme, the Russian "serviceman" survived autocracy and many ideological overlords and even stood up to the state that oppressed him. This uncanny ability to transform the environment, transcend the organic tradition, and press ahead during transitional periods of "radical historical transformation" (Berdiaev) is Russia's greatest historical resource. After all, efforts to break with the past are as much a constant in Russian history as attempts to stem reform and preserve the status quo. Or, as the Slavophile Aleksei Khomyakov pointed out, there was hardly a more typical persona in Russian history than the arch-reformer Peter the Great.

The reform confronting today's Russia, which is not dissimilar to many others that preceded it, can be best described as the "new Westernization." This reform has a decent chance to succeed because it treads familiar territory and represents a return to the well-trodden path from which Russia was pushed by a series of unique historical circumstances. The knowledge the Russians need to see this transition through will be based on their historical experience—their remembrance of things past, remembrance of things future.

Notes

This article was translated from the Russian by Dmitri N. Shalin.

1. See S. M. Solovyov, *Istoriia Rossii s drevnikh vremen*, vols. 1 and 7 (Moscow: Sotsialno-ekonomicheskaia Literatura, 1962).

2. On Chicherin, see B. Paramonov, "Liberalnyi konservator," *Kontinent*, vol. 50 (pp. 279–312).

3. On the seventeenth-century religious schism in Russia, see James H. Billington, *The Icon and the Axe: An Interpretive History of Russian Culture* (New York: Knopf, 1966), pp. 116–62.

4. The very title of Tolstoi's great novel hints at his Slavophile sympathies. The opposition of state and land is tacitly present in the antithesis of "war and peace," where "peace" embodies the celebrated Slavophile "land," which is juxtaposed to "war" or, the same thing, the "state." B. M. Eikhenbaum states that Tolstoi's work is not so much a "historical novel" as an "antihistorical novel." "In a sense, Tolstoi waged war against . . . the very historical process." B. M. Eikhenbaum, *Lev Tolstoy* (Leningrad: GIZ, 1928), p. 288.

5. K. Aksakov, *Polnoe sobranie sochinenii,* vol. 1, *Sochineniia istoricheskie* (Moscow: Universitetskaia tipografiia, 1889), pp. 279, 597–98. Unless otherwise indicated, here and elsewhere in this chapter, translations from the Russian are by Dmitri Shalin.

6. Ibid., pp. 283–84.

7. The Russian commune was not so much an organic expression of Russian folkways as a state-decreed institution created for the sake of implementing state fiscal policies. The Westernizer Chicherin showed this clearly in his work. Yet, Slavophile mystifications succeeded in convincing the authorities that the commune was somehow native to the Russian soil. All this is not to gainsay, of course, that the centuries-old institution of communal village life left its mark on the collectivist psychology of the Russian peasant.

8. See Richard Pipes, *Struve: Liberal on the Right, 1905–1944* (Cambridge: Harvard University Press, 1980), pp. 317–19.

9. Nikolai Berdiaev, "Samopoznanie: Opyt filosofskoi avtobiografii," in *Sobranie sochinenii,* vol. 1 (Paris: YMCA Press, 1983), p. 138.

10. A. Blok, *Sobranie sochinenii,* vol. 6 (Moscow-Leningrad: Khudozhestvennaia literatura, 1962), p. 162.

11. Pyotr B. Struve, *Sotsialnaia i ekonomicheskaia istoriia Rossii* (Paris, 1952), p. 19.

12. S. L. Frank, "Iz razmyshlenii o Russkoi revoliutsii," *Novyi mir,* no. 4 (1990): 215.

13. N. S. Trubetskoi, *K probleme russkogo samosoznaniia* (Paris: Evraziiskoe knigoizdatelstvo, 1927), pp. 42–43, 51–52, 49.

14. Aleksandr Solzhenitsyn, *Bodalsia telenok s dubom: Ocherki literaturnoi zhizni* (Paris: YMCA Press, 1975), p. 400.

15. Nikolai Bukharin, *Zlye zanetki* (Moscow: GIZ, 1927).

16. The book was written in the late 1970s and published in 1988–89 simultaneously by three nationalistic magazines. See, e.g., *Nash sovremennik,* nos. 6, 11 (1989).

17. Shafarevich instigated a noisy campaign against Andrei Sinyavsky's book *Strolls with Pushkin,* which bears an uncanny resemblance to the reception that the Muslim world accorded to Salman Rushdie's book.

18. In the 1970s, Shafarevich distinguished himself with a courageous book exposing socialist fallacies. This book was compared by critics with F. Hayek's *The Road to Slavery*—a comparison designed to dismiss the book and its author as overly partisan. See Igor Shafarevich, *The Socialist Phenomenon* (New York: Harper & Row, 1980).

19. Lev Gumilyov, "Ispoved evraziitsa," *Nashe nasledie,* no. 3 (1991): 25.

20. Georgy Florovsky, "*Metafizicheskie predposylki utopizma,*" *Voprosy filosofii,* no. 10 (1990): 87–88.

21. S. Bulgakov, *Dva grada: Issledovanie o prirode obshchestvennykh idealov,* vol. 1 (Moscow: Put, 1911), p. 198.

22. A. Ageev, "Konspekt o krizise," *Literaturnoe obozrenie,* no. 3 (1991): 17.

23. G. Gachev, "Chastnaia chestnaia zhizn: Alternativa russkoi literature," *Literaturnaia ucheba*, no. 3 (1989): 119, 120, 128.

24. Some years ago, I singled out the evolution of the Communist party nomenklatura system into a nomenklatura capitalism as a welcome scenario for the future. See B. Paramonov, "Kanal Griboedova," *Grani*, no. 138 (1985). My analysis was based on the structural continuity between the old Russian aristocracy and the communist nomenklatura. Today this continuity, as well as that evident in the current transformation of the party nomenklatura into a new economic class of property owners, is commonly acknowledged in the Russian press.

25. G. P. Fedotov, *Novyi grad: Sbornik statei* (New York: Chekhov, 1952), pp. 75–76, 78, 86; and Fyodor Dostoevsky, *Polnoe sobranie sochinenii*, vol. 5 (Leningrad: Nauka, 1973), p. 57.

2

Intellectual Culture

DMITRI N. SHALIN

No group cheered louder for Soviet reform, had a bigger stake in perestroika, or suffered more in its aftermath than the Russian intelligentsia. Today, nearly a decade after Mikhail Gorbachev unveiled his plan to reform Soviet society, the mood among Russian intellectuals is decidedly gloomy. "The intelligentsia has carried perestroika on its shoulders," laments Yury Shchekochikhin, a noted commentator. "So why does it feel so forlorn, superfluous, and forgotten?"[1] Another commentator warns that the intellectual stratum "has become so thin that in three or four years the current genocide against the intelligentsia will surely wipe it out."[2] Andrei Bitov, one of the country's finest writers, waxes nostalgic about the Brezhnev era and "the golden years of stagnation when . . . people could do something real, like build homes, publish books, and what not."[3]

The frustration and self-doubt afflicting Russian intellectuals today might seem excessive, but they are hardly unprecedented. In the last 150 years or so, every crucial turn in Russian history has touched off a new round of debate about the intelligentsia and its role as the conscience of society and guardian of national culture. This discourse by and about the intelligentsia has shaped the distinct themes, literary props, psychological traits, and favored political agendas of Russian intellectual culture. Russian intellectual culture shares with its Western counterpart a belief in directed social change and cultural critique as a tool for social reconstruction. East or West, intellectuals produce a "distinctive culture of discourse,"[4] through which they stake their claim to status and income in modern society. The greater the significance society assigns to the written word, intellectual creativity, and social criticism, the greater the prestige and privilege of the intelligentsia. By keeping critical discourse aflame and promoting high culture, the intelligentsia also increases its cultural capital.

What sets Russian intellectual culture apart is the crying gap between its modern aspirations and the nation's conservative heritage. Its other distinctive feature is the bold, even extravagant, manner in which Russian intellectuals have asserted their vanguard role and claimed moral leadership in society. As Aleksandr Yanov, a prominent Russian intellectual, put it, "One advantage that Russia has over the West is its colossal intellectual wealth."[5] The implication is that if only the Russian intelligentsia could deploy its intellectual resources fully, reforms would have a chance. This sentiment is shared by many Russian intellectuals who continue to search for ways to mobilize culture as a strategic national resource and, in the process, improve their own sinking fortunes.

Whatever their vested interests, intellectuals' yen for stewardship in a rapidly changing Russian society should not be treated lightly. The ongoing discourse about the intelligentsia and its role in current reforms has left a mark on public consciousness and found its way into wider social practice. The question is whether the nation is willing to follow its intelligentsia and, if so, where.

To understand intellectual discourse in today's Russia, we need to examine Russian intellectual culture in its formative years.[6] After tracing the origins of the Russian intellectual tradition, I outline its evolution in the Soviet era. Next, I address the challenges the intelligentsia faces in post-Soviet Russia, the stunning reversal of fortunes Russian intellectuals have suffered in recent years, and their struggle to reassert their critical role in society. Finally, I offer some speculations about the Russian intelligentsia's future.

The Origins of Russian Intellectual Culture

Although the Russian intelligentsia did not evolve into a self-conscious social force until the mid-nineteenth century, its origins can be traced to the early eighteenth century, when Peter the Great embarked on a crash campaign to modernize Russia. Backward, insular, and largely illiterate, Russia was to be brought abreast with the leading European nations through radical reforms in its political, religious, military, and civil service structures. To that effect, Peter I invited experts from all over Europe to Russia, sent young men abroad for study, set up a civil service bureaucracy, reorganized the army and the navy on Western models, established the Russian Academy of Sciences, and encouraged court poets to immortalize the tsar's glorious deeds. This forced Westernization exposed the country to ideas that had no roots in Russia proper and so were met with resistance from its people, who saw the reforms as an affront to Russian Orthodoxy and considered Peter the Great the anti-Christ. But the new class of "servicemen" and courtiers who owed their fortunes to Peter the Great and his successors learned to appreciate the new ways and prided themselves on being the purveyors of European mores in their rough-hewn homeland.

It would be wrong to assume that the proto-intellectual stratum created during Peter the Great's reign instantly produced Western-style intellectuals who embraced the ideals of religious tolerance, political liberty, and a constitutional state. The ruthless manner in which Peter I imposed his reforms on his countrymen was inimical to the Occidental humanistic heritage, with its signature belief in the dignity of every human being. Nor was there any evidence that Russian "servicemen," clerics, academics, and poets had any agenda of their own. Whatever their internal squabbles and personal gripes against the powerful, eighteenth-century bureaucrats by and large identified with the state and its authoritarian domestic policies and imperial aspirations.

As the century wore on, signs began to emerge that the Westernized intellectual stratum was coming into its own and growing uneasy about Russia's backwardness. Catherine II's interest in the French Enlightenment encouraged Russian writers to voice their judgments about the country's social and political affairs. But when some dared to shed their roles as official bards and court wits and venture an opinion mildly critical of Her Majesty's realm, the empress sternly reprimanded them. The dissatisfaction with serfdom that Vasily Kapnist cautiously conveyed in one of his poems was met with a rebuke from Catherine II, who told the writer to mind his own business and barred him from court. Nikolai Novikov, a prominent publisher and educator in Catherine II's reign, was sent to prison after he satirized Russia's gentry. When Western-educated Aleksandr Radishchev wrote a book lamenting the Russian peasants' sorry state, he was stripped of his nobleman's status and sentenced to death (the sentence was changed to life exile with confiscation of property).[7]

During the reign of Alexander I, the gap between autocracy and the Westernized stratum widened. In 1812, Napoleon suffered a crushing defeat. Russian troops marched triumphantly into Paris. As it happened, the occupiers fell under the spell of republicanism. Thirteen years later, the young military commanders attempted to overthrow the tsar and replace autocracy with a constitutional monarchy, dramatically underscoring the extent to which Western ideals had permeated Russia's educated class. The Decembrists' uprising, as this event was called, failed miserably, but in the eyes of many contemporaries and future commentators, it marked a watershed in Russian history. The failed 1825 coup pinpointed the growing alienation between Western-minded intellectuals and a nation still deeply ensconced in its premodern ways, and it presaged the emergence of a politically conscious, socially uprooted, and increasingly radical Russian intelligentsia.

The French Enlightenment, German philosophy, and early socialist teachings were among the most important Western influences on Russian intellectual culture in its formative years. To the Enlightenment, Russian intellectuals owed their preoccupation with constitutional polity and the republican system of government. German philosophy left its mark through a theory that hailed the world historical spirit passing through several progressive stages and elevating humanity to an imminently rational state. The socialist ideas that began to reach Russia in the 1840s furnished fresh rationales for a critique of Russia's backward economy and pervasive inequality.

The term "intelligentsia" has a Latin root and Russian grammatical form, suggesting a hybrid origin. Georgy Fedotov gives a precise date of birth for the intelligentsia: 1837, the year Aleksandr Pushkin died.[8] Pyotr Boborykin claimed to have coined the term in 1866.[9] Its most likely source is the Hegelian philosophy of spirit, which envisioned a superhuman intelligence operating in the universe and inexorably moving society toward an ever more perfect state via the rationalizing activity of self-reflexive minds. From this abstract philosophical doctrine, Russian intellectuals inferred that their country had to be modernized in line with world historical (read "Western European") development and that the elite of Western-educated, publicly minded individuals was best suited for the job. The Westernizers did not seem to be overly concerned that their schemes had hardly any moorings in the Russian political tradition. They had little doubt that their intelligence, theoretical savvy, and boundless energy would surmount the historical obstacles in their path. Hence Georgy Fedotov's famous definition: "The Russian intelligentsia is a group, movement, and tradition marked by the principled nature of its objectives and the unsoundness of its principles."[10] The arrogant stance Westernized intellectuals assumed toward their own cultural heritage had a direct impact on their psychology and behavior. Having sided with progress, Russian intellectuals could not help but feel superior to their society. With the native tradition cast as a fetter on their enlightened spirit, they were apt to scorn as retrograde anyone who saw something valuable in Russia's past. Self-appointed agents of history, they treated all mundane authorities and institutions with contempt and vowed to destroy them. Alas, being ahead of one's time proved exceedingly costly, as critically thinking intellectuals discovered in their struggle with Russia's formidable secret police, called upon to crush these "enemies of the state."

Critical intellectual ferment is already evident in Pyotr Chaadaev, a celebrated nineteenth-century intellectual whose robust critique of Russia's insular ways and longing for European culture so angered Nicholas I that he pronounced Chaadaev a "madman"—the first, though hardly the last, case of its kind in the Russian intelligentsia's beleaguered history. Taking his cue from Friedrich Schelling, Chaadaev extolled "universal intelligence," "universal reason," "one single intellectual force in the whole universe," and "the unique vision of the future granted to some chosen men" whose selfless labors were enlisted to impart world historical wisdom to reality.[11] Chaadaev's views were unabashedly elitist: "I have always thought that humanity could advance only by following its elite, by following those who have the mission of leading it; . . . that the instincts of majorities are necessarily more egotistical, more emotional, more narrow . . . that human intelligence always manifests itself most powerfully only in the solitary mind, center and sun of its sphere."[12]

Once the task of universal intelligence was fully comprehended, everything had to submit to its impersonal dictate. The individual was but a vehicle for divine providence, any private existence largely irrelevant in the face of the universal spirit's transhistorical agenda: "[T]he human being should be understood once and for all as an intelligent being in abstraction, but never as the individual and personal being, circumscribed by the present moment, an ephemeral insect, which is born and dies on the same day, and which is linked with the totality of things merely by the law of birth and corruption."[13] From then on, objective value was to be judged by a person's readiness to subordinate his private urges to universal reason and to fulfill its ultimate goal.

Having set this lofty ideal for himself and his contemporaries, Chaadaev quickly discovered how hard it was to live up to it. In 1836, after his philosophical letters incurred the tsar's wrath, Chaadaev found himself hounded by the police and shunned by the public. Hastily, he renounced his views and retreated into proud solitude. Later, when Alexander Herzen, another prominent Russian intellectual, praised Chaadaev as a precursor of free thought in Russia, Chaadaev dispatched a letter to the political police headquarters, where he denounced his compatriot and swore his loyalty to the tsar in the most abject terms. Asked why he had to abase himself so, he replied that one simply "must save one's skin."[14] This surrender took its emotional toll on Chaadaev, who had foreseen the crushing burden the intellectual would bear in this God-forsaken land: "Where is the man who would be strong enough not to end up hating himself, living in eternal contradiction, always thinking one thing and doing another. . . . What causes this terrible ulcer which is destroying us?"[15] This "terrible ulcer" would eat away at several generations of Russian intellectuals daring to oppose the powerful state. Few would suffer more from it than Chaadaev's friend, Russia's beloved poet, Aleksandr Pushkin.

Educated in the state-run lyceum for young noblemen, in his formative years Pushkin imbibed the free thinking that would lead his friends to Senate Square in St. Petersburg, where the Decembrists staged their

abortive coup. Pushkin did not mince words in his early lyrics, which
breathed regicidal fervor:

> Thou, scoundrel autocratic!
> I hate thy throne and I hate thee.
> My heart feels cruelly ecstatic
> When thy and thy kind's doom I see.[16]

His contemporaries remembered Pushkin in his young adulthood as an
irreverent, Jacobin spirit who did not mince words vilifying the government: "At the governor's [mansion], on the streets, on the square, he was
always eager to explain to anybody that he who did not want to change
the government was a scoundrel. His conversation was replete with cursing and sarcasm, and even his courtesy was punctuated with an ironic
smile."[17] Despite his radicalism, the poet's political preferences were
rather modest: he was ready to settle for a constitutional monarchy.

> · Rulers! your laurels and your crowns accrue
> To your estate from law and not from nature;
> You hover high and mighty over nations,
> Alas, eternal law reigns over you.[18]

Even in the liberal reign of Alexander I (the tsar himself at one point
toyed with the idea of constitutional monarchy), such rhetoric was
deemed highly inflammatory. The tsar had little use for a poet who dared
to put him on notice that

> I cannot force my bashful muse
> Tsars and courtiers to amuse.[19]

Pushkin's verses, widely circulated and popular among future
Decembrists, landed him in exile, which the poet would not escape until
after the Decembrists' failed uprising.

After Alexander I died in 1825, his brother, Nicholas I, ascended to the
throne. Before he brought Pushkin back from exile, he ordered him, along
with a few other free thinkers, to write a report on the linkage between
education and pernicious republicanism, effectively inviting the poet to
repent for his youthful indiscretions. Pushkin's reply was emblematic of
the torturous exercises that Russian intellectuals would have to perform
to save their skins without completely dishonoring themselves. He

charged his friends with "criminal delusions" and "low morals," blamed "foreign ideologism" and "deficient education" for their "wanton behavior," called for "drastic measures" to stem free thinking among Russian youth, and demanded "the end to home schooling," which let minors escape the state's "omniscient oversight."[20] At the same time, he intimated that harsh censorship might have driven honorable men to clandestine publications, that it was better to expose young people to republican ideas in school than make them yield to hostile agitation later on, and that a person's rank in society ought to be made commensurate with his education—quite unorthodox ideas, given the period's reactionary tenor.

About the same time, as if to calm his guilty conscience, Pushkin wrote one of his best-known verses, which he dedicated to his comrades exiled to Siberia:

> Deep down in Siberia's mines
> Sustain your proud, silent patience,
> Your anguished toil will slowly grind,
> Your noble dreams not perish traceless.

Confidently, Pushkin predicted that the time would come when

> Your heavy fetters will fall off,
> The walls of prisons crumble—and freedom
> Will greet you at the gates,
> As friends restore your swords to you.[21]

These words are familiar to all Soviet schoolchildren. Much less known is Pushkin's other side, his secret dealings with the authorities, his endless entreaties to the chief of Russia's secret police: "If the emperor wishes to use my pen, I would be eager, to the best of my abilities and with requisite precision, to fulfill His Highness's will. . . . I offer my magazine to the government—as its tool for shaping public opinion."[22] This is from the man who confessed that he was "tired of depending on the good or bad digestion of one superior or another. . . . All I crave is independence."[23] And again: "What a devil's jest to force me, with my mind and talent, to be born in Russia!"[24] "Of course, I loathe my homeland from head to toe, though I feel annoyed when a foreigner shares this feeling. But you, who are not on the leash," Pushkin queried his friend, "how can you live in Russia? If the tsar granted me *freedom*, I would not stay here a month."[25] Trying to reconcile these conflicting sentiments, Pushkin became ill-tempered and depressed. Freedom from political demands was all an artist should long for, according to the mature Pushkin. This much-quoted verse written in his last year sums up his disillusionment:

> I do not cherish your much touted rights,
> Which set some heads to reeling.
> I do not blame the gods who have denied me
> The sweet pleasure of disputing taxes and meddling
> With tsars forever waging wars among themselves.
> Why should I care whether our press be free
> To fool its readers, if watchful censorship
> Thwarts noisy demagogues' ambitious designs.
> All these, you see, are *words, words, words.*
> Far better, nobler rights are dear to me;
> Far more auspicious freedoms do I crave:
> To bow to the tsar, to bow to the people—
> What difference does it make? God be their judge.
>   To no one else
> Accounting for my deeds, pleasing no other but myself,
> Refusing for gain to bend my neck, my conscience,
>   my belief;
> Wandering here and there as I alone see fit,
> Standing in awe, admiring nature's sacred beauty,
> Beholding artistry's inspired flight, transfixed
> In joy and wonderment by its eternal truth—
> Now, that is happiness! Those are rights . . . [26]

Toward the end of his life, Pushkin grew increasingly irritated with his old friends and unhappy about the real and imaginary slights he suffered from Nicholas I and his servants, who never believed in his conversion. Several times he offered to resign from his lowly position in the court hierarchy but was dissuaded. A notorious womanizer, he found the tables turned on himself when Georges Dantes, a dazzling Frenchman serving in the Russian army, began to court his wife. The duel that followed left Pushkin mortally wounded. On his deathbed, he pleaded with Nicholas I to forgive his indiscretion, asking his friend Vasily Zhukovsky to "tell him that it is a pity I have to die; I would have been his completely."[27] The autocrat struck a noble pose, forgiving Pushkin his sins against the throne, paying off his numerous debts, and promising to look after his wife and children. The foremost poet and intellectual of his time, Aleksandr Pushkin died a broken man.

The First *Intelligenty*

Neither Chaadaev nor Pushkin saw themselves as *intelligenty*—members of the Russian intelligentsia. Both were firmly rooted in the estate system and harbored the same class prejudices against the lower orders that were common at the time. Most contemporary Westernizers resigned themselves to studying the latest foreign theories among like-minded nobles. Nikolai Stankevich, Timofei Granovsky, Ivan Turgenev, Nikolai Ogarev, Alexander Herzen—the golden youth of the 1840s—gathered in small circles where free thinking continued to flourish under the stifling rule of Nicholas I. "What is, is right," pronounced the reigning Hegelian wisdom, from which the Russian intellectuals concluded that they must be patient, that the universal spirit cannot be rushed, that no order was ready to fall until it had exhausted its historical potential.

The revolutionary tide that swept Europe in the late 1840s washed up onto Russian shores socialist slogans that caused Russia's stagnant culture to explode. The case of Alexander Herzen, the brilliant socialist writer and one of Russia's first political exiles to the West, is most revealing here. Son of a Russian nobleman and a German woman, Herzen was schooled at his father's estate in a typically eclectic fashion, learning Latin, German, and French, reading Voltaire and Diderot, soaking up the republican spirit. He enrolled at Moscow State University, where he joined an underground movement of youth looking for ways to snub Russia's hated institutions. The young men's aversion to autocracy was awakened by the Decembrists' uprising and fortified by a heavy dose of Fourierism and Saint Simonism. In 1834, the student group was exposed and its leaders exiled to the east, where Herzen spent eight years working in various provincial administrations and learning more than he cared to about Russia's retrograde customs. After a return to Moscow engineered by his powerful friends, Herzen was exiled one more time, came back again, and in 1847, under the pretext of his wife's poor health, managed to leave Russia, never to return to his homeland.

Residing alternatively in Switzerland, France, Italy, and London, he took active part in the revolutionary upheavals that swept across Europe from 1848 on, and in the process underwent what he called a "perestroika of all convictions."[28] He rejected German idealism as too abstract and consecrated himself to socialism and materialism, convinced that science and education could alleviate absolutism, foster equality, and deliver humanity from its misery. While Herzen's passion for liberalism sometimes approached religious fervor, his caustic, brilliant mind continued to check his theoretical constructs against reality, openly acknowledging wherever the former exceeded his expectations:

Liberalism is the last religion, although its church is not otherworldly and its theodicy is political; it stands firmly on the ground and allows for no mystical reconciliations; it has to reconcile itself with reality in deed. . . . Liberalism has exposed the chasm in all its nakedness; the sickly consciousness of this chasm breeds the irony and skepticism that mark modern man and help him sweep away the remnants of past idols. Irony conveys the disappointment that logical truth is not the same as historical truth, that aside from dialectical development, truth has its passionate and contingent development, that in addition to reason, truth also has its romance.[29]

In the mid-1850s, Herzen started a successful publishing venture, which included his famous magazine *The Bell*, dedicated to three major themes: the institutionalization of *glasnost*, the abolition of serfdom, and the end to corporal punishment. Later he also published *Voices from Russia*, where intellectuals could clandestinely print their philippics against the tsarist state. Issues were smuggled back to Russia, where they were widely read by the regime's proponents and opponents alike, with the top courtiers boasting their familiarity with the latest articles. Herzen was among the very first in Russia to zero in on glasnost as the pivot on which progressive reforms must turn. "Because of censorship, we are unfamiliar with glasnost, which amazes, frightens, and offends us. It is time for the comedians from the imperial secret police to realize that sooner or later their actions, kept secret behind bars and buried in cemeteries, will become known and their shameful deeds revealed in their utter ugliness to the entire world."[30] This would be the central theme of Herzen's magazine throughout its life span. "If we listen carefully to public opinion," wrote an anonymous contributor to the first issue, "we hear one demand: glasnost. If you read underground literature, we come across the same demand: glasnost. Now every fact demonstrates that the only way to fight today's evil is glasnost. . . . The choice is between these two options: cruelty and glasnost."[31]

Herzen's own belief in the power of glasnost and enlightenment remained unshaken throughout his life, but his hope to see liberal ideas triumph in his lifetime gradually faded away. He was also profoundly disaffected with the West and its bourgeois culture—*meshchanstvo*, as the Russians would call it contemptuously. All of Europe, in his estimation, split into two competing and equally philistine camps: "[O]n the one hand, there are philistine-proprietors anxious to hold on to their monopolies; on the other, propertyless philistines [*meshchane*], who strain to but cannot dispossess their counterparts. That is to say, greed on the one side, envy on the other."[32] There seemed to be little prospect of a rational, humane community anywhere in the world. As his hopes waned, Herzen grew ironic, wistful, and sarcastic, as did so many of his Russian contemporaries who had placed their faith in reason only to discover that reality refused to submit to its dictates. Herzen's irritability and unhappiness were exacerbated by personal misfortunes and family problems, as well as generational shifts in values. The new crop of Russian intellectuals found him too liberal and conciliatory. Indeed, toward the end of his life, just as the mood in Russia was becoming belligerent, Herzen renounced revolutionary violence as inimical to constructive social change. Herzen's final judgments read as a warning to the coming generation of freedom fighters who failed to understand that "civilization by the whip, liberation by the guillotine," would spell a new tyranny: "Every cause that requires crazy, mystic, and fantastic means will in the end breed crazy consequences along with the reasonable ones. Clearly, this is not our path; understanding and discussion are our only weapon."[33]

Herzen's social origins and considerable family fortune might have had something to do with his political moderation. But for his successors who could boast neither his pedigree nor his financial resources, moderation in the fight for freedom and equality was no virtue. The new breed of intellectuals known as *raznochintsy* (literally, people from different ranks) came from diverse social and economic strata. One thing these sons and daughters of clergy, servicemen, teachers, or small gentry had in common was that they had severed most of their ties with their social stratum and often maintained a threadbare existence. It was this new crop of déclassé intellectuals who came into their own in the 1850s and blossomed in the 1860s that was for the first time identified as the "Russian intelligentsia." While paying homage to their predecessors and borrowing from them some insights, the new intellectuals spurned noblemen-critics as dreamers, lost souls, or "superfluous people"[34] incapable of linking thoughts with deeds. They considered Pushkin "not serious enough," "too much of an epicurean," "too harmonious by nature to take on life's anomalies."[35] Ivan Turgenev, another nobleman writer with liberal sensibilities and a penchant for compromise, also found himself shunned by progressively militant intellectuals.

Vissarion Belinsky, Nikolai Dobrolyubov, Nikolai Chernyshevsky, and Dmitry Pisarev are key figures who perfected an intellectual style that would dominate high cultural discourse in Russia until the early twentieth century. Here are some key themes and accents that marked their discourse and gave Russian intellectual culture its unique historical flavor:

1. A critical approach that judges every social event or institution from the standpoint of the progressive historical agenda.

2. A moral maximalism or expectation that the *intelligenty* will subordinate their personal needs to public interests, treat everyone according to their contribution to the liberation process, and do everything possible to hasten the arrival of a just society.

3. A vanguardism that calls upon a few educated, conscientious, critically minded individuals to lead the toiling masses toward the final battle against the oppressive and obsolete regime.

4. An ideologically inspired compassion for the toiling classes and oppressed groups who suffer under the autocratic regime without being able to voice their grievances or understand what causes their pains.

5. A programmatic commitment to political, social, and economic equality as the historically most efficient and humane form of societal existence.

6. A readiness to resort to class violence as a necessary evil given a reactionary state that suppresses glasnost and stifles legitimate venues for social reconstruction.

7. A split between word and deed that ascribes to the free word persecuted by the defensive authorities the status of the ultimate deed.

8. An ironic detachment in interpersonal relations and a sarcastic attitude toward all authorities, highlighting the gap between the official roles Russian intellectuals have to play in public and the ideal selves they aspire to be.

9. An opposition to bourgeois culture, or *meshchanstvo*, in all its manifestations in contemporary family life, relations between friends, artistic tastes, and so on.

10. An exalted vision of art and literature as a powerful medium for shaping public opinion and communicating to the masses socialist ideals and ideologically sound attitudes toward society.

This list is not exhaustive; a particular stylistic feature could be present or absent in any given individual. Somewhere at the intersection of these discursive traits, however, emerged the nineteenth-century intelligentsia's creed. The change in the Russian intellectual style could be gleaned from Dobrolyubov's celebrated dictum:

[T]he mass of people who 'think they are above the present reality' is swelling year by year; perhaps everybody will soon outgrow this reality. [But] what we need now are not people who would 'raise us above reality' but who would raise—or teach us how to raise—the reality itself to the level of the rational demands we are making. In short, we need people of action and not just those withdrawn, epicurean individuals who are intent on theorizing.[36]

There was no consensus at the time, or for that matter at any other point in Russian history, as to how reality could be brought in line with reason. But the notion that political means alone might not suffice in bringing about an emancipated society sank roots at this historical juncture. Take Vissarion Belinsky, an iconic figure among Russian *intelligenty*. He started as a moderately conservative idealist, gradually moved toward left Hegelianism, with its maxim, "what is rational must be made actual," then fell under the spell of Saint Simonism, and finally declared himself a social radical. "The entire public foundation of our age requires a painstaking review and radical perestroika," wrote Belinsky in 1840, and this necessitates violence as a tool for social engineering: "It is ridiculous to believe that [social change] could come about on its own, in a timely fashion, without violent uprisings and bloodshed. People are so stupid that they must be led to happiness by force. . . . I am beginning to love mankind as Marat did: to make the least part of it happy, I seem to be ready to destroy the rest of it by fire and sword."[37]

One should resist the temptation to read too much into such inflammatory rhetoric. The mature Belinsky was no more bloodthirsty than the young Pushkin. It must be judged against the backdrop of Nicholas I's suffocating regime, when every independent thought met police punishment, and every free spirit faced ostracism and repression. To be sure, Belinsky was exaggerating when he wrote, "I am mortified by this spectacle of a society in which leading roles are given to scoundrels and perfect mediocrities, while everything noble and talented is hauled away to rot on an uninhabited island,"[38] but he was no malicious slanderer, and he certainly expressed an opinion current among his educated contemporaries. We should also balance the intelligentsia's radical declarations against its commitment to glasnost, art, and literature as vital to social progress, a commitment shared by nearly all Russian intellectuals, even those favoring violence, until the late 1980s. "For us Russians," wrote Chernyshevsky, "literature and poetry have a tremendous importance that is not matched anywhere in the world."[39] The significance that the *intelligenty* assigned to literature in the 1850s and 1860s was far greater than the role they reserved for violence. "For the public, literature is not something that makes it forget life's worries, not a sweet daydreaming in comfortable chairs after a heavy meal," wrote Belinsky. "No, from the stand-point of the public, literature is *res publica*, a public cause, a great deed, the source of moral joy and exaltation. . . . Where there is a public, the writing has a national agenda. . . . Where there is a public, there is public opinion."[40] The mid-nineteenth-century intelligentsia's contribution to the cause of freedom was mostly through literary criticism, which was just about the only semi-legitimate (eased up somewhat in 1865, censor-ship remained strict throughout the nineteenth century) form of critical discourse possible at the time. It was through the painstaking, sometimes forced, occasionally brilliant critique of literary works, theatrical perfor-mances, concerts, painting exhibitions, and the like that the Russian pub-lic learned how to glean the *Zeitgeist* from an artist's work. Through the eyes of Belinsky, Dobrolyubov, Chernyshevsky, and Pisarev, many loyal Russians came to see the corrupt state officials brought to life by Gogol's satirical imagination, to empathize with the yearnings of superfluous people like Mikhail Lermontov's Pechorin and Ivan Goncharov's Oblomov, and to discern the new hard-edged intellectuals exemplified by Ivan Turgenev's Bazarov and Nikolai Chernyshevsky's Rakhmetov.

The last type is particularly interesting, for it embodied the qualities that Russian intellectuals valued in themselves. "Rakhmetov can do with-out what is called personal happiness," wrote Pisarev about a revolution-ary hero pictured in Chernyshevsky's novel *What Is to Be Done*. "He has no need to refresh his strength through a woman's love, pleasant music, a Shakespearian play, or a festive supper with good friends. He has one weakness: a good cigar, which he needs to clear his thoughts. But even this pleasure is but a means for him: he smokes not because he enjoys smoking but because smoking stimulates his mental activity."[41] What is remarkable about statements like this that proliferated in this era is their cultivated asceticism and emotional self-repression. There seemed to be no room for private feelings in the Russian intelligentsia's moral calculus; a person was not to be judged on any other basis than his ideological con-victions. We already saw a hint of this antipersonalism in Chaadaev (though not in Pushkin, the quintessential humanist!), who argued that the individual was but an "abstraction" and "ephemeral insect" devoid of significance apart from his preassigned place in the world historical drama. One senses an even greater stringency in the self-imposed rigors of the intelligentsia. "The death of the particular for the sake of the uni-versal—such is the universal law," intoned Belinsky. "From now on, man is nothing for me; man's beliefs are everything. Conviction is the only thing that can unite me with people or turn me away from them."[42]

One need not be a psychiatrist to suspect that such vociferous opposi-tion to the private sphere and personal pleasures had something to do with the profound emotional disturbances hobbling Russian intellectuals.

This emotional asceticism could be traced in part to the disparity between the harsh realities spawned by quasi-modern Russia and intellectuals' longing for illusive Western liberties, between the communal bliss promised by socialist theories and the punishing discipline imposed on recalcitrant individuals by the tsarist regime. Hence the moralism, defensiveness, self-loathing, and sarcasm directed toward everyone and everything connected with the status quo.

I find Herzen's testimony especially moving here. His passion for justice never throttled his instinct for truth; his demanding attitude toward others never blinded him to his personal shortcomings. His humanism is nowhere more evident than in his brutally honest self-indictment, when he ruminates on the price he and his loved ones had to pay for his endless struggles and sacrifices: "We were born to destroy, our business was to weed and tear down, and for that purpose [we had to] negate and ironize—but even now, after we struck fifteen or twenty blows, we see that we built nothing, educated no one. The consequence—or, to put it bluntly—punishment—can be seen in the people around us, in the relations inside our families, and most of all, in our children."[43] Herzen's balanced insight was not shared by his successors, who reacted with stinging sarcasm and intolerance toward anyone who did not share their convictions. Herzen spotted this personal style in the Russian intellectuals who visited him abroad, such as Aleksandr Engelson and Sergei Nechaev, as well as his fellow immigrant, Mikhail Bakunin. Herzen wrote disparaging the Petrashevtsy, a socialist circle arrested by the Russian secret police in 1849:

> This circle included people who were young, gifted, extremely bright and educated, but also irritable, sickly, and broken. . . . Young emotions, bright and cheerful in their origins, were submerged and replaced by pride and jealous competitiveness. . . . They neither knew what happiness was nor cared to nurture it. On the mildest pretext they struck back ruthlessly and treated those closest to them rudely. They did as much damage and spoiled as many things with their irony as the Germans did with their sugary sentimentality.[44]

Needless to say, not all *intelligenty* personified such qualities. Still, there is enough evidence to be gleaned from their diaries, correspondence, and writings to corroborate Herzen's testimony.[45] Bred into their bones, where it calcified, rage against autocracy drove the *intelligenty* toward self-sacrifice and martyrdom, but it also disfigured their personal lives, stole the happiness of those who loved them the most, and left a trail of bitterness in its wake that no hope for the future could erase.

Soul-Searching and Self-Criticism
Among Intellectuals

By the time the 1860s came to a close, Russian intellectual culture had acquired its familiar traits and every educated person aspiring to be an *intelligent* started to feel its powerful pull. There was still the question of how to bring Russian reality in line with perceived historical demands. The *intelligenty* offered to lead the way, but who would heed the call? According to one Decembrist, "a party of masked men" pouncing on the regal cortege would suffice to set Russia on its modern path. But as Mikhail Lunin (the memorable phrase was his) and the Decembrists learned, remonstrating on Senate Square was not nearly enough.

Then came the familiar saw: the toiling masses—the people—must be roused and turned loose against their oppressors. In the 1870s, the young populists, members of the People's Will, took to the countryside, where they tried to persuade the peasants that their conditions were much too harsh and that they ought to rise up and make their voice heard. The people were to be led by "the critically thinking personality that understood itself as a possible and necessary agent of human progress."[46] The populist campaign was the first concerted effort to foment revolution in Russia. Unfortunately, it failed even more ignominiously than the Decembrists' reckless gamble. The masses did not know what to make of the populists' clamorous agitation. Rebelling against the tsar, the protector of the Russian Orthodox Church, seemed to many blasphemous. No wonder some populists were turned in to the police by the very people they had sworn to liberate. A handful of intellectuals were executed and many ended up in jail or Siberian exile, feeding the image—popular or sinister, depending on one's bias—of the young freedom fighter/nihilist sacrificing his life in the struggle for the people's happiness.

Disgusted with such political turpitude and embittered by the secret police's brutal response to their propaganda, the *intelligenty* sought to regroup. Some hotheads gave up on spreading the word altogether and resorted to propaganda by deed: bombing the royal family, assassinating state officials, sabotaging official institutions. Dmitry Karakozov's unsuccessful attempt to assassinate Alexander II in 1866 opened a new chapter in the intelligentsia's struggle with Russian tsarism. However, by the time the splintering People's Will managed to hunt down and assassinate Alexander II, the public mood in Russia had swung to the right.

As we saw earlier, intellectual culture in Russia received an impetus from Peter the Great's drastic campaign to Westernize Russian society. Radical *intelligenty* were very well aware of this connection. According to Chernyshevsky, it was the task of every critically minded intellectual, artist, and writer "to facilitate in every way possible Peter the Great's cause."[47] Yet, just as the Westernizers were lurching toward socialism and materialism via left Hegelianism, another faction, the Slavophiles, unfurled its banners heralding Russia's cultural superiority and unique path among the European nations. Aleksei Khomyakov, Ivan Kireevsky, Fyodor Tyutchev, and Ivan and Konstantin Aksakov belonged to this influential group, whose members saw the country's past as laden with religious archetypes bearing good tidings for Russia's future. What the Westernizers considered signs of backwardness—a weak legal state, abridged personal freedom, a rudimentary market, constricted property relations—the Slavophiles hailed as the country's traditional strength, in which every Russian should take pride. To the Western preoccupation with the law, the Slavophiles juxtaposed the Russian concern for ethically guided action; the Russian peasants' preference for communal living, they argued, was loftier than European individualism, which was inspired by arrogant humanism; the aversion to private property and competition underscored the Russian peasants' immunity to bourgeois culture. Even the obedience to the tsar and his servants' harsh orders revealed the loyalty and patience of Russia's long-suffering people. This patriotic exegesis that envisioned Russian culture as superior to any Western European model was vividly rendered in Lev Tolstoi's novel *War and Peace*.[48] There was a message for the intelligentsia in these Slavophile musings: Stop imitating the West, do not lead Russia into the abyss, learn from the Russian people. Konstantin Leontiev, a staunch conservative and dyed-in-the-wool Slavophile, wrote, "[H]e who understands how vitally important the cultural, national style is for our state and what a saving grace it could be for the Slavs to shed the *mental yoke* of Europe must wish not to enhance the intelligentsia's impact on the simple folk but, quite the contrary, must look for the best and easiest *ways to emulate the muzhik* (original emphasis)."[49]

The Slavophiles' nationalism was laced with irony, for those nineteenth-century Russian patriots owed as great a debt of gratitude to European thought as did the Westernizers. Slavophilism was propelled into being by the romantic reaction to the French revolution as exemplified by Joseph de Maistre, who lived in Russia for a time, where his words and writings enjoyed considerable influence. Slavophilism was especially indebted to the later Friedrich Wilhelm von Schelling. This eminent German philosopher spurned the Enlightenment and rationalism, elevated mystical and irrational intuition as the surest way to discern the divine will and enjoined each "folk" to carry out God's commandments in its own inimitable fashion. Still, unlike their ultraconservative followers, the original Slavophiles did not deny other nations their special place in world history and urged their countrymen to appreciate other peoples' customs. The point was to find a proper balance between the national and the world historical:

> [T]he advocates of Western Europe tout exclusively the European national form [*narodnost*], which they endow with world historical significance. In its name, they deprive the Russian people of their right to the universally human [*obshchechelovecheskoe*]. . . . But who said that the national view [*narodnoe vozzrenie*] rules out the universal human view? Quite to the contrary. We say "English literature," "French literature," "German literature," "Greek literature," and that does not bother us. . . . Why not grant the same right to the Russians? . . . To deny the Russian people the right to their own national view is to prevent them from partaking in world history.[50]

The great Russian writer Fyodor Dostoevsky articulated a similar view in his famous "Pushkin speech" in which he tried to reconcile Westernizers and Slavophiles. The speech was delivered on June 8, 1880, in connection with the dedication of a monument to Pushkin.[51] It belongs to the venerable Russian tradition, still very much alive, that seeks to fathom Pushkin's legacy for the present, that is, to decipher the cultural/political message to posterity embedded in Pushkin's literary corpus. In Dostoevsky's exegesis, Pushkin went through three stages in his career: (1) a wandering period, when he acted and wrote as a typical Russian intellectual seeking to escape oppressive Russian institutions and find solace in a foreign tradition; (2) a nativist period, when a mature Pushkin discovered that peace was to be found not beyond the country's borders but in Russian popular culture, in its rich heritage of folk tales and other cultural masterpieces and in the imperial glory secured for the nation by Peter the Great and his successors; (3) a synthetic period, when a wise Pushkin summoned his genius to fuse the native tradition with the cultural riches of other nations. In his talk, Dostoevsky warned the intelligentsia ("the Russian wanderers") to reclaim their national roots or risk becoming an albatross around the country's neck. "Humble yourself, proud man; first and foremost break your pride. Humble yourself, idle man; first and foremost come and toil on your homeland's soil."[52] Countering the rising tide of political violence, Dostoevsky deployed his celebrated argument against cruel means as inimical to genuine social reconstruction:

> Let us try to imagine that you are erecting a building that in the end will secure happiness for the entire human race and guarantee people peace and security at last. Imagine, also, that for this purpose you have to torture to death just one human being—maybe even not a very good person, one who might appear downright ridiculous to some. . . . Would

you consent to be an architect in such an undertaking and remain forever happy . . . if in the foundation of the building there were the suffering of just one, if only the pettiest, being ruthlessly and unjustly tortured to death?[53]

What makes the Russians different and what Pushkin's genius revealed beyond reasonable doubt, according to Dostoevsky, was that his countrymen were endowed with the rare ability to empathize with the pain and suffering of all humanity:

Yes, the calling of the Russian is undoubtedly all-European and universal. . . . Oh, European nations—they do not even know how dear they are to us! I believe that in the future we, or rather our successors, the future Russian people, will understand to the last person that to be a true Russian means striving to bring about a final reconciliation of European contradictions, to alleviate the European angst in our universal and all-embracing Russian soul, to absorb [*vmestit*] our brethren in it by means of brotherly love, and ultimately, perhaps to say a final word about the great universal harmony, the brotherly agreement among all tribes that live according to Christian evangelical law.[54]

Flawed though this exegesis may have been (as we saw earlier, Pushkin never completely surrendered his wandering spirit), Dostoevsky rightly sensed a new movement afoot in his land. Indeed, the public was ready to believe that "all our Slavophilism and Westernism is but one great confusion, albeit a necessary one."[55] When the radical intelligentsia began losing its monopoly on high cultural discourse, the intelligentsia began to split into competing camps. Radical intellectuals included old-style populists, anarchists, social democrats, social revolutionaries, and, since the early twentieth century, the Bolsheviks. The liberal camp was mostly inhabited by *zemstvo* activists, who came from the local administrations elected by popular vote from different social strata following Alexander II's cautious political reforms. Moderate conservatives with religious interests centered around the Vekhi group, whose leading representatives—Nikolai Berdiaev, Pyotr Struve, and Sergei Bulgakov—grew away from Marxism while remaining committed to personal freedom and parliamentary institutions. There was also a rightist faction represented by Konstantin Pobedonostsev, Leontiev, and their imitators, which championed ultranationalist causes and encouraged the notoriously anti-Semitic Black Hundreds movement to stamp out foreign influence and eradicate the left.

Any account of this period would be incomplete without mentioning Anton Chekhov, a famous playwright and short story writer. The sickly, somewhat reclusive man commanded respect from nearly all intellectual factions in Russia, even though left- and right-wing intellectuals felt uneasy about his politically noncommittal stance. Chekhov decried the "partisanship and cliquishness" that dominated the contemporary cultural scene and that he found inimical to creativity and fairness: "I fear those who search between my lines in the hope of discovering some tendency and pronouncing me a liberal or a conservative. I am not a liberal, a conservative, a gradualist, a monk, or an indifferentist. . . . My sacred creed is the human body, health, wit, talent, inspiration, love, and absolute freedom, the freedom from violence and lies, whichever form the latter might take."[56] Chekhov's resentment toward the partisan intelligentsia nagging him to choose between political camps would show more of an edge with time. This is what he had to say about left-wing intellectuals a few years before he died: "I do not believe in our intelligentsia, mendacious, sanctimonious, hysterical, bad-mannered, lazy—do not believe it even when it complains and pines away, for its oppressors come from its very depths. I believe only in separate individuals, whether they are *intelligenty* or muzhiks, for they are a real force, albeit a small one."[57]

The first sentence from this passage has been quoted ad infinitum and remains as popular among today's critics of the Russian intelligentsia as it was early in the century. Yet, it is apt to be misinterpreted as a blanket condemnation of all Russian intellectuals. In fact, Chekhov's views were far more differentiated and complex. His writings are filled with passages where he praises the intelligentsia's selfless work and forthright attitudes.[58] More importantly, commentators tend to overlook the evidence that Chekhov's revolt against the intelligentsia represented a revolutionary turn toward the civic virtues that are so vital to a civilized society, which the Russian intellectuals professed to endorse. *Poriadochnost* (decency) and *intelligentnost* (moral intelligence) are two terms that, following Chekhov, Russians would use to denote the new attitudes that the *intelligenty* must cultivate in themselves and display in all life's circumstances. Both words refer to persons who are trustworthy in their dealings, respect people regardless of their status, strive to do justice to an opponent's argument, display professionalism in their work, and seek to practice what they preach. The *intelligenty* who embody these social qualities possess moral intelligence, a trait by no means confined to people with educational credentials, white collar workers, artists, and the like, but widespread throughout the population. Moral intelligence is not a badge of honor that, once awarded, can be proudly displayed on any occasion: it is a claim to be redeemed, an ongoing accomplishment, an identity that is good only until further notice. Raising oneself from depraved conditions and becoming a morally intelligent person—such is the ideal that Chekhov bequeathed to his countrymen, particularly those aspiring to join the ranks of the intelligentsia:

What if you write a story about a young man, son of a serf, ex-shop-keeper, a high school and college student, brought up to honor rank, to slobber over priests' hands, to genuflect before other people's thoughts, who gave thanks for every piece of bread he received, was whipped repeatedly, walked through wet streets in leaking shoes, engaged in fights, tormented pets, loved to dine with rich relatives, casually lied to God and people just because he felt his nothingness. Write how this young man squeezes the slave out of himself, drop by drop, and how one glorious day he wakes up and realizes that it is not slave's blood coursing through his veins but real human blood.[59]

Chekhov's influence would be felt in many subsequent debates about the intelligentsia. A new element in these debates was the strong accent on *intelligentnost* ("moral intelligence" is the best translation I can think of here) as a trait distinguishing genuine *intelligenty*, on the intelligentsia as an ethical rather than a socioeconomic category. Ivanov-Razumnik highlighted this usage in his widely read history of the Russian intelligentsia's political activism, in which he censured those who "equate every 'educated' person with a representative of the intelligentsia, forgetting that no educational certificate can in and of itself turn an 'educated' person into an *intelligent*."[60] Mikhail Tugan-Baranovsky meant very much the same thing when he wrote, "[T]he term 'intelligentsia' is commonly used here to connote not so much a socioeconomic as a socio-moral category."[61]

Characteristically, intellectuals with disparate political agendas sought to appropriate Chekhov's legacy for their cause: those on the right cited his harsh words about the intelligentsia; those left of center recited his paeans to civic virtues. We can see this in two influential volumes that appeared a few years after the revolutionary upheavals of 1905–7 shattered the tsarist authorities' confidence and forced the regime into political concessions. One was published in 1909 by several religiously oriented writers under the title *Guideposts: Essays on the Russian Intelligentsia* (in Russian, *Vekhi*); the other, *The Intelligentsia in Russia*, was assembled a year later by liberals as a response to *Guideposts*.

The first opus launched a frontal attack on the Russian intellectual tradition. Nikolai Berdiaev used the derogative term *intelligentshchina* (rabid intellectualism) to disparage Russian intellectuals for their "cliquishness," "extreme emotionalism," "political despotism," and "artificial isolation from national life." These qualities, according to Berdiaev and his colleagues, had incited the bloody confrontations between workers and the authorities.[62] Pyotr Struve condemned radical intellectuals who breathed "arrogance and haughtiness" and showed "intolerance to dissent." Such intellectuals liked to strike "the proud and offensive pose of savior," to contrast themselves to *obyvateli* (or down-to-earth citizens) preoccupied with their daily routines; yet, their reckless agitation and aversion to acting through normal political venues precipitated chaos and bloodshed.[63] The intelligentsia displayed religious fervor in its political pursuits, but its "asceticism" and "vacuous heroism" was the obverse of the "patient selfless work" (*podvizhnichestvo*) expected from a devout Christian, inasmuch as bellicose intellectuals only paid lip service to "the notion of people's equal worthiness, the absolute dignity of each human being."[64]

In "The Ethics of Nihilism," Semyon Frank endeavored to show that the "intelligentsia's entire attitude toward politics, its fanaticism and intolerance, its impracticality and ineptitude in political matters, its obnoxious penchant for factional fighting, its warped sense of the state's mission—all this flows from its monastic-religious spirit, from the fact that its political activities are undertaken not so much to carry out reforms that are objectively useful in a secular sense as to exterminate the enemies of faith and to convert the infidels by force to its own faith."[65] Mikhail Gershenzon shed light on the intelligentsia's disturbing psychological traits, especially the sharp contrast between its moralism in public affairs and its unscrupulousness in private life. "The intelligentsia's daily life is, on the whole, a terrible mess," charged Gershenzon; its members show "not a trace of discipline, no effort to be consistent even in public (days are wasted God knows how, as the spirit moves them; everything is topsy-turvy); idleness, untidiness, Homeric unreliability in their personal affairs, a naive lack of good faith in their work, an unbridled despotism in politics, a callous indifference toward other individuals, and, before the authorities, sometimes proud challenge, sometimes meek compliance."[66]

The Vekhi authors had their own list of exemplary Russian thinkers—Pushkin, Gogol, Dostoevsky, Fet, Tyutchev—whom they praised lavishly for their nonpartisanship, humanistic beliefs, and universal, often religious, values, all of which were conspicuously absent in left-wing radicals. To head off the intelligentsia's dangerous proclivities, the Vekhi writers exhorted their followers to give up their obsession with politics, look deep inside their hearts, and rediscover the Christian faith from which the spirit of justice and egalitarianism so dear to socialists had originally sprung. "For all those who subscribe to this idea, which in my deep conviction, has religious roots," concluded Struve, "it must be clear that the Russian intelligentsia needs a radical perestroika of its socioeconomic worldview. I think that such a perestroika is already under way."[67]

A year after Vekhi, Russian liberals brought out a volume summing up their political creed. Liberal intellectuals concurred with the Vekhi writers that the left radicals' militancy and partisanship were regrettable, particularly after the 1905–7 upheavals and subsequent reforms opened up the political process, allowing Russian political parties to work together for socioeconomic progress. But the liberals chided the Vekhi critics for seeming to shun politics and disregard the historical context that had exacerbated intellectuals' mores. "[O]ne could not help meeting with disbelief and incredulity this call: be a human being, have faith, learn to love," inveighed Ivan Petrunkevich, "for the inevitable answer is that it is because I treat myself as, and feel like, a human being in solidarity with all other human beings, that I find it necessary to foster the [political] conditions without which human dignity will suffer; it is because I love and have faith that everything that concerns my personal life recedes into the background."[68]

Dmitry Ovsyaniko-Kulikovsky noted with satisfaction the movement away from ideologically rigid platforms to a more tolerant attitude toward opponents. "Since the [18]80s, the call for 'nonpartisanship' [*bespartiinost*] was heard among the intelligentsia, although this nonpartisanship should be understood in an ideological sense, as freedom from the demands of any ideology." He paid homage to Chekhov, whose stance, he insisted, did not mean a wholesale withdrawal from politics: "Among the people who advanced this slogan was Chekhov, who was immediately derided as lacking principles. Now we know that freedom from powerful ideologies does not mean a lack of principles and is far from implying intellectual and social indifference. The *intelligent* without a definite ideology but with definite principles and a thoughtfully chosen social and political orientation is currently becoming more and more widespread."[69]

Pavel Milyukov, a historian by training and head of the Constitutional Democratic party, ridiculed extremists' belief in "panaceas, messianic doctrines, and the immediate and decisive role of personal sacrifice."[70] At the same time, he rejected religious critics' spurious attempts to drive a wedge between the rootless intelligentsia and the patriotic folk, since "the appearance of the intelligentsia is a necessary precondition before a nation can acquire its own self-consciousness. Self-consciousness is a product of consciousness-raising by the *intelligenty*."[71] Milyukov pointed out that overzealous habits had been forced upon the intelligentsia by oppressive political institutions which left few alternatives to the progressive forces opposed to autocratic rule. The situation changed for the better, he went on, once parliamentary organs began to be formed in Russia after 1905, and it would continue to change in the future, as the Russian political process was funneled into more normal channels: "As its influence grows, the sectarian character of [the intelligentsia's] ideology will weaken, its content diversify, its goals become more specific, its immediate task become more concrete, its pragmatic qualities improve, and its public activity acquire continuity, organization, and systematization."[72]

Liberal pragmatism seemed at odds with the Vekhi writers' revivalist tone, but the differences between the two should not be exaggerated. Both groups acknowledged that ideological extremism disfigures those who indulge in it, both emphasized the civilizing effect that the rule of law has on society, and both endorsed reforms carried out through legitimate political channels and urged intellectuals to cultivate civility as a condition for civic society. The primary target audience in each case was the nascent middle class, whose entrance on the political scene had been delayed by the country's autocratic tradition. Moreover, neither program really implied that the Russian intelligentsia would cease to be a political force. Contrary to all appearances, the Vekhi authors remained squarely rooted in the Russian intellectual tradition—witness their passion for justice, exalted view of high culture, and commitment to public discourse as a vehicle for social reconstruction. They endeavored to rid Russian intellectual culture of its ideological intolerance, emotional violence, and heroic grandstanding, points on which conservatives and liberals saw eye to eye.

Such was the era's original contribution to Russian intellectual culture. This epoch started with the Slavophiles' attack on extreme Westernism and Dostoevsky's critique of the intelligentsia's rootlessness; it witnessed Chekhov's appeal for civility and nonpartisanship; and it ended in soul-searching by the Vekhi authors and liberal thinkers. Anton Chekhov was particularly instrumental in exposing the lack of civility among the intelligentsia, its failure to see the link between bourgeois culture and democratic institutions. In rejecting *meshchanstvo*, Russian intellectuals also rejected the civic virtues undergirding bourgeois democracy: respect for law, private property, and the dignity of other people; willingness to compromise and work through legitimate political channels; cultivation of professionalism in one's work. Chekhov's ambivalence toward the intelligentsia reflected the intelligentsia's own ambivalence about middle-class values. Late-bloomers by world historical standards, Russian intellectuals could see not only the glories of capitalist modernity but also its discontents. The intelligentsia might have been a modernizing force in Russian history, but it also wished to prolong the remnants of communitarianism harking back to Russia's premodern past. Hence came its philippics against bourgeois philistinism, contempt for *obyvateli* and *meshchane*, dismal work habits, and bohemian unscrupulousness in personal relations. With Chekhov, the Vekhi critics, and liberal intellectuals, Russia began to inch toward psychological modernity, which grounds civic society in civic virtues. Ultimately, lasting social change must encompass both individuals and institutions, whether one starts with oneself or with the political system. Were it not for the Bolshevik revolution, the liberal program of fostering a middle-class culture and civic society in Russia might have succeeded. Unfortunately, liberal critics never got their message across. They remained marginal in the overpoliticized world of Russian cultural politics and soon yielded to left-wing radicalism.

The Intelligentsia Under Soviet Rule

One reason the nineteenth-century intelligentsia tried to shoulder such a heavy load of responsibilities was that it could not find an ally in its strenuous efforts to bring political modernization to Russia. In Europe, the intellectual stratum grew largely out of the bourgeoisie and more or less faithfully served its needs, but the Russian intelligentsia had virtually no ties to the third estate, which did not come into its own until well into the nineteenth century. Before the intelligentsia could liberate any class, therefore, it had to mold it into a self-conscious political entity. If the Decembrists had any claim to stake concerning class representation, it had to do with the gentry's interests. This claim, made in rather oblique fashion, did have some historical grounds: The Decembrists were committed to liberating their estate from autocratic excesses and to consolidating the gains the Russian gentry made during the reign of Catherine II. For all their republican zeal, however, the Decembrists had no intention of dismantling serfdom; they were also quite content to leave the monarchy in place.

The emancipation schemes favored by the populists were designed to benefit "the people"—the meek, toiling masses believed to be oppressed by the tsarist regime. But the Russian serfs were too amorphous, illiterate, and unself-conscious a social entity to act as an agent of historical change. Liberal intellectuals appealed primarily to the middle class, which stood to gain the most from the intended political reforms. The middle class was an increasingly assertive social stratum at the turn of the century, although its influence was confined chiefly to cities and provincial centers. Conservatives wished to preserve the existing class structure or, better still, revert to more archaic social forms concocted by the conservative romantics' vivid imagination.

There was also a small Social Democratic party, whose followers embraced the Marxist doctrine, pinning their hopes on wage labor—the proletariat. But their claim to "representing a class" was particularly far-fetched given that industrial workers made up barely 3 percent of the Russian population at the century's turn.[73] Aware that nurturing the Russian proletariat was a long-term project, moderate Social Democrats—the Mensheviks—tried to open up their party and turn it into a mainstream organization with a broad socialist appeal. The party's radical wing, the Bolsheviks, remained committed to the dogma that envisioned the proletariat seizing power and freeing the country from the parasitic classes exploiting others' labor. The thankless task of raising the workers' class consciousness fell to the educated party members, who went about their business in much the same way as their populist predecessors, relying primarily on propaganda and agitation but also making a concerted effort to set up a party organization, train professional revolutionaries, and utilize clandestine publications.

From the start, the Bolsheviks' feelings about the intelligentsia were fraught with ambivalence. Vladimir Lenin and his followers understood all too well that an educated elite had to rouse and lead the masses to the barricades. They also acknowledged their debt to the great tradition of Russia's radical democrats. At the same time, the Bolsheviks went out of their way to distinguish themselves both from populist intellectuals, whose program they found unsuitable for the industrial age, and from liberal thinkers, whose middle-class instincts and preference for discursive means were unmistakably bourgeois. As Lev Trotsky (a Menshevik who later joined the Bolshevik faction) noted in an early article about the intelligentsia, because Russia lacked well-organized socioeconomic groups, radical intellectuals were compelled to act as a "class substitute" and to invest much time in training progressive classes for their final assault on the autocratic state. "However great the intelligentsia's role might have been in the past," Trotsky pointed out, "it will occupy a dependent and subordinate place in the future."[74] Thus, the Bolsheviks declined to count themselves among the mainstream intelligentsia. They saw their party as the vanguard of the working class and reserved no special political role for the intelligentsia in a future socialist society, where intellectuals would simply become a service group distinguished by their education and technical skills.

While in opposition, the Bolsheviks listed basic civil liberties among their political demands. They reasserted their commitment to glasnost after the revolution toppled the tsarist regime in February 1917, using newfangled political institutions to buttress their public image as a radically democratic force. Sometime in the summer of 1917, state institutions began to collapse, and on October 26, 1917, the Bolsheviks seized power. Almost immediately, they ordered the closure of hostile publishing outlets, starting with the conservative press, then spread the ban to liberal newspapers, and eventually disallowed all publications that refused to bow to the Bolshevik dictate.[75] The October revolution (critics would call it a putsch), dealt a major setback to the hopes for democratic reform the Russian intelligentsia had nurtured for decades.

The February revolution had been but a few months old when the mood among Russian intellectuals already began to sour. Gone were the boastful declarations about the bloodless revolution brought about by the selfless intelligentsia. In their place we find laments about the diminished role of culture and cultural workers in society. "A mindless crusade against cultured Russia is raging on," wrote one liberal newspaper in September 1917. "The fist—quite literally—is crushing cultural treasures that it took the nation centuries to acquire. A crusade is being waged against the producers of cultural values—against the Russian intelligentsia doomed to suffer under the autocratic regime and now under the triumphant democracy."[76] Increasingly confused in the face of fast-paced events that overwhelmed the fledgling republic, Russian intellectuals felt disappointed with the "toiling masses" they had helped stir into action. The working people's hostility toward the wealthy and powerful stratum spilled over onto all educated classes. Intellectuals protested that it was wrong to lump them together with the bourgeoisie, that they worked hard as custodians of national culture, and that their labor was indispensable to building a civilized society in Russia, but their voices drowned in the revolutionary din. The Bolsheviks' massive attack on civil liberties stunned the already demoralized Russian intelligentsia. For the first time its members were truly frightened by the revolutionary flames they had so enthusiastically fanned.

Zinaida Gippius was right when she claimed that the intelligentsia was "solidly anti-Bolshevik at the time" and that "the exceptions were very few."[77] Virtually all nongovernment newspapers attacked the Bolsheviks, demanding the restoration of glasnost. The nation's leading intellectuals wrote personal letters to the Bolshevik authorities pleading with them to change their misguided course and free citizens arrested on trumped-up ideological charges (the correspondence between the writer Vladimir Korolenko and Anatoly Lunacharsky, head of Narkompros, The People's Commissariat of Enlightenment, is a fine example of this genre). Even some intellectuals close to Lenin were taken aback by his reckless grab for power. Maksim Gorky, an important writer and well-known public figure with links to the Bolsheviks, waged a losing battle against the new regime in the columns of his newspaper *Novaia zhizn'* (New Life). "Lenin, Trotsky and their cronies have already been poisoned by power," wrote Gorky on November 7, 1917. "Witness their shameful attitude toward the freedom of speech, the individual, and the sum total of rights for which democracy fought for so long."[78] Rather than mobilizing the national intellectual resources, charged Gorky, the Bolsheviks had declared war on the intelligentsia. Not only were intellectuals losing their livelihood and their rights, they were also terrorized by the rabble pitted against the middle classes by unscrupulous communists. "Something urgently needs to be done. We have to stop the process that leaves the intelligentsia physically and spiritually exhausted. It is time to realize that it is the nation's brain, which was never more needed than today."[79]

Needless to say, Gorky's newspaper was closed. To his tirade in defense of the intelligentsia, Lenin answered with a well-known quip about those "pathetic *intelligenty*, lackeys of capitalism who pride themselves on being the nation's brain. In fact, they are not its brain, they're its shit."[80] This motto summed up the views on the recalcitrant intelligentsia held by the Bolsheviks during this period. There were concerted efforts to engage intellectuals with valuable technical skills (military officers, railroad engineers, doctors, and so on) in state-sponsored programs, but those with a liberal arts education or a hostile world view were considered a drag on the economy and a dangerous fifth column that had to be neutralized before it began fomenting an opposition. After a brief respite that the communist government gave to the nation in the hope of restoring its economic health, the Bolsheviks renewed their attack on the intelligentsia. In the spring of 1922, Lenin ordered massive arrests among the Bolsheviks' erstwhile allies, the Mensheviks. Some were deported to Russia's Far East, some permanently exiled abroad. The Social Revolutionaries met with the same fate in the fall of 1922. The world was startled when in August 1922 the Bolsheviks put the nation's leading philosophers on a ship (it would become known as the "ship of philosophers") and sent them into exile in the West, with the promise to shoot anyone who dared come back.[81] *Pravda* printed an article on August 31, 1922, to mark the occasion, bearing an eloquent title: "First Warning." About the same time, Feliks Dzerzhinsky, the feared head of the secret police, dispatched a directive to his deputy: "Information must be gathered by all departments and funneled into the intelligentsia department. There must be a file for every *intelligent*. . . . Also, we must keep an eye on all literature in our jurisdiction."[82]

The key elements in Communist party policy on the intelligentsia were to assert strict control over "brain workers," separate the politically reliable from the unreliable intellectuals, instill communist ideology in professional cadres, and raise a new generation of proletarian intelligentsia.[83] "We need intelligentsia cadres that are ideologically trained in a certain way," wrote Nikolai Bukharin, a leading communist intellectual at the time. "Yes, we shall mold *intelligenty*, we shall manufacture them as if on an assembly line."[84] Countering the charge that the Bolsheviks had betrayed the intelligentsia's emancipatory ideals, Lunacharsky wrote that you "cannot expel Bolshevik-*intelligenty* from the intelligentsia and dismiss the great role it played in the history of this 'order.'"[85] He also noted cynically, however, "The more lacking in ideas the person is today, the more valuable he is. That is to say, if a technical specialist [*spets*], say, some engineer, has many ideas, it is worse, for these ideas distract a person from his work. But if he has no ideas, we could let him work right away."[86] The Bolsheviks were setting up a social machine in which each cog and spindle was to serve its appointed task, with the intellectuals doing their job as social technicians under the close supervision of the Communist party's social engineers.

Not all intellectuals immediately rejected the Bolshevik takeover. Some felt that the new regime deserved a chance, that it had to act swiftly to fend off the reactionaries, that civil rights would be restored once the emergency situation eased up. As usual, Russian writers led the way. Vladimir Mayakovsky, Aleksandr Blok, Valery Bryusov, Sergei Esenin, Nikolai Klyuev, Boris Pilnyak, Isaak Babel, and several other prominent literary figures threw in their lot with the Bolsheviks. Poet Bryusov became a censor. Mayakovsky prided himself on dedicating his muse to the proletarian cause. Esenin and Klyuev hailed the revolutionary whirlwind that had stirred the hitherto inert peasant masses into political action.[87] Pilnyiak and Babel wrote novels glorifying Soviet power's early years. Particularly intriguing was the case of Aleksandr Blok, Russia's premier Symbolist poet. Blok greeted the October revolution with a statement in response to a questionnaire published under the title, "Can the Intelligentsia Work with the Bolsheviks?" His answer: "It can and it ought to [for] the intelligentsia hears the same music as the Bolsheviks. The intelligentsia has always been revolutionary. The Bolshevik decrees are the symbols of the intelligentsia. [The latter's] bitter feelings about the Bolsheviks are a superficial phenomenon, and they are beginning to pass away."[88]

Blok's clumsy attempt to justify the October revolt by invoking poetic symbols of "chaos," "storm," and "rebellion" supposedly shared by the revolutionaries and creative intelligentsia provoked a fierce rebuttal from old school thinkers, who accused him of kowtowing to the Bolsheviks, thumbing his nose at the rule of law, and betraying innocent victims to be sacrificed to the revolutionary cause. Ilya Erenburg reminded Blok in his article "The Intelligentsia and Revolution" that violent means compromise sound ends and that the lofty slogans deployed by the Bolsheviks could be just a coverup for their ruthless drive to power. Every time I hear slogans like "peace" and "brotherhood," intimated Erenburg, I cannot help wondering if "they are about to start shooting," "if I am going to be killed."[89]

Blok penned a few more articles on revolution and the intelligentsia and gathered them in a volume bearing the same title, but his enthusiasm for the new regime ebbed as the Bolsheviks stepped up their arrests and expulsions of intellectuals. In his last public speech, he suddenly changed his tune and reverted to time-honored Russian symbols. The occasion could not have been more portentous—the literary gathering commemorating Pushkin's death. Blok quoted Pushkin extensively, citing the famous lines from the 1836 verse where the poet intimated his subversive wish "for no livery/to bend my neck, my conscience, my belief." Also recited were Pushkin's paeans to "a secret freedom" that would take on a new meaning for several generations of intellectuals forced to live under Soviet rule:

> Love and a secret freedom were my beacon,
> They taught my heart its simple tune,

> To all chicanery and flattery immune,
> My voice was the Russian people's echo.[90]

Blok ended his speech with a thinly veiled warning to the authorities never to meddle with the poet's secret freedom: "Let bureaucrats face scorn if they wish to guide poetry into authorized channels, if they violate its secret freedom and try to interfere with its mystic destiny."[91] Soon afterward, Blok's health took a turn for the worse. He applied for a visa to go abroad for medical treatment, but it was denied. After prominent Bolsheviks pleaded his case before the authorities, the Politburo (the Communist party's ruling organ) reversed its earlier decision, but it was too late. Fading away in a matter of months (doctors were never sure what ailed him), Blok died at the age of forty-one, a few days before the state finally issued him a visa. The prophetic words of his last public speech served as the poet's own epitaph: "It was not the bullet of Dantes that killed Pushkin. He died because there was no air left to breathe."[92]

Blok's fate was not unique among intellectuals who disfavored the liberal government brought to power in February 1917 and sided with the Bolsheviks after their October takeover either out of conviction or just to see a steadier hand at the helm. Esenin and Mayakovsky committed suicide. Klyuev, Pilnyak, and Babel died in Stalin's concentration camps along with countless communist sympathizers. Even Communist party intellectuals who pledged to weed out the bourgeois intelligentsia and replace it with proletarian seedlings discovered that they were not invulnerable to the anti-intellectualist forces they had set in motion. Nikolai Bukharin, Karl Radek, Yury Pyatakov, Grigory Zinoviev, Lev Kamenev, Aleksei Rykov, Khristian Rakovsky, and many others perished in Stalin's purges. Lunacharsky died of natural causes, but only because he did not live long enough to see the mass purges. Thanks to his expulsion from the country, Trotsky managed to survive longer: he was murdered on Stalin's order in Mexico, in 1940. The purges came in waves, decimating all classes in Soviet society; among the hardest hit, in relative terms, was the intelligentsia.

Not held in high esteem by Lenin and his comrades, Joseph Stalin went to unimaginable lengths to settle scores with everybody who had ever had the misfortune to doubt his intellect and moral intelligence. In the mid-1930s, he unleashed an unprecedented campaign against the party brass, setting cadres with working-class backgrounds against old-time party theoreticians.[93] By far the most sensational public trial staged by Stalin's henchmen was directed against the so-called Rightist-Trotskyist bloc, featuring as star defendant Nikolai Bukharin, once designated by Lenin as the party's leading intellectual. As one reads the ridiculous charges leveled against the defendants, hears the obsequious praises they heaped on Stalin, and recoils at the way they abased themselves hoping to save their own lives and those of their relatives, one realizes that the *absence* of glasnost is not the worst thing an intellectual can face. Although Bukharin found courage to deny some of the charges brought against him, he confessed to monstrous crimes he never committed:

> I admit that I am guilty of treason against the Socialist fatherland, the most heinous of crimes possible, of the organization of kulak uprisings, of preparations for terrorist acts, and of belonging to an underground, anti-Soviet organization. . . . The severest sentence would be justified, because a man deserves to be shot ten times over for such crimes. . . . I kneel before the country, before the party, before the whole people. The monstrosity of my crimes is immeasurable, especially in the new stage of the struggle for the USSR.[94]

This was the last public statement Bukharin ever made. He knew that his life was about to end, yet he was praising his mortal enemy ("in reality the whole country stands behind Stalin; he is the hope of the world; he is a creator"[95]), because there was still a glimmer of hope—not for himself but for his loved ones held hostage by Stalin. *Golos, glas, glasnost*—the root morpheme is always "voice," the ability to utter, make sense, express oneself. It is this gift of free speech that Lenin and Stalin took away from the people. Worse still, Stalin forced people to say things they did not mean, things they found repugnant. The voicelessness enforced by the autocratic tsars seemed like bliss compared to the perverse glasnost of Stalin's reign: "People gifted with a voice faced the worst possible torture: Their tongues were ripped out and they had to praise their master with the bloody stump. The desire to live was irrepressible, and it coerced people into this form of self-annihilation just to extend their physiological existence. The survivors were as dead as those who actually died."[96] These words belong to Nadezhda Mandelshtam, the widow of Osip Mandelshtam, arguably the greatest twentieth-century Russian poet, who perished in Stalin's concentration camps. Nadezhda Mandelshtam's memoirs are among the most riveting accounts of the intelligentsia's subterranean existence in this macabre age. She wrote about the Russian intelligentsia, who were brought up to revere the spoken word, who saw major strides made toward free expression, and whose members woke up one day in a different country, where the free word had become a capital offense. While some intellectuals publicly attacked the revolutionary decrees curtailing glasnost, other chose to lay low in hopes that Bolshevik rule would not last. In the end, they all were condemned for their "negative attitudes," which earned them the reputation of a reactionary force in the eyes of the new authorities. Since the state quickly asserted its monopoly over employment, intellectuals had little choice but to cooperate with the regime.

"Is there anybody among us," wrote Zinaida Gippius, another survivor from this era, "the most farsighted and incorruptible person imaginable, who is not haunted by the memories of the compromises we were forced to make during St. Petersburg's captivity, who did not plead with Gorky for something or other or eat stale bread from our enemies' hands? I know the taste of such bread, this accursed ration, as well as the feel of Soviet money in my hands."[97] The Soviet government had no intention of making the intellectuals' capitulation easy. It spared no effort in showing them who was boss, in drumming into their heads the conditions of surrender, for which they would be rewarded according to the sincerity of their remorse and willingness to inform on their brethren still persisting in their obstinate ways. Most chose to compromise not out of conviction but out of necessity, yielding to the survival instinct, citing the need to protect children, family. "Theoretically, I know that one should not compromise, but how could I urge somebody to throw caution to the wind and not to compromise, to forget about their children? To all my friends I counsel—compromise," wrote Nadezhda Mandelshtam. "There is one more thing I can add: Do not bring children into this monstrous world."[98]

Writers and artists found it particularly hard to silence their consciences. "I harbor no hatred toward anybody—that is my 'precise ideology,'" wrote Mikhail Zoshchenko in 1921.[99] These words would be dredged up twenty-five years later by Andrei Zhdanov, a party hack in charge of Soviet art and ideology who publicly humiliated the writer for his conciliatory stance and alleged counterrevolutionary sentiments. When Yury Olesha talked about the psychological difficulties that intellectuals faced adjusting to the new regime, he became a symbol of the "rotten [gnilaia] intelligentsia" and subjected to endless derision as an ideologically unstable element (Ilf and Petrov's fictional intelligent Vasisualy Lokhankin bore some traits reminiscent of Olesha). "I seize my own self, reach out to strangle that part of myself which suddenly balks and stirs its way back to the old days," wrote Olesha; "I wish to stifle that second 'self,' and the third self, and every 'self' that comes to haunt me from the past."[100] Vladimir Mayakovsky described the arduous labor of fitting an old self into the new Soviet ideology as "stepping on your own song's throat." His own labor continued until the moment he finally sent a bullet through his head. Maksim Gorky was never forced to do penance in public, for he was too much revered by the Bolsheviks as the first proletarian writer; but when he yielded to tempting invitations and returned to Russia from his exile in Italy, he found himself increasingly isolated, mistrusted, and ignored. Soon after his son was murdered by the NKVD (a KGB precursor), Gorky died under mysterious circumstances—but not before he paid his tribute to the glories of the Stalinist system, the founder of "socialist realism" in literature and the chief "engineer of human souls."

The Bolsheviks stopped exiling their enemies abroad in the early 1920s, although a handful found their way to the West in the mid-1920s. About the same time, officially sponsored trips abroad by Soviet citizens were drastically curtailed (Mayakovsky committed suicide soon after he lost his traveling privileges, when the authorities began to suspect his loyalty). Those who missed the last train or did not wish to taste the stale bread of emigration were forced to collaborate with the regime. Sometime in the early 1930s, poet Boris Pasternak acknowledged that Soviet power was well entrenched, that the Russian people seemed to have sided with the communists, and that it was time for writers to accept the inevitable.[101] Osip Mandelshtam, who worked for various Soviet publications, called himself "a Bolshevik without a party card."[102] Mikhail Bulgakov assured the NKVD that he considered the Soviet regime "extremely stable," that he had "sunk strong roots in Soviet Russia," and that he could "not imagine himself as a writer outside" his homeland.[103] Marina Tsvetaeva, who returned to the Soviet Union after seventeen years in emigration, had to swear her political correctness and the loyalty of her husband, who was arrested by the NKVD soon after his return ("[My husband] served his homeland and the communist idea with his soul and body, word and deed").[104] Anna Akhmatova, whose husband, poet Nikolai Gumilyov, was executed by the Bolsheviks and whose son languished in the Gulag, had to repent in public after being vilified for writing apolitical, decadent verses. Mikhail Zoshchenko contributed stories to Lenin's hagiography and visited the infamous Baltic–White Sea canal project, where political prisoners were used as slave laborers. Yury Olesha penned essays about the happy family of Soviet people and took part in the campaign against composer Dmitry Shostakovich. And these were the best and the brightest, individuals whose personal courage, indomitable spirit, and creative accomplishments—despite their outward obeisance to the state—would be an inspiration for generations to come.

But it would be an oversimplification to dismiss the conversion experiences of some as nothing but protective mimicry. "Mandelshtam," wrote his widow, "always tried to make up his mind freely and check his actions against reality, but even he was not an entirely free person: the noise of time, the noise of life conspired to suppress his inner voice: 'How could I be right if everybody thinks otherwise.'"[105] The cognitive dissonance between their actions and their beliefs, exacerbated by enforced unanimity, wore many down into eventual acceptance of what appeared to be an objective judgment of history.

We should also resist the temptation to erect too sharp a divide between the innocent intelligentsia bludgeoned into collaboration with the regime and the latter's faithful servants. There were many communists, state officials, and lowly bureaucrats who never completely surrendered their "secret freedom" and were perturbed by Stalin's atrocities. We find numerous, often grudging, references in memoirs from this era to the helping hand that this or that Soviet official offered beleaguered intellectuals in times of trouble. It could be Anatoly Lunacharsky, head of the People's Commissariat of Enlightenment, which supervised communist education and propaganda, who bombarded the Politburo with letters demanding an exit visa for Blok and helped dozens of intellectuals to leave Russia when that was still possible. Or it could be the lowly clerk arranging a ration card for a hungry writer and declining to report his angry mutterings to the secret police. "These were people who did quite well 'up there' but who did not forget their old friends. Some of 'us' are still alive thanks to their efforts."[106]

Whether they were on good terms with the regime or languished at its margins, intellectuals led a double or triple existence, thinking one thing to themselves, saying another within earshot of family and friends, and saying and doing something else in public. This multilayered existence left a profound mark on Soviet intellectuals' psyche. They could pride themselves on their "secret freedom," but they also knew that they were compromising their consciences. The pattern familiar to us from the time of Pushkin and Chaadaev blossomed in the Soviet Union, where double-speak and double-think were perfected to an art form. Just consider Mandelshtam's 1934 verse bitterly renouncing Stalin and his 1937 poem praising the tyrant. Bulgakov's novel *The Master and Margarita* satirized Soviet society, but the same author wrote a play, *Batum,* extolling Stalin's virtues. Pasternak's *Doctor Zhivago* could not erase his verses about Joseph Stalin, the nation builder. Anna Akhmatova, a proud spirit steadfastly squelching every temptation to collaborate with the regime, wrote a poem glorifying Soviet Russia's spectacular accomplishments. Most of these writings are unexemplary and better left unread (although Mandelshtam's 1937 "Ode to Stalin" is a work of rare poetic power).[107] Some were written under duress (Akhmatova hoped her verses would buy amnesty for her son), but all testified to the torturous existence led by the Soviet intellectual burdened with conscience and memory.

Even in this eerie age, however, there were certain standards of morality within intelligentsia circles. When Stalin telephoned Pasternak and questioned him about Mandelshtam, who had recently been arrested by the NKVD for his anti-Stalinist verse, Pasternak answered that he did complain about Mandelshtam's arrest and that his friend should be released.[108] No, he did not confront the tyrant; he did not tell him what a disgrace to humanity he was or put him on notice that there was a special place reserved for him in Dante's ninth circle of hell. But Anna Akhmatova and Nadezhda Mandelshtam rightly concluded in their postmortem of this conversation that, under the circumstances, Pasternak's behavior "merits a solid 'B' grade." Agonizing about one's actions in morally charged situations, evaluating and reevaluating an individual's conduct under trying circumstances, would become a sad pastime for Soviet intellectuals.

Mikhail Saltykov-Shchedrin, a famous nineteenth-century satirist, formulated a classic question facing the Russian intelligentsia: What is to be done when there is nothing you can do? As Soviet experience showed, there were things intellectuals could do to salvage their battered consciences. This is the advice Arkady Belinkov offered in his book about Yury Olesha, a brilliant study indispensable to understanding the psychology of the Soviet intelligentsia: "The worst thing an intellectual can do [while working for the system] is to strive to do his base duty with distinction, better than others, to be the top student."[109] In other words, one had to do as little damage to others as possible, take on only such assignments as could not be evaded, and do private penance among friends for one's less than commendable deeds. Mikhail Svetlov joked, "An honest person is one who never does anything dishonest, except when he is forced to, and who is disgusted with himself every time he does do something dishonest."

Irony, sarcasm, black humor, and anecdotes parodying official symbols would become indispensable weapons in the arsenal of the Soviet intelligentsia struggling to maintain a degree of critical distance from inane Soviet realities. Irony is a clue that what seems to be going on is only a front, not to be confused with the true, private self hidden beneath the official uniform. Ironic detachment is worn like a merit badge (or a stigma, depending on how you look at it) that the individual uses to highlight his difference, to let an alternative spiritual reality gleam through the debased discourse. We have seen how this behavioral gambit was used by nineteenth-century intellectuals to rather mixed effect. The Soviet intelligentsia used the same technique.

Nadezhda Mandelshtam recalled her encounters in the early 1920s with Ilya Erenburg, when "he looked on everything as if he were a stranger . . . and hid himself behind ironic omniscience. He had already figured out that irony was the weapon of the helpless."[110] We find brilliant examples of irony and satire in Viktor Shklovsky's novel *The Zoo*, in Mikhail Bulgakov's *Master and Margarita*, and Mandelshtam's *Fourth Prose*. Arkady Belinkov lampoons Soviet reluctance to admit that there might be problems in this most perfect of all possible worlds: "Even in our days, though extremely rarely and only in extraordinary situations, minor contradictions sometimes arise between our bad artists and our wonderful society. Those minor and instantly resolvable contradictions usually arise in connection with the slight incongruity between socialist realism and realistic socialism."[111]

Any Soviet intellectual—or any experienced censor—would immediately recognize such overextended official rhetoric as an irreverent gesture toward official Soviet ideology, which is why none of the works mentioned were published in Stalin's Russia. Written in secret and kept away from outsiders, sometimes even from family and friends, such works should be seen as surviving monuments to "secret freedom," Pushkin's and now the Soviet intellectual's last solace. As for irony, this ultimate weapon of the spiritual proletariat, it was directed mostly at relatives, colleagues, and friends, who bore the brunt of bitterness and alienation that creative spirits suffered in the land of perverted glasnost. Memoirs from this period tell us about the price intellectuals paid for their survival, about their collective "traumatic psychosis," as Nadezhda Mandelshtam called the phenomenon, although we are already familiar with it under the name "terrible ulcer" that Chaadaev gave to it in the nineteenth century. Subsumed under these terms are abnormalities encysted in a psyche that suffered intellectual abuse firsthand or witnessed the ideological bloodbath from afar. A silent witness, points out Igor Kon, a sociologist who survived Stalinism, was worse off in some ways, particularly if he was young.[112] The helplessness and terror experienced by the children whose parents were declared "enemies of the people" induced a trauma they would not be able to shake for life. This grim legacy of political purges will remain with the Russian intelligentsia for some time to come.

The Stalinist era made few original contributions to Russian intellectual culture. It only exacerbated certain traits that were already present during the tsars. Its legacy was apparent in the ever-widening gap between word and deed, in the perverted glasnost imposed on the population by NKVD inquisitors, in intellectuals' spiritual withdrawal ("inner emigration"), in the off-putting interpersonal style aimed at negating fear and debunking official realities through exaggerated irony and sarcasm, and the resultant syndrome of self-loathing displayed by intellectuals alienated from society, from each other, and from their public selves. Stalinist social technologies stifled the personal voice, drove private feelings inside, installed false consciousness in place of freely chosen convictions, and replaced the curative powers of dialogue with the numbing force of propaganda. It would take decades for Russian intellectual culture to free itself from the Stalinist legacy. This process even now is far from complete, although it began many years ago, during the ideological "thaw" that Russia experienced after Stalin's death.

The Intelligentsia and the Thaw

The first step toward sheering Russian intellectual discourse of its Stalinist diction was taken not by an intellectual but by the uncouth, boorish Nikita Khrushchev, Stalin's protégé and temporary victor in the struggle for power that followed Stalin's death.

In 1956, Khrushchev gave a speech at the Twentieth Party Congress in which he denounced Stalin and his terrorist tactics. The speech was secret and the speaker was mainly preoccupied with the plight of innocent communists devoured by the Gulag, but its effect was felt by the entire country. In 1961, at the Twenty-second Party Congress, Khrushchev reaffirmed his commitment to the rule of law, to democratic procedures within the party, to greater freedom for artists, and to improving the welfare of the population as a whole. The "society [that] shoved the flute down the musician's throat"[113] seemed ready to recoil from past horrors and grant its members greater leeway. Khrushchev might not have realized what he was setting in motion, but the seeds of glasnost that he planted survived his reign, sprouted in underground intellectual bunkers, and in time, sapped the communist regime's vitality to the point when it was ready to collapse.

Ever since the Bolshevik takeover, a debate had been raging inside and outside Russia as to whether the old Russian intelligentsia were dead and whether it could be brought back to life. According to Georgy Fedotov, one of the most perceptive historians to study the subject, "The intelligentsia that was decimated by the revolution has lost its meaning and cannot be resuscitated."[114] Other writers disagreed, arguing that the old Russian intelligentsia might be dead but the new one, bearing a strong family resemblance to the prototype, would no doubt emerge. Fedotov himself was ambivalent in this regard; at the end of his career he called for a new "intellectual elite" that could rejuvenate Russia.[115] Whether or not the intellectuals who called themselves *intelligenty* in post-Stalin Russia are related to the old intelligentsia, these intellectuals took pride in calling themselves by this word that commonly had been used as a term of derision in Stalin's time, and they were eager to trace their lineage to their illustrious predecessors and continue their emancipatory work. I cannot do justice here to the diverse intellectual currents that sprang to life in this heady era, but I will try, using broad brush strokes, to paint the major ideological divides along which intellectuals arranged themselves during Khrushchev's thaw and beyond.

The de-Stalinization campaign awakened a great many intellectuals, who realized that the Soviet regime was an aberration. What they could not agree upon was whether socialism was the culprit or just its Stalinist incarnation. Most liberal intellectuals who chose to collaborate with the regime tried to humanize it through painstaking education designed to expose Stalinist excesses and turn the country toward democratic socialism. In his path-breaking book, which set him on a collision course with the authorities, Andrei Sakharov, Russia's leading dissident, spoke about "the moral attractiveness of the ideas of socialism and the glorification of labor, compared with the egotistical ideas of private ownership and the glorification of capital," leaving no doubt as to his own sympathies.[116] Vladimir Lakshin, a widely read liberal critic, described in very similar terms the ideals that animated him and his colleagues at *Novy mir*, a premier literary magazine in post-Stalin Russia: "But we believed in socialism as a noble ideal of justice, we believed in a socialism that was human through and through and not just with a human face. We regarded the democratic rights of the individual as incontestable."[117]

The key element in the program advanced by Sakharov and his liberal followers was glasnost and intellectual freedom, that is, the need to bring all political issues to an open forum and the right to voice one's opinion on any policy matter. From the start, the intelligentsia set out to work within the law, since Khrushchev's reforms contained the implicit promise that one could criticize past mistakes and offer fresh ideas for the future. "The democratic movement," asserted Andrei Amalrik, "intends to operate under the rule of law and glasnost and to work for glasnost, which distinguishes it from small and big underground groups."[118] "*Glasnost*, honest and unabridged *glasnost*," insisted Solzhenitsyn, "such is the first condition of every healthy society, including ours. Whosoever does not want glasnost for our society is indifferent to his homeland and thinks only of himself. Those who do not wish glasnost in our society wish not to cure its ills but to drive them deeper inside where they can fester."[119]

In 1962, *Novy mir* published Solzhenitsyn's powerful novel, *One Day in the Life of Ivan Denisovich*, in which the author, drawing on his own experience in the Gulag, related a political prisoner's daily routine. Khrushchev personally approved the publication, and rumors swirled about the Lenin prize waiting for the author. But the prize went to somebody else, Khrushchev was deposed, and Leonid Brezhnev's conservative regime came to power, dashing hopes for further liberalization. This is when the ideological scales began to fall from the intelligentsia's eyes, and the democratic movement went underground. At this very point, a rift surfaced within the ranks of the intelligentsia, one that is still apparent today. It separated intellectuals who chose to continue working for liberalization through official channels and those who gave up on reforming the system from within.

Among those who took the second route were Andrei Amalrik, Valery Chalidze, Aleksandr Volpin, Pyotr Grigorenko, Vladimir Bukovsky, Vladimir Maximov, Natalya Gorbanevskaya, Viktor Nekrasov, and a few dozen other activists. Their program centered around human rights and the need to hold the Soviet government accountable for its deeds. The idea, which is sometimes attributed to Volpin, seemed simple and unimpeachable: The government must respect its own laws, as well as the international covenants it has signed. The point was to spotlight cases where the state violated legal procedures and to bring the weight of public opinion to bear on the culprits: "We do not have to obey anything but the law. We must defend our laws from abuse by the authorities. We are on the side of the law. They are against it."[120] Demonstrations ensued; petitions were dispatched to the top; courts where political dissidents went on trial were picketed by democratic movement activists, who demanded the glasnost in courtrooms guaranteed by the Soviet law. These courageous efforts drew public attention to the fact that local Soviet authorities routinely used extra-legal means against independent trade union activists, harassed religious worshipers, curtailed political prisoners' rights, and violated the freedoms of speech, political gatherings, and emigration guaranteed by the UN Human Rights Charter, which was signed by the Soviet Union in 1975.

Compelling as the idea behind it was, the democratic movement petered out after several years of fruitful work that exposed to the world numerous abuses by Soviet authorities. The movement's activists vastly underestimated the government's resolve to stamp out political dissent and the KGB's ruthlessness in clamping down on the nonconformist intelligentsia. Soon after Nikita Khrushchev was deposed, the new regime put liberals on notice that it would not tolerate open dissent. In early 1966 the authorities staged the first political show trial of the post-Stalin era, sending Andrei Sinyavsky and Yuly Daniel to prison for publishing their works in the West without state approval. More trials followed. Some democratic movement activists were imprisoned, others sent into internal exile, still others forced to emigrate.

Alongside the democratic movement, other intellectual currents were gathering momentum that advocated ethnic minorities' rights, religious freedom, artistic freedom, freedom of emigration, and so on. Of particular note among these groups was the movement initiated by Aleksandr Solzhenitsyn and his close friend, Igor Shafarevich. Both writers sought to revive the nationalist themes that had lain fallow since the Slavophiles introduced them into public discourse, giving special emphasis to "the traditional ancient Russian notion of *pravda* [truth] as an expression of justice that is superior to any formal law."[121] Solzhenitsyn took issue with Sakharov's notion that intellectual freedom and human rights were key to social reconstruction in Russia:

> Look farther ahead, look at the West. Surely, the West is awash in all
> sorts of freedoms, including intellectual freedom. Did that save it?
> Today we can see the West: its will paralyzed, sinking fast, oblivious to
> the future, its soul neurotic and enfeebled. In and of itself, intellectual
> freedom cannot save us. . . . The absolutely necessary task [facing us] is
> not political liberation but the liberation of our souls from participation
> in the lies imposed on us.[122]

Borrowing from the Vekhi platform, Solzhenitsyn decried the democratic movement's preoccupation with politics and scolded Russian intellectuals for neglecting their national roots. The Russian intelligentsia would have to reinvent itself, he insisted; it had to be reconstituted around "a morally intelligent core [*intelligentnoe iadro*]" distinguished not by its members' "scientific degrees, number of publications, years of schooling . . . but by the purity of their striving, by their willingness to make a spiritual sacrifice—for truth and, most of all, for *this* country where one lives."[123] Solzhenitsyn called the Russians to "national repentance" and urged his fellow citizens not to cooperate with the regime or, to use his memorable line, "live not by the lie."

One more important intellectual shoot broke through the infertile Soviet ground in the post-Stalinist era. It was championed by the creative intelligentsia, mostly writers, like Andrei Sinyavsky, Yuly Daniel, and Joseph Brodsky, who were fed up with politics, shunned official society, and pursued free aesthetic expression. Those who shared this creed had as exalted a view of the artist's place in society as had their nineteenth-century radical predecessors, but they did not want to see art and literature become playgrounds for conflicting ideologies. Whatever literature had to teach society should not be taught through moralizing and didacticism. Here is how Joseph Brodsky framed the idea: "Books became the first and only reality, whereas reality itself was regarded as either nonsense or nuisance. Compared to others, we were ostensibly flunking or faking our lives. But come to think of it, existence which ignores the standards professed in literature is inferior and unworthy of effect. So we thought, and I think we were right. . . . The intuitive preference was to read rather than to act," Brodsky went on. "No wonder our lives were more or less in shambles."[124]

With certain qualifications, though, the same could have been said about any person striving to be morally intelligent under the increasingly oppressive conditions in Russia. By the mid-1970s, the Soviet government had opened a frontal attack on dissent of all stripes, confronting the Russian intelligentsia with the familiar conundrum: What is to be done when there is nothing you can do? Decent choices were few: withdraw from society and become an internal emigré; go underground and keep exposing Soviet power abuses; work through legal channels, doing what one possibly could to educate society, especially the new generation. Dissident intellectuals who tried to keep the government's feet to the fire by exposing KGB abuses in the West resented their liberal colleagues still working for the state. The smoldering debate about the morality of collaboration with the communist government bent on preserving its power at any cost revealed the deepening rift between radical and liberal intellectuals. A defiant Solzhenitsyn broke with his liberal colleagues at *Novy mir* over its cautious editorial policies and challenged every Russian citizen to "fortify oneself and refuse to budge, sacrificing one's life rather than principle!"[125] Solzhenitsyn set an example himself by publishing his works abroad and openly meeting with Western reporters. Like Boris Pasternak before him, Solzhenitsyn was expelled from the Writers' Union, but unlike his predecessor, Solzhenitsyn was deported and became a political exile in the United States. The same fate befell Arkady Belinkov, who, having reached the safety of exile, launched a scathing attack on his liberal colleagues:

> [I]n the concrete history of the 1960s, K. Fedin is worse than N. Gribachev, P. Antokolsky more dangerous than V. Kochetov, E. Evtushenko more repugnant than A. Markov, B. Slutsky uglier than V. Firsov, P. Nilin more base than I. Shevtsov, I. Selvinsky more sinister than A. Sofronov, V. Shklovsky more distasteful than V. Ermilov. All these *carabinieri*, Jacobins, freedom fighters, and daredevils do to [free] public thought what ultramasons, Vendéans, Cossacks, and Black Hundreds did, except that the former crowd does its thing with panache and flare, a sense of poetry, harmony, and charm.[126]

Understandably, the loyal liberals who came into their own in the 1960s (they are still commonly referred to in the intelligentsia parlance as *shestidesiatniki*, the generation of the 1960s) had a very different idea about their mission in society. Efim Etkind, a scholar and literary critic, confronted head on the dilemma that Solzhenitsyn presented to his countrymen: "Aren't the absolute refusal to compromise and the unconditional determination to pursue truth and defend human rights always preferable to the willingness to play politics, make compromises, and show moral flexibility?"[127] Etkind's answer: Solzhenitsyn fell victim to "moral maximalism," which is especially dangerous given the current political climate. No dissident acts in a vacuum; his choices affect other people who might suffer gravely when the individual decides to take a heroic ego trip.[128] Solzhenitsyn, Etkind charged, vastly overestimated the public's interest in challenging the authorities and seriously underestimated the fact that "enlightenment must precede [political] renaissance, [that] underground publications are not sufficient. . . . The first task is to teach, educate, and enlighten. To participate in this centrally important—indeed only—relevant activity in our time, we should be ready to conceal thoughts, yield, and maneuver—of course, within morally acceptable limits."[129]

Lakshin's rebuttal to Solzhenitsyn was even more forceful. Lakshin charged that the eminent author snubbed his colleagues at *Novyi mir*, that his "indifference to means, his psychology of the pre-emptive strike, his cruelty and lying" reflected his prison camp experience, that "Solzhenitsyn had also imbibed the poison of Stalinism," and that "the author who addresses us with his passionate appeal to pursue truth, humanity, and goodness scorns observing these commandments in his own dealings."[130]

Meanwhile, liberals in good standing with the government had to voice their approval when the Soviet Union invaded Czechoslovakia (*Novyi mir* publicly endorsed the invasion), look the other way when Sakharov was forced into exile, keep their outrage to themselves when the state placed dissidents in psychiatric wards, curse the Communist party's harebrained economic schemes in the relative privacy of their apartments, and rely chiefly on the time-honored "secret freedom" (renamed "inner freedom") to keep their sanity intact. Such was the "moral torture," as Etkind put it, that the intelligentsia suffered after Khrushchev's demise. Soviet intellectuals coping with the adversity in the post-Stalinist era reminded one of Spanish Jews forced to choose between their faith and the official state church when either option entailed a prohibitive cost. Thinking one thing, saying another, and doing something altogether different, intellectual Marranos populating Soviet society could not help but lose track of their private and official identities. The recourse to irony seemed natural. "In the atmosphere of mendacity," recalls a veteran of those years, "all-consuming irony becomes a universal self-defense mechanism."[131] But in the end, irony and self-parody did not so much keep official and unofficial selves apart as help the individual cover up the snarled web of his motivation. The burden of affliction from which intellectuals suffered in post-Stalin's Russia might have been somewhat lighter than the "terrible ulcer" that sent Chaadaev into depression, and it was probably less clinically disturbing than the "traumatic psychosis" that disfigured Nadezhda Mandelshtam's generation. Still, it damaged intellectuals' selfhood, sapped their creative energies, and played havoc with their private lives.

If the Russian intelligentsia learned anything in the post-Soviet period, it was to mistrust the leftist radicalism that shaped the nineteenth-century intelligentsia. The break did not come easily or swiftly. "You see," a member of that intelligentsia recalled, "for all our irreverent dissidence (*inakomyslie*), our hearts responded with emotion to the old [communist] symbols, images, and commandments, which—miraculously and in spite of everything—retained for us the purity of that original flame."[132] Even seasoned fighters and internal emigrés with no illusions about the regime resorted to the communist lingo in an effort to explain their ways, as did Brodsky during his 1963 trial, when the prosecutor pressed him to demonstrate how his lifestyle meshed with the Soviet people's efforts to build a communist society: "Building communism is not just operating the machine and plowing the earth. It is also the work of the intelligentsia, which . . . "—that is as far as the judge permitted the future Nobel laureate to take his argument.[133] But by the mid-1970s, when the Brezhnev regime entered the stagnation years and open dissidence was silenced, the liberal intelligentsia began to slip from its socialist moorings.

The preoccupation with moral intelligence inched its way back into existence.[134] Soviet intellectuals sought moral fortitude in the works of Pushkin and Chekhov, placing on their agenda "the acquisition of a 'secret freedom,' through one's own intellectual and moral effort."[135] Camus's "Myth of Sisyphus" captured the intelligentsia's imagination as emblematic of its hopeless existence amid official hypocrisy and corruption.[136] With increased repression came thoughts of emigration (an option that virtually disappeared in the late 1970s) and a longing for the West and distant cultures. "It was not just political anecdotes and irreverent songs that sustained us in those years. It was not just the irony that became the signature trait of our spiritual makeup. It was also the longing for Paris, which we had no chance to see—ever."[137] As before, intellectuals turned their bitterness and anger against themselves and their loved ones. The moral compromises, forced voicelessness, fear of cracking under KGB pressures explain the ambivalence that post-Stalinist Russia and the intelligentsia it engendered continue to elicit in intellectuals who lived in this muddled era.

As for Russian intellectual culture, it did undergo some changes during this period. Khrushchev's thaw left an indelible mark on the new generation of Soviet intellectuals evident in their skepticism about socialist ideologies, their renewed belief in glasnost as a condition for social reconstruction, their willingness to take a public stance, and their narrowing of the gap between word and deed. Other features ingrained in the intelligentsia's collective consciousness—vanguardism, moral maximalism, ironic detachment, contempt for *meshchanstvo*, belief in literature's transformative role—remained largely unaffected, though. If anything, violent emotions, self-loathing, and standoffish demeanor were exacerbated because there was a clear choice, albeit an unpalatable one, between the repression awaiting those who dared to stand up to the authorities and the closet liberalism that relegated the morally intelligent person to an ethical torture chamber. Lakshin had a point when he charged his esteemed colleague, Aleksandr Solzhenitsyn, with reproducing totalitarian stratagems in his own conduct. But did liberal intellectuals free themselves from this syndrome? The test came as Mikhail Gorbachev opened the final chapter in Soviet history.

Perestroika and Beyond

Neither "glasnost" nor "perestroika" are recent inventions. Both terms have a long pedigree in Russian intellectual history. Count Pyotr Vyazemsky, a friend of Pushkin, hailed glasnost and decried its absence in Russia as early as 1831.[138] Later, Herzen, Dobrolyubov, Chernyshevsky, Ivanov-Razumnik, Milyukov, and other Russian intellectuals identified the right to voice one's opinion on the full range of public issues as indispensable for a healthy society. The same applies to "perestroika," which was invoked by politically conscious Russian intellectuals to highlight the importance of making a radical break with past beliefs and practices and setting the country on the path toward political modernization. What made Mikhail Gorbachev's usage different was that he invoked both terms simultaneously and employed them to advance a liberal rather than radical political agenda.

The Soviet leader came to power in April 1985. Within a year he was talking about the need for glasnost in politics and perestroika in the economy, but ideological blinkers were still on tight. Few people inside or outside the Communist party took Gorbachev's musings seriously; they had seen too many government-instigated campaigns peter out in the past. Skeptics notwithstanding, the new rhetoric took wing, generating unprecedented changes in Soviet domestic and foreign policy. That perestroika had plenty of substance could no longer be denied after political prisoners were set free, censorship eased, political dissent tolerated, and emigration allowed to resume; disarmament talks steamed ahead beyond all expectations. The first signs that the intellectuals were taking Gorbachev seriously came about a year and half into his tenure, as some journalists tested the limits of glasnost by bringing up topics previously excluded from public debate. Aleksandr Vasinsky wrote a pioneering article, "The Ballad of Different Opinions," in which he urged that all opinions, including those we passionately oppose, be given the benefit of the doubt. To add extra weight to his argument, Vasinsky dug up a rare quotation from Lenin in which the founder of the Soviet state chastized those who "spread hatred, intolerance, contempt, etc., toward dissenters [*nesoglasnomysliashchie*]."[139] Following Vasinsky, other intellectuals picked up kindred themes with fewer and fewer references to the communist luminaries. "One of the conditions of honesty and directness that our time demands," asserted Sergei Averintsev, a leading Russian philologist, "is to stop confusing the dissenter [*nesoglasnyi*] with the enemy. The intelligentsia must nurture in itself the culture of dissent [*kultura nesoglasiia*], the culture of debate. Not just weak tolerance, but true respect for the opponent."[140] "We still do not have enough courage to say, 'The king is naked,'" charged Vladimir Dudintsev in an article denouncing past abuses in Soviet science, "in spite of the democratic foundations of our society, which requires glasnost, and therefore the freedom to defend one's views. The final judge in any dispute should be the argument, yet it is power and connections, I am sad to say, that often decide the matter."[141]

By 1988, the communist hierarchs realized that Gorbachev's changes had gone too far and started pressuring him to slow the reforms. Immediately, the intelligentsia swung into action, claiming an equal partnership in the reform process. Khrushchev failed to carry out his reform, intellectuals maintained, largely because he turned his back on the intelligentsia and neglected to tap the intellectual resources that had proved indispensable in his earlier struggle with the party hierarchy. The man who started the political thaw after Stalin's death "paid dearly for his mistrust and contempt for the intelligentsia,"[142] charged Fyodor Burlatsky, a former Khrushchev aide, in a statement echoed by many *shestidesiatniki*. This was a thinly veiled warning to the new administration to engage the intelligentsia, to make it a full partner in the reforms. Poet Andrei Voznesensky predicated the success of social reconstruction on the nation's ability to mobilize its intellectual resources and to deploy culture and moral intelligence, two areas in which Russian intellectuals have traditionally claimed special expertise: "A spiritual revolution is stirring in our land, a life and death struggle for a new thinking against the still powerful inertia of the past. This is not a cultural revolution, but a revolution by Culture. . . . Born again is the old Russian word *glasnost*, the word that makes active repentance a norm and that goes back to Tolstoi, whose ideal of fighting evil with active conscience has such resonance today."[143]

Perestroika reignited the old debate about the intelligentsia, its place in the reform process, the linkage between the old and the new intelligentsia, and the troubled relationship between the intelligentsia, the people, and the state. For the first time, the intelligentsia had a chance to settle old accounts, regale with its survival stories, expose the enemies of nonconformist intellectuals. Many established scholars, writers, and artists expressed remorse, or were called upon to repent by their colleagues for past action or inaction. Relishing their newly found freedom and capitalizing on their access to secret archives, intellectuals delved into areas once excluded from public discussion: the famines, economic failures, environmental disasters, forced collectivization, mass purges, Gulag culture, persecution of religious and ethnic minorities. . . .

Intellectuals searched their illustrious pedigree, owned up to their past mistakes, and drew heavily on the Vekhi critique, which exposed the Russian intelligentsia's unsavory practices. Following Chekhov, intellectuals hailed moral intelligence [*intelligentnost*] as a defining characteristic for anyone claiming membership among the intelligentsia's ranks. A highly respected Russian scholar, Dmitry Likhachev, told an interviewer that "an unschooled peasant can be called an *intelligent*, but the same cannot be said of a ruffian, even if he is burdened with intellect, scientific degrees, and official honors. . . . 'Russian *intelligent*' designates a spiritual and moral, rather than cerebral, category. Better put, unless movement of the heart precedes movement of thought, a person cannot be called an *intelligent*."[144] This wording suggests a shift in focus away from the intelligentsia as a corporate group that marked the official Soviet perspective and toward *intelligentnost,* or moral intelligence, as a personal disposition and a pattern of conduct displayed in a particular situation. This theme looms large in a posthumously published note by Aleksei Losev, a celebrated Russian philosopher and survivor of numerous campaigns against the intelligentsia.[145] The title of Losev's article could be freely rendered, "On Feeling, Thinking, and Acting as an *Intelligent.*" In this remarkable piece, the author discusses moral intelligence as a way of life and a peculiarly Russian ideology that "appears out of nowhere, all by itself, acts without understanding its own action, pursues the well-being of humanity, and does so without any clear idea of its actions. The true ideology of true moral intelligence is naive." The *intelligent,* continues Losev, never socially indifferent, is acutely aware of the world's inanities and is determined to "transform reality"—a "person who takes the interest of humanity as his own." Moral intelligence is "conscious spiritual labor to improve oneself and to make the world around us rational." The true *intelligent* is no utopian dreamer but can critically assess reality and knows when to act, when to lay low, where and how to pick a fight. In time, moral intelligence becomes self-reflexive and more assertive. The labor of moral intelligence is the work of reason in history carried out by a particular individual who fights the day's brush fires with sights trained on destiny, which is to be a civilizing force in history. The life of moral intelligence is subject to all the vagaries of everyday life; it is tragic, heroic, and beautiful at the same time.

These ruminations about the intelligentsia's mission in society fall squarely within the Russian intellectual tradition. The all-important difference, however, is that intelligence is perceived here as a moral agency par excellence and the intelligentsia is cast as a social force whose mission is not to drag the unwilling society along a preordained historical path but to ameliorate it via public discourse and personal example. "Jesus Christ," suggested one participant in the ongoing debate about the intelligentsia, "was in essence a prototype of the *intelligent.*"[146] The latter is akin to an individual who is "born again" and who strives to be righteous rather than impose a particular scheme on society (from which it follows that "calling oneself an *intelligent* is like giving oneself a medal"[147]). This and similar statements have familiar messianic overtones, but they are also refreshing insofar as their critical thrust is directed at oneself rather than others. Note, however, that the intelligentsia's commitment to moral means did not slow its enlistment in government-sponsored institutions—ministries, think-tanks, state committees, and other organizations that in the past had been closed to Russian intellectuals practicing moral intelligence. Russian intellectuals took full advantage of the new opportunities. Once intellectuals weaned on hatred toward the state found themselves working for it, they discovered that their ideals did not mesh easily with the demands of power. As Chekhov surmised a century ago, the intelligentsia was hardly immune to the ills of the Russian bureaucracy, from whose head it originally sprang. The way intellectuals in power acted amid the rough and tumble of Russian politics in the Gorbachev and especially the post-Soviet era changed many minds about the intelligentsia's touted virtues.

Never before did the intelligentsia enjoy a greater influence in their homeland than during the heyday of perestroika. Gorbachev's reforms assured intellectuals the right to free speech, unprecedented artistic freedom, wide access to the mass media, and a chance to be elected to the Soviet legislature and to serve in government. In addition to the rights commonly found in capitalist societies, Russian intellectuals still benefited from the largely socialist system, which guaranteed full employment, required little work, and subsidized the intelligentsia's creative pursuits. Thus, throughout the perestroika years, movies continued to be shot, books published, concerts given, research projects publicly funded—all with little regard for the fact that there might be no market for the resulting products. No wonder perestroika received such accolades from the intelligentsia. "There is no doubt," Natan Edelman, a well-known Russian historian, wrote in 1989, "that the intellectuals' support for perestroika is virtually unanimous."[148] Obviously, things could not go on like this for any length of time without a major shakeup, and when it came, the intelligentsia's fortunes sank quickly.

Simply put, for the intelligentsia, glasnost *was* perestroika. It was common for intellectuals giddy from reforms to opine that if they had to choose between glasnost and sausage they would not hesitate to take the former and forgo the latter. For economically more vulnerable social groups, however, perestroika was less of a promise than a threat mounting daily in the increasingly volatile economic environment. The perestroika movement reached its high-water mark in 1989, when political forces in Russia became increasingly polarized. In 1990, the ideological middle ground seemed to evaporate and Gorbachev's political base shriveled to a dangerous point. Whereas his constituents on the left felt irritated by Gorbachev's refusal to dismantle the one-party state, his constituents on the right urged a return to the relative stability provided by the socialist economy. A year later, the situation in the country resembled the disarray that followed the February 1917 revolution. Communist party stalwarts staged a coup against Gorbachev in August 1991, cracking the whip one last time to see whether the Soviet citizen's old reflexes still worked, but it was too late. The failed putsch delayed Gorbachev's exit from the political scene by a few months, but by the end of 1991, the Union of Soviet Socialist Republics had ceased to function, and there began a dramatic reversal of fortunes for the Russian intelligentsia.

The woes that have befallen the intelligentsia in post-Soviet Russia are heavy indeed. The Academy of Sciences had no money to pay its scholars; those who could find employment abroad were already leaving the country in the early 1990s, while their lesser-known colleagues had to look for supplementary employment in the still fragile private sector. The artistic unions that in the past had supported Russian filmmakers, actors, writers, painters, musicians, and others fortunate enough to belong to the so-called creative intelligentsia had lost their state support and could no longer furnish members with lucrative contracts and commissions. Scores of artistic companies, including the world-famous Bolshoi Ballet, went into bankruptcy or teetered on the brink. "Thick" literary journals and high-brow newspapers that had boasted circulations in the millions during perestroika saw their press runs dwindle to a few thousand copies. The Russians, who used to pride themselves on being a nation of readers, theatergoers, music lovers, and art exhibit aficionados, seemed to have lost interest in high culture, as attested by empty theaters, poorly attended shows, unsold books, and so on. To add insult to injury, the intelligentsia was held responsible for every mishap Russia faced after Gorbachev came to power. And of course, there was no longer an overbearing state to kick around, to blame for the intellectuals' misfortunes. The powerful state that the intelligentsia had fought tooth and nail lay in ruins, with the Russian house of intellect buried under its rubble.

The bitterness the intelligentsia once harbored toward the authorities is building up again, but this time its animus is directed against itself. "I detest being an intellectual," confided Aleksandr Panchenko, a prominent Russian scholar and public thinker with liberal credentials.[149] Another well-known writer, Aleksandr Ivanov, told the interviewer who dared to address him as an *intelligent*: "Please do not call me by this disgusting name. I never considered myself an *intelligent* and always viewed this term with contempt."[150] If Lenin ever was right, added Ivanov, it was in his assessment of the intelligentsia as the nation's excrement. Stanislav Govorukhin, a film director, concurs with this assessment, as do several other writers with Slavophile leanings, who desire to restore Russia's former glory. The anger enciphered in such statements has raised the temperature of the debate about the intelligentsia, which has fallen again into the old habit of showering opponents with sarcasm and innuendos. It is as if Russian intellectual culture had suddenly been thrown back to its beginnings. The situation is hardly helped by the fact that now everyone is free to say whatever they like and everybody is talking simultaneously without much regard for their interlocutors or a concerted effort at a real dialogue. The bloody confrontation between Yeltsin's government and the recalcitrant Russian Parliament in October 1993 amplified to a deafening point the over-acidulous invectives Russian intellectuals had been trading since the Soviet Union's demise. The whole situation is eerily reminiscent of the emotional malaise that afflicted the Russian intelligentsia after each previous revolution and that provoked the Vekhi authors' monumental inquiry into the Russian intelligentsia's wayward lifestyle. "Nine-tenths of our intelligentsia is afflicted with neurasthenia," wrote Mikhail Gershenzon, one of the sanest voices in Russian intellectual history, whose insight rings as true today as it did ninety years ago. "There are almost no normal people among us—everybody is acerbic, withdrawn, restless faces contorted in a grimace, because one was either crossed or saddened. . . . We infect each other with bitterness and have so saturated the atmosphere with our neurasthenic attitudes toward life that a fresh person, say, one who lived abroad for a while, could not help feeling suffocated in our midst."[151]

In this din, voices that heed Chekhov's call to civility and emotional sanity, respected voices such as Sergei Averintsev, Dmitry Likhachev, Marietta Chudakova, Viktor Sheinis, and Yuri Levada, use glasnost not to drown out opponents' views but to further dialogue; they continue to urge the return to sanity in public discourse. What draws these very different authors together is the realization that there is more to democracy than constitutional guarantees and representative institutions, that civil society begins with civility, that Russia will continue on its downward path until its citizens can see that, to paraphrase John Dewey, democracy literally begins at home. Marietta Chudakova's article published in *Literaturnaia gazeta* on the eve of the Soviet Union's collapse is as good an example of a clear-headed attitude toward the current chaotic situation in Russia as can be found in recent literature. Chudakova reminds her readers about Olga Fridenberg, a cousin and lifelong friend of Boris Pasternak, as well as a highly regarded scholar of ancient Greek literature, who had this to say about Russian intellectual culture shortly before she died in 1956:

> Everywhere, in all organizations and homes, a nasty squabble [*skloka*] is raging, the poisoned fruit of our social order, a new concept hitherto unknown to civilization and untranslatable into any other language. It is hard to explain what it really is: a mean-spirited, petty rivalry, venomous factionalism that sickens all against each, an unscrupulous envy that breeds endless intrigues. It is sycophancy, libel, informers, the desire to unseat a rival, the deliberate feeding of ugly passions, nerves perpetually set on edge, and a moral degeneration that makes a person or group run amok. Squabbling is a natural state for people who are rubbing against each other in a dungeon, helpless to resist the dehumanization they have been subjected to. Squabbling is the alpha and omega of our politics. Squabbling is our methodology.[152]

The irritability, intolerance, and aggressive demeanor obvious today, Chudakova argues, stem from old habits intellectuals are unable to shed. Now that the ideological husks have been peeled away, the raw anger and bitterness are no longer hiding under the veneer of respectability and politeness. The difference between the past and present discourse, according to Kama Ginkas, a stage director, is the same as between "a philosophical fireside chat and philosophizing with your thumbs slammed in door jambs."[153] The need to pour bitter irony and sarcasm on one's opponent is even more painfully obvious today than in Russia's recent past. Stanislav Rassadin calls it "slovenly irony"; Yury Polyakov laments "the total ironism" that pervades Russian culture today, and Evgeny Shvedov decries "the endless jocularity, the coy and empty irony" that fills the pages of literary magazines.[154] Add to this the devastating impact that market pursuits have had on old friendships, the loss of relatives, colleagues, and friends to emigration, the precipitous decline in the public's interest in high culture, persistent economic uncertainty, anti-intellectualism fanned by the political right, and you will have the picture of a malaise that plagues the intelligentsia's psyche.[155] It is as if someone had suddenly removed the ferment from the perestroika brew, making the drink go sour and giving imbibers a monstrous headache. Intercut with the bitterness widespread among the Russian intelligentsia today is the nostalgia for the good-old-bad-old days before perestroika, when its members knew exactly what they were fighting for and against, when people clung to every word an artist uttered, when there was hope. Some now saw the empire's vices, including the hated censorship, the necessity to speak an Aesopian language and create with no chance of an audience, as hidden virtues.[156] Not surprisingly, Aleksandr Pushkin's verse on Pindemonti is quoted ad nauseam, its author portrayed as "perhaps the freest man in Russia's entire history,"[157] and his "secret freedom" touted as the last refuge of the *intelligent*.

Is this the beginning of the end for the Russian intelligentsia, as many authors inside and outside Russia argue? After all, this ideological order has accomplished its main goals: the overbearing Russian state has been cut down to size and political absolutism broken, glasnost reigns supreme, and Russia is firmly set on its path toward political modernization. As a historical force bearing the birthmark of its premodern origins, the intelligentsia must yield center stage to professional politicians, market-conscious artists, and state bureaucrats. But its historical mission has not been accomplished yet. There is still the unfinished agenda of psychological modernization, of developing a civic culture, which the intelligentsia must take up and which calls for moral as well as emotional intelligence.

Georgy Fedotov saw silence, quietude, holding back one's feelings as a signature trait of Russia's spirituality.[158] Much of what is valuable in

Russian culture, he maintained, comes from this accumulation of emotional and intellectual energy, already evident in early Russian monks. As I have tried to show in this chapter, such voicelessness has a darker side. Too often it has been an involuntary, forced silence that deprived humans of *glas* and *glasnost*, drove their negative feelings inside, and turned their anguish on themselves and others. The emotional abuse that Russian intellectuals casually heap on each other these days is a sure sign that they and their predecessors were themselves abused. All those who survived the Stalinist purges, intimidation by the KGB, or ideologically inspired violence of any kind could not help being deeply troubled by their experiences—particularly if they capitulated by becoming eyes, ears, voices, and hands for the state.

Russian intellectual culture continues to evolve, and there is much of value in it—models of rational, moral, and emotional intelligence that could help Russians rid themselves of regnant obsessions and find the *via media* between facile intellectualism and emotional excess. The agenda for the day is to focus the intelligentsia's attention on its own emotional life, to help it comprehend the distorted communications behind Russian intellectual culture, to make it understand that democracy is also a quality of experience, a sociopsychological culture outside of which democratic institutions cannot sink roots and are sure to wither away. In short, one must balance intellect with emotional intelligence and see to it that emotions are intelligent and intellect is emotionally sane.[159]

Notes

I wish to thank the Russian Research Center at Harvard University, the Soros Foundation, and the International Research and Exchanges Board for support of this project.

1. Y. Shchekochikhin, "Vlast i intelligentsiia," *Literaturnaia gazeta*, July 28, 1993. Unless otherwise indicated, here and elsewhere in the chapter, the translation from the Russian is by Dmitri Shalin.

2. G. R. Ivanitsky, in *Intelligentsiia i vlast'* (Moscow: Soiuz Kinematografistov SSSR, 1992), p. 70.

3. A. Bitov, "Privatizatsiia sovetskoi vlasti," *Novoe russkoe slovo*, January 31, 1993.

4. Alwin W. Gouldner, *The Future of Intellectuals and the Rise of the New Class* (New York: Seabury Press, 1979), p. 5.

5. A. Yanov, "Gde ispytyvaetsia novoe myshlenie," *Izvestiia*, December 8, 1990.

6. There are several important monographs and edited collections on the Russian intelligentsia: Isaiah Berlin, *Russian Thinkers* (New York: Penguin Books, [1948] 1978); Richard Pipes, ed., *The Russian Intelligentsia* (New York: Columbia University Press, 1961); Marc Raeff, *Origins of the Russian Intelligentsia: The Eighteenth Century Nobility* (New York: Harcourt, Brace & World, 1966); Alexander

Gella, ed., *The Intelligentsia and the Intellectuals: Theory, Methods and Case Study* (Beverly Hills, Ca.: Sage, 1976); Abbott Gleason, Peter Kenez, and Richard Stites, eds., *Bolshevik Culture: Experiment and Order in Russian Revolution* (Bloomington:. Indiana University Press, 1985); Marshall S. Shatz, *Soviet Dissent in Historical Perspective* (Cambridge: Cambridge University Press). I particularly recommend the fine work by Vladimir C. Nahirny, who drew attention to the emotional cost of Russian intellectualism in *The Russian Intelligentsia: From Torment to Silence* (New Brunswick, N.J.: Transactions Books, 1983). Among Russian works, of particular interest are the following collections: *Vekhi: Sbornik statei o russkoi intelligentsii* (Moscow: Tipografiia V. M. Sablina, 1909); *Intelligentsiia v Rossii* (St. Petersburg: Zemlia, 1910); *Iz pod glyb: Sbornik statei* (Paris: YMCA Press, 1974); L. I. Novikova and I. N. Sizemskaia, eds., *Intelligentsiia. Vlast. Narod* (Moscow: Nauka, 1993). For the official Soviet perspective on the intelligentsia, see *Sovetskaia intelligentsiia (istoriia formirovaniia i rosta 1917–1965 gg.)* (Moscow: Mysl, 1968).

7. See Nahirny, *Russian Intelligentsia*, pp. 36–49.

8. Georgy P. Fedotov, "Tragediia intelligentsii," in *Sudba i grekhi Rossii*, vol. 2 (St. Peterburg: Sofiia, 1991), p. 142.

9. Pyotr D. Boborykin, *Vospominaniia* (Moscow: Khudozhestvennaia Literatura, [1906] 1965), p. 283. Boborykin states: "I was born a 'citadin,' a city dweller, or what later on in the Russian press I myself christened by the name '*intelligent*'" (p. 283). See also "Russkaia intelligentsiia," *Russkaia mysl*, no. 12 (1904).

10. Georgy P. Fedotov, "Tragediia intelligentsii," in *Sudba i grekhi Rossii*, vol. 1 (St. Petersburg: Sofiia, 1991), pp. 71–72.

11. Peter Chaadaev, *The Major Works of Peter Chaadaev*, edited and translated by Raymond McNally (Notre Dame: University of Notre Dame Press, 1960), pp. 113, 111, 149, 138.

12. Ibid., p. 201.

13. Ibid., pp. 190–91.

14. Berlin, *Russian Thinkers*, p. 15.

15. Ibid., p. 60.

16. Aleksandr S. Pushkin, "Volnost," in *Polnoe sobranie sochinenii v desiati tomakh* (Moscow: Izdatelstvo Akademii Nauk SSSR, [1817] 1962), I: 323.

17. P. I. Dolgorukov, "Kishinev 1822 goda genvaria," *A. S. Pushkin v vospominaniiakh sovremennikov*, vol. 1 (Moscow: Khudozhestvennaia Literatura, 1974), p. 350.

18. Pushkin, "Volnost," p. 322.

19. Aleksandr S. Pushkin, "For N. Ia. Pliuskovoi," in ibid., I: 340.

20. Aleksandr S. Pushkin, "O narodnom vospitanie," in ibid., VII: 42–49.

21. Ibid., III: 7.

22. Pushkin to A. Kh. Benkendorf, July 21, 1831, and circa July 21, 1831, both in ibid., X: 639, 656.

23. Ibid., p. 770.

24. Pushkin to N. N. Pushkina, May 18, 1836, in ibid., p. 583.

25. Pushkin to P. A. Viazemsky, May 27, 1826, in ibid., p. 208.

26. Aleksandr S. Pushkin, "(From Pindemonti)," in ibid., III: 369.

27. V. A. Zhukovsky to S. L. Pushkin, February 15, 1837, in *A. S. Pushkin v vospominaniiakh sovremennikov*, vol. 2 (Moscow: Khudozhestvennaia Literatura, 1974), p. 349.

28. Alexander Herzen, "Byloe i dumy," in A. I. Gertsen, *Sochineniia*, vol. 5 (Moscow: Khudozhestvennaia Literatura, [1862] 1956), p. 98.

22 Ibid., pp. 373–74.

30. Ibid., IV: 401.

31. "Zapiska o pismennoi literature," *Golosa iz Rossii*, vol. 1 (Moscow: Nauka, [1856] 1974), p. 60.

32. Herzen, "Byloe i dumy," p. 383.

33. Alexander Herzen, "K staromu tovarishchu." In A. I. Gertsen, *Sobranie sochinenii v vosmi tomakh* (Moscow: Pravda, 1975), VIII: 335, 325.

34. N. A. Dobrolyubov, *Izbrannoe* (Moscow: Sovremennik, 1984), p. 297.

35. Ibid., p. 437. "Take Pushkin," Vissarion Belinsky once pointed out. "No sooner did he write two or three loyalist poems and put on the court uniform than he lost people's love!" "Vybrannye mesta iz perepiski s druziami Nikolaia Gogolia," in V. G. Belinsky, *Sobranie sochinenii v trekh tomakh* (Moscow: Khudozhestvennaia Literatura, [1847] 1948), III: 712.

36. Dobrolyubov, *Izbrannoe*, p. 295.

37. Vissarion G. Belinsky to V. P. Botkin, December 10, 1840, September 8, 1841, and June 27, 1841, all in V. G. Belinsky, *Izbrannye pisma*, vol. 2 (Moscow: Khudozhestvennaia Literatura, 1955), pp. 133, 173–74, 158, respectively.

38. Ibid., II: 81.

39. N. G. Chernyshevsky, *Izbrannye esteticheskie proizvedeniia* (Moscow: Iskusstvo, 1978), p. 174.

40. Belinsky, *Sobranie sochinenii*, I: 715–16.

41. Dmitry Pisarev, *Literaturnaia kritika*, vol. 2 (Moscow: Khudozhestvennaia Literatura, 1981), p. 11.

42. Belinsky to V. P. Botkin, June 13, 1840, and Belinsky to N. A. Bakunin, November 7, 1842, both in Belinsky, *Izbrannye pisma*, II: 81, 201, respectively.

43. "Letter to N. P. Ogarev, December 2, 1869," in Gertsen, *Sochineniia*, XXX: 271.

44. Herzen, "Byloe i dumy," p. 607.

45. See Nahirny, *Russian Intelligentsia*, pp. 69–86.

46. Pyotr L. Lavrov, "Istoricheskie pisma," in L. I. Novikova and I. M. Sizemskaia, *Intelligentsiia. Vlast. Narod*, p. 51.

47. Chernyshevsky, *Izbrannye esteticheskie proizvedenniia* [1855–56], p. 445.

48. Isaiah Berlin had this to say about Tolstoi's view of the Europeans and their Russian imitators: "Tolstoy looks on them as clever fools, spinners of empty subtleties, blind and deaf to the realities which simpler hearts can grasp, and from time to time he lets fly at them with the brutal violence of a grim, anarchical old peasant, avenging himself after years of silence, on the silly, chattering, town-bred monkeys, so knowing, and full of words to explain everything, and superior, and impotent and empty." Berlin, *Russian Thinkers*, p. 64.

49. Konstantin H. Leontiev, "Kak nado ponimat sblizhenie s narodom," in Konstantin Leontiev, *Zapiski otshelnika* (Moscow: Russkaia Kniga, 1992), p. 510.

50. Konstantin A. Aksakov, "O russkom vozzrenii," in K. S. Aksakov and I. S. Aksakov, *Literaturnaia kritika* (Moscow: Sovremennik, 1981), pp. 198, 197.

51. Fyodor M. Dostoevsky, *Polnoe sobranie sochinenii v tridtsati tomakh* (Moscow: Nauka, [1880] 1984), XXVI: 136–49.

52. Ibid., p. 139.

53. Ibid., p. 142.

54. Ibid., p. 148.

55. Ibid., p. 147.

56. Chekhov to A. N. Pleshcheev, October 4, 1888, in Anton P. Chekhov, *Sobranie sochinenii v dvenadtsati tomakh* (Moscow: Khudozhestvennaia Literatura, 1956), XI: 263.

57. Chekhov to A. F. Marks, February 25, 1899, in ibid., XII: 305.

58. For example, he writes about his town's neighbors: "The intelligentsia here is very nice and interesting. And most importantly—honest." Chekhov to Menshikov, October 12, 1892, in ibid., XI: 593.

59. Chekhov to A. S. Suvorin, January 7, 1889, in ibid., pp. 328–29.

60. Vasily Ivanov-Razumnik, "Intelligentsiia i sotsializm," in Novikova and Sizemskaia, *Intelligentsiia. Vlast. Narod*, p. 218. His two volumes on the history of Russian social thought appeared in 1907; see *Istoriia russkoi obshchestvennoi mysli* (St. Petersburg, 1907).

61. Mikhail I. Tugan-Baranovsky, "Intelligentsiia v Rossii" (St. Petersburg: Zemlia, 1910), p. 248.

62. Nikolai A. Berdiaev, "Filosofskaia istina i intelligentskaia pravda," in *Vekhi*, pp. 1, 2, 9.

63. Pyotr B. Struve, "Geroizm i podvizhnichestvo," in *Vekhi*, p. 41.

64. Ibid., p. 56.

65. Semyon L. Frank, "Etika nigilizma," *Vekhi*, p. 204.

66. Mikhail O. Gershenzon, "Tvorcheskoe samosoznanie," in *Vekhi*, pp. 80–81.

67. Pyotr B. Struve, "Intelligentsiia i narodnoe khoziaistvo," in Novikova and Sizemskaia, *Intelligentsiia. Vlast. Narod*, p. 205.

68. Ivan Petrunkevich, "Intelligentsiia i *Vekhi*," in *Intelligentsiia v Rossii: Postanovka zadachi* (St. Petersburg: Zemlia, 1910), p. 6.

69. Dmitry N. Ovsyaniko-Kulikovsky, "Psikhologiia russkoi intelligentsii," in *Intelligentsiia v Rossii*, p. 217.

70. Pavel N. Milyukov, "Intelligentsiia i istoricheskaia traditsiia. Postanovka zadachi," in *Intelligentsiia v Rossii*, p. 92.

71. Ibid., pp. 151–52.

72. Ibid., p. 92.

73. See Dmitri N. Shalin, "Marxist Paradigm and Academic Freedom," *Social Research* 47 (1980):361–82.

74. Lev D. Trotsky, "Ob intelligentsii," in Novikova and Sizemskaia, *Intelligentsiia. Vlast. Narod*, pp. 115–16.

75. Peter Kenez, "Lenin and the Freedom of the Press," in Gleason, Kenez, and Stites, *Bolshevik Culture*, pp. 130–50.

76. Quoted in Charles Rougle, "The Intelligentsia Debate in Russia 1917–1918," in Nils Ake Nilsson, ed., *Art, Society, Revolution: Russia 1917–1921* (Stockholm: Almqvist & Wiksell International, 1979), pp. 79–80.

77. Zinaida N. Gippius, *Zhivye litsa* (Leningrad: Iskusstvo, [1922] 1991), p. 38.

78. Maksim Gorky, *Nesvoevremennye mysli: Stati 1917–1918 gg.* (Paris: Editions de la Seine, 1971), p. 102.

79. Ibid., p. 244.

80. Vladimir I. Lenin to M. Gorky, September 15, 1919, in Lenin, *Polnoe sobranie sochinenii*, 5th ed., vol. 51 (Moscow: Politicheskaia Literatura, 1965), p. 48.

81. Vyacheslav Kostikov, "Izgnanie iz raia," *Ogonek,* no. 24 (1990): 14–16.

82. Feliks Dzerzhinsky to Unshlikht, September 5, 1922, in Viktor Topolyansky, "Na kazhdogo intelligenta dolzhno byt delo," *Literaturnaia gazeta,* August 11, 1993.

83. See Rougle, "The Intelligentsia Debate in Russia 1917–1918," pp. 54–105.

84. Quoted in Vyacheslav Kostikov, "Volia k vlasti i volia k kulture," *Ogonek,* no. 50 (1990): 17.

85. Anatoly V. Lunacharsky, *Literatura novogo mira: Obzory, ocherki, teoriia* (Moscow: Sovetskaia Rossiia, [1932] 1980), pp. 107–8.

86. Lunacharsky, quoted in Kostikov, "Izgnanie," p. 16.

87. Katerina Clark, "The City versus the Countryside in Soviet Peasant Literature of the Twenties: A Duel of Utopias," in Gleason, Kenez, and Stites, *Bolshevik Culture,* pp. 175–89.

88. Aleksandr Blok, "Mozhet li intelligentsiia rabotat s bolshevikami," in *Sobranie sochinenii,* vol. 6 (Moscow-Leningrad: Khudozhestvennaia Literatura, [1918] 1962), p. 8.

89. Ilya Erenburg, "Intelligentsiia i revoliutsiia," *Literaturnaia gazeta,* no. 10 (March 9, 1994).

90. Aleksandr S. Pushkin, "K N. Ia. Pliuskovoi," in Pushkin, *Polnoe sobranie sochinenii,* I: 340.

91. Blok, "O naznachenii poeta," in *Sobranie sochinenii,* VI: 167.

92. Ibid.

93. See Lewis H. Siegelbaum, "State and Society in the 1920s," in Robert O. Crummey, ed., *Reforms in Russia and the U.S.S.R.: Past and Prospects* (Urbana: University of Illinois Press, 1989), pp. 126–43; and Richard Stites, "Iconoclastic Currents in the Russian Revolution: Destroying and Preserving the Past," in Gleason, Kenez, and Stites, *Bolshevik Culture,* pp. 1–24.

94. *Report of Court Proceedings in the Case of the Anti-Soviet "Bloc of Rights and Trotskyites"* (Moscow: People's Commissariat of Justice of the USSR), pp. 768, 775, 779.

95. Ibid., p. 778.

96. Nadezhda Mandelshtam, *Vospominaniia* (New York: Chekhov, 1970), p. 219.

97. Gippius, *Zhivye litsa,* p. 41.

98. Nadezhda Ia. Mandelshtam, *Vtoraia kniga* (Moscow: Moskovskii Rabochii, 1990), pp. 461, 82.

99. Quoted in Vera von Wiren, "Vvedenie," in Mikhail Zoshchenko, *Pered zakhodom solntsa* (New York: Chekhov, 1973), p. 2.

100. Quoted in Arkady Belinkov, *Sdacha i gibel sovetskogo intelligenta: Yuri Olesha* (Madrid: Ediciones Castilla, 1976), p. 264.

101. Mandelshtam, *Vtoraia kniga,* p. 134.

102. Osip Mandelshtam, *Otklik neba: Stikhi i proza* (Alma-Ata: Zhazushy, 1989), p. 148.

103. Quoted in Marietta Chudakova, "Bulgakov i Lubyanka," *Literaturnaia gazeta,* December 8, 1993.

104. Marina Tsvetaeva, "V sledstvennuiu chast NKVD," *Literaturnaia gazeta,* September 2, 1992.

105. Mandelshtam, *Vtoraia kniga,* p. 231.

106. Georgy Ivanov, "Peterburgskie zimy," in *Serebrianyi vek. Memuary* (Moscow: Izvestiia, 1990), p. 229.

107. Joseph Brodsky once told me that he considered this poem among the very best Mandelshtam ever wrote.

108. "Why didn't you plead for your friend?" Stalin asked Pasternak. "If my poet friend were in trouble, I would have climbed the wall to save him." Anna Akhmatova, "Listki iz dnevnika," in *Serebrianyi vek*, p. 422.

109. Belinkov, *Sdacha i gibel*, p. 167.

110. Mandelshtam, *Vtoraia kniga*, p. 19.

111. Belinkov, *Sdacha i gibel*, pp. 186–87.

112. Igor Kon, "Epokhu ne vybiraiut," *Sotsiologicheskii zhurnal*, no. 2 (1994): 174.

113. Belinkov, *Sdacha i gibel*, p. 382.

114. Fedotov, *Sudba i grekhi Rossii*, I: 100.

115. Ibid., II: 206–27.

116. Andrei D. Sakharov, *Progress, Coexistence and Intellectual Freedom* (New York: Norton, 1968), p. 71.

117. Vladimir Lakshin, in Michael Glenny, ed., *Solzhenitsyn, Tvardovsky, and Novy mir* (Cambridge: MIT Press, 1980), p. 66.

118. Andrei Amalrik, *Prosushchestvuet li Sovetskii Soiuz do 1984 goda?* (Amsterdam: Fond imeni Gertsena, 1970), pp. 7–8.

119. Aleksandr Solzhenitsyn, *Bodalsia telenok s dubom* (Paris: YMCA Press, 1975), p. 541.

120. Vladimir Bukovsky, *I vozvrashchaetsia veter* . . . (New York: Khronika, 1978), pp. 212–13.

121. Aleksandr I. Solzhenitsyn, *Publitsistika: Stati i rechi* (Paris: World, 1981), p. 338.

122. Aleksandr Solzhenitsyn, "Na vozvrate dykhaniia i soznaniia," in *Iz pod glyb* (Paris: YMCA Press, 1974), pp. 21–22.

123. Ibid., p. 251.

124. Joseph Brodsky, *Less Than One: Selected Essays* (New York: Farrar Strauss Giroux, 1986), p. 30.

125. Solzhenitsyn, *Bodalsia telenok*, p. 603.

126. Belinkov, *Sdacha i gibel*, pp. 456–57.

127. Efim Etkind, *Zapiski nezagovorshchika* (London: Overseas Publications Interchange, 1977), p. 247.

128. Etkind cites his own example. In the foreword to his book on poetic translation, Etkind wrote that foreign poets had been lucky with Russian translations of their works because these were often done by outstanding poets in their own right, like Pasternak and Mandelshtam, who were discouraged from writing and publishing their own poetry. Ibid., p. 234.

129. Ibid., p. 249.

130. Lakshin, in Glenny, *Solzhenitsyn, Tvardovsky, and Novy mir*, p. 61.

131. Andrei Kolesnikov, "Chelovek kak tsitata," *Panorama*, no. 659 (November 24, 1939).

132. Anatoly Makarov, "Inye vremena," *Literaturnaia Gazeta*, no. 13 (March 30, 1994).

133. "Vtoroi sud nad I. Brodskim," pp. 348–467, in Etkind, *Zapiski ne zagovorshchika*, p. 439.

134. V. I. Tolstykh, "Ob intelligentsii i intelligentnosti," *Voprosy filosofii*, no. 10 (October 1982): 83–98; V. F. Kormer, "Dvoinoe soznanie intelligentsii i psevdokul-

tura," *Voprosy filosofii*, no. 9 (September 1989): 65–79 (published posthumously, originally written in 1969).

135. Makarov, "Inye vremena."

136. A. Lebedev, "Apologiia Sizifa," *Literaturnaia gazeta* (February 14, 1990).

137. Makarov, "Inye vremena."

138. Pyotr A. Vyazemsky, "Mnenie eshche odnogo grazhdanina" [excerpt from Vyazemsky's diary], *Smena*, August 8, 1991.

139. Aleksandr Vasinsky, "Ballada o raznykh mneniiakh," *Izvestiia*, October 22, 1986.

140. Sergey Averintsev, "Po linii naibolshego," *Sovetskaia kultura* (February 21, 1987).

141. Vladimir Dudintsev, "Genetika sovesti," *Izvestiia*, February 17, 1987.

142. Fyodor Burlatsky, "Ispoved reformatora," *Literaturnaia gazeta* (July 19, 1989).

143. Andrei Voznesensky, "Pered stykovkoi vekov," *Sovetskaia kultura* (February 21, 1987).

144. Dmitry Likhachev, "Nelegkaia nosha akademika Likhacheva," *Moskovskie novosti*, September 18, 1988. The words are a partial paraphrase of Likhachev's by the interviewer, A. Chernov.

145. A. F. Losev, "Ob intelligentnosti," *Sovetskaia kultura* (January 1, 1989).

146. K. M. Kantor, "Stenograficheskii otchet," *Intelligentsiia i vlast* (Moscow: Soiuz Kinematografistov, 1992), p. 60.

147. Natalya Ivanova, "Prezentatsiia apokalipsisa, ili kto ne uspel, tot opozdal," *Literaturnaia gazeta* (September 8, 1993).

148. Natan Edelman, in *Strana i Mir*, no. 1 (1989).

149. Aleksandr Panchenko, "I Detest Being an Intellectual," *Moscow News*, no. 50 (1991).

150. Aleksandr A. Ivanov, "Interviu s A. A. Ivanovym, intellektualom iz Rossii," *Novoe russkoe slovo*, March 1, 1994.

151. Gershenzon, "Tvorcheskoe samosoznanie," pp. 89–90.

152. Olga Fridenberg, in Boris Pasternak: *Perepiska s Olgoi Fridenberg*, edited by Elliott Mossman (New York: Harcourt, Brace, Jovanovich, 1981), p. 291. Quoted in Marietta Chudakova, "Blud borby," *Literaturnaia gazeta* (October 30, 1991).

153. Kama Ginkas, "Vysokoe kosnoiazychie," *Literaturnaia gazeta* (December 25, 1991).

154. Stanislav Rassadin, "Prodazhnye i zaprodannye," *Literaturnaia gazeta* (November 3, 1993); Evgeny Shvedov, "Utonchennaia ubogost sverkh ironii," *Smena* (May 29, 1992); Yuri Polyakov, "Ia ne liubliu ironii tvoei," *Literaturnaia gazeta* (August 18, 1993).

155. M. Berg, "Plius emigratsiia vsei strany . . . ," *Moskovskie novosti*, July 19, 1992.

156. Andrei Konchalovsky, "My ishchem schastia na storone i nekhotim naiti ego doma," *Izvestiia*, September 24, 1992; A. Bitov, "Privatizatsiia sovetskoi vlasti," *Novoe russkoe slovo*, January 31, 1993.

157. Stanislav Rassadin, "Dzyk, dzyk," *Literaturnaia gazeta* (February 17, 1993).

158. Fedotov, *Sudba i grekhi Rossii*, II: 175.

159. See Dmitri N. Shalin, "Critical Theory and the Pragmatist Challenge," *American Journal of Sociology* 98 (1992): 237–79; and "'Skazkobyl': Zametki o retsessivnykh genakh russkoi kultury," *Zvezda*, no. 2 (1995).

3

Psychological Culture

ALEXANDER M. ETKIND

"National character," "modal personality," "collective unconscious," "ethnic mentality," and "cultural identity" are notions designed to capture psychological traits that distinguish one social group from another. Attempts to isolate such hypothetical qualities are no different in principle from efforts to describe religious, legal, or other social patterns found among people who have lived together for a length of time, except that psychological constructs tend to focus on subjective characteristics and are somewhat harder to identify.[1] The link between culture and psychology first came under close scrutiny in the nineteenth century. German linguists H. Steinthal and M. Lazarus and psychologist Wilhelm Wundt made an elaborate case for *Folkpsychologie,* a discipline that examined the interfaces between folklore, language, social institutions, and psychological traits. In this century, around World War II, much attention was given to the "modal personality" and "national character" that purported to describe the ways in which other people, often belonging to enemy nations, raised their children and behaved in their daily life. Margaret Mead, Clyde Kluckhohn, Geoffrey Gorer, Henry Dicks, and other social scientists developed a concept of the Russian national character that sought to explain the contradictions in the overt behavior of America's arch-enemy in psychological terms.[2] In more recent decades, scholars began to pay closer attention to the role of culture and psychology in nation-building. As economic differences between nations level off, less tangible cultural characteristics—emotional, cognitive, aesthetic, axiological—have come to the fore as key factors determining national peculiarities. Ernest Gellner put it most provocatively when he said that cultures produced nations, not vice versa.[3]

Like any field dealing with human behavior, cultural psychology has its share of methodological and ideological difficulties. Scholars tend to gloss over considerable psychological variations within human groups, and this is a source of many questionable generalizations about ethnic psychology, national character, and so on. Complicating the situation are differences between how individuals perceive themselves and how they appear to outside observers.[4] We tend to comprehend other people's actions in terms of their motives and fundamental personality traits, whereas we attribute our own actions to external circumstances beyond our control. Few insiders in a society agree with the judgments nonmembers pass on local mores. What appears odd and problematic to those looking from without seems self-evident and natural for group members. When things go awry, insiders are likely to excuse themselves and blame conspiracy, foreign interference, or bad luck for their problems. By contrast, an outside observer is apt to spot bad habits, ingrained ineptitude, or some other questionable personality traits behind the problems at hand and to assign much responsibility for these problems to group members themselves. Take the Marquis de Custine, a French writer who visited Russia in 1839 and returned from his trip disgusted with what he had seen. He did not care for Russian customs and was convinced that the Russians brought on their own misfortunes. His conclusion was a classic case of blaming the victim: "The oppressed have always merited their sufferings."[5]

This propensity to impugn other people's motives and exonerate one's own conduct is the source of many ethnic and racial biases in cross-cultural perception. Cultural psychology frequently has been employed by those who seek scientific justification for anticultural policies. The Nazis, for example, expressed great interest in Carl Jung's theories about the spirit of the race and the collective unconsciousness. This does not necessarily disqualify Jung's theories, but it does call for caution: Cultural psychology can be used to fan ethnic hatred.[6]

To counter Jung's theory of national psychology, Freud and his followers developed a sort of biological internationalism that ruled out any cultural specificity of mental processes. Alfred Adler and Wilhelm Reich took a keen interest in Marxist theory and even tried to help the Soviet government employ psychology in the cause of socialism. Denying any cultural specificity to psychological phenomena can present its own problems. This century knows several utopian projects designed to unify all mankind on the basis of common political (Marxist), mystical (Free-masonry), religious (the Reverend Moon's Unification Church), linguistic (Esperanto), and other supposedly universal qualities lying dormant in human nature, waiting to be summoned forth by skillful manipulation. The manner in which such projects have been implemented at times has matched the ruthlessness of the politics of racial and ethnic exclusion. German Nazis and Russian communists entertained conflicting views on human nature, but they relied on the same mass violence to implement their political schemes. Which brings us to the central theme of this essay.

There is a difference between "psychology" as an academic discipline and "psychology" as a shorthand for personality traits common in a given population. This difference is not especially pertinent when it

comes to traditional, preindustrial societies, which did not evolve their own psychological science. But in modern societies that have established psychology as an academic discipline with a strong applied dimension we have to deal with a peculiar situation in which "scientific knowledge" about the individual and group psyche is fed back to group members and to some extent informs their self-perception, if not their actual behavior. A case in point is academic psychology in the Soviet Union, which from the start was entrusted with the political task of creating a "New Soviet Man," a model personality suitable for a future socialist society. We can speak in this connection about "psychological culture," by which we shall understand a set of theories and practices that describe, prescribe, and facilitate the formation of certain cognitive, emotional, and behavioral traits in a given population. Psychological culture is not identical with the way particular individuals feel, think, and act, but it offers them ready-made models for self-understanding and thus enters their psychological makeup. We should bear in mind, also, that the term "psychology" did not carry the same meaning in the Soviet context as it did in the West. There was no sharp line separating psychology from other "social sciences." All these disciplines functioned as branches of "ideology," an overarching field that encompassed political theory, moral philosophy, historical science, applied psychology, and other subservient domains of knowledge reinforced by the government propaganda machinery and penal institutions. To understand Soviet psychological culture, therefore, we need to take a broader look at the political context within which it came into existence and how it was made to serve the system.

In this chapter I examine systematic efforts on the part of Soviet authorities to formulate, shape, and enforce a specific personality type in the Soviet population. I begin with a brief overview of stereotypes about the Russian psyche as it appeared to foreign observers and survey the precursors of Soviet psychology in prerevolutionary Russia. Next, I turn to the Soviet era and the competing political-psychological projects for raising a New Soviet Man. I analyze the model Soviet personality envisioned by Stalin and the evolution of this model in post-Stalinist Russia. Finally, I discuss the implications that decades of Soviet efforts to mold human psyches have for the current project of forming a democratic society in Russia.

The Russian Psyche from the Outsider's and the Insider's Points of View

Popular stereotypes differ from scientific concepts in at least one important respect: They are not meant to predict actual conduct or to test a theory. Their main function is to reduce complexity to a neat scheme, to make odd behavior understandable, and quite often, to disparage out-

siders for their alien ways. Stereotypes are influenced by political attitudes, artistic accounts, and exemplary personalities, as well as by the
past and present relationships between the groups to which both an observer and an observed belong. Notoriously unreliable as guides to understanding other cultures, stereotypes tell us something important about
both the culture observed and the observer's own culture.

For centuries, Russian culture has fascinated people in the West, who
have expressed alternating admiration and disgust for its inimitable
ways.[7] Diderot and Voltaire looked to the Empress Catherine the Great to
realize Enlightenment ideals. Marx held a lifelong contempt for Russia
and its rulers, but shortly before his death he was so impressed with the
inroads that socialist ideas had made in this country that he set himself
the task of learning the Russian language. In modern times, this interest
would occasionally take on sexual overtones. Nietzsche fell in love with a
Russian woman, Lou Andreas-Salomé, asked her to marry him, and, dis-
tressed by her refusal, commenced his magnum opus *Thus Spoke
Zarathustra*. Carl Jung was similarly captivated by Sabina Spielrein, another Russian woman, who had a great impact on his personal life and
professional career.

Stereotypes about the Russian psyche popular in the West ascribe to
Russians a bewildering mix of qualities, such as laziness and hard work,
dependency and disobedience, moodiness and exaltation, mysticism and
realism, shrewdness and impracticality, plus abundant and wild sexuality. For Madame de Stael, who traveled to Russia in 1812, "in every way
there is something gigantic about these people: ordinary dimensions have
no application to them. . . . If they do not attain their goals it is because
they exceed them."[8] George Brandes, a Danish literary critic, emerged
with a different impression from his 1887 trip to Russia: "[I]ntellectually,
the Russians impress the stranger by their realism, their practical, positive
taste for the real."[9] Yet the same author described Russians as "radicals in
everything" and insisted that "when a Russian has got hold of a thought,
a fundamental idea, a principle . . . he does not rest until he has followed
it out to the last results."[10] So much for Russian realism and practicality.
Another (stereo)typical statement comes from a group of Americans writing under the pseudonym E. B. Lanin, who noted in 1891 that Russians
were "a good-natured, lying, thievish, shiftless, ignorant mass."[11] Such
Western opinions about Russia and the Russians could be multiplied at
will.

This may or may not be a coincidence, but Western intellectuals promoting radical psychology spent a surprising amount of time pondering
the Russian psyche as it is depicted in the novels of Dostoevsky and observed in the country's infamous personages (Rasputin is still the most
widely known Russian name in the West). In the process, they revealed

much about their own psyche projected onto the Russians. Some of the most horrid actions in the novels written by the Marquis de Sade (whose father was ambassador to Russia) were committed by Russians. Leopold von Sacher-Masoch, of sadomasochism fame, was also a great admirer of Russian culture; his erotic novels were filled with Russian personages and loving descriptions of Russian sexual mores. Freud, who had many Russians in his Vienna circle, once noted that "even those Russians who are not neurotics are deeply ambivalent."[12] His favorite patient, known under the pseudonym "Wolfman," was a Russian man who provided Freud with the model case of neurotic hypersexuality. Apparently, the founder of psychoanalysis initially felt more comfortable assigning these psychosexual dynamics to exotic Russians rather than to the more staid Austrians.

Contrary to the popular view, Russians themselves had mixed feelings about psychology.[13] "People call me a 'psychologist,'" complained Dostoevsky. "It's not true; I'm only a realist."[14] Tolstoi inveighed against psychology as a false science. The Russian literary critic Mikhail Bakhtin claimed that "every psychologist is a spy." In the early twentieth century, during the Silver Age, a period of major cultural developments that culminated in the Russian revolution, many intellectuals expressed a similar ambivalence about psychology. Vasily Rozanov, an influential literary figure of this era, thought that Russians did not need any science of psychology because they had an innate "psychological acuity," a natural ability to empathize with others, which could only be smothered by rational psychology. After describing in his novel the onset of menses in a young girl, Boris Pasternak made a characteristic comment that she had no need for psychology, which could lure her away from wondrous nature, which was perfectly capable of running its course without any aid from psychology. Vasily Ern, a neopopulist philosopher of the first decade of the century, made a similar point to disparage what he called "psychologism," which would only restrict the natural flow of subjectivity, arrest human will, and stop the miracle of "immediate psychic action."[15]

There was, of course, another intellectual strand among cultured Russians that hailed psychology as an indispensable instrument for understanding the world and coping with social problems. This strand became more prominent in the 1910s, as chaos gradually enveloped the country, making more common economic and political explanations sound increasingly implausible. Poet Zinaida Gippius made this diary entry about revolutionary Petersburg in 1918: "The reality is so bizarre that it is impossible to believe in facts as they are. Only psychology provides understanding."[16] More subtle—psychological—hypotheses were called upon to make sense of a society hurtling into a political abyss. This movement away from rationalist schemes favored by modernity toward more irrational, postmodern explanations is indicative of the crisis of modernity in Russia and elsewhere in the world at the time. The depths of the human psyche would be plumbed in search of more radical explanations and cures for the ailings of the age.

The turn toward psychology as a handy tool not only for understanding but also for reshaping human nature had several important precursors. One of them was Nikolai Fyodorov, a Russian philosopher who in the mid- to late nineteenth century championed a utopian project of future society based on the principle of "psychocracy" and guided by a new science designed to make all people genderless and immortal. Odd as it may sound, Fyodorov had many followers in Russia, including Dostoevsky and Vladimir Solovyov. As late as the 1930s, Russian emigré political thinkers (Pavel P. Suvchinsky was the most prominent among them) swore allegiance to Fyodorov and his philosophical social psychology. Fedorov's project had its historical counterpart in the psychological-religious program of the Skoptsy, a radical Russian religious sect whose members practiced voluntary castration of men and degendering of women (who had their breasts and clitoris amputated) as a path to sanctity. The ideas and rituals of this sect curiously adumbrated certain cherished Bolshevik ideals, such as shared property, the end to competition, overcoming of gender differences, and blind loyalty to the leader. V. Bonch-Bruevich, a friend of Lenin and secretary of his cabinet, took a lifelong interest in Russian sectarians, apparently hoping to apply their experience to the monumental tasks facing socialist building.

Psychological Science in Service of Communism

It might seem odd at first that Bolsheviks, the standard bearers of Marxism in Russia, would give credence not to economics and politics but to psychology as a primary instrument for social reconstruction. But in retrospect, this fact is not all that surprising. After the Bolsheviks seized banks, factories, and communications and declared their victory, they expected human behavior to change accordingly. They quickly discovered, however, that political and economic power was not enough: To change old habits, one had to reach deeper into the human psyche than politics or economics could. This is where "progressive psychology" came into full view as a supreme science, called upon to accomplish the task that the old Russian culture reserved for tradition, religion, and common sense. Recognizing the failure of objective economic and political conditions to effect the desired behavioral changes, the party shifted its hope toward the psychology of hunger, pain, and death. This psychology was to help party experts disabuse Soviet citizens of obsolete beliefs, to reduce each individual to bare physiological reflexes, and to inculcate "progressive" forms of behavior that would be conducive to socialism. Bolsheviks insisted that everything should be planned and nothing remain unconscious, and they were convinced that the new science of the human psyche would be the key to the success of their plans.

Before the revolution and throughout the Soviet era, Russian Marxists shaped the new discipline as a useful tool for future reforms. In their quest for a new psychology, the Bolsheviks tapped one unlikely source: Friedrich Nietzsche. Coming from an entirely different tradition, this German thinker nonetheless suited Bolshevik ideology, with his views on psychology as a science of the future, capable of revolutionizing the entire society: "[P]sychology shall be recognized . . . as a queen of the sciences, for whose service and preparation the other sciences exist. For psychology is now again the path to the fundamental problems."[17] Bolshevik intellectuals, most notably Lev Trotsky, Aleksandr Bogdanov, and Anatoly Lunacharsky, accepted this Nietzschean precept and consciously sought to splice Marx's socioeconomic utopia with the Nietzschean psychobiological one. Unlike Nietzsche, they believed that the technical problems of implementing this idea could be solved within a few years with the help of psychological science. What other Europeans saw as metaphor and hyperbole, Bolsheviks took as a guide to action.

Although the ideological goals were perfectly clear to Russian Marxists, the practical means were still problematic. However, the optimistic leaders of the new order considered the task at hand to be a technical one. Neither Nietzsche nor Marx nor Freud confronted the problem head on. Nietzsche's Superman was couched in mythological terms and his arrival relegated to a somewhat indefinite future. Marx thought that human nature would change more or less automatically as soon as the new social and economic relations were formed. Freud seemed to have relevant methods, but they were not easy to apply.

"The [new] man has not come yet, but he is not far away, and his silhouette is looming over the horizon," Aleksandr Bogdanov, a Marxist theoretician and psychiatrist by education, wrote in 1904.[18] "To publish a new, improved edition of Man," intoned Trotsky, "is the next task of communism."[19] The Soviet era's most brilliant psychologist, Lev Vygotsky, fully concurred: "In the new society, our science will be at the center of life. . . . It will be the last science in the historical period of Mankind. . . . The new society will make a new human being. . . . This new science of the new man will be nothing other than psychology."[20] In 1929, an ex-psychoanalyst, Aron Zalkind, formulated the main task of the new psychological discipline as the "mass construction of the New Man."[21] Anton Makarenko, who succeeded Zalkind as a guru of Soviet psychology, explained the purpose of his "pedagogical science" this way: "We should take as our task the formation of that type of behavior, those characters and qualities of personality, which are necessary for the Soviet state."[22]

Eugenics—the biological science of breeding a better human specimen—also drew the passing interests of Bolsheviks. In the mid-1920s, Nikolai Koltsov, a brilliant researcher whose studies received full support from the authorities, sought to apply genetic methods for the artificial selection of future mankind. Ilya Ivanov, a biology professor, petitioned the People's Commissariat of Enlightenment with a more radical idea: cross-breeding African apes and Russian citizens. His proposal was approved and financed by the government, which gave Professor Ivanov hard currency and sent him to Africa. This at a time when Ivan Pavlov, the Nobel prize–winning physiologist, had no food to feed his experimental dogs.[23] The program of building the New Soviet Man would be continuously adjusted in its technical details, but its main thrust remained unchanged throughout the Soviet era. Years after Stalin's death, a prominent Soviet philosopher, Evald Ilenkov, restated the original program as follows: "Formation of the personality of the new, communist-type man on a mass scale . . . now becomes a practical task and the immediate goal."[24]

Implementing this ambitious program for educating a new man required extensive logistical arrangements. The civil war was not yet over, but the spectacular institutional buildup in psychology had commenced. Six times more students registered as "pedagogic" majors in 1921 than in 1914. In 1922, Moscow alone sported over twenty institutions devoted entirely to research and higher learning in psychology and pedagogy.[25] Four federal commissariats—of Education, Health, Railways, and Heavy Industry—had their own pedological services. In 1923, the Russian Psychological Association, the Russian Psychoanalytical Association, and the Russian Association for Experimental Psychology were founded in Moscow. In 1927, the Moscow Testing Association was formed, along with the All-Russian Psychotechnical Association and the Soviet Pedological Association, which had their first congresses the same year. This bloated establishment helped the Communist party select leaders, place people in appropriate positions, and develop their natural abilities.[26]

Human Nature and Bolshevik Culture

The term "human nature" generally connotes stable biological and psychological traits beyond social control. In this sense, "nature" is opposed to "culture." This usage, which goes back to Rousseau, is very common in liberal and skeptical discourse. Freud referred to human nature each time he wished to make a point about how difficult it was to change man and society. Radical thinkers and totalitarian politicians valued psychology more than liberal ones. If you think that human nature is a constant and more or less perfect, you need no radical psychological intervention to make it better. Thus, Fritz A. Hayek rejected Freud, B. F. Skinner, and psychology in general as a tool for social reconstruction.[27] The more one despairs about human nature and wants to see it ameliorated, the more likely one is to invest in psychology. Radical psychology and radical politics went hand in hand throughout this century. For political extremists, human nature was not a nature anymore; rather, it was equated with culture and reduced to an underlying sociohistorical context. What was made by history, the radicals surmised, could be remade in the new historical circumstances through conscious efforts. Understood in this fashion, human nature presented itself as suitable object for political manipulation. More and more, Soviet theoreticians would look on it as just another word for human culture. This transformation of the familiar nature-culture construct[28] infinitely enlarged the scope for radical intervention in human affairs and offered endless creative possibilities for early twentieth-century Russian intellectuals.

When economic determinism proved rather helpless to affect the human psyche, Bolsheviks turned to behavioral science for theoretical concepts and technical solutions to complement Marxism. All these thinkers saw human nature as a culture in disguise, an infinitely malleable substance ready for social amelioration. Such was the broad ideological consensus that united otherwise diverse thinkers of this period. Said Vygotsky, "When we speak about the transformation (*pereplavka*) of man as a quality unquestionably required by the new mankind, about the artificial selection of the new biological species, we are dealing with a truly unique situation: man is the first and only biological species that makes itself."[29] "Psychotechnique" (*psikhotekhnika*) was among the most popular words of the epoch. Each major theorist construed it in a somewhat different way, but they all believed in the magic of "scientific" transformation to be accomplished with the aid of a well-tested psychological tool. For Vygotsky, it was "concept," for Lysenko "genes," for N. Marr "language," for Makarenko "groups." Responding to the official critique of his pedology, Zalkind sought to reassert his political credentials: "I have always worked to prove the extraordinary sociogenic conditionality and plasticity of human behavior."[30] In 1931, Zalkind attempted to formulate the principles that would become the methodological canons for Soviet psychology, which included "activity," meaning that the individual should be studied as an active and not merely contemplative being, and "plasticity," implying that human nature was "not a warehouse" of ready-made traits but a store of dynamic potentialities.

Trotsky's ideas were especially informative in this context. "Man is purging himself from top to bottom. He purged himself of God, State, and the Tsar, he freed the economy of chaos and competition, and he is now purging his inner world of unconsciousness and obscurity."[31] Effortlessly, Trotsky crossed the line between the commonplace and utopian, economy and psychology, Marxism and Freudianism. Everything inherited from the past was to be "purged" from top to bottom. It was not long before Trotsky discovered that the metaphor of "purging" could be applied to him as well. While still in power, Trotsky sought a shortcut to the Bolshevik scientific utopia via psychoanalysis, which he had become familiar with during his Viennese emigration in 1908. Alfred Adler and his wife were his personal friends; he attended psychoanalytical meetings and left remarkable memoirs on this subject. In 1931, Trotsky sent his own daughter to Berlin to undergo psychoanalytic treatment. His disciple, friend, and lifelong collaborator, Adolf Ioffe, was a patient of Adler's. In September 1923, Trotsky wrote a letter to Ivan Pavlov advising him to synthesize his physiology with Freudian psychoanalysis. Both Pavlov and Freud, Trotsky reasoned, were exploring the depth of the human spirit, although Freud did so from above and Pavlov from below. Trotsky's passion for psychoanalysis was infectious, as attested by the creation in 1923 of the State Psychoanalytic Institute in Moscow. At that time, too, the Russian Psychoanalytic Association had more top Bolsheviks as board members than professional psychoanalysts. Yet this institution for psychologically molding the New Soviet Man did not survive Trotsky's political downfall.[32] We might add in passing that Trotsky's link to psychoanalytic circles had an ironic and rather dark side. Naum Eitingon, the head of Stalin's counterintelligence service, who personally supervised Stalin's plot to assassinate Trotsky, had an indirect link to the psychoanalytic establishment: his brother and business partner, Dr. Max Eitingon, was president of the International Psychoanalytic Association.

Stalinist Psychology and the Psychodynamics of Soviet Power

Like several other undertakings pioneered by Trotsky, the applied science of the human psyche was first rejected, then simplified, and finally put into action by Stalin. After the downfall of psychoanalysis and with encouragement from Stalin, pedology took its place as the chief psychological theory, with Aron Zalkind as its official leader. Pedology, supported by Nikolai Bukharin, Nadezhda Krupskaya, and Anatoly Lunacharsky, enjoyed a boom around 1930. Many psychoanalysts and psychologists, among them Sabina Spielrein in Rostov and Lev Vygotsky in Moscow, found refuge in the institutions working under the banner of pedology. In 1936, the party rejected pedology and replaced it with Makarenko's pedagogy [or pedagogic principle]. Makarenko's normative vision for the New Soviet Man followed the familiar Bolshevik blueprint. He was to love work for its own sake and be both unswervingly devoted to the communist cause and enthusiastic about any assignments the party might give him. The transformation of an ordinary human into a model Soviet citizen was to be radical and swift. The New Soviet Man's psyche would enable him to believe in the incredible, to endure the unbearable, to love things people normally hate. Sexual libido had to be reduced to a minimum along with other human needs, so as not to dissipate the individual's energy on trivial pursuits. Interpersonal feelings were supposed to give way to "collectivist" identifications. Aggression and competitiveness were to be neutralized in everyday life and reactivated when the country had to fight its foreign enemies. We can summarize the quasi-scientific concept of human nature and psychology espoused by Soviet theoreticians of this era as follows:

1. Human nature is far from perfect; its spontaneity is dangerous; like children, human beings should be kept under constant supervision; they require guidance and firm direction from knowledgeable adults.

2. Human nature is not fixed, but plastic and malleable; it can be changed in a methodical way; people, like children, are open to the molding influence of environment, culture, and society.

3. Transforming human nature is a complicated task; its ultimate aims and scientific procedures might not be fully understandable to the uninitiated; political education is a job for highly skilled and ideologically astute professionals.

4. Human beings owe their essence to society; the transforming power of society is vested in social groups or "collectives"; a suitable paradigm for a collective is an army unit or a work brigade; families, peer groups, and other primary group formations do not qualify as collectives.

5. Concepts and words are primary psychological phenomena; personal experiences are verbally recoverable; the verbalization of personal attitudes is to be encouraged in order to facilitate official monitoring; nonverbal, unconscious, uncontrollable psychological processes are to be stamped out by the scientific manipulation of the human psyche.

Not to be outdone by Trotsky, Stalin professed himself a proponent of "scientific psychology."[33] It was with his approval that psychology was added to the school curriculum as a mandatory discipline, an unprecedented measure that remained in effect until Stalin's death. With Stalin consolidating his power over the Communist party and the country, the blueprint for raising the New Soviet Man changed somewhat, becoming even more rigidly ideological and, at the same time, more personalized. Elaborate networks of personal relations sprang up without which nobody could successfully exercise power and climb up in the hierarchy. It is tempting to compare this tangle of political, economic, and personal relations to the operations of a mafia family. To be sure, the members of the latter do not seek to take over the entire society; they prey on society at large rather than trying to transform it from scratch, as the Bolsheviks set out to do. Nonetheless, some instructive similarities are apparent in the sustained efforts to impart the organization's ethos to its younger members, the initiation rituals symbolizing the individual's dedication to the organization, the emphasis on personal trust and undivided commitment to the leader, the relentless power struggles and endless fights for the position closest to the chief, the readiness to cut old ties on a moment's notice and to rededicate oneself to a new power configuration. Learning these rules by heart was as much a condition of success as a matter of survival for those caught in this deadly game.

The mafialike pattern of personal bonds was reproduced at all levels of power in Stalin's Russia. Each ministry, industry, army unit, work brigade, office, or scientific division identified with its chief, who was a role model for his subordinates. A trusted comrade, such an exemplary individual could accomplish any task by the sheer strength of his character. A strong leader could meet any goal, even without technical expertise, as long as he possessed the right psychological stuff.[34] A strong will, intimidating demeanor, and heavy hand were expected from a person aspiring for a leadership position in Soviet society.

Not surprisingly, the parent-child relationship became the paradigm for all social ties under Stalin's rule. Stalin's image was drummed into the nation's psyche as a paradigmatic father figure, while Lenin was widely perceived as a grandfather of sorts. Freud also noticed this pattern of leader-follower relationships, which he thought common to all politics. In the West, though, such psychological mechanisms were not altogether apparent; rather, they represented a fairly sophisticated analytical construct. In Stalin's Russia, on the other hand, people openly declared their love for the nation's pater familias. A Soviet professor could praise Stalin-the-father leading his grateful citizen-children to a bright future, and nobody in the audience would see anything wrong with this locution.

"Some people say that thoughts appear in the human mind before they are uttered, outside of language, naked, so to speak," opined Stalin in a broadside against Freudian Marxists and all wayward psychologists, linguists, and philosophers interested in the notion of the unconscious. "It is absolutely not true. Whatever thoughts man might have exist only on the basis of language, on the basis of language terms and phrases. There are no thoughts naked and free from language material."[35] This strategic idea perfectly suited Stalin's totalitarian political aspirations. During his reign, anything that eluded ideological control and resisted correct political formulation was to be barred from existence, or at least from psychological textbooks. There is nothing in the human mind that is closed to the party's watchful eye, that could not be revealed and corrected. Society, or what was the same thing for Stalin, power, is in a position to program and reprogram human psyche. Whatever man conceals from himself, he conceals from the authorities. To postulate anything unreadable and unrecoverable in the human psyche was to doubt the party's omnipotence. This precept survived many transformations in Soviet psychology and remained central in the works of such diverse thinkers as Lev Vygotsky, Aleksei Leontiev, and Evald Ilenkov. Thinking was nothing but inner speech, and concepts were interiorized social hierarchies.

Nature as Culture:
Dimensions of a Metaphor

Sexuality, senility, mortality—all natural phenomena that could not be readily squeezed into an ideologically correct schema—were suspect in Soviet psychological culture. The fact that high ideological discourse systematically ignored low bodily functions did not mean, of course, that the latter were wished away. Hidden in the interstices of an omnipotent culture were the incorrigible facts of human nature, which kept intruding into life despite all efforts to sanitize it, to purify it from natural imperfections. Thus, Soviets never managed to abolish death; when a person died, the rituals of grieving and burial were performed, just as they were centuries before the October revolution. Despite repeated attempts, no cultural forms pertaining to birth, marriage, or burial rituals emerged in the Soviet Union that bore an unmistakable imprint of Soviet ideology, which failed to leave any noticeable traces because the human life cycle had no recognized place in Soviet ideology. Ideology had a lot to say on how humans should live, work, struggle, and cherish the motherland, but nothing at all on how they should go about giving birth and facing death.

Compromises with nature were only temporary; ultimately, culture would overcome its inertia and make every bodily function follow a correct ideological blueprint. What follows is an attempt to codify some of the most salient characteristics that Soviet culture sought to impart to human nature, an ideal type of fully realized Soviet being toward which Soviet citizens were to move under the guidance of their spiritual leaders.

Power as Supreme Value

Human needs and values are many, but as far as Soviet ideology was concerned, none came close in importance to power: acquiring power, wielding power, enjoying power. Power was more important than love, respect, and health and gave more pleasure than family, creativity, and sex. The reason for this imperative was simple: Power guaranteed its owner access to all other values. Education, career, friendship, economic security, and sexual pleasure could be exchanged for power, as measured by one's proximity to the party and state leaders. A luxurious life (by Soviet standards at any rate) awaited high officials—summer cottages, limousines, opera boxes, ostentatious culinary feasts, the company of artistic celebrities—just about anything except private property. Losing one's power base meant giving up everything of personal value. The "cult of power" had a psychological counterpart in the "cult of personality," which Nikita Khrushchev denounced as the essence of the Stalinist political system. In the words of Pierre Bourdieu, all forms of capital—economic, cultural, psychological—correlated with and derived from political capital in Soviet society.[36] The case of Stalin's henchman, Lavrenty Beria, comes to mind, his fabled sexual exploits being greatly aided by his powerful position as head of the Soviet secret police.

The Soviet authorities' uncompromising attitude toward private property and independent cultural pursuits makes perfect sense in this context, for these could not help but undermine the party faithful's monopoly on power and sever the link between a person's place in the political hierarchy and the quantity of pleasure meted out to this person. Of course, some values are difficult or impossible to redistribute, such as health, youth, and physical beauty. These belong to nature, which places severe limits on how much cultural manipulation can enhance them. This is why the Communist party perceived such values as a threat to its total power. Unable to control these values, the regime methodically sought to devalue them in the public mind and deprive them of their traditional cultural meaning. Biological universalities and constants of human existence were given new cultural interpretations that undercut their natural significance.

The Subject as Absence

Power was there to be wielded and enjoyed, but not conspicuously, for it did not belong to any particular individual. Contrary to the "cult of personality" thesis, Soviet power was not vested in a person; it derived from the state and the party, whose comrades had to exude modesty and reticence and act as conduits for its collective wisdom. Trotsky showed too much personal ambition, which violated the Bolshevik's cherished beliefs. He acted like a master seducer conquering the feminine crowd, to use the image Freud employed in his essay on "group psychology." Trotsky's comrades never forgave him his charisma and mass appeal and ditched him at the first opportunity. Stalin, by comparison, was a paragon of modesty and collegiality. His demonstratively noncompetitive style in public suited the spirit of the time well. All top Soviet leaders had to suppress their ambitions and appear to the populace as humble servants of the state. Carefully planned and consciously constructed, Soviet power was modeled not so much on sexual conquest as on a long bureaucratic climb by leaders who proved themselves in office, showed respect for their organization and its ethos, and were finally rewarded with the mantle of leadership.

The subject, the flesh and blood human being, was conspicuous for its absence in official Soviet life, as was reflected in Soviet political speech, which proscribed the use of "I." The plural form, "we," implied that an infinite number of other comrades would have said the same thing under similar circumstances. Passive voice and impersonal forms are ubiquitous in Soviet political jargon. "It is proposed that . . . ," a typical sentence would commence, leaving the uninitiated to wonder who exactly was proposing. The English language does not quite capture these subjectless grammatical constructions, which are so pervasive in Russian speech. Some languages may be better equipped for power play than others, although any language can be twisted to convey power symbolism.

The Soviet leader was always a symbol for something other than himself. He embodied the idea of Soviet power and was subject to instant recall whenever he failed to communicate the proper message to his underlings. A replica of power rather than a self-motivated agent, the leader served not as a prototype but as a monument to be worshiped in lieu of the original. It would be unseemly for a portrait, a replica, a copy to speak out on its own behalf. In fact, the original was power itself, and the Soviet state could be seen as a shrine where citizens worshiped power.

The Psyche as Discursiveness

The New Soviet Man had to be a supremely discursive creature capable of verbalizing his innermost feelings and thoughts. No event of his psyche could escape notice—his own or other responsible comrades'. Psychological processes were to be recovered through speech. To control is to know, and to know is to verbalize. This is why confession qualified as the ultimate proof in Soviet legal practice. True, the confession might have been extracted by torture, but pain and suffering, being nonverbal psychic events, were meaningless in themselves.

The emphasis on discursiveness did not improve the quality of verbal production in the Soviet Union. Soviet leaders were as verbose as they were inarticulate. To an extent, this was true of the Soviet people in general.[37] The content of a speech meant little compared to the fact that this person was authorized to speak publicly, to voice an opinion. Public ceremonies—from Communist party congresses to meetings of local party cells—were transformed into endless verbal exercises. Speeches were tedious, speakers repeated each other, and little hard information was presented, but that was beside the point. What really mattered was who got to the podium, in what order, for how long, and so forth. An experienced observer could instantly infer a speaker's place in the pecking order, his closeness to the higher-ups, the amount of political capital at his disposal, and so on. Generally, the more often a person spoke in public, the more importance people assigned to him. In his waning years, handicapped by numerous illnesses, Brezhnev felt obliged to give six-hour long speeches before the national audience, making uneasy viewers wonder whether he could survive the ordeal.

Speaking took precedence over writing in Soviet society. Speechwriters were invariably lower in the social hierarchy than speechmakers. Published work also enjoyed a lower status than public speaking. Intellectuals engaged in writing and publishing wielded minimal political power. Their skills could bring them a decent living, but with very few exceptions (Maksim Gorky, for example), Soviet writers did not ascend to the pinnacle of power and were never deified as were Soviet political leaders given to public oratory.

The right to voice an opinion in public was reserved for trusted comrades. The common folks had the right—and duty—to demonstrate their approval for the leaders and their public pronouncements. Characteristically, the very idea of democracy is linked in the Russian language with speech: *golosovat*—to vote—in Russian literally means "to exercise one's voice." People deprived of voting rights in the 1930s due to their bourgeois origins or similar political indiscretions were referred to as "deprived of the right of voice." Gorbachev's campaign for openness—*glasnost*—was construed as an effort to restore the people's voice and encourage unauthorized speech.

Body as Pain

Soviet art often featured the heroic deeds and titanic efforts of individuals struggling, suffering, and overcoming pain to achieve worthy goals. Rarely did it depict pleasure. Eating, dreaming, sex—any activity that did not pursue a public agenda and could be enjoyed for its own sake was suspect. Soviet psychological culture was allergic to pleasure. The familiar Soviet formula, "With a feeling of deep satisfaction it is stated that . . . ," hints at this ascetic sentiment, this aversion to pleasure. This verbal cliché has no grammatical subject. It is not the speaker who feels satisfaction; whatever positive emotions are registered here, they have nothing to do with the human body. Soviet citizens were expected to be motivated in their endeavors by sheer enthusiasm for a collectively approved goal. Heroism Soviet style consisted in overcoming human nature and acting as if the body did not matter, like the famous veteran pilot who took to the air to pursue enemy airplanes after losing his legs in battle. A common scene in Soviet war movies featured a proud soldier or resistance fighter refusing to reveal state secrets while being tortured by fascists.

To be sure, the body stripped of its natural functions, immune to pleasure, and desensitized to pain was only a cultural metaphor. People never stopped eating, imbibing, defecating, or copulating, just as they continued to love, dream, and think silly thoughts. It is amazing, Pasternak once said, that amid all this madness, people could still have normal dreams.

Death as Silence

A voiceless individual was much less of a threat to the state than one who did not surrender this party-given gift. A careless joke, a complaint about working conditions, an approving reference to genetics, which had been denounced as a bourgeois science—any statement that did not meet with official approval could cost an individual his voice. And when the party wanted to silence individuals permanently, it deprived them of their body, as well. A dead body is a silent body. In Soviet society, death was commonly the ultimate form of censorship imposed on discursively imprudent citizens. Any strong voice that stood out in the chorus and sang an unfamiliar tune was in danger. That is, unless the voice belonged to a beloved leader, like Lenin or Stalin, in which case death was but a temporary impairment to be rectified by the advancement of Soviet science. The bodies of the deceased leaders in the Soviet Union were preserved in the best possible conditions for more than just ideological-propaganda reasons. This practice goes back to the early Bolsheviks, who, like the prerevolutionary Skoptsy and visionaries such as Fyodorov, entertained serious hopes that one day mortal comrades would be brought back to life. The mausoleum on Red Square in Moscow where the bodies of Lenin and Stalin were placed after their death is a monument to this quest for immortality.

As to the rank-and-file builders of communism, they had to face death on their own, unaided by official guidelines as to its meaning or the prospects of life after death. The nearly total absence of grieving rituals or even simple explanations pertaining to death in official Soviet culture is stunning. Political leaders did not fare much better in this department: They repeatedly revealed themselves unprepared for death, leaving the nation without a clue about its future and setting in motion protracted fights between potential successors to the leadership mantle.

Age as Power

Consider the ageless portraits of Soviet leaders. The authorities detested aging as a biological process immune to cultural manipulations. Determined efforts to overcome aging were mounted in the 1920s, when a surgical procedure for rejuvenating testicles became popular among some Bolsheviks, but the efforts apparently failed, so Bolsheviks chose to ignore aging as a phenomenon worthy of serious attention. The natural stages in the human life cycle—childhood, youth, old age—were virtually unknown to Soviet ideologists and for a long time were downplayed by scientists. Nobody outlawed the different ages, but the distinct stages in personal growth were never given positive acknowledgment either. Childhood and youth had value as transitory periods allowing humans to practice their future roles as adult citizens. Age-specific subcultures were suppressed. Soviet youth had significantly less peer-group interaction than did their counterparts in the West, and whatever experience they did have was frowned upon by adults. For a long time, the country had no discernable youth fashion or holidays geared toward children. Medical facilities for children were inadequate and counseling services nonexistent. By the same token, the authorities made no concerted efforts to build facilities for the elderly, to insure access for the handicapped to public areas, and so on. Adulthood emerged here as a supreme value and a power base. However infirm or old Soviet leaders might appear, they were hailed as productive adults.

Gerontocracy is a pattern commonly found in nondemocratic polities, but few modern societies pressed it as far as the Soviet Union, whose leaders continuously exhorted the younger generations to become more ideologically vigilant, economically efficient, and public-spirited. In fact, most of the talk about the New Soviet Man was addressed by elderly leaders to the country's youth. Officially approved organizations like the Octobrists, Young Pioneers, and Young Communist League replicated the Communist party organization and adhered in their practices to adult values and tastes. Mandatory military service provided one official outlet where Soviet youth engaged in what seemed like age-specific activities, but its heavy ideological indoctrination, sadistic initiation rituals, and brutal disciplinary practices turned it into a powerful mechanism for instilling rigid collectivist principles in Soviet youth. In fact, the armed forces duplicated the age bias found in Soviet society at large, as senior conscripts were allowed to brutalize their junior comrades at will.

Gender as Maleness

Officially, Soviet ideology tended to minimize gender differences. Men and women were expected to subscribe to the same values and beliefs, have the same psychological qualities, and engage with the same enthusiasm in building a future society. In practice, however, gender-based inequality pervaded Soviet society. The people in power were predominantly males. The dominant culture was produced by and for males. Women labored as hard as men did, but they had to carry a double burden—at work and at home. In a way, women were allowed to stay closer to nature than men, as they continued to give birth, care for children, prepare meals, and participate in the natural life cycle in ways that could not be abolished by official decrees. Women worked in agriculture, education, or as general practitioners in medicine, leaving to men the areas of cultural creativity, industrial production, and military service. Males' alienation from nature was self-imposed; they were perfectly happy to let women take care of such natural functions, while they concentrated on cultural pursuits. As a result, the cultural violence unleashed by the Bolsheviks consumed more men than women. It is this closeness to nature that helped women survive the madness of Soviet civilization better than their male counterparts.

The End of Stalinism and the
Transformation of Soviet Psychology

Violence has been practiced as an instrument of social change since time immemorial by people subscribing to disparate ideological agendas. In this century, the Nazis used it extensively to exterminate undesirable political (communist), racial (Jewish and Gypsy), and sexual (homosexual) groups. These narrowly targeted groups were supposedly impeding the transition to a glorious state of the future. The very predictability of this violence gave untargeted German citizens a sense of security. What made Stalin's terror different and profoundly affected the Soviet psyche was its randomness. Nobody was immune from the purges; every person was a potential target, and every group had to offer up its share of sacrifices on the altar of power.

There was no way to predict who the next victim would be. Sometimes verbal violence preceded physical violence, as was the case with the political trials unleashed during the campaign of mass terror in 1936. At other times, verbal attacks hinting at incarceration and death failed to inflict the expected damage. Thus, the vociferous campaign against pedology and its practitioners ordered by Stalin in 1936 stopped short of arrests and executions. In other cases, deadly violence was applied without any verbal warning. A person or entire ethnic groups could vanish from their homes and sometimes from the face of the earth, as did Jewish writers in the late 1940s and Crimean Tatars during World War II, to name just two examples. The sheer randomness of the violence infused the Soviet people with unimaginable horror and left an indelible mark on their psyche. If fear is an expectation of punishment and guilt is an internalization of this expectation, then the Soviet psyche was permanently afflicted with both. Most people knew that they could be punished and felt guilty before they were actually accused of any wrongdoing. Soviet propaganda, in turn, worked over time to ensure that each person remained vigilant and ready to meet his fate if need be. A great terror without systematic deception would be mass murder. Propaganda without terror would be a massive lie. But deception and violence working in tandem created a new psychological reality for their victims. The two reinforced each other and supported the system, which would have collapsed without these props. When the Soviet regime gave up on random terror and concentrated mostly on deception as its instrument of social control, it doomed itself to an imminent demise.

Altering adults' behavior is a complicated business. Witness all the efforts to alter eating, drinking, and sexual habits, which were met with only marginal success. The chief stumbling block here is that humans are supposed to change their mind-sets and behavior while their environment remains basically the same. Moving an obese person into a famine area would surely produce dramatic results in reducing the person's weight. Moreover, attitude and behavior modification accomplished in such a dramatic manner often meets with less psychological resistance than a change that is supposed to be entirely voluntary. If people in Stalin's Russia adapted to the ideological demands without much resistance and even felt nostalgic about Stalinism, it is in large measure because the psychological changes sought by the regime were reinforced by drastic environmental changes, the total mobilization of resources, and the massive use of violence.

Having renounced Stalinist methods, Soviet leaders had to place even greater emphasis on psychology, propaganda, and agitation. A slate of Stalin's successors, with the possible exception of Khrushchev, fancied themselves experts in human psychology and touted their administrative and public relations skills as an asset in implementing the scaled down communist agenda. Brezhnev is reported to have bragged to his buddies that he might be weak in economics but that psychology and the art of governing were his strong suits. Konstantin Chernenko, Brezhnev's successor, tried to reanimate the moribund Soviet society with yet another crack at "communist upbringing" and "instilling right values" in Soviet youth. Yury Andropov, the ex-KGB chief, was a recognized master of deception. But the efforts to achieve change without violence, by relying chiefly on rhetoric and deception, failed. When ideological vitriol and politically correct ranting are no longer followed by action, punitive or otherwise, they lose their persuasive power and sooner or later ring hollow.

This is what happened in the post-Stalinist era, when the level of verbal violence visibly escalated but the authorities' ability to move people around vastly diminished. Beginning in the late 1950s, the monolithic psychological culture began to give way to one dominated by doublethink. In public, people still had to convey their enthusiasm for socialism, appear to be hard-working, demonstrate moral fiber, exhibit gender-free qualities, and so on. But in private life they could think and behave pretty much as they pleased, as long as they did not let their private actions spill over into the public arena. The opposition between nature and culture transformed itself into the opposition between public and private. Culture reigned over the public sphere; nature took over private life. In contrast to the public sphere, where transactions grew excessively formal and ritualized, private life promoted unusually close emotional ties, which flourished undisturbed by envy and competition given forced egalitarianism. Emotional bonding, personal commitment, aversion to cold calculation, penchant for improvisation, and lifelong friendships became especially prominent among the intelligentsia. In private settings, Soviets often seemed to prefer singing to speaking, perhaps because music entailed a strong nondiscursive element. These characteristics would be strikingly apparent to Western visitors, who learned to appreciate the company of intellectuals and the emotional intimacy of the vast interpersonal networks that sprang to life in post-Stalinist Russia.

But there was a price to be paid for these seemingly congenial and nonutilitarian personal bonds. The gap between word and deed, a deep contempt for the system, and a forced public silence bred hypocrisy and encouraged self-hatred. When the gap became intolerable and someone dared voice dissent in public, the authorities moved to silence the nonconformist. Even if the person did not resemble a New Soviet Man in private life, the pretence was still required in public appearances. The handful of dissidents who openly dared to challenge the Soviet system found this out the hard way. After denouncing Stalin's violence, Khrushchev and his successors did not shy away from the old punitive ways, even though they hesitated to practice violence on a mass scale and never dared to reintroduce random terror. From that point on, only public dissent would be a punishable offence.

Psychology was fully institutionalized as an independent academic discipline in post-Stalin's Russia. The first psychology departments were established at the Moscow and Leningrad state universities in 1964, a generation before the first sociology department was created in 1986. The discipline's premises remained more or less unchanged. "Our entire nature might be constructed," wrote Aleksei Leontiev, a leading psychologist of this period, "and this is especially true about the psychological nature of man."[38] In his early research, Leontiev tried to show that humans can be taught to discriminate color by touch. His findings were never confirmed, but Leontiev remained convinced throughout his life that human nature was an infinitely malleable social construct that could be made and remade at will. Another prominent Soviet thinker, Evald Ilenkov, expressed similar convictions that the human psyche could be shaped according to an ideological blueprint. He sought to prove his thesis through a study of congenitally blind-deaf-mute individuals, whose progress he guided and monitored for a number of years. The results seemed impressive: several of his subjects enrolled in Moscow State University and successfully completed their undergraduate education. "In spite of obstacles that seemed insurmountable—the complete and innate absence of both vision and hearing—it was shown possible to . . . shape a highly sophisticated human psyche."[39] His sensational theories fell apart, however, when his subjects confessed that their defects were not congenital but acquired between the ages of four and six.[40]

A more sinister role in shoring up the official lies was accorded to Soviet psychiatry. Its chief exponent, Dr. A. Snezhnevsky, came up with an idea that political dissent in Soviet society was usually an indication of psychiatric abnormalities. He discerned the early signs of schizophrenia in patients who "develop an odd . . . interest in abstract problems and harbor naive ideas about their resolution. In particular, [such patients] spend much time reading philosophical, psychological, sociological, and aesthetics treatises."[41] This doctrine rationalized the psychiatric abuses in the Soviet Union, the longstanding practice of institutionalizing political dissidents, labor organizers, religious activists, and simply independently minded people who refused to acknowledge the party line and dared to voice unauthorized views in public. Consciousness that failed to acknowledge Soviet reality in all its official glory was pronounced delusionary and subjected to medical treatment. The plight of dissidents committed to psychiatric facilities was in many ways worse than that of dissidents thrown to prisons, for as patients in psychiatric wards, dissidents were isolated from normal human beings and had to endure the application of mind-altering drugs. They could also be kept in mental asylums indefinitely. The only way for a patient to get out of the psychiatric prison was to renounce incorrect views and embrace the official line.

Again, the healthy psyche was equated with discursiveness, the ability to spout correct verbiage, the eagerness with which one was willing to present ideologically correct precepts as personal convictions.

Wearing pious masks in public and cursing the regime in private would become a norm, and this pervasive double-think could not help leaving its mark on the Soviet psyche. One of its insidious consequences was alcoholism, which afflicted high-brow intellectuals and common folk alike. In the intoxicated state, Soviet citizens could transcend the fundamental duality of their being and achieve the unity of mind and action that the mendacious realities of everyday life denied them in their sober moments. This was also a way, however fleeting, to break through culture and reach out to nature inside and outside oneself.

By the early 1980s, the New Soviet Man's existence was as threadbare as that of the senile Soviet leader, Leonid Brezhnev, whose barely functioning body was kept alive by the valiant efforts of doctors and faith healers. A cultural construct that came to life in extreme historical conditions and required mass terror to prop it up, the New Soviet Man transpired as a pathetic monster whom nobody took seriously any longer, not even experts from the Department of Propaganda and Agitation, who kept themselves busy propagating the familiar nonsense but for all practical purposes ceased agitating the populace. Soviet citizens contemptuously referred to the New Soviet Man as "Sovok"—a little shovel handy for collecting dust or absorbing ideological garbage. Such was the ignominious end of the communist superman—Homo Sovieticus—that Trotsky and his comrades had dreamed of at the dawn of Soviet civilization.

Conclusion:
The Unbearable Lightness of Human Nature

Among the causes contributing to the demise of the Soviet empire one has to count the psychological crisis that gripped Soviet society in the early 1970s and wore it down through the 1980s. Apathy, cynicism, and alcoholism had as much to do with the collapse of the Soviet regime as falling prices on world oil markets and corruption among Soviet officials. Mikhail Gorbachev set out to lead the country out of its malaise and managed to breathe some new life into old political forms. But in the end, perestroika failed to deliver on its promise, not just because its architect was too slow to jettison obsolete ideological schemes, but because he underestimated the depth of the anger that enveloped Soviet society after its cherished myths were exposed.

Some found postcommunist reality to their liking, but most cringed. The deadlocked political process, the fluctuating economic reforms, and the mounting chaos in daily life left many feeling nostalgic for the certainties of the bygone era. The breakup of the Soviet empire had a particularly strong effect on the Russian psyche. Even people who detested communism were troubled by the collapse of the Soviet Union and the nation's loss of its superpower status. From the psychological viewpoint, ex-Soviets found the diminished sense of security and sudden loss of personal identity most upsetting. However arduous life was under the *ancien régime*, it accorded the individual a place in the social system and guaranteed employment, minimal standards of living, free health care, a chance to get ahead for those willing to play by the rules, and a sense that one belonged to a great nation. When wild capitalism replaced cradle-to-grave security, many people were frightened by the revolutionary forces they had helped unleash. Blue and white collar workers now faced unemployment; intellectuals found their spiritual bonds threatened by inequality; artists lamented their lost state subsidies; the once pampered military forces saw their prestige take a nose dive; collective farmers felt reluctant to strike out on their own as private producers; and nearly everybody felt the void inside. To fill this void, some turned to the discrete pleasures of private enterprise. Others sought refuge in nationalism and religion. Still others vowed to bring back the good old days of socialism and restore the Soviet empire to its former glory. Everyone had to master the difficult art of private living, with all its headaches, uncertainties, and opportunities. But identities, like new shoes, do not always fit. People are still groping for a self they can be proud of or at least comfortable with. Hopes are riding high for a miraculous cure to deliver the country from its present morass and reinvest personal life with meaning. One indication that people are vying for a quick fix is the spreading hatred toward minorities, who are blamed for current problems. Another is the proliferation of psychics and fortunetellers in Russian society. Anatoly Kashpirovsky, an immensely popular faith healer who made his name during the late perestroika era, was invited by Vladimir Zhirinovsky to run as a representative of his "Liberal Democratic" party. Kashpirovsky agreed and was elected to the Russian Parliament. More sound liberals gathered around Yeltsin yearn for a miracle of their own—the miracle of a free market. Yet the liberal idea that the free market would speedily transform the Soviet psyche into something more benign proved to be as misplaced as the radical claim that the socialist economy would deliver a new man. Which brings us back to the question of human nature in its relation to culture.

In previous sections, I examined the blueprints for the New Soviet Man, the techniques used to implement it, and the outcome of efforts to engineer a communist social species. The Soviet experiment was based on the assumption that human nature is flexible, malleable, and passive, that it is shaped anew in each historical era according to specific cultural blueprints. Indeed, human behavior can be influenced by social forces and changed on a mass scale, provided the efforts are reinforced by total control over society and its members. But all such efforts are predicated on a willingness to use both violence and deception. As soon as the authorities begin to let up on violence, humans recoil from extremes and revert to more common attitudes and actions. Even under extreme conditions, people are likely to change their habits rather than their motives, their ideological verbiage rather than their bodily functions, their cultural forms rather than their natural desires. What Soviet experience appears to teach us is that revolutions against human nature are doomed. Culture might disguise nature, but it cannot abolish it altogether. This is not to gainsay that sex, gender, family, and work patterns bear a distinct historical and cultural mark, only that the variability in these patterns is limited by the universalities of human nature. For all the resources the Soviet regime brought to bear on modifying human conduct, it had very little to show for its efforts. Soviet citizens emerged from the historical experiment that began in October 1917 demoralized, but they had not lost their ability to love, laugh, kibbitz, hope. With time, they will form new habits to satisfy their basic needs. I do not know how the Russian psyche will evolve in the next few decades, but I am convinced that Russian citizens will resist the temptation to succumb to yet another overarching ideological blueprint for a happy future.

Notes

This chapter was translated from the Russian by Alexander M. Etkind and Dmitri N. Shalin. The author wishes to thank Dr. Leonid Gozman, Moscow State University, for years of fruitful collaboration during which some of the ideas formulated here were developed; Dr. Lee Ross, Stanford University, for his interest in this project and valuable feedback; and Dr. Dmitri N. Shalin, University of Nevada, Las Vegas, for his generous attention to the language and substance of this chapter, far beyond routine editorial work. I also want to express my gratitude to the George Soros Foundation and its Central European University program, as well as to the International Research and Exchanges Board, for their support.

1. See James W. Stigler, Richard A. Shweder, and Gilbert Herdt, eds., *Cultural Psychology: Essays on Comparative Human Development* (New York: Cambridge University Press, 1990).
2. For example, Margaret Mead, *Soviet Attitudes to Authority* (New York: William Morrow, 1951); Geoffrey Gorer and John Rickman, *The People of Great Russia* (London: Norton Library, 1949); Henry V. Dicks, "Observations on Contemporary Russian Behavior," *Human Relations*, no. 2 (1952): 111–75.

3. For an overview, see E. Gellner, *Nations and Nationalism* (Oxford: Blackwell, 1983); and *Culture, Identity and Politics* (New York: Blackwell, 1987).

4. See L. Ross and R. E. Nisbett, *The Person and the Situation* (New York: McGraw-Hill, 1991).

5. F. Wilson, *Muscovy: Russia Through Foreign Eyes* (New York: Praeger, 1970), p. 223.

6. Jung's psychological ideas and political affiliations are discussed in Andrew Samuels, *The Political Psyche* (London: Routledge, 1993). See also Alexander M. Etkind, *Eros nevozmozhnogo: Istoriia psikhoanaliza v Rossii* (St. Petersburg: Meduza, 1993).

7. For a recent example, see Ronald Hingley, *The Russian Mind* (New York: Scribner, 1977).

8. Wilson, *Muscovy*, p. 188.

9. George Brandes, *Impressions of Russia* (New York: Crowell, 1966), p. 18.

10. Ibid.

11. E. B. Lanin, *Russian Traits and Terrors* (Boston: B. R. Tucker, 1891), p. 3.

12. Sigmund Freud and Arnold Zweig, *Correspondence* (New York: Harcourt, 1988), p. 55.

13. See Alexander Etkind, "Kultura protiv prirody: Psikhologiia russkogo moderna," *Oktiabr*, no. 7 (1993): 168–92.

14. Mikhail Bakhtin, *Problemy poetiki Dostoevskogo* (Moscow: Sovetskaia Rossiia, 1979), p. 71.

15. Vasily Ern, *Sochineniia* (Moscow: Pravda, 1991), p. 388.

16. Zinaida Gippius, *Chernye tetradi: Zvenia*, vol. 2 (Moscow-St. Petersburg, 1992), p. 53.

17. Friedrich Nietzsche, *Beyond Good and Evil: Prelude to a Philosophy of the Future* (New York: Vintage Books, 1966), p. 32.

18. Aleksandr Bogdanov, "Novyi mir," in *Voprosy sotsializma* (Moscow: Politizdat, 1990), p. 28.

19. Lev Trotsky, "Neskolko slov o vospitanii cheloveka," in *Sochineniia*, vol. 1 (Moscow: GIZ, 1927), p. 110.

20. Lev Vygotsky, "Istoricheskii smysl psikhologicheskogo krizisa," in *Sobranie sochinenii*, vol. 1 (Moscow: Pedagogika, 1982), p. 435. See also "O L. S. Vygotskom: Zabytye teksty i nenaidennye konteksty," *Voprosy psikhologii*, no. 4 (1993): 37–55.

21. Aron Zalkind, "Psikhonevrologicheskie nauki i sotsialisticheskoe stroitel-stvo," *Pedologiia*, no. 3 (1930): 309–22.

22. Anton Makarenko, "Tsel vospitaniia," *Izvestiia*, August 28, 1937.

23. The relevant materials can be found in the Central State Archives of Russia, fund 298, opis 1, delo 1, p. 135. Ivanov's expedition is described in by G. Faiman, "Dnevnik doktora Bormentala. . . ." *Iskusstvo kino* (1991): 7–10.

24. Evald Ilenkov, "Chto zhe takoe lichnost?" in *Filosofiia i kultura* (Moscow: Politizdat, 1991), p. 387.

25. Among them, Advanced Studies in Pedology, Advanced Studies in Psychology, Central Institute for Public Education Organizers, Academy for Social Training, Pedagogical Institute of Child Deficiency, Institute of Psychology of the First Moscow University, Moscow State Institute for Psychoneurology,

Central Institute for Pedology, State Institute for Medical Psychology, Laboratory of Experimental Psychology and Pediatric Psychoneurology at the Neurological Institute, Medico-Pedagogical Clinic, Central Psychological Laboratory for Special Learning Schools, Experimental Laboratory of Psychology of General Headquarters, Central Institute of Labor, Laboratory of Industrial Psychotechnique of the Ministry of Labor, Central Institute for Humanitarian Pedagogy, Museum of Preschool Education, and Institute for Social Psychology.

26. For more information, see *Pedagogicheskaia Moskva: Spravochnik-kalendar za 1923* (Moscow: Krasnaia Moskva, 1923), p. 435; Etkind, *Eros nevozmozhnogo*.

27. Fritz Hayek, *The Political Order of a Free People* (London: Routledge, 1979).

28. C. Lévi-Strauss, *Anthropologie structural* (Paris: Plon, 1958).

29. Lev Vygotsky, "Istoricheskii smysl psikhologicheskogo krizisa," in *Sobranie sochinenii*, vol. 1 (Moscow: Pedagogika, 1982), pp. 2–3.

30. A. B. Zalkind, "O metodologii tselostnogo izucheniia v pedologii," *Pedologiia* (1931): 2–3.

31. Lev Trotsky, "O kulture budushchego," in *Sochineniia*, I: 460. See also "Trotsky and Psychoanalysis," *Partisan Review*, no. 2 (1994): 303–8.

32. See Etkind, *Eros nevozmozhnogo*.

33. Stalin's interest in psychology was noted by Western observers. See Robert C. Tucker, *Stalin and the Uses of Psychology* (Santa Monica: Rand, 1955).

34. The main features of totalitarian consciousness are discussed in Leonid Gozman and Alexander M. Etkind. *The Psychology of Post-Totalitarianism in Russia*, translated by Roger Clarke (London: Center for Research into Communist Economics, 1992).

35. Iosif V. Stalin, *Marksizm i problemy iazykoznaniia* (Moscow: Gospolitizdat, 1949), p. 66.

36. Pierre Bourdieu, *Homo Academicus* (Stanford: Stanford University Press, 1988).

37. George Brandes made a similar observation in 1887, pointing out that "with the exception of the lawyers, no man in Russia has the talent of speaking, nor the courage to try." See Brandes, *Impressions of Russia*, p. 60.

38. Aleksei N. Leontiev, *Izbrannye psikhologicheskie proizvedeniia*, vol. 1 (Moscow: Pedagogika, 1983), p. 139.

39. Evald Ilenkov, "Stanovlenie lichnosti: K itogam nauchnogo eksperimenta," *Kommunist*, no. 2 (1977): 69.

40. *Slepoglukhonemota: Istoricheskie i metodologicheskie aspekty* (Moscow, 1989), p. 93.

41. A. Snezhnevsky, "Skitsofreniia: Formy i techenie," *Bolshaia meditsinskaia entsiklopediia*, vol. 31 (Moscow, 1963), p. 267.

4

Religious Culture

JERRY G. PANKHURST

The former Soviet Union is undergoing a religious revival. People inside and outside the Russian Orthodox Church are reexamining its ancient ways, rediscovering its long-forgotten saints, and searching its institutional memory for answers to urgent questions facing the nation. The Western reaction to this remarkable resurgence of religion in Russia has been mixed. All observers welcome the fact that free inquiry about religion and free religious worship have been restored in the Russian Federation. At the same time, many are concerned about the xenophobic tendencies that have accompanied the religious revival in Russia and that became especially evident after the liberal forces suffered a defeat in the December 1993 parliamentary election. Calls to restore the great Russian empire sounded by the winners brought to mind the old slogan, "Moscow, the Third Rome," that spurred Muscovy in the sixteenth and seventeenth centuries to expand its dominion over neighboring countries. The situation is further exacerbated by a few archbishops and metropolitans who exhort the Russian people to bring their orthodox, unchanging faith—*pravoslavie*—to the world.

Western evangelicals who flock to Russia hoping to save it from itself find themselves in an awkward position. Ironically, they act as a missionary force trying to sever Russian Orthodoxy from its traditional moorings, but in the process they could inadvertently transform the present religious revival into yet another victory for secularism. Just as their well-meaning counterparts are intent on building capitalism in Russia (a project no less heroic than that of building communism), Western religionists are determined to bring reformation to a country that missed its chance at religious reform in the sixteenth century. But the Russians have seen all this before. Was not the Bolshevik revolution a drive to impose Western enlightenment on the dark East and to replace its backward mores with imported prescriptions for universal happiness?

While we cannot—and should not—avoid passing judgment about the path the religious revival has taken in Russia, we need to resist the temptation to impose our ready-made schemes on a vastly different country without doing justice to its unique religious culture. It would be prudent to defer our judgment until we had a chance to examine the origins of Orthodoxy and the role it has played in the nation's history, including the transformation that the Orthodox faith and church institutions underwent during the Soviet era.

The term "religious culture" refers here not only to the life of the Russian Orthodox Church—its religious corpus, worship rituals, and organizational principles—but also to a wider range of social practices that bear the imprint of Russian Orthodoxy. Russian religious culture has left its mark on every cultural domain in the nation. Its pervasiveness has much to do with the fact that the Russian Orthodox Church had been the favored religious organization in the land since at least the tenth century. Adopted as the official faith of all Russias, Eastern Christianity remained inexorably tied to the state. When the state faltered under invasion and foreign control, the Church continued to nurture a sense of nationhood for Russians, preventing society from splintering and disintegrating. When the state regained its strength, the Church lent its considerable legitimizing power to the government and the state's imperial expansion. Hence the strong historical bond that was formed between Russianness as an ethnic or national identity and Russian Orthodoxy as a religious affiliation.

By certain Western Christian (e.g., evangelical Protestant) standards, membership in a church is realized through regular participation and overt commitment to the church's values and goals. The Russian Orthodox Church adopts a far broader perspective on membership. One gains membership in the Russian Orthodox Church first and foremost through baptism performed at birth and only secondarily through participation in religious worship. The latter could be very sporadic without affecting the person's standing as an Orthodox faithful. Barring explicit evidence to the contrary, one's membership in the Orthodox Church was presumed to be established if one was born Russian. This applied not only to Orthodox Christians accepting the Church's authority but also to the "Old Believers"—religious sectarians who refused to honor the church's innovations in liturgy and swore to uphold the old faith in the face of excommunication and persecution from the official church.

The contiguity between the boundaries of ethnicity and religion in Russia had important implications for other religious confessions, be they Catholic, Protestant, Muslim, Jewish, or Buddhist. All those espousing non-Orthodox beliefs (*inovertsy*) were hard pressed to maintain their national identity as Russians and to act in a manner at least outwardly consistent with certain Orthodox ideas about propriety, authority, and loyalty. The right wing within Orthodoxy frequently saw conspiracies by the non-Orthodox, especially Jews, Masons, and Catholics, as great threats to Mother Russia herself. Hence, such *inovertsy* experienced themselves and were perceived by others as not fully Russian—a stigma they continue to carry today.

In this century, communist authorities worked hard to stamp out religious beliefs and replace old notions about Russian nationhood with the internationalist identity deemed proper for Soviet citizens. However, the old religious demarcation lines were not erased completely. The atheist state professed by Stalin could not escape completely the formative influence of Russian Orthodoxy. Its vestiges shone through the public rituals and were clearly visible in the communist craving for political monopoly, cultural orthodoxy, and sanctimonious rigorism.

How did Orthodox customs manage to survive in atheistic Soviet society? To understand this phenomenon I will invoke Clifford Geertz's concept of "spiritual afterimages," which refers to "reflections, reverberations, projections" of religious experience in daily life.[1] Formed in an earlier era, such reflections, reverberations, and projections often resurface at a later point in a nation's history as moral imperatives and sentiments that continue to guide national development. These imperatives may lack the clarity and purpose that distinguished the original precepts, but they leave a distinct mark on successive generations, on the country's political, social, and economic practices. During periods of religious revival, spiritual afterimages regain much of their original vitality, sometimes suppressing secular social forms and spurring powerful fundamentalist movements.

Along these lines we should see the current religious renaissance in Russia—the increased church attendance, the desire to learn about the ancient saints, the longing for the wonders wrought by holy people in the distant past, the renewed pilgrimage to holy places like Valaam (the monastery complex at the north end of Lake Ladoga) and Sarov (the home of Saint Serafim). Through these practices, the spiritual afterimages of Russian history are revitalized and reincorporated into the nation's psyche. Besides these obvious stirrings, there are more subtle ways in which religious culture affects, and in turn is affected by, the developments in other domains of Russian culture. This confluence is not always benign. Given the historical precedents, we have to wonder whether the authority of the Russian Orthodox Church will once again be used to legitimize the state's imperial ambitions, whether the Church is ready to make concerted efforts to regain its spiritual autonomy, to encourage the growth of democratic political culture, to facilitate the transition to a market economy, or to serve as a unifying force in these times of trouble. Such are weighty issues that have direct bearing on the future of Russian civilization. I cannot pretend to have answers to all the relevant questions, but I hope that the following discussion will clarify the stakes that Russian society has in these issues and shed some light on the future of Russian Orthodoxy.

The Origins of Russian Religious Culture

In 1988, the Russian Orthodox Church marked its first millennium. The festivities commemorated the time when Grand Prince Vladimir committed himself and his nation to Eastern Christianity, making it the official faith of ancient Rus. Vladimir did not seem to meet much opposition to conversion from the population, but it would be a mistake to conclude that conversion was always voluntary. Vestiges of ancient folk religion survived for centuries in Russia, suggesting that it was deeply established in the lands of Rus. The chronicles and legends record many instances when severe force had to be used by both Vladimir and his lieutenants. Novgorod's conversion in particular was accompanied by a great deal of violence, and 100 years later everyone in the city, except the clergy and the nobility, remained pagans, not Christians.[2]

The paganism of Rus was weakly institutionalized—there were no priests, temples, or regular forms of worship, no complex mythology— but it seemed to have resonated deeply in people's hearts. As was generally the case with the Christianization of pagan nations, the new religion became more palatable through syncretism. Thus, "Perun the god of thunder becomes Elijah, with his chariot of fire; Veles becomes St. Blaise, and is still the patron of cattle."[3] As Fedotov pointed out, ancient Rus blended the Christian cult of Mary with the Mother Earth and the female goddesses cult, which revolved around birth and the governing of individual destiny, so that Mary was cast as the mother of all mankind in Russian Orthodoxy.[4] That is to say, when Christianity came to Rus and the Divine Motherhood cult was transferred to center on Theotokos ("Mother of God"), the old pagan mythology continued to evolve in the new Christian context.

Local cults multiplied in response to this syncretism, and the religion of Rus was in effect a "dual faith" (dvoeverie), with Christian ritual and ceremony overlaying pagan holidays and festivals.[5] It took about six centuries for Christian piety to sink roots in the Russian people's heart, but once it did, it emerged in a stark form of severe ritual observance, constant crossing of oneself, genuflections, long night services, and the like.[6] At first, only the upper class had any clear idea about Christianity. The ruling class's religious knowledge remained insular because the clergy, drawn primarily from Constantinople, often did not speak Russian and communicated chiefly with the elite. Those Russians deeply involved in

religious life sought to emulate, however unsuccessfully, the extreme asceticism of the Eastern Christian monastics, which further distanced them
from the population.

Over the next few centuries, the level of piety among the Russian clergy
declined, as it absorbed more native Russians, lost its penchant for asceticism, and gradually switched to serving the ritual needs of the population. Whether or not anyone understood the ritual was not an issue anymore. Noted Russian historian Pavel Milyukov pointed out that the
clergy stratum became rather illiterate at this time (which is why many
Church historians decried this period as that of decline in the Church).
Just as the clergy began to lose its cultural and educational edge, the population as a whole noticeably increased its level of Christian observance.
By the fifteenth or sixteenth century, the clergy and the people converged
on a middle ground, reaching a level of religious consciousness not deep
enough to satisfy the ascetics but considerably loftier than the one common at the earlier *dvoeverie* stage: "It was the magic significance of the rite
which became the cause and condition of its popularity [consistent with
the old folk cult]. Therefore the rite served also as a middle course upon
which met the upper and lower strata of Russian faith: the former gradually losing the true conception of the contents, the latter gradually gain-
ing an approximate understanding of the form."[7]

During this first 600 years of Christian influence, three major political
developments had great significance for the fate of religion in Russia: the
steady decline of Constantinople, the conquest of Rus by the Mongols,
and the shift of Rus's cultural-political center from Kiev to Moscow.

Since Rus had allied itself with Byzantine Christianity centered in
Constantinople, it was bound to feel the effects of Byzantium's steady political decline. In 1453, the Turks finally captured Constantinople. Greek
influence was not strong enough to smooth out the coarseness of Russian
civilization before the thirteenth century, when the Tartars spread their
yoke over Russia, drastically reducing its contacts with the Byzantines.
Nevertheless, the Byzantine tradition and church administration left their
distinct marks on Russia. This heritage of Eastern Christianity comes to
the fore in the Church's subservience to state authority, a theme that acquired its very Russian overtones during the next 600 years. The second
major legacy of Constantinople was the notion that the Greek Church was
the only true church, all other Christian churches having fallen to heresy
or corruption.[8] Constantinople continued to be the reference template for
the Russian Church for many more years, but by the mid-fifteenth century it had lost whatever formal control it had had over the Russian
Church. The failure to unify the Eastern and Western branches of
Christianity at the Council of Florence sealed the transformation of the
Russian Orthodox Church into an autocephalic religious body.

The choice of Eastern Christianity as a model for ancient Russia had a profound impact on the Russian Church, its spirituality, and the culture it fostered. First, there is the forcefully uprooted paganism present in the syncretic elements and manifest in the magical conception of the rites of the Church. However sincere and devout the Russian Christian, there is a sense in which he or she is living an unstable faith that could at any moment devolve into untamed pagan practices. This might be part of the reason why the Russian Orthodox Church has always been so adamant about the eternal verities of the faith and the absolute truth it claims to hold in every religious sense. This persistent claim may reflect the need to control the undisciplined pagan within. Hence, doctrinal rigidity and inflexibility in ritual practice are part of Russian religious culture.

Second, Constantinople's claim that it is the only true successor to the ancient Christian Church, a claim that denigrated the Western Christian tradition, undercut the diversity within the Russian Church. Even minor doctrinal or ritual disagreement among the faithful was feared as inviting a schism. Christian movements outside the Orthodox Church could only be judged as heresy, thus subject to repression. Virtually no diversity in religious perspective or practice could be accommodated. Intolerance of dissent, therefore, could be listed as another distinct characteristic of Russian religious culture.

Third, Eastern Christianity accords central importance to the principle that the church must be unequivocally subordinated to the state. This precept was consistent with the Byzantine principle of symphonia, symbolizing the ultimate harmony of religion and government. As the patriarch of Constantinople was required to submit to the Byzantine emperor, so the metropolitan and later patriarch of Russia was to submit to the tsar. The Eastern Churches were all built around a national conception of church. There was no central authority like the Catholic Pope, but there was a strong authority structure in each national church, which maintained respectful and concilliar relations with the other national churches of the Eastern communion. The head of state had to confirm—and sometimes directly appointed—the head bishop for a national church. Church and state leaders were to represent for their people the spiritual unity and truth of the one true church; therefore, there could be no major disagreement or separation between them. This principle produced a church subordinated to political authorities, a condition firmly established in Russia at least from the time of Peter I through the communist period. In more general terms, this practice informed a culture in which a discourse about political, economic, or social issues could easily acquire an extra-mundane significance and generate a quasi-religious zeal. This propensity to raise ideological stakes, to treat routine differences as if they pertained to sacred matters, would become typical of Russian culture in general and Russian religious culture in particular.

Finally, there was the sharp opposition to the West that reflected the split of the Christian church into Eastern and Western churches. When the Western European Middle Ages exploded into Renaissance, Reformation, and Enlightenment, the wall between East and West kept these great social upheavals from infecting Russia. And when the shock waves from these momentous developments finally reached Russia, their effect was only partial, often distorted, and sometimes the opposite of what transpired in the West. Thus, when Peter I imported Western European innovations in secular and religious governance to Russia—most notably, the senate for the state and the synod for the church—they were turned into instruments of greater authoritarian control rather than broader popular participation. The state's dominion over the church is still among the most acute problems facing Russian Orthodoxy.

It would be a mistake to view Russian religious culture in negative terms, to judge it exclusively by the extent to which it approximates Western beliefs and practices. Nurtured in the cradle of Eastern Christianity, Russian religious culture emerged extremely rich in its spiritual values and aesthetics. It produced artistic works that continue to inspire us today. It had its share of saints and religious workers who spurred the faithful to keep the nation together when its breakdown seemed imminent. At the same time, we cannot close our eyes to the fact that its spirituality was flawed by the state, which harnessed Orthodoxy for its imperial purposes, that Orthodoxy did not always provide moral guidance to the faithful in their everyday lives, that it failed to explore the interfaces between religious spirituality and personal freedom implicit in the Christian faith. These paradigmatic features of Russian religious culture were further reinforced during subsequent periods of national expansion under the tsars and the communists.

National Expansion and Orthodox Culture

By the end of the fifteenth century, ancient Rus had been transformed into the sovereign state of Muscovy. Although there were still the neighboring states of Crimea, Astrakhan, and Kazan, which threatened the Russian state, Tatar domination, with its cultural and political insularity, came to an end after the Golden Horde was defeated by Ivan III in 1480. With Constantinople vanquished by the Turks and Orthodoxy coming into its own, the links with Russia's old benefactor were now only symbolic. Even though the patriarch of Constantinople reinstituted communion with Moscow and repudiated the Council of Florence after 1453 (the move had been motivated largely by the vain hope of military aid from Rome), the Greek Church had irreversibly lost its prestige in Moscow's eyes.

Nevertheless, the idea of Greek Christianity as the only true religion had taken deep root, and Muscovy saw itself, after the seeming self-betrayal and ignominious demise of Constantinople, as the last representative of the true faith. Popular piety at the time consisted chiefly in formal adherence to ritual and the magical notion of rite, reflecting the pagan legacy. Very little room was left for the spiritual dimension of the Christian faith. Authority in the Church was now vested in an indigenous hierarchy. The lower clergy remained largely illiterate, while the upper clergy and hierarchs were preoccupied with pleasing the princes who held the power of appointment and removal. When there was no more Byzantine emperor to control the appointment of the metropolitan, the job quite naturally devolved onto the grand prince, soon to be called tsar.

At this juncture, political aspirations and accomplishments merged with religious ideology to produce a peculiar national imagery captured in the heady slogan, "Moscow, the Third Rome." Its express function was to symbolize Muscovy's direct succession from the great apostolic see. Rome, it was reasoned, had fallen to papal heresy and corruption and was succeeded by Constantinople. Now the same diseases had subdued fair Byzantium. Was not its conquest by the heathen Turks proof of God's wrath at its heinous departure from the orthodox faith of the apostles and Holy Councils? And who else but Muscovy matched in dignity and orthodoxy the prior supreme sees? Given its cultural and religious background, these ideas made good sense to fifteenth- and sixteenth-century Russians. Such ideas furnished fertile grounds on which political absolutism could flourish. Absolutism in politics had as its natural counterpart a status quoism in popular piety, a kind of religious formalism that replaced Christian spirituality and subordinated religious authority to state imperatives. Now all dissension could be nipped in the bud and ruthlessly expunged by a sacredly legitimized state power. And since the tsar was sanctified by Church authority, any political opposition could easily be interpreted as apostasy or heresy: "[Thus the Russian Church] was now left for the first time face to face with the formidable power of Muscovite absolutism, with neither Constantinople nor Sarai to defend its ancient privileges against possible encroachments by the grand dukes [of Muscovy]. The Church chose the road of submission and threw its influence to the support of the ambitions of the Moscow dynasty."[9]

The removal of three metropolitans from their posts during the sixteenth century signaled the dynasty's willingness to exercise its powers as a divinely appointed authority.[10] That religious and state powers fully merged became obvious when the Church canonized Prince Vladimir, who had turned Russia into a Christian state and the Russian state into a Church-anointed power. Forever after, the religious afterimages embedded in the Russian faithfuls' psyche reminded them of the state's supremacy in all spiritual matters. Through the period of expansion following the defeat of the Tatars, the Church added new saints who likewise elevated state authority in the spiritual world of the faithful Orthodox believer. Many princes and tsars were canonized as saints, and especially important were those who served as warriors preserving the integrity of the Russian nation. Whatever their personal learning and holiness, Dmitry Donskoi, Aleksandr Nevsky, and Saint Sergius of Radonezh (who counseled Dmitry Donskoi and blessed his troops as they went to battle) distinguished themselves as actors who aided Russia's military and political expansion.

Under the reigns of Ivan III (1462–1505) and Vasily III (1505–33), a reconsolidated Rus made its debut upon the diplomatic stage of Europe as it expanded westward into the lands controlled by Lithuania. Contacts were established with the Holy Roman empire, the Pope, France, Denmark, and other countries of Western Europe, as well as with Muscovy's immediate neighbors, Poland, Lithuania, Sweden, Hungary, and the Ottoman empire.[11] Under Ivan IV (1533–84), also known as "Ivan the Terrible" or "the Dread," Russian hegemony expanded southward to the Caspian Sea, including much of the older Tatar lands. Now, the Russian ruler could claim control as far as the Arctic Ocean in the north. Clearly, for Russia this was a time of great political success, which extended into the field of religion: Job, the metropolitan of Moscow, was consecrated Patriarch of Moscow and all Russias in 1589 by Constantinopolitan Patriarch Jeremy. This act, which confirmed the separation of the Russian Church from Constantinople, must have buoyed the Russian psyche, for "the Russian Church felt ashamed to be under the authority [at least technically] of a subject of the sultan."[12] Vasily Klyuchevsky attributes this consecration and the psychological boost it gave to the nation largely to political, rather than religious, developments.

Towards the opening of the seventeenth century that community [of Rus] was "thoroughly permeated with religious self-confidence, but a self-confidence which was fostered, not by the religious, but by the political, progress of Orthodox Rus, as well as by the political misfortunes of the Orthodox East."[13]

From a religious point of view, the only blemish on Russian Orthodoxy's supremacy in the Orthodox communion was that the Moscow patriarchate ranked fifth in the formalized hierarchy of Eastern Christianity, after the ancient patriarchates of Constantinople, Alexandria, Antioch, and Jerusalem, although before the older patriarchate of Serbia.[14] Russia's assertion of its religious superiority and its insistence on being the only universal church were not without serious drawbacks, however: "As soon as Orthodox Rus proclaimed herself the sole possessor of Christian faith, that means of correction [of local devia-tion by universal Christianity] became lost to her, since, once it had de-clared itself to be the Church Universal, the Russian Church community could not very well permit any extraneous examination of its beliefs and rites."[15] This effectively arrested the development of the Russian Orthodox religion at the point where the Church Universal doctrine com-menced, that is, in the fifteenth and sixteenth centuries. Thus, the grand-son was obligated only to believe and practice as his grandfather had.[16] Ivan IV's strict formalism left a strong impression on the Church of his time,[17] and the pattern of strict outward piety (ritual, crossings, genuflec-tions, and so forth) became fully established as in the Russian Orthodoxy under Tsar Alexis (1645–76), whose police measures forced it upon a pre-viously lax and often indifferent population.[18]

In fact, under the first Romanov tsars, Michael (1613–45) and Alexis, "The Church . . . was more than ever subservient to the wishes of the Kremlin."[19] Florinsky contends that in trying to cope with the post–"Time of Troubles" political unrest and the contemporaneous enserfment of Russian peasantry, Michael and Alexis established a "totalitarian state" in which the church was deeply implicated. In particular, vast ecclesiastical landholdings tied the Church to pro-serfdom policies: "In the manhunt for fugitive serfs, which was one of the distressing characteristics of this period [seventeenth century], ecclesiastical dignitaries and the monaster-ies vied with the lay landlords both in savagery and in resourcefulness."[20]

The reign of Alexis was marked by one of the most important events in the history of the Russian Orthodox Church, the "Great Schism" of the Old Believers. This rupture, which shattered the unity of the Church, was not the first expression of dissent in religious matters. Russia had had tastes of religious fissure with the movements of the Strigolniki, the Judaizers, and the Volga Hermits. The religious ferment in the Polish areas in the sixteenth century especially reminded the Russians that they were also subject to nonindigenous religious traditions. In addition, resi-dents of the larger cities saw Protestant and Catholic traders and diplo-mats, and, beginning with the reign of Michael (1613–45), Westerners brought their own faiths along when they were invited to modernize the military and the related economy. However, foreigners lived in segre-gated areas, thus reducing the impact of their cultures on local communi-ties. There were important consequences of the imported and dissenting religions, but the problem of diversity came to a head only in the Old Believer schism.[21]

This schism tells us a great deal about the nature of Russian Orthodoxy. The split occurred in reaction to reforms implemented by Patriarch Nikon. What did Nikon want to change? Looking at the specific reforms, the modernized Westerner is struck by their apparent insignificance to overall faith. The reforms centered on local practices that had become customary in Russia and had acquired an official sanction. The questions at issue were which icons to use and when, how to spell the name "Jesus," how many "alleluias" to say, how many wafers to use in a mass, how many fingers to extend while crossing oneself, and so on—matters pertaining to external observance of rite and requiring no alteration of dogma.[22]

The reaction to such seemingly innocuous reforms, however, was virulent. Old Believers contended that the things Nikon wanted to change were essential to salvation and thus immutable. For its part, the Russian Church hierarchy countered that the Old Believers had too narrow a mind-set to distinguish the essential from the superficial and accidental. However, the most important consequence of the Nikon reform was not for theology or Church practice but for Church–state relations and, less directly, for the possible opening to Western influence on Russian society and culture. The Nikon reforms "impinged upon the most sensitive chord in the attunement of the Russian Church community—namely, upon its national self-complacency in ecclesiastical matters."[23] The schism splintered the Church community and weakened its political voice, allowing secular power to emerge as a sole arbiter in religious disputes. Because many of its most avid believers went into schism, the Church was left chiefly with those "lukewarm" and indifferent in religious matters. This led to greater reliance on the state, police, and army to enforce the faith.

The council that condemned both Nikon and the schismatics seemed to have been animated by a spirit of special service to the tsar, some delegates candidly stating their wish to please him. Patriarchal authority vis-à-vis the tsar was greatly diminished. Furthermore, a major decision of the council was to eliminate the parish election of priests, which had been traditional in Russia, yielding to the bishops the task of assigning priests to parishes. With the state virtually dictating episcopal appointments, state control over the Church grew at the grass-roots level as well. Thus, the council's main outcome "was to establish the clear subordination of church to state by flooding the church bureaucracy with priests who were, in effect, state appointed."[24] In sum, the schism reinforced the Church's subservience to the state and ceded more sanctity to state authorities.[25]

Seen across the thousand years of Russian Church history, however, the Great Schism testified to the growing strength of popular Christian sensibilities. Even in their confused religiosity, the masses were finally identified with the Christian church. The Old Believers took the extreme path, often being pushed to suffering and martyrdom by the oppressive practices of the Church and the state. However, the plight of Old Believers dramatized the fact that the broader populace in Russia had been finally

Christianized. Although there were to be some important religious developments for the elite, the faith of the common people was established at its general level for the next 200 years. And while the Old Believers found themselves repeatedly at the core of peasant revolts, the regularity with which such revolts were crushed testified to the impracticality of popular movements in the face of overwhelming state power. That pattern lasted into the twentieth century. The reorganization carried out by Peter I settled the Church's subordination to the state for the remainder of the period of the Russian empire. First refusing to appoint a new patriarch upon the death of Hadrian in 1700, then replacing the patriarchate itself with the Holy Synod in 1721, the emperor took total control over the Church into his own hands. Appointments to the Holy Synod and the synod's agenda were supervised by a lay officer, the over procurator, who was himself an appointee and servant of the emperor. Consequently, until the revolution of February 1917, the Church structure was an arm of the government bureaucracy and the popular faith languished in its seventeenth-century form.

In the two centuries between Peter's reign and 1917, two other developments took place that had implications for the modern religious culture. First was the appearance of a small population of Protestant and some Catholic believers on Russian soil. Found among German and other foreign peasant farmers imported by Catherine II to foster efficiency in agriculture, these faiths slowly began to mix with indigenous sectarians and Orthodox believers, offering them a glimpse of alternative religious cultures. Facing strong constraints against growth, including (especially in the mid-nineteenth century) legal and police barriers against proselytizing, these tiny groups began to breathe and act a touch freer in the early twentieth century following legal reforms in 1903 and 1905. Still, at no point did they pose a significant threat to the established order.

Another interesting development goes back to the late nineteenth and early twentieth century, when the elite showed new willingness to explore the frontiers of faith and engage in a serious discussion about the indigenous religious culture. The reign of Alexander I held some precursors, but Nicholas I closed off most avenues for innovation, even as its harsh rigidity provoked a revolt among the intelligentsia that was finally ready and willing to confront Western European ideas on their own merit. In the second half of the nineteenth century, the clash of the Slavophiles and Westernizers was in full swing, with some intellectuals moving toward full secularization and others, especially toward the end of the nineteenth century, increasingly drawn to their Christian roots. I cannot dwell on this richly nuanced era of philosophical and theological revival. Let me just note the relative liberality that marked the reign of Alexander II and that provided a hospitable environment for a creative inquiry into religious matters. Had historical circumstances gone in other directions, this flourishing of religious discourse might have served as a launching pad for a true reformation in Russian Christianity. The Slavophile position had in itself currents of illiberality, but the arguments of the intellectuals of the era had begun to grapple with the most negative of these in a constructive way. At the beginning of the twentieth century, the philosophical and theological renewal clashed with the extreme nationalist, anti-Semitic and xenophobic forces of the "Black Hundreds," which legitimized the pogroms and reveled in the struggle against all sorts of conspiratorial enemies of Russia.[26] Too often, churchmen were heard in support of the scapegoating of Jews by the tsars and the assertions of special Russian privilege in a multiethnic empire and multinational world. Other things being equal, the renewal might have won out against such forces. Instead, Russia slid into the disorganization and revolts that engulfed the European continent in the wake of World War I. When the communists took power, the Church's dependence on the state proved exceedingly costly. The state triumphant was the state that bound the Church in chains and left the religious institution without the energy and resources to fend off perhaps the most devastating secularizing force in history—Marxism-Leninism.

Religion Under Soviet Rule

Among the features of communist society that continuously fascinated Western observers was an ambitious Soviet policy aimed at transforming the human personality. Soviet ideology mandated that the "New Soviet Man" be created from the raw materials of the Russian citizenry.[27] The builder of communism was to be peace-loving, internationalist, patriotic, law-abiding, collectivistic, hard working, and—militantly atheist.

To promote atheism and stamp out "religious superstitions" among its citizens, the state authorities and the Communist party established a comprehensive educational program, *ateisticheskoe vospitanie*, a term usually translated as "atheist upbringing." The Russian word *vospitanie*, for which there is no exact equivalent in English, refers to the general blueprints for character formation contrived by the Soviet authorities.[28] As conceived and carried out by Communist party experts, an atheist upbringing was not a simple educational program, although it was included in school curricula and the pedagogical propaganda for the general public. More than that, *ateisticheskoe vospitanie* spurred a multifaceted effort across the lifespan to nurture atheism, to turn it into the way of thinking for every Soviet citizen.

Normally, socialization is designed to inculcate some new knowledge or skill in the fledgling generation. Atheism, by contrast, is not so much a new knowledge to be imparted as an old belief to be expunged. Since religious knowledge of some sort is generally widespread, pursuing atheist upbringing in the Soviet Union was similar to trying to create a vacuum. The ultimate Soviet Marxist aim was to develop a purified environment where the particles of religious faith were so rarified that the vacuum in the religious area could become self-sustaining. In the ideological imagery, such a situation would represent a pure environment where the full character development of the New Soviet Man could proceed unhindered. Soviet atheist upbringing, therefore, was not simply the obverse of religious socialization in the West. The forces working against atheism were no less entrenched in Soviet Russia than, say, in the United States, where organized atheism and atheist convictions have been historically weak in both numbers and popular support. Routing popular religiosity in the Soviet Union, therefore, was a truly daunting task.

Furthermore, although atheism is not inconsistent with the secularizing trends set in motion by urbanization, industrialization, and modernization,[29] Soviet ideological interpretation was unique in its stated agenda of speeding up and deepening general secularization, the latter being construed as a precondition for the emergence of a well-rounded personality. An atheist upbringing, consequently, went far beyond attempts to neutralize religion, relegate it to a private corner of the individual's spiritual life; it implied a coherent antireligious "world view" and an appropriate agenda for action without which Soviet society could not reach its ultimate—communist—developmental stage.

Finally, and perhaps most importantly, an atheist upbringing in the Soviet Union differed from religious socialization in the West insofar as it was a planned effort organized and orchestrated by the Soviet state and mandatory for every segment of the Soviet population. In other words, it was state policy and, as we shall see, politics. Thus, even in its basic form, the "scientific atheism" propagated by Soviet ideologues fundamentally diverged from the largely voluntaristic and diverse activities carried out in the West under the banners of parochial education, proselytization, and evangelization.

Political Factors

State atheism varied in its nature, focus, and intensity over the course of Soviet history. This shifting policy meant that succeeding generations did not experience the atheist program in the same way, that the program had varying impact on Soviet citizens. We can count three major antireligious campaigns and one period of dramatic letup in antireligious zeal in the pre-Gorbachev period of Soviet history.[30] The first attack on religion came immediately after the October 1917 revolution. Its primary targets were the Orthodox Church and the Muslim establishment; its immediate aim, to sap the sources of real and potential counterrevolution. By the mid-1920s, a *modus operandi* for religious activities, albeit much more limited and controlled than before the revolution, had been established. This rather shaky status quo was disrupted with a crackdown on religious institutions during the "forced collectivization" (1928–33), when many churches and religious establishments were closed, most significant religious leaders imprisoned, and religious activity in the country reduced to a bare minimum. This campaign was followed by a period of severe restrictions of all religious activities during the 1930s.

As World War II broke out, however, party leaders realized the Church's potential as a cradle of patriotic sentiments and dramatically reversed their stance on religion. Although Stalinist police closely supervised the reinvigorated religious groups to ensure that the religious revival would not get out of hand, relative peace prevailed in state–Church relations from 1943 until Stalin's death in 1953. This period ended when the Khrushchev regime set in motion a new antireligious campaign fully comparable to the one that rocked the country in the early 1930s. Subsequently, with the demise of Khrushchev in 1964, the campaign was modulated. The Brezhnev era ushered in some new openings for the private practice of religion and for official religious organizations, although pressures continued against religious dissidents and those who would seek to expand the sphere of religious activities into evangelization, religious education for children, and Church expansion.

In contrast to problems of military security and national economic development, Soviet state atheism was a relatively minor policy issue. According to Bohdan Bociurkiw, the fluctuations in religious policy largely reflected factors outside the religious sphere, such as nationality, peasant, industrial, and military policy.[31] A closer look at these factors suggests that Soviet state atheism was largely political in its nature and influence upon the population. Many factors extraneous to religion proper affected religious policy and thus altered the impact of state atheism upon the people.

Social and Institutional Factors

An atheist upbringing was shaped by and, in turn, shaped many social circumstances that had a bearing on antireligious socialization patterns. Important in this respect is to distinguish between the individual and collectivist aspects of socialization:

> Relative to the individual, socialization means all those processes
> through which the individual in interaction with the environment and
> with himself develops relatively enduring patterns of behavior which

enable him to take part in societal life and in certain cases, to participate in its change. Relative to the collectivity, socialization indicates the differentiated, and under certain conditions contradictory, interaction of all those societal institutions which express the economical, political and cultural conceptions of the task of caring for and educating children, who are ultimately individuals with identities.[32]

Central in this insight is that socialization involves institutional interactions that may be contradictory at times. The potential for "contradictory" socialization is something we should acknowledge from the start. Anyone who visited the Soviet Union could have sensed these contradictions in the atheist upbringing of Soviet citizens. The Soviet propaganda's manifest message was unambiguous: religion was to be stamped out as a vestige of the past impeding progress toward the future society envisioned by Marx, Engels, and Lenin. However, latent messages conveyed by the same propaganda were rather confusing to Soviet citizens. For example, the state-sponsored movement to salvage and restore national monuments and artistic works extended to certain religious artifacts. It did not escape notice at home or abroad that the Soviet authorities adopted the onion dome of the Orthodox church as the nation's aesthetic emblem.

In a similarly contradictory way, Soviets celebrated events and heroes closely aligned with the nation's religious history. One case in point was the state-sponsored festivities surrounding the inauguration of the monument to Prince Vladimir, long ago canonized by the Church and now holding aloft the very same cross that once topped the Novgorod monument dedicated to 1,000 years of Russia. Similarly, the communist authorities honored the Russian icon with its resplendent Christian imagery—by far the best-known form of visual art in Russia—as a national aesthetic treasure. Literary works by Dostoevsky, Tolstoi, and lesser writers continued to feed religious themes to Soviet readers. Through such diverse channels, religious symbols, myths, and institutional memories were preserved in the nation whose leaders had dedicated themselves to atheism. Thus, the authorities themselves kept religious sentiments alive by their inconsistent actions.

In these and many other ways, the institutional context of Soviet atheist socialization remained highly schizophrenic, causing problems for atheistic propaganda. While pedagogical institutions doggedly pursued the atheist upbringing, other institutional spheres acted at cross-purpose. Literature and the arts proved particularly recalcitrant in this respect, their practitioners unable and unwilling to ignore the religious and mystical wellsprings of earlier creativity. The Russian grandmother—the *babushka*—played a special role that ran contrary to atheistic propaganda.

The *babushka* was the major source of primary bonding in Russia, the kind that social psychologists find most effective in shaping individual character in its formative stages.[33] Undaunted by official propaganda, the *babushka* crossed herself, went to church, told her grandchildren old tales, and in the long run quietly undid what endless lectures and required readings tried to achieve through formal atheist upbringing. Soviet authorities were well aware of this menacing presence. In 1966, one V. G. Shtyuka wrote: "Study of the population's religiosity shows that the religious and cultural activities that are solidly rooted in everyday life and have become family traditions are the most tenacious. Here lie the broadest channels for the penetration of religious ideology and the religious world view into the people's consciousness."[34] In the landmark studies of displaced persons from Russia that were carried out following World War II, Harvard Project researchers made a special effort to assess the impact of Soviet socialization on various social domains, including the religious sphere. Alex Inkeles and Raymond Bauer reported that emigrés experienced conflict in socialization related to traditional values such as religion. Some (especially people from peasant and working class backgrounds) intimated that the public atheist education had led to clashes at home, with parents and grandparents often looking askance at the atheistic beliefs children acquired at school.[35]

To assess the impact of atheistic education on Soviet citizens we need to take a closer look at the educational practices insofar as they entail what Ernest Q. Campbell calls the social control imperative and the socialization objective.[36] The former refers to *vospitanie* as it endeavored to squelch religious impulses and relied on punishments for religious behavior and attitudes. The latter involved building the free atheist character, that is, rewarding atheist and antireligious behavior and attitudes. Some aspects of the atheist upbringing seemed to mix negative and positive elements of socialization. Both punishment and reward factors were evident when it came to the legitimation problem that established authorities faced in their antireligious propaganda. Rebellion or less dramatic disregard for authority could lead to punishment, but acceptance and recognition of official messages could provide direct rewards. Let us review each major aspect of atheist upbringing—building legitimacy, socialization objectives, and social control requirements.

The Problem of Legitimacy

To legitimize itself in the public mind, a state (government, party) cannot rely exclusively on force; it must socialize the populace into believing that its cause is a righteous one. Thus, all children, future adult citizens, must learn to think that the state knows the best, acts in everybody's interests, and can improve social conditions in an efficient manner. Up to a point, the state can count on loyalty of its citizens simply because it holds power and performs routine tasks without which life would be difficult. The state's legitimacy has to strike deeper roots, however, if it is to be based on any other foundation than force, and that means suppressing alternative sources of legitimacy, most notably, the belief that governments rule by the grace of God and require divine consent. The Soviet version of "civics class," therefore, had to absorb the atheistic education that was designed to clear up "old religious prejudices" and make room for the doctrine that propped up the communist government.

More than that, Soviet educators sought to coopt religious sentiments by creating quasi-ritual and ceremonial activities organized into so-called "new socialist traditions."[37] The state sanctioned numerous common Soviet institutions and rites:

1. Sometime after World War II, "wedding palaces" sprang to life to accommodate the secular marriage ceremony, in which newlyweds dedicated themselves and their future children to building communism and cultivating communist habits and beliefs. To inject a patriotic element into marriage, Soviet couples were encouraged to visit local war memorials in conjunction with their weddings.

2. Secular funerals replaced appropriate religious ceremonies; the deceased were celebrated for their contribution to the socialist state, and the survivors pledged to continue their patriotic deeds.

3. Elaborate rites of passage solemnized such occasions as starting school, graduating, entering the workforce, joining the Octobrists, Pioneers, or Young Communist League (Komsomol), acquiring identity papers (internal passport), and the like.

4. The old religious holidays (like Christmas and Easter) were replaced with New Year celebrations, May 1 demonstrations, the Bolshevik Revolution Anniversary parade, Lenin's birthday festivities, and so on.

The success of these "new traditions" varied widely, but they seemed to attract considerable popular participation. It is not clear whether they effectively replaced comparable religious rites and ceremonies, but they certainly helped cement the emotional bond between citizens and the state. To the extent that such socialist rituals turned into public habits, they enhanced the state's legitimacy. Most certainly, they strengthened other messages the state sought to convey to its citizens, including those with an expressly antireligious content. By providing a positive emotional bond with the state, which itself promoted atheistic and antireligious behaviors and attitudes, the new ceremonies and celebrations helped ingrain atheism in the individual's self-identity. Being religious and at the same time enjoying socialist rites would have created a psychological dissonance. We know from many studies in social psychology that it is difficult to maintain such inconsistencies for long periods without damaging personal consequences.

Socialization Objectives

The atheistic socialization agenda included a wide range of positive incentives. Proper behavior and attitudes were reinforced by legitimate authority and thus carried a positive emotional charge. Atheistic socialization had as its ultimate goal what Soviet writers called "a scientific atheistic world view," which included the following elements:

1. Strong scientific training awaited all students, starting from the earliest grades. Science was always taught as an indubitable and entirely sufficient way of understanding the world that left no room for alternative orientations. All other perspectives, most notably religion, were said to be incompatible with science and to distort reality.

2. A special emphasis was placed on the notion that humans make their own futures. No supernatural forces or divine entities had any relation to the world. In Marxian terms, science was the surest basis for building the future because it recognized the true nature of the world.

3. Atheistic socialization required teaching about the history of freethinking and atheism, as well as about "religious obscurantism," which undermined the progress of science.

4. Atheism had to have its own "positive heroes" such as Charles Darwin, Galileo, and Copernicus. The abundant literature on such figures served the important socialization goal of creating "reference idols" to encourage young people to emulate atheistic values.[38]

5. Movies and newspapers, television and radio, literature and painting—all forms of mass culture—had to be upgraded in content so as to woo the population away from religious spectacles. For instance, during the Easter holidays the state would show especially popular programs on TV and keep movie theaters open late to keep the populace from attending all-night Easter services.

6. Atheist propaganda was carried out by a sprawling set of agencies and organizations, such as the Museum of Religion and Atheism

and the Knowledge Society,[39] which printed pamphlets and books and offered public lectures and presentations.

Through all these socializing institutions and practices the authorities sought to provide models of atheist behavior and attitudes for average Soviet citizens, to turn them into "good atheists" intolerant of *religioznoe mrakobesie* (religious obscurantism). But the same outcomes could be— and sometimes had to be—accomplished through other means, such as punishments and costs inflicted on believers to discourage them from practicing proscribed behavior.

Social Control Imperatives

Soviet believers who evaded the state's socialization efforts had to bear excessive costs for their religious activities. The state did everything it could to "overcome" religion peaceably, to make it "wither away," but when its "constructive" efforts failed, it was ready to deploy a vast array of social control devices to stamp out religious customs. Here are some of the more important social control venues favored by the Soviet state:

1. Forbidding formal religious education for children, that is, any group classes, Sunday schools, and the like.

2. Hindering the participation of children in religious activities by pressuring and intimidating clergy, parents, and children themselves (usually in school).

3. Controlling baptism rites by requiring a formal "registration" and a "permit" for a baptism ceremony.

4. Ridiculing or criticizing believers in the public press.

5. Intentionally and actively seeking out believers and attempting to "re-educate" them. Schoolteachers played a particularly important role in this regard, as did Pioneer and Komsomol cadres and party and trade union activists in the workplace. Adults could also be forced into one-on-one sessions with atheist activists.

6. Publishing and disseminating antireligious propaganda through literature, lectures, newspaper articles, radio, and television programs. The Knowledge Society must be singled out here for its relentless efforts on behalf of "scientific atheism," although the trade unions, party cells, atheist clubs, and antireligious museums did not lag far behind.

7. Manipulating religious leaders so as to limit their personal influ-

ence and their ability to organize and disseminate religious influence.

8. Limiting the prospects for appointment and job advancement for religious believers. Since most high-level positions required party membership, believers were naturally excluded from advancement to such levels. In some cases, believers were denied routine pay increases and promotions because of their "backward views." Although this was not universal practice, it encouraged believers to be less visibly active religiously or to hide their faith altogether, and it intimidated those who were not active from becoming so.

In these and perhaps other ways, the Soviet state barred children from sympathetic exposure to religion and punished those who defied the state and sought to exercise their nominal constitutional rights. Needless to say, children who passed through this elaborate system of antireligious propaganda were less likely to become religious adults, whereas those who persisted in their religious beliefs and practices could expect the state to curtail their life options severely.

The Fate of Religion in the Post-Soviet Era

The atheist upbringing in Soviet society was fraught with many problems and, as time revealed, had little resonance among the general population. However, it had been undertaken in the context of the Russian religious culture and, as such, was bound to have reverberated throughout society. We recall that *pravoslavie,* or Orthodoxy, was imposed upon the pagan population from above and never fully replaced ancient religious customs with the new forms of spirituality and spiritual discipline. Cultural development nearly stopped at the point where Christian rituals were implanted in everyday consciousness without transforming its spiritual content. The Orthodox Church tended to equate religiosity with ritual. The Church never made any attempt to foster a religiously literate population. In fact, for a long time Russian Orthodoxy eschewed general literacy as a worthy goal. Even less was the religious establishment in Russia committed to critical inquiry into its spiritual moorings, to instilling an open-minded attitude toward religious practices among its participants. The religious renaissance that the intellectual elite experienced before the revolution of 1917 came to a grinding halt after the Bolsheviks came to power and made it all but impossible to convert this movement into a popular religious renaissance. The communists' attack on the Church exhausted its leadership and sealed its subservient status in a relationship that harkened back to the Byzantine principle of symphonia. Dogmatism, religious formalism, intolerance of dissent—some of the salient features of the Russian religious culture—were further reinforced by autocratic communist practices. With religious leaders and intellectuals effectively silenced, the common faithful had few means of preserving anything more than a flawed memory of Orthodoxy along with the sentimental attachment to the beauty of the Russian Orthodox liturgy. By the end of the Soviet era, Russians were a religiously malformed people who had sustained heavy damage, both individually and institutionally, from the decades of party-sponsored atheism overlain upon centuries of religious submission to autocracy.

Orthodoxy is prone to celebrate its martyrs above all saints, but nobody is denying the blessings that religious freedom gave to the believers in the mid-1980s. Religious freedom arrived, first surreptitiously, as the state lapsed in its efforts to enforce antireligious laws, then more openly, beginning with the decision to release religious prisoners of conscience in the period 1986–87. From that point on, believers faced fewer problems registering their congregations. Liberalization gained momentum after the 1988 festivities surrounding the millennium of Russian Orthodoxy. This glorious event opened auspiciously with General Secretary Gorbachev granting an audience to the patriarch and chief bishops. About the same time, drafts of new laws on "freedom of conscience and religious organizations" reached the public. After extended public discussion, final versions thereof were adopted by both the Soviet Union and the Russian Republic in October 1990. These laws eliminated the primary means by which the Soviet government had waged its war on religion since the end of the 1920s and finally permitted—for the first time in over fifty years— what most people elsewhere in the world would consider normal religious worship.[40] Orthodox and other religious believers in the Soviet Union were just getting adapted to the new circumstances when the whole structure of the Soviet state collapsed in late 1991.

Seldom does a religious institution find itself in such a truly historic circumstance as the Russian Church does in the post-Soviet era. The changes engulfing Russia have portents not only for its citizens but for the whole world. A vigorous, decisive, democratic church might wield great influence on the direction those important changes take. Such a church would possess a social ethic conducive to democratic ideology and free market entrepreneurship. It would spearhead a debate about society's values and goals, as well as spell out its own agenda in the various arenas of policy planning. It would exercise its spiritual influence on the population and shape the spiritual identity of the newly emerging autonomous nation. To paraphrase Richard John Neuhaus, a Protestant theologian, such a church should be a visible presence in the public square. Has the Russian Orthodox Church established a permanent residence there?

Physically, the Russian Orthodox Church is quickly re-establishing itself on the town square. Since 1988, when Gorbachev and the leaders of the Russian Orthodox Church met for the first time, the number of congregations and operating churches has burgeoned. According to one source, this number nearly doubled between 1985 and 1991, from 6,806 to approximately 12,000.[41] However, the costs of this expansion have been extremely high. Without many outlets for its resources, the Russian Church had grown used to being relatively well off under the Soviets. Now, the Church has been essentially bankrupted by its rapid expansion. We should bear in mind that institutions are real and organized societal beings, that they are in conflict and competition for the hearts of the people. So far, the state has been a big winner in its competition with the Russian Church. The question now is whether the religious institution has the means to mount a new drive to better counterbalance statism in society.

The Church's bankruptcy is apparent not only in monetary terms. The Church's spiritual and theological resources are stretched to the limit as well. First, there are not enough clergy to serve all the new parishes. Second, the Church does not have the ability to compensate adequately those who are serving. Third, to satisfy the growing demand for clergy, priests work excessive hours, with very little time left for new initiatives or even simple reflection. Furthermore, the Church has yet to address fully and effectively (especially under the present trying circumstances) the serious issue of theological preparation for the clergy. As in the past, the Church has stressed the liturgical preparation of its clerics over their intellectual or spiritual preparations. Recognizing that the people of the parishes want someone to provide the sacraments, to baptize, marry, and bury them, the Church has responded by enlarging seminary classes without the requisite increase in faculty and staff. New teaching resources are sorely lacking; there is a tendency to fall back on the nineteenth century and earlier precedents. Very little constructive energy has been expended to find the meeting ground between *pravoslavie* and twentieth-century religious experience. In other words, while the Church may be reoccupying the public square physically—by breaking into the open, reaching out to the public, reclaiming property once confiscated by the state—it has yet to occupy the square spiritually, as a social force to reckon with in the giant reconstruction now facing the nation.

We cannot be too harsh in our judgment, though, for the problems facing the Russian Orthodox Church are enormous, indeed. The devout Russian Orthodox believer needs first and foremost a "spiritual father"; he needs to restore the historical bond with a priest or monk with whom he has a special relationship of trust and confidence. Unfortunately, the clergy today are overburdened with the ritual services to provide inspiration, spiritual guidance, and a clear vision of the future to everyone. We need to remind ourselves, however, that Russia is not the only place where religious institutions show signs of exhaustion. Richard John Neuhaus expressed his deep concerns about the disappearance of religious values and symbols from public discourse in America in the 1980s.[42] We can hardly expect such values and symbols to spring to life overnight under the extreme conditions in today's Russia. Moreover, we have to be concerned about the abuse of religious rhetoric by the leaders of nativist, ultraconservative movements. Numerous right-wing political and nationalist groups have risen up in Russia since the onset of perestroika, some of them tracing their roots back to prerevolutionary movements. Some of the leaders of such groups have begun utilizing religious language in their calls for Russia's return to her "greater destiny," and there are noteworthy proponents among the clergy and hierarchs of the Russian Orthodox Church who appear to be supporters. Traditional Russian Orthodox anti-Semitism has not been bridled on the extreme fringes, and it supports the reappearance in bookstalls of the scurrilous *Protocols of the Elders of Zion* and other hate literature. Although Patriarch Aleksii II has denied anti-Semitism in Church affairs, his administration has not mounted a direct attack on this problem. Without Church leadership in this regard, Pamyat and similar nationalist-patriotic groupings have pursued their dark agendas with the support of extremist churchmen who experience no censure from their spiritual authorities.[43]

In the legal arena itself, the Church has decided to keep silent. Several major churchmen were elected to the Gorbachev and then Russian Federation Parliament, including the patriarch, the most powerful bishops, and a number of priests. Yet, in the early 1990s the patriarch ruled that clergy were no longer permitted to run for such offices. When Father Gleb Yakunin defied the decree, he was defrocked and publicly humiliated by the patriarch. Ironically, Yakunin had been at odds with the Church hierarchy for nearly all his adult life. In 1991, he revealed some KGB records (since sealed) that indicated the close cooperation between several key bishops and the Soviet secret police. In 1993, from his seat in the Russian Parliament, Father Yakunin vigorously opposed the legislation on religious affairs sponsored by the Russian Orthodox Church. The law would have reinstated registration for all religious groups and organizations, limited the activities of foreign missionaries in Russia, and restored the Russian Orthodox Church's privileged position in the land. The manner in which the Patriarchate treated Father Yakunin indicates its unwillingness to engage in debate over its own position in Russian society, its freedom to stamp out dissent among its ranks, and its right to limit alternative forms of religious expression. This stance showed no tolerance for diversity, nor did it encourage constructive debate with its opponents inside and outside the Church. Dissenting views were handled in sadly familiar ways: exclusion, condemnation, excommunication.

Only in areas of direct interest has the Church taken an active role in the political process. Otherwise, as the run-up to the December 1993 elections demonstrated, Church authorities failed to connect their faith and their politics. No sense of moral obligation seemed to inform the clergy's politics, which are conspicuous for their absence in the seminaries, where no attempt is currently under way to initiate a coherent political discussion. This public square was naked indeed. The predominant impulse was to escape from the tough political fray into the comforting spiritual ether of the liturgy. Perhaps these developments will take time to unfold, but a religious culture that could sustain them is yet to take root. The cultural history I have sketched above does not bode well for the Church's action in the public arena, certainly not in the immediate future. Still, there is room for hope.

In its struggle with adversity, Russian Orthodoxy evolved a spiritual style that offers a special solace to its adherents, a religious culture that stimulates a transcendent experience all its own. To paraphrase one Soviet sociologist, a Russian Orthodox service is a crowd scene in the presence of a great mystery. The crowd scene might have something to do with the repression that the Soviet regime unleashed on religion and that drastically curtailed the number of active churches and clergy in the land, but the feeling of great mystery surrounding its religious rites is indeed an enduring legacy and the core strength of the Russian Orthodox tradition. Faith encourages the feeling of awe before the divine presence, which is magnified by holy icons and the flickering glow of candles lit by the faithful. More than any other major branch of Christianity, the Orthodox tradition cultivates the mystical experience of divinity, an experience central to all religion, according to Emile Durkheim. The Russian Orthodox Church excels in the rituals that bring the faithful to the threshold of the sacred. The Orthodox faith makes use of liturgical solemnity, unified group prayer, and the urge to experience the inner silence of holiness to solidify the group and reinvigorate the social bonds among its members.

In cultivating this mystical dimension of religious experience, Russian Orthodoxy has inspired generations of Russian artists working in the most diverse media. In addition to great icon painters, the Russian mystical tradition is palpable in the spiritual density of Russian literature and the soulful sounds of Russian music. The aesthetic impulse that animated the great works of Russian art has inspired the faithful and is felt by non-believers as well.[44] These aesthetic sensibilities are quintessential to

Russian Orthodoxy, and they are likely to be an important resource in the revitalization of Russian religious culture.

We can see some signs of religious revival in the nascent debate about the relationship between Russian Orthodoxy and the other historical branches of Christianity. A tiny minority of Orthodox did join Protestant and Catholic dissenters in movements of protest in the 1960s, 1970s, and 1980s; the dissidents of the 1990s challenge the Church to lay out a new path through Russian nationalism or secular democratic institutions that meets current needs and fills the spiritual vacuum left by the collapse of Marxist ideology. Gleb Yakunin and his colleagues among Christian democrats are trying to include religious values and ideals in the public debates about Russia's future. Scattered priests and lay activists are embarking on programs of direct involvement in sociopolitical life through community or educational initiatives.

Another interesting portent is the widespread Sunday school movement, which could foster a religious literacy previously unknown among the Russian Orthodox. It could also encourage a religious voluntarism that offers a healthy antidote to excessive hierarchical control.

Another bit of evidence that some believers in Russia are rising to the occasion and meeting current challenges is the spread of charitable projects enlivening churches around the country. Still in its infancy, the movement to set up special services for the elderly, the imprisoned, the infirm, and the impoverished may invigorate Russian Orthodoxy as a whole. Together with international organizations and services, it may help spread a new social ethic of responsibility.

Finally, there are some signs that the crusty Church hierarchy is not totally inflexible. The Patriarchate itself sponsored a major interfaith conference in June 1994 dedicated to the search for solutions to interethnic and other conflicts on the territory of the former Soviet Union. It was noteworthy that representatives of all major confessions from the former Soviet territory were invited and included among the delegates. The conferees strongly expressed an ecumenical spirit concerning the solution of these conflicts; such cooperative efforts may bear fruits even in the more directly religious sphere itself. This conference was particularly important in that it broke the mold of the communist past, when discussions were limited to restricted topics and Russian churchmen were compelled to keep public statements in line with party doctrine. This time, conversations in the halls and hotel rooms were frank, and disputes were publicly aired in ways not thought possible before the last few years.

In the meantime, the Church establishment has tended to revert to ancient patterns, seeking to maintain or reestablish its privileged status in Russian society. It is particularly incensed with the non-Orthodox religious groups engaged in a major push to convert Russians to a different view, to offer the population a new way in the context of religious freedom. Seeing the troops of the Western evangelistic crusade gathered in stadiums in prayer, the Russian Orthodox Church hierarchy launched its own campaign to put up barriers between the spiritual invaders and the Russian people. The summer of 1993 saw a fascinating legislative battle waged in Moscow in which Orthodox spiritual discipline was at issue. The Church hierarchy sought to construct a wall between the missionaries and the Russians, to keep the missionaries at bay, to keep the Russian spiritual menu clear of unsafe (though savory) contaminants such as Western religion. Had it not been for the confrontation between President Yeltsin and the Parliament in early October, legislation limiting access for Western evangelicals to Russia might now be on the books. Yeltsin had opposed this legislation on several grounds but might not have been able to reject it completely in the end. The Church's determination to limit religious freedom is facing great criticism from democrats inside Russia as well as outside advocates of individualistic human rights.

The path ahead is a tortuous one. Old elements must be purged, to be sure, but the bedrock of the tradition cannot be abandoned. The cultural transformation required is vast; it may be excruciatingly painful, given that *pravoslavie* faces its reconstruction exhausted by the communist era, and now further drained by the huge costs of energy, time, and money required for rebuilding its crumbling infrastructure. Although thousands of church buildings have been returned to the Church, most of them are in need of extensive and costly repair; many are, in the words of one bishop, "simply ruins," which must be totally reconstructed. There is an acute shortage of clergy, so the Church has to focus on the quick training of ritual specialists. Yet, somehow, the Church must develop the broader pastoral, theological, and philosophical concerns that could fill the public's needs the most. Can the Church find the resources to serve the great spiritual needs of the liberated population? Or will other aspirants to the status of religious supplier to Russia become more successful in fulfilling these yearnings, thus leading the transformation of Russian religious culture away from its historical Orthodox roots?

Experience in other countries suggests that, if general religious freedom persists, Russia is likely to become a great deal more diverse in its religious culture. While Orthodoxy recuperates its strength, other "religious entrepreneurs" will win a significant share of the religious market in Russia. Still, the daunting question persists: Will the Orthodox Church continue to stress the form, encourage nativistic elements in the government, and deny newer groups access to the population? Stated differently, will the Church put nationalistic goals and Church–state unity above service to the spiritual needs of the population?

One element that is affecting the Russian religious scene these days as never before is international religious culture. Historically, Russia was insulated from outside religious currents. Now, it cannot afford to be completely isolated. Although the Russian Orthodox Church has grown weary of ecumenical efforts, this international element gives one hope that the Church will continue to evolve in order to serve better its members' spiritual needs. Global culture may provide some of the innovations that will stimulate the broader revival of religion in Russia. The mature postcommunist Russia that one day will emerge after this present period of massive reconstruction will not simply ape Western society, as so many outsiders who put their entire stock in capitalist economics insist. We cannot say what shape the Russian civilization will take in the future, but we can venture a guess that it will reflect both the nation's historical religious afterimages and its present religious experience, which whittles away at the old religious culture and broadens the horizons of Russian Orthodoxy.

Notes

The broader research upon which this chapter is based has been supported on different occasions by travel grants from the International Research and Exchanges Board and from the Faculty Research Fund and Faculty Development Organization of Wittenberg University. Interviewing in the summer of 1993 was carried out jointly with Jeffrey K. Hadden, and his contributions to my thinking are reflected in parts of this chapter. Long-term research assistance by Carolyn Welch is gratefully acknowledged.

1. Clifford Geertz, *Islam Observed: Religious Development in Morocco and Indonesia* (Chicago: University of Chicago Press, 1968).

2. Bernard Pares, *A History of Russia*, definitive ed. (New York: Vintage, [1926] 1965); Michael T. Florinsky, *Russia: A History and an Interpretation*, vol. 1 (New York: Macmillan, 1953). Historical information is found in numerous sources. I will try to cite only the most readily available and useful ones, although others should be consulted as well.

3. Pares, *History of Russia*, p. 32.

4. George P. Fedotov, *The Russian Religious Mind* (New York: Harper, 1946).

5. This issue is explored dramatically in the modern classic film about Andrei Rublyov, the great monk icon painter, who struggled mightily to overcome the seductive pull of pagan rites. Some authors have questioned the quality of paganism involved in *dvoeverie*. Compare Eve Luria, "*Dvoeverie* and Popular Religion," pp. 29–52, in Stephen K. Batalden, ed., *Seeking God: The Recovery of Religious Identity in Orthodox Russia, Ukraine, and Georgia* (DeKalb: Northern Illinois University Press, 1993).

6. Paul Miliukov, *Outlines of Russian Culture, Part 1: Religion and the Church* (Philadelphia: University of Pennsylvania Press, 1942), p. 11. The term "dual faith" is widely used by Florinsky, *Russia*, p. 129.

7. Miliukov, *Outlines of Russian Culture*, p. 11.

8. Compare Florinsky, *Russia*, pp. 139–40.

9. Ibid., p. 165.

10. Ibid., p. 142.

11. Ibid., pp. 163–64.

12. Pares, *History of Russia*, p. 136..

13. V. O. Klyuchevsky, *A History of Russia*, vol. 3 (New York: Russell and Russell, 1960), p. 304.

14. Timothy Ware, *The Orthodox Church* (Baltimore: Penguin, 1964), p. 119; John Meyendorff, *The Orthodox Church: Its Past and Its Role in the World Today* (New York: Pantheon, 1962), pp. 107, 109.

15. Klyuchevsky, *History of Russia*, p. 305.

16. Ibid., p. 395.

17. Florinsky, *Russia*, pp. 196–97.

18. Ibid., p. 129.

19. Ibid., p. 283.

20. Ibid., p. 284.

21. James H. Billington, *The Icon and the Axe: An Interpretative History of Russian Culture* (New York: Knopf, 1966), p. 84; Florinsky, *Russia*, p. 296; J. S. Hebly, *Protestants in Russia*, translated by John Pott (Belfast: Christian Journals, 1976), p. 18; Klyuchevsky, *History of Russia*, pp. 331–75; Pares, *History of Russia*, pp. 184–89.

22. Billington, *Icon*, p. 133; Florinsky, *Russia*, p. 287; Klyuchevsky, *History of Russia*, p. 295; Pares, *History of Russia*, 165; Ware, *Orthodox Church*, p. 122.

23. Klyuchevsky, *History of Russia*, p. 323.

24. Billington, *Icon*, pp. 144–45.

25. Compare Florinsky, *Russia*, pp. 294–95; Billington, *Icon*, p. 145; Donald Treadgold, *The West in Russia and China: Religious and Secular Thought in Modern Times, Vol. 1: Russia, 1472–1917* (Cambridge: Cambridge University Press, 1973), p. 72; Ware, *Orthodox Church*, pp. 124–25.

26. Walter Laqueur, *Black Hundred: The Rise of the Extreme Right in Russia* (New York: HarperCollins, 1993).

27. Richard T. DeGeorge, *Soviet Ethics and Morality* (Ann Arbor: University of Michigan Press, 1969), pp. 83–125; Jerome M. Gilison, *The Soviet Image of Utopia* (Baltimore: Johns Hopkins University Press, 1975); Alex Inkeles, *Public Opinion in Soviet Russia: A Study in Mass Persuasion* (Cambridge: Harvard University Press, 1958); Ludwig Liegle, *The Family's Role in Soviet Education* (New York: Springer, [1970] 1975), pp. 117–20; Felicity O'Dell, *Socialization through Children's Literature: The Soviet Example* (Cambridge: Cambridge University Press, 1978), pp. 32–44.

28. Compare Urie Bronfenbrenner, *Two Worlds of Childhood: U.S. and U.S.S.R.* (New York: Pocket Books, 1973).

29. Compare Alex Inkeles, "The Modernization of Man in Socialist Countries," in Mark G. Field, ed., *Social Consequences of Modernization in Communist Societies* (Baltimore: Johns Hopkins University Press, 1976).

30. Bohdan Bociurkiw, "The Shaping of Soviet Religious Policy," *Problems of Communism* 32, no. 2 (1983): 37–51; Jerry G. Pankhurst, "The Orthodox and the Baptists in the USSR: Resources for the Survival of Ideologically Defined Deviance," Ph.D. dissertation, University of Michigan, 1978.

31. Bociurkiw, "Soviet Religious Policy."

32. Kurt Luscher, "Knowledge of Socialization," Working paper no. 3, "Familienforschung" project, University of Konstanz, 1977.

33. James C. Davies, "The Family's Role in Political Socialization," *Annals of the American Academy of Political and Social Science* 361 (September 1965): 10–19.

34. V. G. Shtyuka, *Byt i religiia* (Moscow: Mysl, 1966), p. 3. Translation from the Russian by the author.

35. Alex Inkeles and Raymond Bauer, *The Soviet Citizen: Daily Life in a Totalitarian Society* (New York: Atheneum, [1959] 1968).

36. Ernest Q. Campbell, *Socialization: Culture and Personality* (Dubuque: Wm. C. Brown, 1975). Compare John A. Clausen, ed., *Socialization and Society* (Boston: Little, Brown, 1968).

37. Christel Lane, *The Rites of Rulers: Ritual in Industrial Society—The Soviet Case* (Cambridge: Cambridge University Press, 1981); Jennifer McDowell, "Soviet Civil Ceremonies," *Journal for the Scientific Study of Religion* 14 (1975): 266–79; I. S. Sukhanov, *Obychai, traditsii i preemstvennost pokolenii* (Moscow: Politizdat, 1976).

38. Alan McEvoy and Edsal L. Erickson, "Heroes and Villains: A Conceptual Strategy for Assessing Their Influence," *Sociological Focus* 14 (1982): 111–22; compare Felicity O'Dell, "Socialization in the Children's Literature Lesson," pp. 92–109, in Jenny Brine, Maureen Perrie, and Andrew Sutton, eds., *Home, School and Leisure in the Soviet Union* (London: Allen and Unwin, 1980).

39. The Knowledge (Znanie) Society was the principal public organization for ideological and scientific propaganda. It maintained an extensive network of activists in every part of the Soviet Union. See David Powell, *Antireligious Propaganda in the Soviet Union: A Study of Mass Persuasion* (Cambridge: MIT Press, 1975), pp. 48–51.

40. See Jerry G. Pankhurst and Carolyn Welch, "Religion under Gorbachev," pp. 323–36, in J. Wieczynski, *The Gorbachev Encyclopedia* (Los Angeles: Charles Schlacks, Jr., 1994), for a more detailed treatment of the provisions of the new laws and other developments in the era of perestroika.

41. Igor Troyanovsky, *Religion in the Soviet Republics: Christianity, Judaism, Islam, Buddhism and Other Religions* (San Francisco: Harper, 1991).

42. Richard John Neuhaus, *The Naked Public Square: Religion and Democracy in America* (Grand Rapids, Mich.: William B. Eerdmans, 1984).

43. Laqueur, *Black Hundred*, p. 239.

44. A good example is composer Nikolai Rimsky-Korsakov, who drew heavily on religious themes and symbols even though he considered himself an atheist.

5

Everyday Culture

SVETLANA BOYM

Soviet Everyday Culture: An Oxymoron?

Mikhail Mishin, a Soviet satirist, wrote that Russians recognize themselves in the famous fairy-tale character Ivan the Fool. He bides his time napping atop the heating stove and gets up only to undertake major heroic feats. Ivan the Fool might be a great hero, but he has no idea how to survive his everyday life. Everyday life, captured in the Russian word *byt*, is a more dangerous enemy to him than the multiheaded fire-breathing dragon. The everyday is Russia's cultural monster. The nation might worship its heroes and their fabled ability to withstand hell or high water, but it also celebrates their impracticality and helplessness in the face of everyday life.

The distinguished linguist and literary critic Roman Jakobson claims that the Russian word for the everyday, *byt*, is culturally untranslatable into other languages: in his view, only Russia among all the European nations was capable of fighting "the fortresses of *byt*" and of conceptualizing radical alterity to the everyday (*byt*).[1] The opposite of *byt*, spiritual, poetic, or revolutionary being (*bytie*), is at the heart of Russian culture. In a similar way, Vladimir Nabokov claims the Russian conception of "banality," *poshlost*—a word that refers at once to artistic triviality, lack of spirituality, and obscenity—to be absolutely original. In Nabokov's view, only Russians were able to devise neatly the concept of *poshlost*—because of the "good taste of old Russia."[2] (This is perhaps one of the least ironic sentences in Nabokov, bordering on the banal.) No wonder, another word that was claimed to be untranslatable is *podvig*—heroic feat, dynamic force. It does not necessarily refer to a specific courageous accomplishment; rather, it embodies the notion of unlimited dynamism, perpetual movement (*dvizhenie*) itself.[3] Two Russian "untranslatable" words, then, one referring to the everyday and the other to the heroic feat, are closely linked and reflect what Russian and Soviet Russian critics perceive to be a fundamental feature of the Russian mentality. For many Russian and Soviet cultural critics, the expression "everyday culture" would appear problematic, if not oxymoronic, because culture in the Russian context, in the singular and with a capital "C," has been defined as a heroic battle against the everyday.[4]

Thus, there are radical differences between the "American dream," the dream of the private pursuit of happiness in the family home, and the Russian dream that—at least in the conception of Dostoevsky and his great admirer, the philosopher of the "Russian idea," Nikolai Berdiaev—consisted of spiritual homelessness and messianic nomadism. In Russia, the preoccupation with the everyday was frequently conceived as petit bourgeois (marked by the derogatory term *meshchanstvo*), inauthentic, unspiritual, or counterrevolutionary: It was fought against by Westernizers and Slavophiles, romantics and modernists, aesthetic and political utopianists, Bolsheviks and monarchists alike. To some extent, the modern concept of a secular everyday culture has never sunk roots in Russia.

If the American dream is pursued in the individual family house, the Soviet dream can only be fulfilled in the communal home. The central archeological site of our study of Soviet civilization is the communal apartment. It is at once a memory of Soviet collective home, the institution of social control, and the breeding ground of grass-roots informants in Stalin's times. We will eavesdrop behind the flimsy communal partitions on the "private" collections of "domestic trash" and kitschy souvenirs. Those everyday rituals, the practices of deviation and secrecy, reveal how the official ideological designs were inhabited. As such, they seem to precede and survive both the Soviet ideology and the communal apartment itself. I will combine the perspective of a cultural critic with my own memories of a former communal apartment resident who never fulfilled her "communal duties" and was frequently chided by watchful neighbors.

Any discussion of everyday culture is inevitably anachronistic; it raises issues of continuity and change in the national self-definition and daily practices in Russia, from prerevolutionary to post-Soviet times, from the time when there was no single word for "privacy" to the post-Soviet era, when privatization became a buzz word. If *byt* exemplifies the collective Russian mentalities, which have survived long durations of time, wars, uprisings, and revolutions, so does the opposition to *byt*, the critique of the everyday life that is also a part of the Russian collective mentality. Boris Uspensky and Yury Lotman insist that the binary opposition between *byt* and *bytie* is a fundamental feature of Russian culture; they point out the crucial difference between the Western medieval "world beyond the grave," divided into three spaces—heaven, purgatory, and hell—and the Russian medieval system, which was based on a fundamental duality. In Russia, the everyday could not therefore be perceived as the neutral sphere of human behavior where the concepts of civil society and private life originate.[5] Do the critics of culture *describe* the historical situation of the past, *perpetuate* cultural mythology, or both? In other words, is there, in fact, no neutral sphere of behavior in early modern Russia, or has it simply been insufficiently described by Russian cultural historians and hence not integrated into the Russian cultural identity as constructed in literary and political writings?[6]

The Soviet construction of the "new *byt*" did not escape the old dichotomy of *byt* and *bytie*. In this respect, there is a clear ideological continuity between the nineteenth-century Russian intelligentsia and the early Soviet leftist theorists.[7] The Soviet iconography of the new *byt* was thought through to the last detail—or, as Mayakovsky put it, "to the last button on one's suit." The new *byt*, one of the early Russian revolutionary dreams, was based on the complete restructuring of both time and space; from Aleksandr Gastev's utopian schedules of everyday life to the total design of the new communist space, from the all-people's house-commune to the making of new men and women. But can everyday life be contained by a utopian topography? Perhaps it is not surprising that in the twentieth century hardly anywhere else in the modern Western world did such a precise construction of ideologically correct everyday life exist; nowhere else were there so many deviations from this utopian construct.[8]

The New *Byt* and Stalinist Domestic Bliss

Let us begin the discussion of iconography of Soviet everyday life with a picture of a Stalinist domestic idyll as represented by Laktyonov's programmatic painting "Moving to the New Apartment." The room is cheerfully lit, although the source of light is hidden. It is the *natural* light of the bright socialist realist future. In the center is a middle-aged woman wearing a war medal, proud mistress of the new apartment, who seems ready to break into a Russian folk dance. Nearby is her son, an exemplary boy and Pioneer. A portrait of Stalin takes the place of the father. The gazes of this Soviet family do not meet; the mother looks out at the audience as if inviting our approval; the son looks up to his proud mother; and Stalin looks in the opposite direction, as if watching us through the half-open door, guarding the limits of the visible. The scene appears to belong to a familiar totalitarian sitcom: The characters wear appropriate Soviet uniforms and freeze in the established theatrical poses known from films and paintings, as if waiting the predictable canned applause. A few neighbors with whom the family will share the communal apartment gather at the door, jolly smiles frozen on their faces. The furniture in the room is very sparse and the private objects are limited to books, a radio, toys, a political poster, a globe with the largest country of the world usually colored in bright pink, a mandolina, and a sickly looking rubber tree plant (*Fikus*) in the foreground.

"Moving to the New Apartment" (1952 painting by Alexander Laktionov, Tretyakov Gallery, Moscow). Photo by author.

The painting is neither reflective nor self-reflective; people and objects hardly cast any shadows, and there is no mirror hidden in the corner. The scene flaunts the perfect transparency of its meaning. Michel Foucault's *The Order of Things* (Les mots et les choses), with an icon of early modern civilization—Diego Velázquez' "Las Meninas," which tests the rules and limits of representation—exposes *trompe l'œil*, and at the same time pays homage to the patrons of art—in this case, the royal couple. "Moving to the New Apartment," although similarly an icon of Soviet civilization that prescribes the order of everyday things, carefully hides all visual and ideological manipulations. This is the way a culture wishes to see itself and be seen, without thinking about the act of seeing. There are no uneven brush strokes and no blind spots; rather, everything is made readable in a didactic way, to the point that nobody has to bother reading it. The books near the rubber plant are all works by established Russian and Soviet classics, among whom the revolutionary poet Vladimir Mayakovsky stands out, and on the poster we can read the slogan, "Glory to our beloved Motherland!" The painter cannot afford to be suggestive or to allow anything contingent or accidental to appear on the canvas.[9] This is a perfect socialist realist genre scene reminiscent of the old Academic paintings.[10] This is not merely a private family festivity but a celebration of the Soviet collective in miniature, in the newly repaired communal apartment. There is no distinction between public and private here, only one fluid and seemingly cheerful ideological space.

It is difficult to imagine what could have been judged "ideologically incorrect" in this painting that is so carefully and moderately ideological. Yet its seamless surface was censored twice from two different sides: first for the rubber tree plant; and later for the portrait of Stalin. One could draw a mental diagonal to connect those two iconographically incorrect images. When the painting was first exhibited in the early 1950s, it was the rubber plant in the foreground that rubbed critics the wrong way. The painting was accused of celebrating the petit bourgeois values embodied in the rubber tree plant and of "varnishing Soviet reality." The rubber tree plant was regarded as a symptom of counterrevolutionary and petit bourgeois tastes, a personal item that should not be a part of the collective iconography. But what is so wrong with rubber tree plants?

When I have explained this painting to my American students, they have attempted to figure out what specific to this plant made it into a symbol of bad taste. But no knowledge of horticulture was helpful in this case. The "rub" is not inherent in the rubber plant; it depends fully on context. It turns out that the rubber tree plant is a part of American mythology of the 1950s as well, but there its meaning was completely different. Here is a passage from a song featuring a rubber tree plant very popular in the 1950s, "High Hopes": "Just what makes that poor little ant/Think he can move that rubber tree plant. / He's got hi-i-i-gh hopes, he's got hi-i-i-gh hopes. . . ." Here the plant is a symbol of *natural* obstacles to be overcome by confidence and hard work, a milestone on the way to the American dream.

The portrait of Stalin is located on a direct diagonal from the rubber tree plant; it almost appears as if the "great leader of all people" is averting his eyes from this bourgeois "flower of evil." In albums of Soviet art during the 1960s, after the half-hearted official de-Stalinization campaign, the painting appeared without the portrait of Stalin that had been deemed in bad taste, a kind of historical embarrassment implicating the painter and his audience in the Stalinist compromise. By covering up the compromise of mass collaboration with Stalin, the critics of the 1960s engaged in another compromise: forgetting. Erasing the portrait continued a long tradition of erasing and remaking history that originated in the 1920s and continued through the late 1980s and that consisted of omitting historical embarrassments and—to use the term of a Stalinist art critic—of "varnishing" the reality of authoritarian representation. Since this is a didactic painting, we are supposed to learn a lesson from it, and the lesson is that the everyday is as natural as the rubber plant, that history and ideology are as hidden as the portrait of Stalin, and that the relationship between the everyday and ideology is as "seamless" as the painting.

As we begin to uncover the ideological roots of the rubber plant, the cultural plot thickens, reflecting many paradoxes in the Soviet construction of the "new everyday" (*novyi byt*). The iconography of the rubber plant is ambiguous. It might have been regarded as the last sickly survivor of the exotic palm trees from the imaginary "greenhouses" of the upper bourgeoisie, or a poor relative of the infamous geranium on the windows of the merchant dwellings that were purged and physically eradicated in the campaign against "domestic trash" in Stalin's time. The rubber plant, an iconographic blemish on the image of socialist realist domestic bliss, and perhaps the only true-to-life object in the painting, can function as a trigger of cultural memory and a key to the "archeology" of Soviet private and communal life. This cultural archeology is not without contradictions.[11]

The communal apartment depicted in the painting is a far cry from the house-commune imagined by revolutionary architects in the early Soviet era. In the postrevolutionary period, architecture became a major art—an arch-art, a material embodiment of the revolutionary superstructure, a foundation of the social order. It was a rational art involved in conquering and reconstructing the mysterious, the unresolved, and the chaotic. Since Marx and Engels did not develop a specific picture of communist life, postrevolutionary visionaries turned to utopian writers like Thomas

Moore, Tommaso Campanella, Robert Owen, and Charles Fourier and tried to adopt for practical use their exemplary Ikarias and Cities of the Sun. The modern utopia, called the *sots gorod* (socialist city), was expected to multiply around the whole world through the "socialist resettlement of mankind." The house-commune was envisioned as a microcosm of the *sots gorod*. The *sots gorod*, in turn, served as a microcosm of Soviet society as a whole. Elaborate projects for house-communes were developed by Konstantin Melnikov, Semyon Ginsburg, Moisei Vengerov, and others. The nucleus of the new utopia, the "house-commune," reflected an ideal of "socialism in one building," to use the expression coined by Richard Stites.[12] The house-commune, also known as the "new proletariat house," aimed at replacing the familiar bourgeois family structure with "proletarian comradeship." In the house-commune, children were to be cared for collectively to alleviate the burden that once fell upon the bourgeois family's individual members. A popular slogan made headway at the time, "Down with the dictatorship of the kitchen!" The individual kitchen was denounced as a symbol of the nuclear family and women's enslavement to *byt*. By contrast, the communal home was not just a retreat for the individual, a place marked by personal traces and memories; rather, it was a public and therefore ideologically charged site. The communal dwelling's simple and stark geometry had to be enjoyed for its own sake. Characteristically, contemporary Soviet theorists praised empty spaces shot through with light, uncluttered by objects and personal artifacts that could spoil the dwelling's pristine purity. Where domestic objects appeared, they were to be strictly nonrepresentational and antirealistic, hinting at alternative spatial dimensions that transcend industrial domesticity. El Lissitsky compared the room of the future "to the best kind of traveling suitcase." He wrote that, for a modern person, it was enough to have an empty room, a mattress, a folding chair, a table, and a gramophone.[13] (The gramophone was his concession to popular taste.)

The campaign for the new *byt* began with the debunking of the old *byt*. Both the new and old *byt* acquired their specific features in the 1920s, when the revolutionary intelligentsia joined in the Bolshevik attack on *byt*. In his suicide note, Vladimir Mayakovsky, Soviet society's foremost revolutionary poet, wrote: "The love boat has crashed into *byt*." This was not only the fate of his personal "love boat." In the poet's eyes, the revolution itself was being held hostage to everyday life. Mayakovsky feared that communism would be murdered by yellow canaries and the revolution would be betrayed by a Marx framed in crimson in a cozy petit bourgeois interior. The poet fought against all signs of postrevolutionary domesticity, such as rubber plants, lyrical gramophone songs, and all kinds of pets, dead or alive—kittens, canaries, and the infamous elephant figurines. Porcelain elephants, symbolizing private happiness, would be-come notable enemies of the Soviet regime from the 1920s to the 1990s. No other animal, except perhaps for a few birds in bad taste—like pink flamingos or yellow canaries—was to receive such shabby treatment from revolutionary artists.

In the period 1928–29, responding to the poet's call, *Komsomolskaia pravda* started a campaign, "Down with Domestic Trash": "Let us stop the production of tasteless bric-a-brac!," urged the newspaper. "All these dogs, mermaids, figurine devils, and elephants only help smuggle back petit bourgeoisie. Clean your room! Summon bric-a-brac to public trial!"[14] The campaign recreated the rhetoric of the civil war and cultural revolution. In 1929, plans were laid for a series of exhibits "On the Manifestation of *Meshchanstvo* in Art" and "On Anti-Aesthetic Objects in Worker's *Byt*." The exhibits could be compared with the Nazi exhibit of "Degenerate Art," except that the Soviet exhibit was supposed to be about the "degenerate everyday." Actually, the Soviet project never got off the ground because cultural politics had changed drastically by the late 1930s. The war against the "little gods of things" was a war against fetishization, reification, and objectification of life's simple pleasures, but it was also a war for war's sake, a nostalgia for the nomadic lifestyle of the true revolutionary. Which is why the furniture had to be simple and portable, always ready to be folded up and carried along during some major political offensive, economic drive, or military campaign. Many leftist artists who were bent on designing the authentic revolutionary everyday were purged during this era. Ironically, the war against "do-mestic trash" outlived its idealistic proponents.

By the mid-1930s, the trashing of domestic life and the critique of philistinism temporarily subsided. The new acquisitiveness of Soviet citi-zens was cautiously encouraged in official writings, partially in order to justify and partially to disguise the legitimation of the new order of social inequality, which allocated special privileges for the Stalinist elite (who usually resided in spacious private apartments).[15] Yet, there was tension in the official acceptance of domesticity, and the depiction of its ideal iconography was unstable. In the period of High Stalinism, especially after the war, there was an attempt to create a different iconography of the everyday, in not an avant-garde but an imperial Socialist Realist style designed to benefit the privileged few; yet some iconographic elements—including rubber tree plants, those peculiar Soviet flowers of evil—sur-vived. The purging of the rubber plant, from the 1920s avant-garde to 1950s socialist realism, reveals some paradoxical continuities of the utopian vision, although the styles of those two utopias were quite differ-ent. It also points to some tragic paradoxes in socialist realist culture, which, in a rather cruel manner, realized the old dream of the Russian intelligentsia—the dream of creating a unified "people's culture" by abolishing the distinction between "high" and "low."

During the 1930s, intrusion into the everyday became more than rhetorical—the home search became an ordinary occurrence during the new Stalinist perestroika of everyday life. The brightly lit room of "Moving to the New Apartment" is so paranoidly codified because beyond the threshold there is another scene—"removing someone from an old apartment"—the scene of the search and arrest.

The 1950s saw a brief domestic revival, a new infatuation with pink-shaded lamps and escapist sentimental romances about "banana-lemon Singapore," sung by repentant Russian emigré and born-again patriot Aleksandr Vertinsky. The intelligentsia of the 1960s criticized the collaborationist philistinism of Stalinist culture and recreated the spirit of nomadic romanticism characteristic of the 1920s. It sang about trips "in search of the fog and the smell of taiga," about the romances of mountaineers, geologists, and flight attendants, and launched its own "campaign against domestic trash." This was a peculiar romantic crusade against domestic coziness, against not only pink lamp shades and porcelain elephants but also all kinds of comfortable furniture—soft sofas and armchairs, love seats, and velvet curtains—based on the belief that there was no need to cultivate domestic nests. Although the 1960s returned in many ways to the revolutionary and very mildly avant-garde discourse of the 1920s (mildly, because most of the art works and texts remained unavailable), yet this return was in many ways revolutionary, particularly in the understanding of the self and private life. The official "collective" was rewritten as an unofficial association of friends, a rather casual community of transient soul mates. Occasionally, one soul mate would report on another soul mate, occasionally the other soul mate would be called into the KGB, but as the Soviet anecdote has it, great progress was made under Brezhnev: the ten-year prison sentence joke became a three-year one. In some ways, this imaginary community of the 1960s ironically flaunted its own fragility. By the late 1960s, "privacy" had begun to be seen as the only honorable and uncompromising response to the system of public compromise. Not an escape, but a way of carving out an alternative space, a way of personalizing and de-ideologizing (to use a favorite term of perestroika intellectuals) the official maps of everyday life.

In the 1970s, after the Soviet tanks had trundled into Prague, a different kind of "nomadism" emerged. Members of intelligentsia went into a private retreat and questioned the imaginary "kitchen communities" of the 1960s. Some became dissidents and experienced violent invasion of privacy, including KGB home searches, while others conformed to a life of stagnation, and a few emigrated abroad—to capitalist lands where "privacy" is protected by law and elevated to the status of a state religion—and observed the collapse of Soviet civilization.

From the ideal image of Soviet collective bliss, marred only by one ideologically incorrect plant, we will move to its less ideal representation in the communal apartment of the former Leningrad. My "thick description" of the communal apartment and the Soviet home—to borrow a term from cultural anthropology—combines utopian designs and revolutionary genealogy with an examination of actual everyday practices that reflect the tragicomedies of Soviet communal living. I will supplement the discussion of the utopian house-communes envisioned by revolutionary architects with a few glimpses into the tragic comedy of actual communal living. The story of Soviet domestic life and communal apartment challenges familiar conceptions of domesticity, privacy, and commodity. From Gogol to Chekhov, domesticity in the Russian tradition was connected not only with "family values" but also with *poshlost* and with a routine both endearing and stifling. The communal apartment is at once a result of the revolutionary war on commodity fetishism, domestic kitsch, and *poshlost*, a fortress of commodities and kitsch in its own right. My description will be shaped by inevitable personal memories intended to provide the necessary balance between familiarity and defamiliarization, between homesickness and the sickness produced by being home.

The Archeology of the Communal Apartment

Here is another version of the Soviet family romance. Instead of a portrait of Stalin, there is a television image of Brezhnev, who is not listened to but merely present as background noise. My parents were having foreign guests for the first time in their life in our room in the communal apartment. Our neighbors, "Aunt Vera" and "Uncle Fedya," were home. Russian children call their adult neighbors "aunts" and "uncles" euphemistically, as if they were members of one very extended family. Uncle Fedya usually came home drunk, and when Aunt Vera would refuse to let him in, he crashed right in the long corridor, the central "thoroughfare" of the communal apartment, obstructing the entrance to our room. As a child, I often played with the peacefully reclining and heavily intoxicated Uncle Fedya, with his fingers and his buttons, telling him tales to which he probably did not have much to add. This time we were all in the room, listening to music to muffle the communal noises, and my mother was telling our foreign guests about the beauties of Leningrad. "You absolutely must go to the Hermitage, and then to Pushkin's apartment-museum and, of course, to the Russian Museum. . . . " As the conversation rolled along and the foreign guest was commenting on the riches of the Russian Museum, a narrow yellow stream slowly made its way under the door of the room. Smelly, embarrassing, intrusive, it formed a little puddle right in front of our dinner table. This scene, with the precarious coziness of a family gathering, both intimate and public, and a mixture of ease and fear in the presence of foreigners and neighbors, remained fixed as a memory of home. The family picture is framed by that inescapable stream of Uncle Fedya's urine effortlessly crossing the minimal boundaries of our communal privacy, disrupting the fragile etiquette of communal propriety. (And the smell was too bad to be domesticated or turned into a metaphor.)

If there was such a thing as a Soviet cultural unconscious, it must have been structured as a communal apartment with its flimsy partitions between the public and private, between control and intoxication. The Soviet "family romance," to use Freud's phrase, now in its melancholic twilight stage, was punctuated by the fluttering sound of a curious neighbor's slippers or by an inquisitive representative of the local Housing Committee. It was a romance with the collective that was equally unfaithful to the communitarian mythologies and to traditional family values.

In 1926, Walter Benjamin wrote a provocative and laconic sentence in his essay about Moscow: "The Bolsheviks have abolished private life." Private life in Soviet Russia, Benjamin felt, was to be eliminated along with private property. Anything private was denigrated as politically dangerous, literally de-prived of social utility and significance. Benjamin astutely noticed that just as private life was collectivized, public cafés tended to disappear as well. Somehow, the two were linked. A public sphere embodied in café culture shriveled away along with excised private life, and critical intellectuals became an endangered species on their way to extinction.

Privacy is notoriously difficult to translate into Russian. All examples given in Dal's famous dictionary of Russian under "private life" seem tendentious and negatively colored.[16] From Denis Fonvizin and Alexander Herzen to Fyodor Dostoevsky and Nikolai Berdiaev, Russian thinkers ridiculed the Western middle-class ideal of "a chicken in every pot and a little house of your own." The Russian soul was supposed to be homeless and impervious to the middle-class appeal of private life. The latter seemed alien to Russian mores by definition, or perhaps it is the lack of definition that made it appear non-Russian. Russian writers declared private life as practiced in the West to be "inauthentic" and unspiritual. By the same token, Western travelers to Russia, from the Marquis de Custine to Benjamin, lamented its inhabitants' flagrant disregard for private space. (Custine observed that the bed is among the least used items of Russian furniture, acquired mostly for public display.[17])

The Russian *kommunalka*, a term of both endearment and deprecation for the communal apartment, is not only a result of a housing crisis but also a product of a revolutionary experiment in collective living. Since very few house-communes were actually built, the authorities resorted to a cheaper option: reconstructing and partitioning existing "bourgeois quarters." Like so many other things in Soviet Russia, the *kommunalka* sprang from Lenin's head. A few weeks after the October revolution, Lenin drafted a plan to expropriate "large apartments." Any apartment was considered large if the number of rooms in it equaled or exceeded the number of its regular residents.[18] (Russian poet Joseph Brodsky once called his family's living quarters "a room and a half.") Lenin's decree reflected a different perspective on home and space than that found in the West. A person, or rather an impersonal statistical unit, was entitled not to a room or a private space but to a certain square footage. The space was divided mathematically and bureaucratically, as if it were not a "living" space, a real home once inhabited by real people, but some topological abstraction. As a result, countless apartments in major cities were partitioned in the most bizarre manner, creating unlivable spaces, long winding corridors, back entrances, and labyrinthine interior yards.

In the literature and art of the 1920s, the search for the dwelling place lost appears to be an all-embracing passion, and the identity crisis is closely linked to the housing crisis. In the literature and film of the 1920s, "defamiliarization" is not simply a metaphor for a literary device but also a central thematic preoccupation, a frustrated attempt to create a new Soviet family in the context of the housing shortage. Love and hatred are secondary passions; it is usually love of "dwelling space," envying those who have such space, and melancholy for housing lost. The quest for housing space and furniture appears to be the major driving force for plot in 1920s literature and film.

Structurally, many literary works and films of the 1920s are organized around a very desirable object of furniture. The celebrated film *Bed and Sofa* (Tretia meshchanskaia, 1928) portrays a peculiar love triangle—a young woman, her husband (the representative of the new Moscow proletariat), and his friend, a printer with whom he fought in the civil war. The friend moves in with the couple because he simply has no other place to live. The bed and the sofa are like musical chairs; the husband and friend switch from spousal bed to marginal sofa as the plot of the film unfolds. Neither the English nor the Russian title names the heros but rather the symbolic names of the street they live on or the prominent objects in their household. At the end, the heroine abandons the uncomfortable communal arrangement, leaving the two men in their rather unusual male bonding over a cup of tea with jam. The satirical tales of the late 1920s and early 1930s contain abundant tragicomic images of neighbors persuading each other to commit suicide for their sake, of publicly shamed intellectuals composing iambic tetrameters in the communal closet while their neighbors are busy expropriating the rooms of absent explorers of the North Pole, or subletting six single beds in one communal apartment.[19] In Mikhail Bulgakov's novel, *Master and Margarita*, the communal apartment turns into the most fantastic place on earth, more fantastic than the palace of Pontius Pilate. The Satan's ball takes place in the "fifth dimension" of the Moscow communal apartment. The devil himself is amazed at the tricks of Moscow "apartment exchange" and the dwelling space's ability to expand and divide in the postrevolutionary capitol.

Beginning in the late 1920s and especially during Stalin's times, the communal apartment became a major Soviet institution of social control and a form of constant surveillance. The laws of strict "residency permits" and the campaign against those deprived of the rights of citizenship (*lishentsy*) were all connected to the consolidation of the communal apartment. Communal apartments were under the observation of the local Housing Committee and were a training ground for grass-roots informants in Stalin's times. By the mid-1930s, "separate apartments" came into being and became a sign of a special privilege, or occasionally, special luck.[20] Only in the late 1950s did a new revolution in Soviet daily life begin with the resettlement to the "micro-districts" in the urban outskirts, where for the first time in their life many were able to have a state-owned separate apartment. These newly built buildings were given the unflattering name *khrushchoby*, a neologism formed from *Khrushchev* and *trushcheby*, or slums. Until 1990, about 40 percent of the population in urban centers like Leningrad lived in communal apartments. The communal apartment combined futuristic designs and premodern ways of living that were reminiscent of leprosiums, hospitals, camps, and other earlier forms of imposed communality. In a sense, the communal apartment was Soviet society in miniature, a leap of faith from utopian theory to everyday reality.

The Soviet *kommunalka* shared more than a linguistic root with the house-commune (*dom kommuna*). It was engendered by the same revolutionary topography as the house-commune and propelled by the same utopian longing for unfettered collectivity. Architecturally, both were alike in two crucial respects: the communal kitchen (although each family had its own pots and pans and a gas burner on the shared stove); and the corridor clearly marking (although never fully separating) the public and private spheres. If the house-commune was a microcosm of the ideal revolutionary universe, the communal apartment was an actual Soviet microcosm. Economic hardship was not the sole reason why the purist socialist idyll turned into a social farce. The problem is that any utopia, be it social, political, or architectural, is a u-chronia, forced atemporality, interrupted time-flow, life standing still. What the architectural utopia does not take into account is history; both in the broad sense of social history and in the sense of individual history, with its multiple narratives of everyday life.

The Psychopathology of Soviet Everyday Life

The partition is the communal apartment's central architectural feature. Made of plywood and oddly positioned, the partition marks the intersection between the public and private spheres within a communal dwelling. Because of the chronic housing shortage, old rooms and corridors were endlessly partitioned and subdivided, creating angular spaces, windowless living quarters, and rooms overlooking half-lit back yards. Tenants strained their imagination by inventing all manner of curtains and screens to mark minimal privacy. A plywood partition was a far more tenuous barrier against the invasion of privacy than a wall, more a *sign* of the division than a division itself. Too flimsy to keep secrets from your neighbors, the partition served to create an illusion that some intimacy was possible after all.

Privacy in the communal apartment was often equated with secrecy. The secret was a way of life, a form of resistance to forced communality. I recall how in the kindergarten we used to play "secrets." We would go to the far end of the park somewhere near the fence off the public paths and perform a ritual burial of secrets in the ground. The "secret" could be a fragment of colored glass, an old stamp, a discarded candy wrapper, an old badge—any useless "found object" that exerted a peculiar fascination on us. The "secret"—something to be hidden in order to be shared—served to affirm a bond of friendship, to escape an imposed collective sociality, to create an alternative community. The game of secrets was opposed to the official game of hide-and-seek, where there was nothing to conceal and therefore nothing to uncover. The real secret in our game was the voluntary community of friends that we built. Adults in the communal apartments would play their own games of secrets, trying to establish unofficial communities, but not necessarily individual privacy.

One of the main features of communal interactions was "performance disruption." Sexual disruption or a sudden invasion of the couple's intimate life was comically featured in Soviet fiction and films. Soviet sexologists consider the lack of privacy, coupled with the deeply internalized fear of interruption, to be the major source of sexual dysfunction and neurosis among Soviet people. Embarrassment is endemic to communal life. One could not be embarrassed in complete solitude. Embarrassment requires an audience; it is an exemplary trope for social theatricality. Etymologically, the word "embarrassment" signifies physical obstruction. It was first applied to human relations only in the eighteenth century. Ever since, it has been inexorably present wherever the private and public spheres rub against each other. The incident with Uncle Fedya's urinating in the communal corridor is embarrassment Soviet style. The embarrassment my mother felt in front of honored guests, along with the nonchalance she tried to feign to cover up Uncle Fedya's "impropriety," was familiar to every Soviet citizen. Embarrassment was such a commonplace that it became ritualized and internalized in the Soviet psyche. It might have even engendered a kind of communal tolerance, an attitude of benign neglect that the collective adopted in the face of an odd scene or awkward circumstances. But it also concealed repressed anger that could break out into the open at any moment.

Communal apartments were communal by necessity, not by choice. Communal neighbors were joined together in a kind of "mutual responsibility" (*krugovaia poruka*); they shared the duties, used each other's property, and partook of domestic gossip. This resembles a premodern type of collectivity and centralized control that had spread in Russian villages since the time of Mongol invasion. Yet, the comparison can be made only with the village commune stripped of its romantic and patriotic idealization; moreover, the central feature of the communal apartment was precisely the clash of different classes and social groups, between people with different backgrounds, unlike the fairly homogeneous neighbors of patriarchal village communes. The main features of village life that influenced Russian political "folkways" included: "a strong tendency to maintain stability, a kind of closed equilibrium, risk avoidance, the considerable freedom of action and expression 'within the group,' [and] a striving for the unanimous and final resolution of potentially divisive issues."[21] The inhabitants of communal apartments adopted various survival strategies to help mitigate the harsh realities of communal living. The very deficiencies of communal living were sometimes turned upside down and used to accentuate inhabitants' individuality. Thus, neighbors would often exaggerate their separateness by mounting their own individual door bells, vociferously guarding their exclusive access to a particular gas burner, or setting up personal electricity meters. At the same time, residents in communal apartments tended to internalize the communality as a fact of life and a guarantee of stability.

The communal apartment was a classical Soviet stage where the chorus of conservative public opinion prevailed and where many, though not all, impossible conflicts were resolved. For instance, public opinion would compel an intellectual residing in an apartment to refrain from reading in the communal water closet; the drunkard would be assigned a special kitchen corner where he could rest while sobering up; kids were expected to wheel their bicycles in the communal corridor very quietly, and Aunt Shura reported only every other political joke to the local KGB officer, not every one. The communal stage was a field of compromise as well as battle. Alcoholism, which became rampant in Brezhnev's times, was tolerated as a fact of life. Social psychologist Alexander Etkind sees alcoholism as a metaphor for stagnation (in Russian *zapoi*, "an alcoholic binge," and *zastoi*, "stagnation," rhyme). The alcoholic was not compelled to sober up, and a consistently sober person was looked upon with suspicion: nobody should stand out in the collective and be better than the next person. In a way, alcoholic intoxication was a state of mind most adequate to the bizarre Soviet reality. "The best moments in the life of an alcoholic are not his sober achievements but his drunken unity with his equals."[22] No wonder Gorbachev's reforms began with the anti-alcoholism campaign.

Individualism and uncommon behavior were discouraged in communal apartments, just as they were in the old village commune, and envy permeated relations between residents. "Envy" is the title of one of the earliest Soviet novels about Soviet cohabitation that preceded communal apartments. Although envy is by no means peculiar to Soviet everyday life, it was marked by what Igor Kon, a leading Russian sociologist, calls "historical immaturity." It is akin not so much to the competition present in developed capitalist societies but to interactions found in preindustrial communities, where relationships are governed by a "zero-sum" presupposition: one person's gain is regarded as the other's loss. According to Kon, "the dictatorship of envy, disguised as social justice, efficiently blocked individual efforts to do better and to rise above the average," and it disclosed "a general mistrust of individual achievement and fear of social differentiation."[23]

Any communal apartment dweller was permanently frightened by that symbolic "mutual responsibility," the double bind of love and hatred, envy and attachment, secrecy and exhibitionism, embarrassment and compromise; people in collective dwellings professed to hate any form of communal interaction, yet they often internalized communal structures and later recalled them with nostalgia. An elderly woman, a Russian emigré now living in the United States, suffered all her life in horrendous communal apartments. Now she complains of solitude: "Worse come to worst, even after peeing in your teapot, they [my neighbors] would call you an ambulance when you needed one, or lend you a pinch of salt for your cooking. . . . It is this spoonful of coarse salt that I miss so much."

Communal apartments had no living rooms, bedrooms, or studies, only "rooms," so the traditional "bourgeois division of labor" and the separation of domestic spheres were supposedly banished. The room was a transformable stage fit for all occasions. It could be a bedroom, a guest

room, a dining room, a nursery, or a salon. The kitchen was not a communal meeting place; quite to the contrary, it was a place of forced communality that must be avoided. One recently interviewed communal apartment resident called it the "domestic Nagorno-Karabakh" (a region in the
former Soviet Union torn by an ethnic strife). The communal kitchen was
a battleground of petty rivalries. What was at issue here was who burned
more gas, whose turn it was to cook or clean, and who was to blame for
the breakdown in communal etiquette. Each family had its burner and a
designated time to use it. When the cooking was done, family members
made sure to carry all their pots and pans to their rooms so that nobody
else would use those scarce personal belongings. In the same way, toilet
paper, a rare commodity in the Soviet Union, was kept in the room and
carried inconspicuously to the toilet. However, for those who could not
procure toilet paper, there was usually a stack of *Pravda* in the bathroom
to be read or put to another functional use. The intellectual in the communal water closet—in the literal rather than literary sense—was a character
prominently featured in Soviet literature.

In the 1960s, following Khrushchev's "thaw," an alternative kitchen
culture began to appear in Soviet society. It was widespread among
Soviet intellectuals, especially those lucky enough to have an apartment
of their own. The kitchen functioned as an informal salon for the intelligentsia in the 1960s. The most important issues were discussed in these
overcrowded kitchens, where people "really talked," shared news, flirted,
and occasionally munched on whatever the family's refrigerator had to
offer. The kitchen salon of the 1960s was a perfect site for grown-up children to continue to bury their secrets and celebrate shared escapes from
the predictability of Soviet life.

Soviet Interiors:
Aunt Lyuba's Still Life

Benjamin wrote, "To live is to leave traces."[24] Perhaps this is the best definition of the private—to leave traces for oneself and for others, memory
traces of which one cannot be deprived. A room in the Soviet and post-
Soviet communal apartment reveals an obsession with leaving traces,
with commemoration and preservation in the most ostensible fashion.
The campaign against "domestic trash" failed miserably in most communal apartments. Indeed, we can discern signs of rebellion in the conspicuous accumulation of "domestic trash" (the expression derives from a
well-known Mayakovsky play), which survived all ideological purges
and changes in leadership. A secret residue of privacy, it defended people
from externally imposed and internalized communality.

Let us enter the room of a sixty-year-old widow, "Aunt Lyuba," whom I visited in the summer of 1991 and 1992. Lyuba N. came to Leningrad from Belarus after World War II. She was assigned a room in a communal apartment and found a job as an accountant in the medical students' dorm. Aunt Lyuba's room contained nearly everything that was considered to be in bad taste from the 1920s to the 1970s, including the infamous rubber tree plant. She did not move to a newly renovated apartment, as in the exemplary Stalinist painting, but continued to live in the old communal flat for about thirty years, from the late 1950s to the 1990s. Her room appears untouched by both the 1960s campaigns for good taste and more recent trends in fashion. Although the city and the country where Aunt Lyuba lives have recently changed their name, her room preserves a certain domestic mentality that has survived historical upheavals.

This is how the room looked the first summer after the dissolution of the Soviet Union. In Aunt Lyuba's only room of some 13 square meters, there is a cupboard (a kind of a wardrobe) made in the early 1960s, a bed, a table, and an old-fashioned TV set. The television stands in the center of the table on a Russian shawl that serves as a tablecloth and is treated like an altar of modern conveniences. The television set is covered with a special lacy cloth that used to cover icons and, later, gramophones, all of which were treated with a peculiar reverence. Aunt Lyuba's room reminds us of many traditional Slavic dwellings, except that the functions of the stove and the "red corner" (where icons were displayed) are now taken up by the television and the display shelf of the cupboard, where all the most precious items are stored for everyone to see. The television's blinking artificial light is reflected in the cupboard's glass doors, casting bluish shadows upon personal possessions.

The cupboard is the most important piece of furniture in the old-fashioned communal apartment room. It has survived the campaign against domestic trash, the civil war on *meshchanstvo*, and ironic debunking by high brow writers. (At the end of Erdman's play *The Suicide*, the main character, the would-be suicide Semyon, begs his neighbors and friends to spare him and not to force him to kill himself. He is ready to sign off everything to them, to refuse food, enslave his wife, send his mother-in-law to work in the mines, and . . . to sell his cupboard.) The genesis of the cupboard symbolizes the development of both the bourgeois commodity and of the conceptions of comfort, home, and interiority. If the mid-nineteenth century was the historical moment when, in Benjamin's words, "the private individual enters the stage of history,"[25] then the mid-1920s was a turning point when that private individual went backstage in Russia. And yet, the old and rather modest cupboard found in Soviet communal apartments reminds us that personal pride and the desire for individuation have not died.

Detail of Aunt Lyuba's still life (Leningrad, 1992). Photo by author.

Aunt Lyuba has carefully arranged the objects on her cupboard. There is a big plastic apple brought from her native Belarussian village, a Chinese thermos with bright floral patterns, a naturalistic porcelain dog, three bottles containing different glass flowers (daisies and more exotic red flowers with a touch of elegance), a samovar, a set of folk-style Soviet porcelain cups. "You see I have it all here, it's my still life," she tells me proudly as I photograph her room. Curiously, she uses the artistic term "still life" to describe this corner of her quarters. In fact, she says *natiur mort*, a Russian Gallicism that might have reflected the high school tours of painting galleries obligatory for Soviet students. The display is clearly tinged with an aesthetic quality in her mind, as well as with personal memories. Indeed, there is something pleasing and cheerful in the brightness and unabashed eclecticism of her collection, which contrasts sharply to the bleak uniformity of the communal corridors.

In Russia, one can only speak about nostalgia for the still life, nostalgia for a sustained and sustaining materiality of everyday life that withstands the winds of time and never-ending crises. Lyuba's collection of Soviet ready-mades exemplifying her trivial private utopias and everyday minor aesthetic, framed by the glass of the cupboard as if it were a museum exhibit, is a monument to that desire for a still life, for a life that does not rush anywhere amid the whirlpool of social metamorphoses. Lyuba's "still life" has no masterpieces or truly exotic items: her beloved objects are all mass-produced and slightly out of fashion, giving the whole scene an aura of time past. The woman has gathered together all her beautiful and memorable things. The ornaments clash, recreating distant images of the village home and prerevolutionary images of cozy merchants' dwellings; their covers, napkins, and laces give the feeling of "completeness and personal touch."

Lyuba's room is full of flowers: Soviet Victorian roses on the communal wallpaper; exotic red glass flowers and simple plastic daisies on the shelf; stylized gold and yellow daisies on the porcelain, red floral decorations on the painted wooden spoon. The only real flower is a little rubber plant comfortably perched on the window sill (I was glad to find this old friend here). Aunt Lyuba's carefully gathered exhibit presents a daunting challenge to the theoretical framing of domestic objects.

From the 1920s and through the 1970s, the domestic object was a precarious possession in Soviet homes, an endangered species constantly threatened by ideological, social and economic conditions. This was not only a social deprivation but also a sensory deprivation, a thwarting of sentience, human contact, the powers of projection and reciprocity. The war on fetishism carries a different meaning in a country where most people have experienced the loss of domesticity at least once in a lifetime and where the preservation of domestic objects has spelled not so much consumerism as survival.

The artifact on communal display is an object preserving private memory, a souvenir to privacy itself, a remnant of a pre-industrial and possibly a prerevolutionary world. The souvenir moves the object from common into individual history. The souvenir's owner becomes the author who reinvents the objects and their uses and refuses to accept the official "system of objects," whether that system be capitalist commercialism or frugal collective ideology.

The personal domestic objects of Aunt Lyuba are difficult to theorize about. They are too useless for either use- or exchange-value theories. They are impure and outmoded on all grounds. The analysis of Aunt Lyuba's still life reveals everyday resistance to sociological theories, yet her objects can tell us a lot about eclectic Soviet cultural mythologies. They are not about defamiliarization but rather about the domestication of estranged ideological designs. Lyuba's objects are not bare essentials, but they are also not objects of status or conspicuous consumption. If they do represent a need, it is first and foremost an aesthetic need, a desire for beauty given minimum available means, an aesthetic domestication of the hostile outside world.

In the rooms inhabited by ex-Soviet intellectuals, by contrast, we do not find cheap old-fashioned chests of drawers. What we encounter here are the 1960s-style wall units and shelves designed in the modern functional fashion and made in the "developed Socialist countries," such as Hungary or even Yugoslavia. The wall units and ample bookshelves popular among the intelligentsia were also status symbols, fetishes of rediscovered modernist functionality. Hard-to-get books and collected works of foreign authors signaled one's membership in the esteemed status group of the intelligentsia. Given the material scarcity in the post–World War II era, personal possessions were hardly acquired exclusively for "conspicuous consumption." The space between the folding glass on the bookshelf, an ephemeral space, where the owners would typically display especially meaningful personal objects, such as photographs, images from travel, baby pictures, portraits of Ernest Hemingway or of the popular Soviet bard Vladimir Vysotsky (both with beards and with or without cigars), snapshots of faraway friends, occasionally toys or souvenirs from the Crimea or Suzdal, envelopes with foreign stamps, loose pages from dismembered old books, dated newspaper clippings, and so forth. This two-dimensional space behind the glass door of the bookcase reflects the image of the resident; it is his or her carefully arranged interface with the world. The narrative of the treasured objects cannot be easily reconstructed by the outsider, for it is nonlinear, unreadable, with many blank spots, oddly meaningful banalities and mild obsessions. It does not reveal a person's biography but rather a biographical legend, a story of inner life externally fashioned, a record of what really matters, assorted traces of lived or vicariously experienced life that have survived the drudgery of dailyness. Sometimes, it is a story of travels—real or imaginary—of journeys to exotic places and escapes into wishful thinking. In the 1960s and early 1970s, when traveling abroad was nearly impossible, the Soviets engaged in "virtual travel" by watching an immensely popular television program, Cine-Travelers Club, a Soviet version of *National Geographic* that offered everyone free transit to the West and beyond.

There appeared to be an unwritten law of fashion that told everyone when Hemingway and Pasternak were out and Vysotsky and Solzhenitsyn were in. With the passage of time, Solzhenitsyn also became passé, supplanted by a photoreproduction of the exotic and apolitical Nefertiti, the mythical beauty queen of ancient Egypt whom Soviet intellectuals inherited from the traveling exhibit, "The Treasures of Tutankhamen." Now side by side with Nefertiti there is a half-dressed foreign pin-up with a non-Russian smile that has replaced all past political and poetic heroes. Private memorabilia are not deprived of cultural myths; they are separated from the dominant discourses only by a fragile plywood partition. The objects/souvenirs are often the only personal possessions, offering us erratic narratives of utopian coziness and homeliness. Both priceless and cheap, conspicuous and private, they make us question some cherished precepts of the commodity theory.

The Ruins of Soviet Communality

The communal apartment was always an exemplary metaphor for Soviet communality, official and unofficial. Nowadays, it is a frequent subject of editorials in the post-Soviet press. When Stalin was taken out of the mausoleum, people joked that Khrushchev had resettled Lenin's communal apartment, which (the joke is updated in the post-Soviet era) could now be fully "privatized."[26] Writer Aleksandr Kabakov ridiculed Russian ultranationalists for their "communal apartment tactics." By mobilizing neighborhood bullies (*kham*), Kabakov argues, ultranationalists hope to force intellectuals into playing by their boorish rules of insult and coercion.[27] Like chronic diseases, memories of the communal apartment cannot be cured; communal apartment strategies of attack, survival, and resistance shaped the mentality of several Soviet generations.

Once a realm of powerful myths, the communal apartment itself is on its way to becoming a myth. From a forward-looking utopia, it has evolved into a nostalgic memory of Soviet communality. Some former communal apartment neighbors remember it with a mixture of anger and endearment, not merely as a "domestic Nagorno-Karabakh" but as the site of their old-fashioned Soviet childhood and youth, when life was difficult, pleasures simple, and—for better or worse—there did not seem to be any way out. A recent article in the popular weekly *Ogonek* remembered the communal apartment with bittersweet irony as a never-never land where one could be happy with so little. This precarious Soviet happiness is now largely extinct, and to many former Soviet citizens deprived of privacy in the past, the old miseries seem less frightening than the incoming privatization.

Although the communal apartment lost its status as an officially sanctioned institution at the end of Gorbachev's reign, it has survived as an unfortunate fact of life reflecting the continuous housing shortage. Radical perestroika brought down many old partitions in former communal apartments. This latest revolution in everyday life had to proceed slowly, for it had to grapple with the consequences of the older campaigns, such as the drive for a new *byt* that brought forth the communal apartments and Khrushchev's reforms, which moved about 30 percent of Soviet urban dwellers into private apartments on the cities' outskirts. Before the privatization campaign, there were 300,000 communal apartments in Moscow. According to official statistics, 40 percent of the population in Leningrad, recently renamed St. Petersburg, still live in communal apartments. Housing conditions are particularly harsh in the city's center. Privatizing apartments has turned out to be an excruciating task, straining the emerging post-Soviet legal culture, which has stumbled into unpredictable (or rather very predictable but never legally accounted for) webs of Soviet everyday practices. In 1988, the Council of Ministers approved an amendment to existing laws that allowed citizens residing in private apartments to buy them from the city government. There were very few takers at first. In 1989, only 0.03 percent of all apartments and 0.07 percent of apartment residents turned their apartments into private property.[28] In July 1991, the Supreme Soviet adopted a new law designed to speed up the apartment privatization process. Rooms in communal apartments still could not be privatized.

The privatization policy encountered much popular criticism reflecting not only Soviet prejudices but also the traditional Russian suspicion of private property. A friend of mine reports a conversation on the trolley overheard in 1991: "They are going to get privatization vouchers; we are going to privatize!" To which another person replied, "You should be ashamed to use such words in the presence of women." "Privatization" remains a bad word for many ex-Soviet citizens. An aging schoolteacher wrote a letter to *Ogonek*, complaining that she was ostracized by other dwellers residing in the same housing project when she decided to privatize her one-room standard apartment. She was called "a NEP woman, a capitalist, and a private property owner"—words that sound derogatory if not obscene in Russian and come directly from the vocabulary of the political insults that carried a mortal threat in the Stalinist epoch.

By 1990, only a few completely dilapidated and substandard (even by Soviet standards) communal apartments had been taken over by artists and, later on, almost like in downtown Manhattan, reclaimed by newly emerging shady businessmen, real estate operators, and "astrologists anonymous." After the 1991 law on domestic property privatization went into effect, a new wave of housing "gentrification" (to use the American term) began in Russia, which left in its wake a clearly visible trail of bribery and coercion.

Imagine a post-Soviet nouveau riche, a young woman who works as a financial director for an international "joint venture" and falls in love with a dilapidated but spacious Moscow communal apartment featuring bay windows and a Neoclassical facade. She would have to pay each communal apartment resident a hefty fee *and* supply each of them with a separate apartment where they would be willing to move. Moreover, she would have to find her way around (usually by bribing) the obsolete yet fully functional Soviet bureaucrats from the housing committee. Also, still in place is an old Soviet mechanism of social control, the residency permit, without which a person is not allowed to settle in a given city. "A birthmark of the past," this residency permit is a bureaucrat's dream opportunity to extort. In one of the many stories I have heard on this subject, an apparatchik from the Housing Committee demanded a bribe of no less than $20,000 (probably more than a year's income for all the building's residents) for the permit to privatize a particularly attractive apartment on Arbat Street. When the would-be owner refused to pay the bribe, the bureaucrat resorted to threatening phone calls demanding that his terms be met. The harassment ceased only when the aspiring owner solicited help from the wife of a prominent Russian politician.[29]

These stories point out that the old Soviet ways are far from dead. The old techniques of coping with the Soviet bureaucracy come in handy when ex-Soviet citizens have to battle for their newly acquired rights. The dream of a Western-style private dwelling is still just a dream for most Russians who have survived socialism. By the same token, many post-Soviet reforms are but legal abstractions and nobody knows how to put them into practice. "Free market" and "democracy" remain empty foreign words in the minds of the Russian people, just as "socialist political economy" and "communism" used to be.

In these post-Soviet, postcommunist, postmodern times, all the words formerly deemed untranslatable into Russian are finding their way into post-Soviet discourse: *mentalnost, identichnost, manadzher, sponsor*. Once ubiquitous adjectives like "collective'" and "communal" are out of fashion; everything that starts with the foreign prefix inter (like "international") is in. International companies, joint ventures, and cooperatives are in vogue, as is privatization in all its numberless forms. In the Soviet past, private life was forbidden in public, but now there is a newspaper called *Private Life* (*Chastnaia zhizn*), which specializes in personal ads, cries of loneliness, and searches for "Western" husbands and wives. In response to the newspaper's verse contest, one female reader wrote a funny, teasing line that reflects all the ambiguities and paradoxes of the new and still untranslatable (or at least unprecedented in any Western language) post-Soviet *byt*: "So, what can I do? Oh, well, I won't despair. I don't have a personal life, but *Private Life* I do." "Private life" is only the name of a newspaper, a new cliché in the post-Soviet language not yet the "property" of the still-deprived Russian citizens.

Notes

The research for this chapter was made possible by ACLS/SSRC Fellowship for 1990–91 and an IREX short-term grant in the summer of 1992. For a more extensive discussion of Soviet everyday life and its myths, see my book, *Common Places: Mythologies of Everyday Life in Russia* (Cambridge: Harvard University Press, 1994).

1. Roman Jakobson, "On the Generation that Squandered Its Poets," in Krystyna Pomorska and Stephen Rudy, eds., *The Language in Literature* (Cambridge: Harvard University Press, 1987).

2. Vladimir Nabokov, "Philistines and Philistinism," in *Lectures on Russian Literature* (New York: Harcourt Brace Jovanovich, 1981), p. 313.

3. Nikolai Rerikh complains that the Oxford English Dictionary includes only two Russian words, *ukaz* and *sovet*, both connected to Russian and Soviet systems of power and bureaucracy (quoted in Dmitry Likhachev, *Zametki o russkom* [Moscow: Soviet Russia, 1984], p. 11). Likhachev also writes that two Russian words—*volia* (freedom) and *udal* (courage)—are connected to the Russian landscape and emphasize the enormity of the central Russian plain.

4. In response to a questionnaire on mass culture offered to prominent Soviet writers, artists, and intellectuals, Tatiana Tolstaya, a contemporary Russian writer, wrote that mass culture is "not a culture by definition." Mass culture is a contradiction in terms, which Tolstaya dismisses as "kitsch." *Iskusstvo kino*, no. 6 (June 1990): 69–70.

5. Yuri Lotman and Boris Uspensky, "Binary Models in the Dynamics of Russian Culture," in Alexander Nakhimovsky and Alice Stone-Nakhimovsky, eds., *Semiotics of Russian Cultural History* (Ithaca: Cornell University Press, 1985), p. 32.

6. A similar description/perpetuation of the extraordinary Russian resistance to ordinary life can be found in the writings of Nikolai Berdiaev, but with an additional twist. Berdiaev insists that the opposition between *byt* and *bytie* is rooted in the Russian apocalyptic conscience; see Nikolai Berdiaev, *Russaia ideia* (Paris: YMCA Press, 1946). Russia's conception of national identity depends on its extraordinary deeds (*podvig*) and on its eschatological mission, not on its everyday. Real life and true happiness is only possible in the "future perfect" of the utopia or the apocalypse, not in the transient present of everyday life. Russia herself is frequently personified as a flying troika that escapes the limits of this world and runs away without aim or restraint. In Blok's *fin de siècle* vision, Russia appears as a spiritual dancer who has given away her flesh and now dances accompanied by a sad song about escape from the everyday (*bez-byt-nost*) and fleeting moments. As she dances, an apocalyptic horseman lurks in the twilight. So, Russia is defined by her perpetual nomadic spirit, wanderlust, and liberation from everydayness. In this iconography, the everyday (*byt*) is perceived not just as unspiritual but also as non-Russian in a higher, poetic sense of the word.

7. Sergei Tretyakov, the propagandist of *Left Front*, redefines the opposition between *byt* and *bytie*, in which *bytie* turns from a spiritual into a revolutionary being. The dynamic force of the revolutionary *bytie* is opposed to the materialistic *byt*, the realm of those petit bourgeois kitschy objects—romantic postcards, gramophone records, porcelain peasants and gypsies, pink ivory elephants, and all those other "enemies of the people" that do not simply comprise a private world but also profane the revolution.

8. Modern secular everyday life was defined as the residue of theory and metadiscourse. Michel de Certeau describes everyday life as a series of minor practices of ruse and *braconnage*, the arts of survival that undermine the prescribed Art of Life, official ideologies, and some sociological theories. In other words, this conception of everyday life (which derives from French rather than Russian intellectual history) is anti-utopian by definition. The everyday and its cultural descriptions were regarded as resistance to utopia both in practice and in

theory. Hence to write the history of the everyday means to go against the grain of Russian cultural myths and the many paradigmatic descriptions of Russian cultural history that reproduce them. For European theories of everyday life, see Henri Lefebvre, *Everyday Life in the Modern World*, translated by Sasha Rabinovitch (New Brunswick, N.J.: Transaction Books, 1984). For the development of Lefebvre's theories, see the special issue of the *Yale French Studies* on the Everyday (*YFS*, edited by Kristin Ross and Alice Kaplan, no. 73 [1987]). Michel de Certeau, *L'invention du quotidien/Arts de faire* (Paris: Union Générale d'Editions, 1980).

9. The painting seeks to convince us that it is not about painting but about life. It is a blueprint for life, not the way it is, and certainly not the way it was, but the way it should be.

10. In contrast to the art of Nazi Germany, we find hardly any depiction of private or domestic life in the Soviet art of the 1920s and 1950s, which was primarily dedicated to epic subjects. This is a painting about *moving* to domestic life, about domestic life-to-be in a victorious postwar Soviet Union. It portrays domesticity not as a given but as an award presented by the party for heroic deeds.

11. The archeology of the everyday offers us neither a complete reconstruction of the past nor a single authorial explanation, neither a comforting taxonomy nor a scientific periodization. It only helps to unearth a few material exhibits, like the rubber plant, that illuminate twisted plots of forgotten cultural history. Walter Benjamin compares archeological digging to the operations of memory. In his view, the archeologist "must not be afraid to return again and again to the same matter: to scatter it as one scatters, to turn it over as one turns soil. For the matter itself is only a deposit, a stratum which yields only to the most meticulous examination what constitutes a real treasure hidden within the earth; the images, severed from all earlier associations that stand like precious fragments of torsos in a collector's gallery — in the prosaic rooms of our later understanding. Walter Benjamin, "A Berlin Chronicle," in *Reflections*, edited by Peter Demetz (New York: Schocken, 1986), p. 26. For the notion of archeology in contemporary theory, see Michel Foucault, *The Archeology of Knowledge* (New York: Pantheon Books, 1982); and for a critical discussion of the concepts of "history" and "archeology," see Domenick LaCapra and Steven L. Kaplan, eds., *Modern European Intellectual History* (Ithaca: Cornell University Press, 1982).

12. For a historical description of revolutionary utopias, see Richard Stites, *Revolutionary Dreams: Utopian Vision and Experimental Life in the Russian Revolution* (New York: Oxford University Press, 1989); V. E. Khazanova, *Iz istorii sovetskoi architektury, 1917–1925* (Moscow: ANSSSR, 1963); Khazanova, *Sovetskaia arkhitektura pervykh let oktiabria* (Moscow: Nauka, 1970); Khazanova, *Sovetskaia arkhitektura pervoi piatiletki* (Moscow: Nauka, 1980).

13. *Kultura zhilia, stroitelnaia promyshlennost*, no. 12 (1926): 881. Quoted in Khazanova, *Sovetskaia arkhitektura pervykh let oktiabria*, p. 220.

14. *Komsomolskaia pravda*, November 4, 1928.

15. On the "new deal" Stalin style and the "new acquisitiveness" in the 1930s, see Vera Dunham, *In Stalin's Time* (Cambridge: Cambridge University Press, 1976). See also Sheila Fitzpatrick, "Becoming Cultured: Socialist Realism and the

Representation of Privilege and Taste," pp. 216–17, in *The Cultural Front: Power and Culture in Revolutionary Russia* (Ithaca: Cornell University Press, 1993).

16. Vladimir Dal, *Tolkovyi slovar zhivago velikorusskogo iazyka* (St. Petersburg: Volf, 1882), p. 259. Other examples include "personal insult" (*lichnoe oskorblenie*): if a clerk is insulted in the workplace or because of his position, this is not a personal insult (*oskorblenie chinovnika po dolzhnosti ego ne est obida lichnaia*) and "personal responsibility" (*lichnaia otvetstvennost*). The latter offers the only example that is not defined in opposition to the community, but here the responsiveness to the community is internalized. Hence Russian personal life, *lichnaia zhizn*, seems more like a realm of publicly sanctioned guilt and a heightened sense of personal duty.

17. It is symptomatic that in the *History of Private Life* (Cambridge: Harvard University Press, 1987–91) recently published in France and the United States there is almost no mentioning of Russia. Perhaps the editors conceived private life exclusively in Western terms and now it is time to issue a complementary volume on the "history of communal life," with Russia as the case in point.

18. Quoted in Vladimir Paperny, *Kultura dva* (Ann Arbor: University of Michigan Press, 1986), p. 83.

19. I refer specifically to Ilya Ilf and Evgeny Petrov's satirical novels *The Twelve Chairs* and *The Golden Calf*, Nikolai Erdman's play, *The Suicide*, and Mikhail Zoshchenko's short stories. I offer a more detailed examination of the literature of the communal apartment in chapter 2 of *Common Places*.

20. The establishment of new privileges allowed certain groups of the population—party apparatchiks, intellectual and artistic elites that collaborated with the regime (and were not arrested)—additional "living space." Living in a separate apartment was a mark of prestige. Yet, elements of the Soviet communal mentality persisted beyond communal apartments.

21. Edward Keenan, "Moscow Political Folkways," *Slavic Review* 45 (1986): 128.

22. Alexander Etkind, "Psychological Culture of the Soviets," Paper presented at the Nevada Conference on Soviet Culture, Las Vegas, November 1992.

23. Igor Kon, "Soviet Moral Culture," Paper presented at the Nevada Conference on Soviet Culture, Las Vegas, November 1992.

24. Walter Benjamin, "Paris, the Capital of the Nineteenth Century," in *Reflections* (New York: Harcourt Brace Jovanovich, 1989), p. 155.

25. Ibid., p. 154.

26. See Robert Vikkers, ed., *Istoriia SSSR v anekdotakh* (Smolensk, 1991).

27. Aleksandr Kabakov, "Na chuzhom pole," *Moskovskie novosti*, no. 49 (December 6, 1992): 5.

28. These figures are cited in *Ogonek*, no. 38 (September 1991): 18.

29. See Celestine Bohlen, "Moscow Privatization Yields Privacy and Problems," *New York Times*, February 28, 1993.

6

Moral Culture

IGOR S. KON

What could be worse than socialism?—
Whatever comes after it.
—Contemporary Russian joke

When Mikhail Gorbachev unfurled his reform banners in the late 1980s, many observers inside and outside Russia hailed perestroika as a moral renaissance. The Soviet Union was indeed a spiritually bankrupt society at the time, its citizens demanding a clean break with the past and yearning for a better future. Despite the new openness, or glasnost, changes have been slow and often very controversial. A public opinion survey conducted in February 1991 showed the country morally adrift and deeply divided about the course of reforms.[1]

"What do you think about public morality in our country?" the researchers asked a cross-section of the Russian population. Thirty-one percent answered that there had been a sharp moral decline in the last few years; 35 percent claimed things had not changed much, except for the fact that what had earlier been hidden had come to the fore; 21 percent said that public morals had definitely changed, mostly for the better; and 13 percent could not answer.

As these findings suggest, moral malaise is widespread in post-Soviet Russia. This is in large measure the legacy of the country's communist past. We shall examine this legacy and its impact on the country's future, but first a few words need to be said about the difficulties that students of moral culture face in dealing with such a complex phenomenon.

A historical, interpretive approach to Soviet moral culture should distinguish several interrelated yet analytically separate levels of morality. First, there are official norms and principles that elucidate the "communist morality" and that are spelled out in party documents, such as "The Moral Code of the Builders of Communism" and speeches and pronouncements by party leaders. Second, there is the theoretical/philosophical discourse where these moral norms are systematically interpreted and presented to the public through newspaper accounts, journal articles, textbooks, dictionaries, and the like. Third, we have to distinguish everyday moral consciousness—moral beliefs and values as reflected in the mass media, literature, and art. And fourth, we should address personal, subjective attitudes and the motives that guide the individual's moral behavior and that can be judged only indirectly, through the person's conduct and stated reasons. The relationship between these four levels of morality is complex, often muddled, and sometimes plainly contradictory.

The easiest to grasp is the official moral ideology, which tends to be rigid and formal in communist societies. Yet its real meaning could hardly be understood without any reference to ethical discourse, which is more sophisticated, flexible, and context dependent and often reveals subtle differences of opinion. Neither official ideology nor formal ethical discourse exhausts everyday moral consciousness, which assumes certain official principles, pays lip service to others, and ignores inconvenient moral imperatives altogether. Quite often—and not only in authoritarian societies—people think one way, talk another, and act a third. What makes repressive societies different is that double-think is a matter of survival for those living under dictatorial regimes. Saying what you really think and acting on your convictions in public could be ruinous. Henceforth, we must be careful about passing moral judgments on people in communist societies. If such a judgment is attempted, it must take into account the political context and specific circumstances within which a particular action (or inaction) took place.

Clearly mistaken are those Western observers who viewed Soviet society as a monolith, who bought the Soviet propaganda line about the internal unity and stability of Soviet society. Equally wrong-headed are attempts to divide Soviet citizens into honest prisoners and dishonest jailers: under the Soviet regime, each person was likely to be both a victim and a jailer. Finally, we should be skeptical about excommunists who now profess their undying hatred for communism. They have been too quick to exonerate themselves from past abuses while condemning Soviet society and its members as morally corrupt. While it is true that this society forced everyone to partake in the official hypocrisy, if only passively, it is not true that everyone shares the same burden of responsibility for the past.

A joke that dates back to the 1950s captures the peculiar moral situation that confronted the Soviet people. "God gave man three virtues—intelligence, honesty, and Communist party membership. He stipulated, though, that any one person could choose only two of these three virtues." That is to say, a party member who is an honest person must be a fool. A bright person and a party member is, by definition, dishonest.

And a person who is bright and honest could not be a Communist party member. Now, when my Russian colleagues insist that they were always honest and had acted on their convictions, I have to question either their intelligence or their credulity. As an old Russian proverb goes, "A drunk will sleep off his drunkenness, but a fool is a fool forever."

As a Soviet intellectual and once a member of the Communist party, I realize that the above considerations apply to myself. When an American colleague familiar with my work recently wrote a reference letter on my behalf in which he stated that Dr. Kon was a man of integrity who "never compromised" with the Soviet system, I told him that I felt honored but that his evaluation was basically wrong. Throughout my life, I have had to make compromises, sometimes very painful ones; otherwise, I would have been unable to work under the Soviet censorship system and publish my research, which made a difference for my people. Life without moral and political compromises is impossible even in a liberal democratic society. So what do you expect from us poor devils from a totalitarian/authoritarian country? Why should we pretend to have been better than we actually were, better even than an average person in your country? Please do not hold us up as a role model; we have our own lives to live. Besides, an uncompromising stance praised by all revolutionaries, including Bolsheviks, would be a poor foundation for a liberal democracy. Moral values may be absolute and moral judgments categorical, but what about moral action? Whenever we convert our beliefs into actions, we have to take risks, calculate the consequences, judge the lesser evil. The question, therefore, is not whether good, moral people should compromise but which compromise can be ethically justified and which one cannot.

With these considerations in mind, let us now turn to moral culture and moral reasoning in Soviet society.

The Foundations of Communist Morality

Moral reasoning conceals within itself a contradiction. On the one hand, there are ultimate values, absolute norms, and rigid imperatives that furnish standards for separating good from evil and determining ethical conduct. On the other hand, moral reasoning presupposes free will and personal freedom as a basis for individual moral choice and responsibility. The relationship between these two sides of morality is a dialectical one; it is bound to produce paradoxes and complicate practical moral judgment.

The moral system generated by communist ideologies is rather unique in that it seeks to dispense with both key elements of traditional morality. Marxist sociological historicism does not recognize any absolute, extra-social, transhistorical moral values. At the same time, communism is decidedly anti-individualistic and antilibertarian. By placing social (state, party, group) loyalties above individual rights, Marxist collectivism tends to nourish moral irresponsibility and expedient conformity. In its infancy, the Soviet regime denounced any morality as a bourgeois invention, a vestige of religion alien to a society undergoing a communist revolution. Disputes about the revolutionary proletariat and a new morality that might replace the traditional one were extremely popular in the early 1920s. As soon as the revolutionary order stabilized, however, Soviet ideologists came to the conclusion that the new society needed moral legitimation.

In his famous speech at the Third Congress of the All-Russian Communist Youth League, on October 2, 1920, Lenin announced that all education and teaching of contemporary youth should be an "education in the spirit of communist morality."[2] He hastened to add that the proletarian morality would have nothing to do with the old moral systems. "Our morality is completely subservient to the interests of the proletarian class struggle. Our morality is deduced from the interests of the proletariat"; "the fundamentals of communist morality help us strengthen and complete our struggle for communism."[3]

This relativistic formula lends itself to different interpretations, including a humanistic one. Insofar as the Marxist social utopia—communism—aims at universal justice and seeks to abolish all exploitation, it can be taken to mean that "only that which is moral expresses the proletariat's interests and strengthens communism."[4] However, this liberal paraphrase only serves to show how loosely and arbitrarily the Marxist dogma was interpreted in the Soviet Union, especially in its waning years. We should bear in mind that Lenin's formula was not just a theoretical statement, an abstract philosophical doctrine. It should be judged against the backdrop of ruthless Bolshevik practices. In this specific historical context, Lenin's reduction of morality to class interests and the subordination of ethics to political expediency should be taken literally. Neither Lenin nor his successors ever reasoned morally. Moral language simply helped the authorities legitimate their political interests and justify their policies.

Having dispensed with God as an ultimate value-giver and the individual as a free agent responsible for his or her action, communists confronted the problem of grounding their moral values. In the 1920s, it was a messianic class—"the proletariat"—that was proclaimed to be the repository of the new moral vision. In the 1930s, the party paid only lip service to "the interests of the working class." Undivided loyalty emerged as the cardinal virtue—loyalty to the Communist party, which proclaimed itself "the mind, honor, and consciousness of our time," and to the state, which took the place of civil society. There was no place left for privacy (the Soviet citizen had no right to lead a private life hidden from or unaccountable to the party) or for moral decisions (the party, the state, and the working collective were always right). The individual's civic duty was to the state, his political loyalty to the Communist party. Even at the peak of the totalitarian repression, however, elements of moral culture survived in the mass consciousness.

Basic moral feelings such as compassion and solidarity lingered. Publicly, everybody was applauding the infamous show trials against political dissidents that shook the country in 1937 and demanded death for "enemies of the people." But privately some people tried to help the victims in spite of great personal risks. Maksim Gorky's formula, "If the enemy does not surrender, it must be liquidated," did not stamp out compassion for the innocent victims who suffered during the political purges.

Another factor that spared traditional morality from total extinction and that became the trademark of Soviet moral culture was what George Orwell called double-think—the capacity to rename things and to combine, quite sincerely and without guilt, incompatible beliefs about the same subject. To some extent, double-think was really a condition for survival. Official values were to be taken on faith and obeyed unswervingly. Yet anybody naive or stupid enough to do so would be doomed, for the Soviet system never functioned in line with its official pronouncements. At the same time, rejecting official values in toto would have been socially dysfunctional: everyone had to use the official language, and it was easier to do so automatically, without much reflection. Complete and self-conscious cynicism, with its sharp division between public and private life, would be unbearable for most people.

Double-think is fundamentally amoral. It is incompatible with individual self-realization and moral responsibility. Yet, paradoxically, it could occasionally provoke reflection on the reasoning and language that best applies to the given context and circumstances, and by their very nature, reflection and doubt are subversive and antitotalitarian. Thus, double-think is a doubly manipulative strategy: it helps the system manipulate individual consciousness, but it also allows the individual to evade the pressures of the system and to turn subservience into lip service.

Official pronouncements on Soviet moral culture were always internally contradictory, and, as in every orthodoxy, the changing interpretations of the dogma were more important than the dogma itself. After Stalin's death, Soviet society grew more socially, politically, and culturally heterogeneous. This is when conflicting interpretations of communist morality emerged. It became increasingly difficult to figure out what "genuine communist morality" was all about. As contradictions mounted, so did conscious and unconscious hypocrisy. The growing normative uncertainty, rightly perceived by party watchdogs as a sign of moral crisis, accorded a greater freedom of choice to individuals, who could no longer blame their own action or inaction on harsh reprisals and were increasingly confronted with the need to rationalize their conduct in moral terms. Indeed, freedom of choice is the very essence of morality. It is absent in a truly totalitarian culture, where you either have to accept the dominant ideology in its entirety or renounce any chance to work constructively within the existing society. Once the Soviet Union began to shed its Stalinist legacy, moral reasoning grew in prominence among Soviet citizens and even inside the Communist party itself.

The gradual emancipation of moral consciousness from political expediency was slow and painful. The first breakthrough came in the 1950s, when a relative autonomy and independence of morality from the economy and politics was reaffirmed.[5] The first sign of the revival of moral reflection was the emergence of ethical discourse. Intellectually primitive at first, it raised some new or, to be more precise, quite old but completely forgotten questions. Critically important in this respect were the liberal reforms attempted by Nikita Khrushchev.

The Communist party was interested not in changing society but in preserving its rule. The language of universal moral values suited this purpose much better than did relativistic class consciousness. The moralization of Soviet ideology meant its partial depoliticization, as well as the recognition of private life. Still, the private sphere was understood quite narrowly as encompassing primarily marriage and the family, and even then the individual was expected to follow the general guidelines laid down by the Communist party. It is remarkable that neither the *Philosophical Encyclopedia* published in the 1960s nor six consecutive editions of *The Dictionary of Ethics* that appeared between 1965 and 1989 had an entry on private or personal life, which was mentioned only in passing, with the standard reminder that private life should not be opposed to public life. Notice that these were among the most liberal publications of their time.

The Communist party had its own reasons for emphasizing the moral underpinnings of reforms. For one thing, moral reasoning was aimed at the excesses of revolutionary morality, which claimed countless victims, including devoted party members, during the Stalinist era. Also, the moralization of politics was meant to tap new sources of productivity in the labor force. A good example of how the party used morality was the Moral Code of the Builders of Communism, which was incorporated into the Communist party program in 1961. While emphasizing the importance and specificity of moral norms, this code presented morality in a formal and authoritarian manner as a set of prescriptions for moral conduct, which, the document claimed, had already been realized in Soviet society. Public opinion in the Soviet Union did not buy this premise. The Moral Code was generally perceived as a clumsy piece of propaganda and a monument to official hypocrisy.

From the party's standpoint, the Moral Code was chiefly a new ideological tool for social control, but liberal intellectuals managed to use it as an instrument of social criticism. The emphasis upon universal human values made more evident the unfulfilled promises and moral inadequacies inherent in the Soviet regime. Such concepts as "personality," "self," and "moral responsibility," which had been very much suspect in the 1930s and 1940s, got a foothold in public discourse in the 1960s. Conformism was openly spurned and personal integrity and autonomy highly praised. The notion of alienation also made a comeback, as did the ideas of human rights and religious freedom.

In 1964, Khrushchev was ousted from power, and the country entered the stagnation era marked by the inept leadership of Leonid Brezhnev. This shift made all the more painfully evident the tension between the developing moral consciousness and amoral social practices. At the level of mass consciousness, "morality was put on the very top of the value pyramid; it emerged as the fundamental hidden truth if not of all being, then at least of spiritual life."[6] Yet, socially and economically, Soviet life amounted to highly institutionalized inefficiency and corruption.

Judged against the backdrop of daily life, the new morality itself was exceedingly contradictory. Already in the early 1970s, sociological research could not support the official propaganda claim about the total incompatibility of the Western/capitalist and Soviet/socialist ways of life. Soviet laborers were expected to be motivated chiefly by moral incentives in their work, by the commitment to building a glorious society of the future. In fact, research showed that industrial workers considered a "good salary" and "their families' interests" to be the most salient factors contributing to their job satisfaction. And since a "good salary" was hardly ever paid, work was losing its centrality in laborers' value system. This shift in Soviet workers' attitudes was consistent with the trends that Western researchers found in the capitalist labor force.[7] Surveys of Soviet workers and engineers conducted in the 1970s showed that the values of creativity and initiative topped the list in the hierarchy of personal values, while self-discipline, meticulousness, and punctuality bore chiefly a negative connotation. A distinct shift in personal interests away from the sphere of work and public affairs to family life and consumer activity was undeniable.[8]

For the ruling Communist party, this shift was ideologically subversive and economically dysfunctional. The official ideology exhorted workers to improve labor discipline, to do more for less. This communist work ethic very much resembled the Protestant work ethic in its emphasis on symbolic rather than material rewards. The latter were denounced as hedonist and bourgeois-decadent. This moralizing propaganda was highly inefficient. Nobody, including party officials themselves, took it seriously. People did not want to work for the glory of the communist future and sought to escape from hopelessly bureaucratized public life into private worlds, where they could pursue personal and spiritual interests—literature, music, family life, sex, drinking. Everyday moral culture was becoming more and more individualistic. This trend could be defended theoretically using the Marxist theory of alienation, which decried work under conditions of exploitation, work devoid of meaning and precluding the all-round development of the personality.

To sum up, the moral language that became popular in the 1960s and 1970s served both conservative and critical purposes. While the party used it to relegitimize its rule, liberal forces employed it to highlight the country's problems and push it toward further reforms. Yet, when social, economic, and political issues are couched in moral language rather than treated in their own terms, you can be sure that nobody takes them seriously enough or is earnestly trying to solve them. Moral reasoning is no substitute for serious economic and political thinking. It may express a general discontent, but it does not offer constructive solutions. Moral criticism is often utopian and implicitly conservative, even when its explicit thrust is critical.

Before the 1970s, moral opposition to the regime relied chiefly on communist terminology and on juxtaposing "humanist" Marxism to Stalinist "distortions." This situation changed in the 1960s, when pro-Western dissidents singled out human rights as the central political and moral issue, thus elevating individual freedom above state interests. On the other side, Christian morality revitalized the discourse about absolute, eternal, and transhistorical moral values. Looked at from both these perspectives, the Soviet regime appeared economically moribund and morally depraved beyond salvation. Meanwhile, social escapism and passive resistance to the regime gained momentum among the general population.

Postcommunist Moral Culture

Changes in the former Soviet Union have been fast and dramatic, permeating all spheres of social and private life. People had no time to adjust to these changes gradually, to internalize them in succession. These transformations left in their wake a political turmoil that ripped at the fabric of society and hastened the collapse of the Soviet Union. No nation could take these momentous changes in stride, and the Soviet people were exceedingly ill prepared by their history for this rapid transformation.

Soviet culture and personality were geared not to innovation and change but to stability and stagnation. For many decades, communist ideology remained extremely conservative. Even minor innovations provoked suspicion. Social and cultural life was dull and tedious. A "secure future"—the main advantage that socialism had to offer over capitalism—had in practice meant an endless repetition of the past. This climate was suffocating for every creative personality, but for ordinary people this stagnant lifestyle became the norm, and when the winds of change finally began to sweep through society, they caught the vast majority of the population totally unprepared for the new challenges and opportunities.

Social change is inseparable from self-change, from experimentation with new identities. Yet the Soviet system systematically discouraged such experimentation. Individuality was suppressed as a sign of bourgeois individualism incompatible with the virtues of the New Soviet Man. The primitive egalitarianism in wages, the fear of competition, and especially the bureaucratic mentality that equated the individual with a "cog" in an impersonal clocklike social mechanism conspired to stifle personal initiative. The category of human rights, which historically had helped the individual to hold his own against the state, was eclipsed by the concept of the individual's obligations to society. The monistic world view endemic to Soviet Marxism—"one party, one truth, one leader"—bred a rigid, authoritarian personality impervious to doubt and militated against the cognitive complexity and intellectual tolerance sorely needed in times of rapid change. No wonder the reforms plunged the average Soviet into a state of confusion and made perestroika seem a menace or, to use Aleksandr Zinoviev's word, *katastroika*.

Loss of Identity

According to official propaganda, "Soviet man" possesses the following unimpeachable traits: he accepts the party's goals and principles and elevates society's interests over personal ones; work for the public good is for him the major source of meaning, dignity, and fulfillment in life; solidarity, collectivism, and internationalism are the norms that guide his relations with other people.[9] Needless to say, hardly any Soviet person took this ideological fiction seriously. At best, it was a vague normative statement telling people what they were supposed to be or, rather, appear. More often than not, this was mere ideological verbiage with no direct link to reality.

As an antidote to this irritating ideological cliché, an ironic version of Soviet man, or Homo Sovieticus, took shape in the public mind. The more popular term, Sovok, emerged in the 1980s. The word means a little shovel, which can be used for any purposes, especially for collecting dust. The Sovok was a personological correlate of the Soviet lifestyle, a model personality marked by conformism, laziness, inefficiency, hypocrisy, and irresponsibility. These traits were attributed to others. Nobody ever said,

"I am a Sovok." The retort—"Oh yes, you are!"—would be terribly insulting. One could openly acknowledge and discuss these traits without any damage to one's self-esteem. The guilty party was the social system; its victims were other individuals, never whoever used the term. This was a more or less conscious strategy of self-alienation that dispirited Soviets used to distance themselves from their society and its official values.

Few people would actually lament the disappearance of the Soviet man so defined. But the adjective "Soviet" also designated a certain civil (citizenship) and geographical (country) status. Now this connotation has been rendered meaningless and useless. Many other terms describing social roles and statuses associated with the Soviet system (party membership, academic degrees, social privileges, public prestige) have lost their power to confer a meaningful identity on the individual. Urgently needed are new self-definitions framed in more personal, nonbureaucratic terms. Finding them, however, has proven a daunting task for many people.

Let me offer a personal example. Who am I? In the past, while traveling abroad, I would usually mention my formal Soviet identity first. Now my identity is far more problematic. Am I a Russian? First and foremost, this term signifies an ethnic identity, and claiming to be a Russian, I would seem to renounce my half-Jewish origins. Am I a Jew? Psychologically, such a claim would be dubious. My language, culture, and education have been Russian. Long ago, I learned to feel Jewish because of anti-Semitism and discrimination, but an identity so acquired tends to be tenuous and negative. My political identity is also problematic. After leaving the Communist party in 1990, I lost a formal political affiliation and no longer wish to have any. My basic values are democratic and pro-Western, but I don't believe that Russian society can transform itself into a democracy overnight. I have written many books and articles; some, I believe, are reasonably good; but the criteria by which I judge my past work have changed and a critical self-examination is now clearly in order. I was born and lived through most of my life in Leningrad. Now my city is called St. Petersburg. Yet for me, whatever my attitudes to Lenin, Peter the Great, or Saint Peter, this name has only a dim historical connotation. I have been deprived of my birthplace—symbolically. So everything in my life is problematic; whatever self-definition comes to the fore, I could never help feeling like an impostor.

This self-reflection is more than the usual intellectual autoerotic play with existentialist categories. People who, unlike myself, cannot indulge in translating their uneasiness into theoretical concepts may want to take revenge upon someone they think had ruined their country, stolen their glorious past, and destroyed their familiar selves. I do not share these feelings, but I can understand them.

Adolescent Syndrome

This syndrome is marked by several interrelated qualities, such as a lack of historicity ("before us, there was nothing valuable"), maximalism ("all or nothing"), impatience ("everything immediately"), and negativism ("nothing is working and everything should be changed"). A trait found in all revolutionary visionaries and reinforced by the messianic attitudes of the pre-1917 Russian intelligentsia, the adolescent syndrome is unmistakable in present-day radical democrats.

The 1917 vintage Leninists believed that all previous world history was merely a prehistory and that "genuine history" began only with themselves. The old world injustice should have been completely destroyed and the brave new socialist world built on its ruins. The results of this reckless attitude are well known. Present-day anticommunists believe that seventy years of Soviet history were completely wrong and everything done during that time should be redone from scratch and as soon as possible. This is the old communist mentality in reverse. Before 1987, everything Soviet was by definition good and everything Western was bad. Now it's just the opposite: everything undesirable, including global problems (like pollution and drug addiction) is attributed to bad communist policies. The market economy, on the contrary, is seen as a synonym of humanism and social justice.

Envy

Like the adolescent syndrome, envy is a global phenomenon. It is much easier to love a stranger, someone you do not know, than your own neighbor. According to an old Moslem joke, Allah once decided to reward a holy man: "For your holiness," he told him, "I will fulfill your every wish, but on one condition. Whatever you ask for, your neighbor will receive twice as much." After long deliberation, the holy man said: "Oh, Allah! Take out one of my eyes!"

There are two strategies for coping with this grudging attitude. One is predicated on competition: "I'm better than my neighbor, and I will prove it by working harder and having more than he has!" The second strategy is envy: "I'm better than my neighbor, and I will not permit him to have more than I have!" It is a social as well as a psychological phenomenon. In preindustrial—*Gemeinschaft*—societies, individuals were very tolerant of outgroup inequalities, which were based on estate/status differences and held to be natural, immutable, and unquestionable. The individual's aspirations were strongly related to his or her social origin and status. Peasants did not compare themselves with the nobility; they inhabited very different social and cultural worlds. Yet the same people were extremely sensitive and intolerant to the good fortune of those around them (communal envy).

This phenomenon can be interpreted in several ways. In preindustrial societies people tend to believe that one person's gain means somebody else's loss: the quantity of available goods being limited, valuables can be obtained only through redistribution, at somebody else's expense, which is judged to be socially and morally unjust.[10] People shun social differentiation; they have a generalized mistrust of any individual achievement because it threatens to undermine familiar power, prestige, and authority relationships. Being a "greedy institution,"[11] *Gemeinschaft* "requires complete involvement of the individual, stability of social relations, and lack of differentiation of the personality as well as of the labor performed."[12] Because public, personal, anonymous, and face-to-face relations are relatively undifferentiated in preindustrial societies, a change in somebody's wealth or status undermines not only the power structure but the entire network of interpersonal relations within the community. People do not want these changes, hence their strong envious reactions.

These conditions change with the onset of the market economy, social mobility, urbanization, and the attendant growth in anonymity. Social stratification is no longer taken for granted and seen as something natural and immutable; social origin does not predetermine the aspirations of the individual, who can compare himself or herself to and compete with anybody within and outside his group. The growing competition breeds intergroup, class, and status envy, but these social conflicts are less likely to be personalized. The public consciousness accepts the fact that social and financial success can result not only from someone's unseemly action but from personal initiative and industry, which are redefined as positive qualities. Intragroup rivalry and envy do not disappear but become less odious, as well as a less efficient means of social control.

Now, turning to Russian history, we discover that the traditional peasant community existed there much longer and was considerably stronger than in the West. Egalitarian attitudes were further legitimized by the Russian intelligentsia's anticapitalist mentality, which idealized the village commune. The independent farmer—the kulak—was the most hated figure in early twentieth-century Russian classical literature. The leveling mentality sanctified by communist ideology served to reinforce these negative attitudes and further discourage personal initiative among Soviet citizens. An old anecdote captures the situation well. As the 1917 revolution rages in the streets of Petrograd, a countess asks her maid about the noisy crowds outside: "What do these people want?" "They urge that there be no more rich people." "Isn't that strange?" asks the puzzled old lady. "We always dreamed that there should be no poor people."

Marx himself was well aware of envy's corrosive power. He defined primitive egalitarian "barracks communism" as "envy institutionalized as a force."[13] Yet the abolition of private property and forced collectivization undermined individual autonomy and industry in the Russian population, infusing it with the vicious, militant, envious lumpen mentality, which effectively blocked every individual effort to do better and to rise above the average. Not to permit anybody to get ahead of you was psychologically more important than to move up personally and improve everybody's well-being. Combining hatred toward higher-ups with envy toward social equals, this mentality had a disastrous impact on the fate of perestroika itself. In retrospect, the privatization campaign should have been carried out first not in state-owned industry but in agriculture. Gorbachev's rather timid steps toward individual farming were undermined by the party and collective farm bureaucracies as well as by envious neighbors who dreaded the changes and cast independent farmers as their worst class enemies. Envy, disguised as social justice, is the most powerful enemy of social and economic progress.

Privileges Versus Rights

The Soviet mentality resembled that of a feudal society insofar as it elevated the particularistic norm of group privilege over the universalistic principle of human rights. Each social group or stratum in the Soviet Union had its own set of privileges. Some privileges were legal and open; others, illegal and secret. For example, high-level party and state officials received the so-called *kremlevka*—an assortment of high-quality food items for a symbolic price that hardly changed over some forty years. The material advantages residing in one's status were often far more substantial than anything one could purchase on a salary. Lost status meant lost privileges. Exercising your privilege was both your right and your duty. Privilege distribution worked as a powerful lever to ensure an individual's loyalty.

Years ago, someone I knew was appointed a special consultant to the Central Committee, a position that entitled him to a *kremlevka*. Being a bachelor and a human being of unusual moral qualms, he decided not to exercise this privilege. After he failed to collect his package the first time, an administrator politely reminded him about it. The second time around, his boss summoned him:

"Do you like your new job? Is everything okay?"

"Yes, I do. Thank you very much."

"Then why don't you claim your kremlevka?"

"I don't need it. I eat in the cafeteria."

"A lot of people in Moscow would be grateful if you gave them this food. It's up to you. But when you don't take it it looks like you want to be different and better than your colleagues here, and that is unacceptable. We hope that this issue will never come up again."

Economically, the highly stratified system of privileges resulted from the permanent shortages endemic to Soviet society. It was a particular way of rationing and distributing scarce goods. Yet, the symbolic meaning the privileges carried outweighed their material value. Hard work did not suffice if you wanted to get access to a certain good; you had to "belong," to find your way into a prestigious organization. In the early 1930s, the famous Soviet satirists, Ilya Ilf and Evgeny Petrov parodied this system by concocting an announcement: "Beer is sold only to trade union members." The more prestigious an organization, the more sophisticated its privileges. The party's Central Committee was especially ingenuous in marking status differences without any concern for the communists' professed egalitarianism. Even the smallest change in ritual was a serious social event. According to Fyodor Burlatsky, a noted Soviet journalist, a department head in the Communist party's Central Committee was entitled to have lunch in his office; his deputy could order for himself and his visitors a free cup of tea and cookies; and a subdivision head could count on a cup of tea, but without the cookies. One day a liberal ruling was handed down the line: from now on, the subdivision head could request cookies along with his tea. To mark the difference between him and his superior, however, the administration would provide a genuine cloth napkin to go with the deputy's tea cup, whereas the subdivision head had to make do with just tea and a simple paper napkin.

A similar hierarchy reigned in academic institutions, universities, and industrial plants. The National Academy of Sciences, for example, had two medical centers: one for simple mortals, and a special one (everything privileged, exclusive, and superior in quality was dabbed "special") for the most distinguished full professors. Yet within the special dispensary there was—and still is—its own hierarchy. If a professor was waiting for his turn at the doctor's office (the lines generally were not too long) and a corresponding member of the Academy came along, the last person to show up would go first. If a full member of the Academy showed up, he had clear precedence over a corresponding member. Status was more important than appointment. So, sometimes these highly esteemed gentlemen would have to explain to each other who was who: "Excuse me, please, I am a full member of the Academy and have to go first." "I beg your pardon, I am also a full Academy member and director of the Institute, so you will have to wait."

I once heard about a jocular announcement posted in the campus store at the Novosibirsk branch of the Academy of Sciences: "Imported furniture is now in stock and will be available for sale. Academicians are entitled to a dining room; corresponding members to a bedroom; professors with doctorates to a study; candidate-doctorate to an office desk; and junior research associates without scientific degrees to a kitchen stool."

The hierarchy of privileges embedded in the Soviet distribution system had a direct bearing on a person's self-esteem. But the same people who resented the privileges accorded to a higher stratum, were convinced that their own privileges were richly deserved: "Surely, these lazy and arrogant party apparatchiks have too much. But I am a full professor. My time is more valuable than that of a young assistant. Why should I wait in line? I have a legal and moral right to be served first." That is to say, Soviet citizens were fighting not for rights but for privileges, and the acute sense of identity loss in today's Russia is more than a little tinged with a nostalgia for lost privileges. This particular form of distributive justice was a part of the ancient bureaucratic ethos. It is still very much alive, and it constitutes a formidable barrier to market reforms and advances in human rights.

Learned Helplessness

For many decades, Soviet economic and social life was a highly institutionalized inefficiency, every individual initiative being directly or indirectly punishable. The harder one tried, the more frustrated and helpless one was made to feel. Everything progressive was doomed in advance. In the late 1970s, struggling for the recognition and institutionalization of Soviet sociology, my colleagues and I used to cheer, "Let's drink to the success of our hopeless endeavor!" One of my friends used to quote the advice an old prostitute gave her young colleagues: "First of all, girls, don't make a fuss when you are under the customer!" However boundless, sooner or later your energy would run out and you would get tired of fighting the authorities. Productive social activity was being gradually eliminated and replaced by bureaucratic simulation and meaningless rituals. The predominant and ever growing feeling in the 1970s and 1980s was social apathy.

This situation taught the individual "learned helplessness," which also functioned as a rational strategy for survival and, paradoxically, for getting ahead. People with ideas and ambitions were frowned upon, but politically savvy mediocrities were in demand. Complete social and moral irresponsibility went hand in hand with low-level aspirations, expectations, and performance. A worker's salary was virtually unrelated to either quantity or quality of work, and the worker knew that all elementary needs would be met by the state. An independent person would find this situation humiliating and intolerable, but most people learned to play the game and wait for the authorities to improve their lot.

The Soviet Union was a country of petty bureaucrats. Everybody, from industrial worker to university professor, was a state official. Both the Soviet social system and the system of socialization were essentially maternalistic. Like an authoritarian mother, the Communist party knew your "rational needs" better than you did yourself. She might have punished you for your mistakes, but she always had "your best interests at heart." The party and the state took care of you, and this authoritarian care and control were accepted as natural. In the 1990s, nobody seems to care, and many people feel abandoned and helpless, seeing no better future ahead. Hence the widespread pessimism, fear, and apocalyptic expectations, which sometime turn out to be self-fulfilling prophesies.

Traditionalism

The current Russian reforms are both democratic, insofar as they are directed against authoritarianism, and conservative, because they seek to restore the presocialist, capitalist social order. But how far back should we go? If postmodernism is a drive into the unknown future, then postcommunist traditionalism, like Moslem fundamentalism, is a groping for the unknown past. The recent past is rejected in favor of something more distant, something thoroughly forgotten. It is a return not to the "real" historical past but to the idealized, imaginary past, when everything was moral and beautiful.

This conservative utopia is multifaceted. On one side, it reflects the global disillusionment with modernity, a response to its contradictions and excesses. On the other side, it is a continuation of the Brezhnev era's social inertia, with its emphasis on stability and continuity. Finally, it is a specific form of anticommunist ideology.

Traditionalism is usually presented as a renaissance of spirituality, of universal (read "religious and moral") values and national traditions distorted or suppressed by the communist regime. But very often traditionalists appeal not only to presocialist but to precapitalist and preindustrial times and mores, conceived in exceedingly idealized terms. The traditionalist utopia is both unrealistic and authoritarian; you cannot turn history back and make people live according to rules that became problematic or lost their legitimacy centuries ago. But the greatest danger of traditionalism is that it is strongly linked with primitive and militant nationalism.

Prospects for the Future

The attitudes bred by the Soviet system do not bode well for Russia's moral rejuvenation and its ambitious economic and political reforms. The question is how—some would ask whether—this social heritage can be overcome.

On methodological grounds, I am skeptical about the view that paints "Homo Sovieticus" as an immutable entity. "National character," "modal personality," and similar concepts do better as loose metaphors than analytical concepts. This is not to suggest that historical continuity in the Russian or any other case is a fiction.[14] The interrelated syndromes mentioned above were spotted long before the Bolsheviks came to power and described by the Russian writers as *Oblomovism* (passivity, indecision, an incapacity for action), *Manilovism* (daydreaming and castle-building as a substitute for practical deeds), and *Khlestakovism* (irresponsibility, boastfulness, and cheating). But then, early twentieth-century Russian capitalism was not created by Oblomovs, Manilovs, or Khlestakovs. Envious and passive at home, "Sovok" is often quite successful after he has left Russia and settled in the United States or Israel, where the standards and expectations are different and where his efforts are duly rewarded. If people can be competitive, industrious, and thriving in emigration, why could they not do the same back home now that the social system is being changed? Perhaps they could, but first they have to confront the legacy of the past, and that means reinventing themselves.

The loss of identity is particularly hard on the old people and for those with a vested interest in the communist system: party and state officials whose bureaucratic mentality and experiences became useless and dysfunctional. Any intellectually rigid person is likely to find adaptation to the changing conditions a trying task. But let us not overlook private entrepreneurs, independent managers, and others who have found the personal resources to meet the new challenges head on. Age difference is a major factor in predicting an individual's response to the economic, political, and moral upheavals in postcommunist Russia.

What for people of my generation might be a disaster, young men and women often see as an opportunity. Without established social identities and privileges, they have nothing to lose. Recent public opinion polls show a sharp contrast between the older, less-educated, rural population, on the one hand, and younger, better-educated, urban respondents, on the other. Of the respondents below twenty-five, 63 percent had a positive attitude toward private property and the market economy, compared to 19 percent among those sixty years and older.[15] In another survey conducted in 1992, three-fifths of the respondents answered no when asked whether perestroika was a worthwhile undertaking. Several months later, 80 percent said that life was better before perestroika. Younger, better-educated, and urban dwellers, as well as individuals with connections to private and joint enterprises, strongly disagreed with that opinion.[16] People from this category were more willing to take personal risks in economic competition and strenuously opposed egalitarianism.[17] Young people tended to be more optimistic about their own future. When pollsters asked them, "Are young people capable of hard work?" 71 percent answered yes, and 79 percent believed that young people could show initiative.[18] These high hopes on the part of young people are more important for the country's future than the fears and anxieties that beset the older generation.

Age and education are also linked with the general shift to postmaterialist values. A 1990 survey conducted in the European part of the Soviet Union and another carried out in the Russian Federation in January 1991 showed an upsurge of postmaterialist, spiritual values. "Like other advanced industrial societies," the researchers conclude, "Russia seems to be undergoing an intergenerational shift from overwhelmingly Materialist values to increasingly Postmaterialist values—and this shift brings with it growing mass pressures for democratization."[19] Postmaterialists are much more likely to support core democratic values—free speech, pluralistic politics, independent mass media, competitive elections, and political tolerance.

All this sounds promising, but Russian youth have been shaped in the post-Soviet years not by the nascent social order but by the decomposing old system. As the sociological research by Ronald Inglehart and his associates show, the high levels of trust and subjective well-being necessary for economic and political cooperation flourish in times of economic prosperity and individual security. Yet the data from the 1990 World Values survey in Eastern Europe

> reveal the lowest levels of subjective well-being ever recorded. . . . In the surveys carried out in Russia, Belarus, Bulgaria, Latvia, and Lithuania, about as many people describe themselves as "unhappy" as "happy," and about as many say they are "dissatisfied with their lives as a whole" as say they are "satisfied." This is an extraordinary and alarming finding. In 1990, these societies ranked far below much poorer countries such as India, Nigeria or China. . . . We view this as an indication of profound malaise among the general public.[20]

Young people are not exempt from this malaise. There is a tremendous gap between their ultimate values and long-term goals, on the one hand, and their short-term plans and available means, on the other. Postcommunist youth are decidedly materialist and procapitalist in their broad outlooks, but their capacity for honest, hard work is less than obvious. The commonly expressed desire is to get rich quickly, without much effort or sacrifice. According to a Russian public opinion survey conducted in September 1991, the most popular answer (53 percent) to the question, What is most important to young people? was "material well-being," and the least popular (3 percent) "public activity." And this is not just an over-reaction to the old hypocritical communist clichés.

Young people mature quickly. As the 1993 national opinion poll shows, getting an education and a steady job for a certain salary has lost its appeal, whereas the prestige of going into business has gone up. Of those polled, 35 percent said that the best thing for a man sixteen to eighteen years old to do today is to study, 8 percent mentioned getting a job, and 19 percent of the young men singled out business (only 5 percent of the respondents felt that business was a sound option for a young woman). Of the respondents in this poll, 24 percent could not decide, and as many listed another venue as the most promising opportunity in the early 1990s.

Comparative analysis of job motivation and long-term life plans among Russian and Ukrainian teenagers (high school students) in 1985 and 1991[21] reveals these three consistent trends: (1) a growing concern with money and other material values; (2) a sharp rise in social expectations, be it salary, prestige, or power position; (3) a drastic drop in the willingness to take on hard or unpleasant work. But if in 1985 high school graduates' expectations were reasonably realistic, that is, they hoped for what they could realistically achieve, in 1991 their expectations surged dramatically and became utterly unrealistic. Now teenagers want to have everything, to have it immediately, and without extra effort. They also expect more help from their parents and public institutions than is possible in these troubled times. These hedonistic and dependency-bound expectations are dysfunctional for both socioeconomic and moral development. Such an orientation is more likely to get a young person involved in crime than in constructive efforts. And the crime rate in Russia is growing dangerously high.

Another dream for young people is emigration. Eighty-five percent of Magun and Litvintseva's respondents declared that they would like to go abroad to work temporarily, 49 percent want to leave the country permanently, provided a decent position is available, and 19 percent want to emigrate at any price.

In a survey conducted in October 1994 that asked Moscow high school students whether they would like to emigrate and live in another country, 16.5 percent answered yes without hesitation, 21 percent preferred to do so, 18 percent were uncertain, 23.5 percent preferred to live in their homeland, and only 21 percent said they definitely wanted to live in Russia.[22]

All this should come as no surprise. Russia's economy is sputtering. The country lacks a legal or binding moral order. Internal standards were compromised long ago by the hypocrisy of the communist elite and overly stringent external control. To cheat on or withdraw from the all-powerful Soviet state was risky but not amoral; in a way, it was the only chance to feel free. Now external control is loose and there are neither moral restrictions nor role models. There is much public talk about morality, universal human values, and religious renaissance, but the real situation is that of complete anomie, lawlessness, and normlessness.

Although the old communist bureaucracy is bankrupt, the "democrats" are not much better. All too often they come across as irresponsible chatterboxes full of false promises. Once swept to power, some proved to be even more corrupt than their predecessors. Ironically, there is more corruption and cynicism in post-Soviet society than under Brezhnev's rule, when officialdom paid some homage to appearances and feared losing its privileges. Before 1985, the Soviet Union was the most hypocritical country in the world, now it is the most cynical.

According to a 1994 national opinion survey, Russians feel that the situation has improved considerably in such areas as religious freedom, freedom of speech, political association, and individual choice. But when asked whether people have more influence on governmental policies, only 6 percent discerned any improvement, 47.5 percent saw no change, 20.2 percent believed the situation was worse, and 26.6 percent did not have an opinion. By the same token, only 7.4 percent felt that the government was equally fair and just with all the people, 38.4 percent saw no change, and 31.8 percent said that the situation was now worse than before.[23] A television poll done in October 1994 revealed that 95 percent of respondents were convinced that real power in their country belonged not to the president or Parliament but to criminal capital. I tend to share this opinion.

The moral lesson young people are likely to learn these days is every man for himself, or, as Ilf and Petrov put it long ago, "Rescuing a drowning man is the task of the drowning man himself." As a survival strategy in times of cataclysm, this is better than learned helplessness, but it hardly qualifies as a moral imperative.

In its developed form, Western individualism presupposes not only "freedom from" but also "freedom for," the latter requiring self-control, respect for social rules, moral norms, and a sense of personal responsibility. New Russian individualism is basically a product of anomie. In the absence of an established value hierarchy, the breakdown of external control spells anarchy and chaos. Hence the talk about "the banditization of the whole country" so common today.

Such pessimism is not universal, however. According to data compiled by the National Center for Public Opinion Research, 43 percent of individuals polled in 1994 agreed that it would be better if things today were the way they were before Gorbachev came to power in 1985, but 45 percent rejected this view, and 16 percent did not have a definite opinion. Moreover, the younger, the more educated, and the more socioeconomically secure the respondent, the more likely he was to be optimistic about the current situation and confident about prospects for the future. Social changes that were judged to be natural and inevitable by well-adjusted social strata were likely to be seen as a tragic mistake and a product of conspiracy by the advantaged. Indeed, older respondents in the above poll felt more vulnerable and helpless today than in the past.[24] Pessimism, fear, and apocalyptic expectations often function as self-fulfilling prophecies; they are also apt to be exploited by self-styled "prophets" and "saviors." Widespread among Russians in the mid-1990s is the belief in supernatural powers, which can be seen as just another manifestation of learned helplessness.

The moral situation in Russia is muddled to the point of being schizophrenic. The law is routinely flouted, property-grabbing passes for privatization, disoriented people search desperately for ways to stay afloat, hurting each other in the process. The prescribed remedies are extreme and contradictory. Absolute individual freedom and total self-reliance are praised in the same breath as stern discipline and Christian virtues. The individualistic, liberal position seems to be more in line with the market economy, democratic pluralism, and values espoused by the younger generation. Contemporary Russian youth look more pragmatic and down to earth than idealistic and romantic. Now that the familiar order has dissolved and nothing is guaranteed, a return to the materialistic values of economic and physical security seems natural and inevitable. Yet this trend may be temporary. When—and if—a certain standard of living is recovered, a global shift toward postmaterialist values, including moral pluralism, may well be the order of the day.

Current socioeconomic trends in Russia do not lend themselves readily to unambiguous judgment. We know where we are coming from, but we are less sure where we are heading and where and when we will get there. It would be naive to mistake primitive capital accumulation and the upsurge in organized crime in the country for a moral renaissance and a restoration of "universal values." Thomas Hobbes's dictum—war of each against all—describes the current realities well. The Russian word for this situation, when there are no moral limits, is *bespredel*. The word comes from criminal slang and tells us a great deal about the moral state of the country. For the young, the strong, and the predatory it is a state of unlimited possibilities checked only by those stronger than them. For the old, the weak, and the nonaggressive, the same situation means helplessness and hopelessness from which only death can spell relief.

For those determined to survive under the current conditions, a clear consciousness of private stakes and group interests (along the lines enunciated by Marx in his theory of class struggle) are more useful than abstract talk about universal human values, particularly when those values are expounded by the political jackals and economic gangsters who have built their fortunes on the general suffering.

In fairness, we should say that a class analysis does not preclude the possibility of agreement. Some positive experience in consensus-building has accumulated in the last few years, and herein lies hope for the future. Even in its most primitive form, the institution of private property encourages the owner to take personal initiative and gives him sense of dignity unknown to a people enslaved by a totalitarian state. The revolutionary situation has also taught the individual to assume personal responsibility, as the resistance to the 1991 and 1993 coups testify. Unfortunately, neither individual nor collective egoism can furnish a foundation for morality. Several generations are likely to pass before basic moral feelings, such as respect for human dignity, labor, and property, come back to life. Along the line, one would have to contend not only with the communist legacy but also with the harrowing memories of the current *bespredel*. Given the criminal and highly distorted character of the Russian anticommunist revolution, I suspect that the moral consciousness in Russia will remain tinged with antibourgeois sentiments for quite a while. It is likely to vacillate between two poles: the conservative-religious and the socialist (though not communist!). Primitive moralizing, leveling distributive justice, and religious authoritarianism are easier to comprehend and practice than autonomous morality and social realism. Does this scenario offer welcome portents for the future? As a French proverb says, "Qui vivra verra."

Notes

I want to thank the George Soros Foundation and the International Research and Exchanges Board for their support of this study.

1. Unpublished data. Quoted with the permission of the National Center for Public Opinion Research.

2. V. I. Lenin, "Zadachi soiuzov molodezhi," *Polnoe sobranie sochinenii,* vol. 41 (Moscow: Politizdat, 1962), p. 309. Here and elsewhere, the translation from the Russian is by Igor Kon, unless otherwise indicated.

3. Ibid., pp. 309, 313.

4. A. A. Guseinov, "Kommunizm i nravstvennost," *Eticheskaia mysl 1988* (Moscow: Politizdat, 1989), p. 9.

5. A. A. Guseinov, "Perestroika: Novyi obraz morali," *Eticheskaia mysl 1990* (Moscow: Politizdat, 1991), p. 11.

6. Ibid.

7. See Ronald Inglehart, *Culture Shift in Advanced Industrial Society* (Princeton: Princeton University Press, 1990).

8. See V. A. Iadov, "The Social Personality Type," *Soviet Education*, no. 9 (September 1989).

9. G. L. Smirnov, *Sovetskii chelovek: Formirovanie sotsialisticheskogo tipa lichnosti* (Moscow: Politizdat, 1980), pp. 231–51.

10. See George M. Foster, "Peasant Society and the Image of Limited Good," *American Anthropologist*, no. 2 (April 1967): 293–315. See also James Dow, "The Image of Limited Production: Envy and the Domestic Mode of Production in Peasant Society," *Human Organization*, no. 4 (Winter 1981): 360–63; Siegfried-Rudolf Dunde, "Symptom oder Destruktivkraft: Zur Funktion des Neides in der Gesellschaft," *Sociologia-Internationalis*, no. 2 (1984): 217–33.

11. See Lewis A. Coser, *Greedy Institutions* (New York: Free Press, 1974).

12. Rose Laub Coser, *In Defense of Modernity: Role Complexity and Individual Autonomy* (Stanford: Stanford University Press, 1991), p. 138.

13. K. Marx. "Oekonomisch-philosophische Manuskripte aus den Jahre 1844," in Karl Marx and Friedrich Engels, *Werke*, Erganzungsband, Erste Teil (Berlin, 1968), p. 534.

14. See, for example, Edward L. Keenan, "Muscovite Political Folkways," *Russian Review* 45 (1986).

15. *Mir mnenii i mnenia o mire*, Sluzhba VP, Bulletin no. 8 (August 1992): 6.

16. *Mir mnenii i mnenia o mire*, Sluzhba VP, Bulletin no. 2 (February 1992): 1.

17. *Mir mnenii i mnenia o mire*, Sluzhba VP, Bulletin no. 9 (November 1991): 4.

18. Ibid., p. 6.

19. See James L. Gibson and Raymond M. Duch, "Postmaterialism and the Emerging Soviet Democracy," Paper presented to the 1991 Annual Meeting of the American Political Science Association, Washington, D.C.

20. Ronald Inglehart, "Democratization in Global Perspective," Paper presented at the Annual Meetings of Midwest Political Science Association, Chicago, April 9–11, 1992, p. 35.

21. See V. Magun, *Motivatsiia truda i trudovaia moral v postsotsialisticheskom rossiiskom obshchestve i ikh predistoriia* (Moscow: Institut Sotsiologii RAN, 1992); V. S. Magun and A. Z. Litvintseva, *Zhiznennye pritiazaniia rannei iunosti i strategiia ikh realizatsii: 90e i 80e gody* (Moscow: Institut Sotsiologii RAN, 1993).

22. *Tsenter-plus*, October 10, 1994.

23. *Izvestiia*, October 26, 1994.

24. Lev Gudkov and Vladimir Shokarev, "Mnogie gorozhane toskuiut o proshlom," *Segodnia* (June 25, 1994).

7

Popular Culture

ZARA ABDULLAEVA

"Morality? Do you want to know about morality? Well, we believe that morality is not to be found in virtue, that is, not in reason, discipline, good manners, or honesty; quite to the contrary, we find it in sinfulness, in danger to which one exposes oneself and evil which could devour us. We believe it is morally loftier to perish, to drive oneself into the ground, than to save one's soul."
—Shosha, the Russian heroine of Thomas Mann's *The Magic Mountain,* explaining to the German Hans Castorp what Russians mean by morals

Well known is Fyodor Tyutchev's maxim that "Russia is baffling to the mind." Indeed, any knowledge adequate to this mysterious subject is bound to be indirect and marred by contradictions. Perhaps the most promising approach to Russian Soviet reality is through its folklore. In its fairy tales, songs, customs, and jokes, Russian culture discloses its generative code, its secret meaning, which has remained unperturbed by all the revolutions and perestroikas. The fabled realm inhabited by this nation is indeed enchanted: the most common things go astray here, while extraordinary ones come to pass. Cause–effect connections have been severed for good, common sense casually defied, and some impenetrable magic rules that fools smart people and gives fools a break.

Neither logic, nor psychology, nor positivist science can do justice to the bizarre laws that govern life in this wondrous domain. Artistic intuition alone can catch the elusive meaning of the ambivalent Russian psyche. Characteristically, writers and artists have been Russia's best interpreters, its true phenomenologists and sociologists. Folklore has furnished us a superindividual narrative in which the peculiarly Russian reality found its conscious expression. Let us set aside methodological prejudices, then, take another look at what we have seen so many times before, and try to fathom what has been so "baffling to the mind." Just as a pain in the solar plexus points to something beyond the muscle itself, our intuitive knowledge reveals a region of pain undeniably real to those who feel it, even if the region itself is phantom.

> Alas, a fairy tale's a lie, but there's a clue in it,
> A lesson to be learned by all you valiant lads.[1]

Although every fairy tale is, strictly speaking, a lie, a truth is to be extracted from it. What we find here is a subtext for the text, a clue that beckons us. The fairy tale is beyond the truth/falsehood dichotomy; it wrenches the duo from its habitual context and places it in a new one—say, the context of Soviet civilization.

"A fairy tale," wrote renowned folklorist Vladimir Propp, "reflects not only prehistoric times but also medieval mores and customs and feudal social relations, as well as the relationships found under capitalism."[2] And, we should add, under socialism, which built a feudal society according to mythological blueprints deeply rooted in the past and fully realized in Soviet folklore.

The folk spawned their fairy tales, tried to bring them to life in a magnificent experiment, and got a hernia in the process, but did not break down completely. They harnessed life's destructive forces in the creative power of the anecdote and sublimated into song their heroic dreams and romantic temperament, their perennial loneliness and desire for intimacy, their public-mindedness and individualistic urges.

In a mass culture, popular songs play the role once reserved for folk songs, and Soviet folklore is more than just a subterranean anecdote culture, an unofficial realm that serves the nation as a testing ground for its history and geography. Soviet folklore also includes the song—the tried and true hero of this surreal history and geography. The song is an abject necessity for us, an almost physical need, a ritual of everyday culture and a symbol of faith. Since singing and fibbing have always been favorite pastimes in which we engage with ardor and passion and without any prompting from the outside, we, as a nation, can attain happiness, or rather dissipate our grief, not in some distant future but in the present, in the here and now of the moment. As the saying goes, "Dear is the spoon when dinner's ready."

Our fairy tales nourished the arrogant conviction that any fool could master the world in an instant. The fools and heroes could be robbed of their prospects—for in the end, cadres did determine everything ("cadres are everything," Stalin said)—but anecdote sarcastically elevated the slaves in their own eyes, turned them into kamikazelike heroes, and simultaneously mocked and deflated the sinister jesters lording it over them. The song was always generous and giving, comforting the folk while they were being decimated.

Of course, it was not the lyrics alone that made Soviet popular songs so vitally important. The brilliant music by Isaak Dunaevsky, the Pokrass brothers, Vasily Solovyov-Sedoi, and others had much to do with their success, but this should be the subject of a separate musicological study. By the same token, I leave unexplored the songs by Aleksandr Galich, Bulat Okudzhava, Vladimir Vysotsky, and other Soviet bards who wrote authorial songs distinguished by their creators' inimitable individuality. Their songs gained wide circulation after Stalin's death, especially among the educated strata, but they stood somewhat apart from mainstream Soviet popular culture, which is the focal point of this chapter.

* * *

A well-known avant-garde painter, Sergei Mironenko, coined the term "alcoholic consciousness" to describe the state of mind peculiar to "Homo Sovieticus." I think the artist gave us a scientific definition of Soviet mentality. Soviet lore has its direct equivalent: To make heads or tails of this takes a quart of vodka. This paradox has its roots in Russian fairy tales, where the anonymous narrator invariably lapses into alcoholic consciousness as he recounts the incredible feast he chanced to attend: "And I was there, drank wine and beer, it all poured down my whiskers, none landed in my mouth." This line, familiar to every Russian child, blurs the distinction not only between truth and falsehood but also between sane and insane, victors and victims, drunk and sober. Which is why it is said, "What is on a sober man's mind is on the drunkard's tongue." Actually, the two are one person. And the reality such a person confronts is the same. What is different is the amount of alcohol consumed, which could radically alter one's state of mind and attitude toward reality.

"In a sense, reality was separated from the state, evolving by itself according to fairy-tale logic. Thus, the Soviet artist, insofar as he exemplified Homo Sovieticus, developed a peculiar double-mindedness. Truth and lie were mere conventions to him, and good and evil traded places all the time."[3] Aleksandr Zinoviev made a similar observation: "In regard to the Russian mentality, the fundamental dilemma, 'To be or not to be,' amounts to this: 'To drink or not to drink.' The answer is self-evident: 'To drink, of course!'"[4]

To drink is to be alive. No wonder that in the early perestroika years vodka was rationed and citizens were given coupons for this most basic of all staples. The "alcoholic consciousness," blending fairy-tale and everyday reality, is also a utopian consciousness, the state of mind that tends to erase the fine line between the real and the unreal. Hence, every Soviet citizen was, by necessity, an artist and an alcoholic, a hero and a villain, a left-handed and a right-handed person at the same time. And until very recently, a romantic. Lenin's formula that "art belongs to the people" is quite literally true in a nation where people, like genuine artists, live an imaginary life. And this people's art is rightfully tagged socialist realism—a fabled reality (*skazkobyl*), a truthful lie. Being determines consciousness, and alcoholic consciousness determines an otherworldly being, an aesthetic reality that blends metaphoric life with realistic art.

The Russian fairy tale culminates in the popular festival with the obligatory feast where the new king generously treats his people to food and drinks. With the goods given away, the hero ends his path as the fairy-tale character and begins his happy life in . . . song, in our Song of Songs.

"It's hard to live by song alone," sang the popular bard Aleksandr Vertinsky. But then, it is harder to survive without it. Drinking and singing are the two constants firmly embedded in our national character and fully independent of the changing political climate. You can lose yourself in a song just as well as in wine. The song heals your wounds like a proven folk medicine. You pour your heart into it, you struggle and rejoice, you live and you die, and you come back to life with every song you sing: "For only song, and song alone, will always stay with you!" Such is the sum of wisdom one gleans from Russia's long and troubled history. As a popular song goes,

> This song is faster than a bird,
> It makes our oppressors tremble,
> The riksha and the coolie sing this song,
> And so does the Chinese rifleman.

Again, this is hardly a metaphor. In 1940, a Chinese composer implored Dunaevsky, who was an immensely popular Russian composer, to send him sheet music, which would enable the Chinese "to make their own weapons, which would seal the enemy's defeat."[5] In 1955, Tokyo Orchestra musicians rehearsing with David Oistrakh, a Russian violinist, greeted the maestro with a patriotic Soviet tune "Broad Is My Native Land," surprising him with this "very unusual way to express their feelings and sympathies."[6] Paul Robeson confessed that among his favorite tunes was the Soviet "Song of the Motherland": "I know some people will say this is not a genuine 'folk' tune," explained Robeson. "But . . . the people took this song close to heart, made it their own, and so it is as much a folk song as the American song about the Mississippi."[7]

The song is the ultimate proof of the Russian Soviet people's boundless generosity. The song will never betray you. It is "your friend forever and ever." It is always on your side, whether you are a winner or a loser, an executioner or a victim:

> Sometimes, when responsibility weighed too heavily on the General Secretary and President of the USSR, M. S. [Mikhail Gorbachev] poured his soul and all his emotions, bottled up inside him during the endless political battles, into a heartfelt song. Just before his resignation, Gorbachev received Chancellor Helmut Kohl in the luxurious mansion that once belonged to the former first secretary of the Ukrainian Communist party. By then, the two were on quite friendly terms, calling each other "Helmut" and "Misha." And so they were chatting about things. Deep down they both knew that Gorbachev's days were numbered, that the man could not stay much longer as his country's President. . . . Then, all of a sudden, M. S. burst into song. At first, he sang Ukrainian songs, then switched to those of his native South Russia, the songs from the Kuban river region. Good-natured Kohl, who mellowed quite a bit, tried to sing along, though he did not know the words. They sat there, arms around each other, for quite a while, as I was listening for the last time to Gorbachev's soft, pleasant baritone.[8]

> You don't bid farewell to the song,
> The song will never say good-by to you!

Without a song, the image of the Russian/Soviet man would remain incomplete. Not only did it accompany him wherever he went, "The song is marching down the street, it bids you to follow suit." Like a shadow in a fairy tale, the song is capable of miraculous feats. In one of Evgeny Shvarts's plays, *The Shadow*, a simple country girl tells a near-sighted scholar: "Can't you see? We live in a very special country. What is but a fairy tale in other places, what other folks would see as just a fable, happens around here every day."[9]

Our people's fondness for songs signals the triumph of fairy tale over reality, poetry over truth. Consider the following historical fact: "Toward the end of the national congress of Stakhanovites [laborers who routinely exceeded their daily production quotas] who had gathered at the Kremlin in November 1935, the audience unanimously broke out into singing the march from a popular movie, *The Merry Boys*."[10] It is no accident that the best workers, who were "born to make a fairy tale come true" and who learned from their own experience that the harder the work, the merrier the life, found it most natural to sing, as though enchanted by the miracle of their daily labor and their magic helper—the song.

"Your songs," a young Pioneer from Voronezh once told Dunaevsky, "are cheerful and combative, tender and lyrical. They show us how beautiful our young lives are and help us live."[11] Like a wise teacher, the song conveys the boundless beauty of our life, "where every man can breathe so freely." Truly, one might have suffocated without it.

Take a closer look at the confession with which the narrator typically ends the fairy tale, "And I was there, drank wine and beer, it all poured down my whiskers, none landed in my mouth." Such clumsiness! It surely sounds peculiar. The narrator assures us he was there at the feast, he claims to have partaken in it, yet his stomach is empty. The phantom reality we encounter in this story perfectly fits the familiar stereotype about "the mysterious Russian soul"—and "body," for it presages famines in a country with fabulous riches.

A saying hints at the mystery not only of the Russian "soul" and "body," but also of their *locus operandi* ("in every fairy tale one finds a germ of truth," said Lenin). Let us keep scanning our fairy tale for further clues about the Russian soul and body and the country they inhabit. There must be a blinking light in this archetypical paradox of drinking without imbibing, a fateful insight into the Russian curse—the other side of this blissful life, where we (the collective, the folk) are born to make the dream come true, where I (the individual) was at this feast, drank wine and beer, but went to bed with an empty stomach.

A modern paraphrase translates this sacramental insight from Russian into Russian: "We are born to make Kafka come true." This saying resonates with another archetypical task-setting derived from ancient Russian lore: "Hurry I know not where, bring me I know not what." Here is a variation on the same theme gleaned from a Soviet song:

> "How will I find you? Where shall I write you?"
> "Doesn't matter," he quietly said. "Just send your letter some-where."

The fairy-tale hero has no idea where he is going or what he is expected to do, but in real life he has managed "to make Kafka come true." The hero is doomed to an unhappy ending. Some earthly powers might be singled out for the blame, but in fact there is an anonymous curse hovering over the land like a dark cloud, condemning its people to lawlessness and chaos, a sentiment that a contemporary anecdote plays upon:

Two men are walking on the streets:
"The weather is terrible. Rain with snow!"
"Those big shot bastards! They do whatever they want to us!"

Although the nation did not read Kafka, it did turn into a collective Kafka and transformed its world into an exquisitely absurd place. The nation bowed not so much to natural or social forces as to magic existential powers. There may be no place for common sense or reasoned action in this spellbound world, but there is plenty of room for imagination and creative narrative.

The sagacious Marquis de Custine had this to say about the Russians: "They have more finesse than tact, more plasticity than sensitivity, more flexibility than spontaneity, more grace than tenderness, more insightfulness than ingenuity, more quick-wittedness than imagination, more perceptiveness than wit, but the quality that distinguishes the Russian the most is shrewdness."[12] The last point sounds odd: the ability to figure out one's best interest must be the last trait this patient folk possesses. Yet Marquis de Custine guessed the secret deeply buried in the Russian psyche: in order to survive, this nation had to exercise its uncommon rationality—irrational rationality. It is this peculiar brand of rationality that bred some supernatural mutations:

Says Rabinowitz, looking at his reflection in the mirror:
"One of us has got to be a snitch!"

Dualism became the inalienable property of the Soviet monolith. It is present in larger-than-life heroes and ordinary people—and these are but the two sides of the same coin.

* * *

Just as the fairy tale helped people creatively transform life, the song helped transform the fairy tale. If anecdote was a manifestation of collective neurosis and a form of individual protest, then song served both as a powerful collective tonic and as a means of personal relaxation.

For many years we stumbled "wherever my eyes led me." You cannot reach such a murky destination while traveling a common road. Nor can you rely on the consciousness or conscience favored by a socialist society. Rather, you must entrust yourself to the "collective unconscious," which replaces social imperatives ("you ought to do this") with the notion of predestination. In other words, you need to follow the creative path charted in folk art:

> He who cannot sing and hear those songs,
> Will never know how to be happy.

This line from a Soviet song comes across like an official directive, a lesson taught "to all you valiant lads," a warning as well as a promise of salvation. "State aesthetics," explains Vladimir Paperny, "sanction the production of life according to the laws of the epic. The epic in Culture-2 [official Soviet art] is the composition of folk songs as prescribed by the orders of state power."[13]

The nation that sang at home and at work, by the campfire and on the train, in a mud hut and in the streets, was performing a magic rite that fulfilled the soul's innermost needs and marked important milestones in national history. The result was a fairy tale that displaced real life, a ritual behavior that charmed and ultimately conquered space and time. After all, "We are only a geological product of vast spaces into which we were thrown by some enigmatic force, nothing more than a curious wrinkle in the physical geography"[14]:

> Vast and boundless is the Russian land . . .
> You're rich in your fairy tales, you live by your songs.

Fairy tales are our gold reserve, a vital mineral resource. But we ourselves are also like the fossils that come to life by singing. In our songs, we transcend the mundane reality and build a fabled one:

> Life is fine, living is fine.
> For some it's fine, for others it's shit.

Just as Fedya Protasov, the living corpse in Tolstoi's play, used to forget his troubles while listening to Gypsy songs, Soviet man drew his strength from and realized his dreams in songs.

The right to sing is the only inalienable right guaranteed to the Russian people. It is also their duty. In the 1920s, the right to fairy tales (like the right to tell jokes in the 1930s) was suppressed. "Fairy tales have had their day," charged the anti-fairy-tale campaign, "Down with the fairy tale. The literature of the future must be freed from this anachronism." "The magic tablecloth will never feed us, and Cinderella will not drop her shoe around here again," lamented poet Ilya Selvinsky. "Along with fairy tales, all books in which the element of fantasy exceeded the officially approved dosage were removed from children's libraries."[15] Then, in 1933, there was a sudden about-face: the Communist party's Central Committee passed a resolution declaring fairy tales to be "an important genre of literature for children."[16] But it was the song, this powerful pedagogical tool, that transformed the fairy tale and turned it into a tale for adults who were to retain their childish fantasies, playfulness, and vulnerability.

> We will sing and laugh like children,
> As we move and toil through the day.
> That's the way we were born —
> Never to give up anywhere.

Notice the song's dominant spatial-temporal pattern: "never ... nowhere," which has its logical counterpart in "always ... everywhere."

Songs about the revolution traced the unhappy history of the hero. But from the 1930s on, Soviet songs marked a new page in the hero's biography—his bright and cloudless "life after death." Those born to make a fairy tale come true were actually destined to bring Kafka's world to life, which is why the Soviet hero gradually evolved into a dead man, an inanimate object—a "Sovok," literally, "dust pan," the term designating "Soviet man" in contemporary Russian slang. This word play is emblematic of Soviet realities, and it is widely reflected in common parlance:

> Reagan, riding through the streets of Moscow, turns to Brezhnev:
> "What are these people lining up for?"
> "Shoes have just been thrown out in the shoe store."
> "Good for you. In America shoes like that are thrown out, too."

In Russian parlance, "to throw out" means "to put on sale," and "taking" is a synonym for "buying." The product thrown out is taken by Sovok (dust pan):

> "What is a cut-rate joke?"
> "A joke that gets you only three years in jail instead of ten."

When Soviet power came tumbling down, all it left behind was "bare facts" that could not explain anything. By contrast, jokes reflected the nonexistent being or the being of the nonexistent. Recorded and published in the post-perestroika period, jokes have become a collection of corpses, akin to the collapsible sculptures in conceptualist art. They are the most stunning, though unseen, monuments on our common grave.

The genre that gave everyday Soviet culture its most eloquent expression was doomed from the outset. This culture's pretended reality, or, better still, its nonbeing (*nebytie*) was faithfully preserved in its jokes, but the joke itself fell by the wayside once its time had run out. The anecdote vanished along with its raconteur, who recognized the curse of his (non)existence sublimated in a fairy tale and a song. When folklore merged with the culture of letters, the joke lost its meaning. The joke has now been relegated to the past, permeated with a romantic nostalgia for the brave and gifted Soviet man, who never parted with the song. The Soviet song, with which he "lived, toiled, and loved" and that helped him "make fairy tales come true," fulfilled the American dream—the Russian-style dream, that is, or the Russian fairy tale:

> Remember, there once lived a girl called Alyonushka?
> She took me by the hand and led me to a fairyland.
> Trust me, you'll find your happiness there,
> Enchanting is the fairy tale's magic.

Songs made up for whatever the sloppy narrator failed to eat or imbibe at the fabulous feast. When you sang, you embraced the world as a feast, a nonstop holiday amid arduous labors: If there was nothing to eat, there was still a song to get us through the day:

> Forever and ever will our folk be happy.
> Our dreams are daring and will not be denied.

The boundless hope of happiness turned into unhappiness without bounds. When workdays are holidays, you learn to revel in misery:

> Oh, mother Russia! You are like no other place.
> I can't live without you, I can't sing without you.

To sing is to live, to live is to drink, from which it follows that to drink is to live and sing. This is the tragic but dignified choice of the centaur—the heroic Sovok.

While the fairy tale nagged the listener to "go I know not where," the path charted by the song always led either up or down, straight to the heavens or all the way to hell. Meanwhile, here on earth, there were purges going on.

* * *

The scientific experiment designed to make this life a fairy tale unfolded under the watchful eye of the helper from beyond the grave, who volunteered to aid the simple folk in their appointed task. The Russian fairy tale spelled out in significant detail the road leading to the magic kingdom. It also teaches us about the kingdom's topography, its distinguishing traits, as well as its location, be it on the top of a hill, in the netherworld, or underworld.

The hero's adventures usually began in the woods. "In fairy tales, the wood symbolizes an obstacle."[17] The labor camp to which Soviet prisoners were sent to cut wood can be seen as a stopover on the way to the other world. The wood was the entrance to the kingdom of Hades, where coveted magical objects were stored and languishing princesses waited to be freed. Hence, the prominence that cutting wood was accorded in Soviet mythology (the film *Kommunist*) and that was captured in this familiar adage: "The chips fly when the wood is cut." That is to say, the innocent will suffer when the grand battle is waged, or, as the English proverb has it, "You cannot make an omelet without breaking eggs."

Meanwhile, the fairy-tale hero enters the wood and meets the witch, Baba Yaga. The success or failure of his mission is in her hands. From this point on, the hero need not worry about anything and can rest. Once he has secured the right helper, the battle was practically won. This fairy tale's prerequisite was dutifully observed in building the new socialist society. Beautiful palaces are filled with eternal lights in the fairyland, wherever it might be located, even in the netherworld. Gardens are in full bloom there, inspiring the poet's imagination:

> I know there will be such a city,
> I know our garden will bloom,
> When our Soviet homeland
> Is teeming with such people.

The subway of Hades, the Garden of Eden—this is the netherworld of Stalinist mythology, uncannily blending the symbols of life and death.

The decision to blow up Moscow's Church of Christ the Savior and erect the Palace of Soviets in its place was a logical step toward the glorious future. But since the soil there proved ill suited for the palace, the authorities settled on a compromise—a swimming pool, a kind of underwater palace in an invisible city. The subway and the swimming pool symbolize an invisible yet real kingdom. Building both took some real effort, though. Alas, "Nothing can stop us on land or at sea."

The Exhibition of Economic Achievements, better known by its Russian acronyms, VDNKh, was the third metaphor of this fairyland topography, symbolizing the nation's countless victories and fabulous riches. The VDNKh was an architectural ensemble embodying an "otherworldly kingdom," as well as a frontier between the world at hand and the world to come. The skyscrapers, the subway, the VDNKh, the place where the wood is cut—these are the fairy-tale palaces and gardens, the magic grounds where Soviet heroes could prove their mettle. The visible and invisible worlds merge when the Palace of Congresses rises in the old Kremlin, when Kalinin Avenue displaces the Old Arbat, when the rivers are forced to reverse their flow—wherever a perestroika of one kind or another has been unleashed on this country and its people.

In the long run, the fairy-tale hero "proves that either he has reached the other world (fulfilled all assignments, descended to hell, and so on) or that his own nature is like that of a dead man."[18] That is why we have turned our world into a fairy tale. We are heroes. Dead man's nature is our nature. Some of us have been to "the other world" and seen hell with our own eyes; others have labored to make "the other world" their own. But just as our dreams have come true, we have stopped reveling in myths and fairy tales and plunged into reality. We may yet pay dearly for our inability to remember that at the core of our "historical reality" is a myth. "Disavowing the myth," wrote Propp, "would strip the myth of its sacred nature, its magic, or as Lucien Lévy-Bruhl liked to say, its mystic power. Without its myths, the tribe could not possibly continue to exist."[19]

It was indeed glasnost that began to tear the masks off cherished social and cultural myths, depriving the folk of its stable world view and plunging the nation into chaos. This demythologization from above was aided by Soviet man's unusual genealogy:

> Where did I come from? From the anecdote.
> Where did you come from? From the anecdote.
> Where did we all come from? Just the same,
> We all come from the anecdote, from the anecdote.
> (N. Gorbanevskaia)

What is this strange medium that spawned them all, causing them to rise like Venus from the sea foam? According to Dostoevsky's classic and time-worn formula, Russian literature emerged from Gogol's story, "The Overcoat," from the anecdote about the man who lost his most valuable possession, that is to say, from "laughter through tears." Like the man stepping out of his overcoat, Russian literature emerged from the anecdote. Then, as if shedding police surveillance and leaving his underground existence behind, Soviet man came into being, again owing his birth to a joke. To come out of the anecdote was to acquire freedom, to sever the umbilical cord with the motherland, to demythologize one's existence. The joke derives its roots from the collective antimythology, or, if you wish, from the anecdote about "the father of all nations" begetting all sorts of bastards and "children of the underground." To come out of the joke also means to stop being an anti-Soviet man and become "just another man."

Paradoxically, getting a jail sentence for telling a joke is a joke in itself, although a sad one. Laughter (liberation) is punished by tears (imprisonment).

This, it seems, was possible only in the Soviet land. As a modern proverb has it, "Soviet means excellent," that is, something truly beautiful and inimitable. Thus, the anecdote became a password for entering the taboo-laden culture, a culture open to every Soviet person, regardless of social, class, or intellectual background. The Soviet civilization's hieroglyphs were penned in the invisible ink of anecdote that is so deeply rooted in the nation's subconscious. Once deciphered and interpreted, however, the anecdote—this basic staple of urban folklore—vanishes without a trace. The jokester's muse is spewed out into the air; you cannot catch her in a net like a butterfly:

> "What is the theory of relativity?"
> "I'm not sure, but if I were you, I would have emigrated long ago."

The joke is not just a uniquely Soviet comic strip but also a ubiquitous oral journal in which real characters acquire the status of mythological heroes.

Anecdote situated itself in the underground of official mass culture, but it also served as its avant-garde. Unlike works produced by Soviet underground artists, anecdote could not be smuggled abroad, for it was alien to Western civilization's semiotics. Unable to profit from their jokes, the people repeated the experience of the "lost generation": "the victors received no spoils from their victory." The folk's heroic efforts were appreciated and properly assessed only by the KGB, which kept a watchful eye on vanguard folklorists. Eventually, the joke was objectified, turned into a personified object that could be stolen or thrown out as useless:

> From Brezhnev's interview:
> "Do you have a hobby?"
> "Yes, I am collecting jokes about myself."
> "Really? How many have you gotten so far?"
> "Enough to fill a couple of labor camps."

People's fate was measured by their right to tell jokes. Soviet civilization must be credited with this fundamental discovery, which transcends the boundaries of the merely political and enters the domain of the purely existential:

"Why is living so expensive these days?"
"Because it has become a luxury."

The joke faithfully mirrors the ongoing transubstantiation of life into commodity, word into action, literature into life, human being into object. Soviet jokesters cultivated an astounding detachment from actual events, and their Olympian aloofness (divine omniscience?) secured their triumph over reality. Their disengagement and passivity, honed to a fine art, were largely responsible for the exceptional perception, embedded in the anecdotal narrative, which itself evolved into a unique language based on the modernist principle of "missing links" ("I write in missing links," said Osip Mandelshtam):

"The Sun has set."
"Don't you think that's a bit much?"

The link missing in this case is highlighted by the word "to set" (*sest*), which is also Russian slang for "to be imprisoned."

* * *

The unusual characters, odd circumstances, and misbegotten actions so typical of Russian fairy tales and songs were absorbed into Kafkaesque Soviet reality as norms or ideals. But then the tale, according to an expert's opinion, is recounted "as if all that happens in it had once taken place in real life, although neither the teller nor the listener believes the tale. This discrepancy highlights the fairy tale's humor."[20] Place, time, and circumstances narrated in the fairy tale are conventions allowing for the temporary suspension of disbelief. The fairy tale's humor stems from the tension between its truthful form and its improbable content. The reader laughs whenever the tale begins to resemble the truth. But when the fairy tale was transformed into an official ideology, literature and art, that is, when it was entrusted with a serious mission, humor branched off into anecdote and saved itself in a joke. Humor, resulting from the perception of tension between reality and the official fairy tales about happy life could incur serious consequences for the humorist: he could end up in jail. The formal (and not merely literary) opposition between good and evil, laughter and tears, was being eroded.

A joke disrupts reality, forces destiny to stumble at the very point where fairy tale and reality are supposed to merge seamlessly. Through the anecdote, the individual mocks the familiar stereotypes buried in the collective unconscious, shakes them loose, and turns them around. The humorist violates the conventions of typical reality, whittles away at their foundations through the unsanctioned word. But as Baba Yaga could smell a human being miles away, so the authorities could sniff out the unsanctioned word. The innocent jokester sentenced to correctional labor is Ivan the Fool who has worked his way up through endless ordeals to become a hero, if only posthumously.

The genealogy of Soviet man brings us back to the fairy tale, to its temporal dimension, and specifically to the fact that the most complicated tasks are accomplished by its heroes at night. It was at night that the "free slaves" undertook their honest labors and managed to carry out the impossible tasks that the king-despot set them. In 1936, a well-known architect, M. Ginzburg, already knew that the dead of night was the time most suited for serious labor: "Hundreds of leading architects are now living through the most extraordinary time, working the nights through, giving all their thoughts, all their strength, to their work."[21] Nocturnal labors are carried out in fairy tales with the help of magical powers and are accompanied by a distinctly sexual pleasure. No wonder Stalin was called "the father of all nations." This strong metaphor proved its continued fecundity by yielding "Stalin's children," then "Stalin's grandchildren," the "children of the Twentieth CPSU Congress," and so on and so forth. The greatest progenitor, Stalin preferred to work at night. By morning, one is either a hero ("I am a master, or I am doomed") or a dead man ("Here is my sword. Off with your head"). Nocturnal labors are propelled by the seminal powers that brought into being generations of Soviet workers who died with the name of "the great father" on their lips or endeavored to start a new life by denouncing their paternity.

Vanguard workers and farmers who toiled to make a fairy tale into reality owed their life not only to "the father of all nations" but also to other fairy-tale heroes: Maria the Queen, Vasilissa the Beautiful, and their numerous descendants from the supernatural world—sorcerers, witches, and dragons. Propp calls all these characters "grantors." Thus, Baba Yaga functions in the fairy tale as the hero's mother, mother-in-law, aunt, or wife's sister. Whoever came into contact with the inhabitants of the netherworld—fabled or communist—was infused with remarkable spirit and stamina: the labors of the dead were vast, unceasing, and invariably successful. The farther away the fairyland, "the land of the dead," the more woods cut down and wood chips wasted, the quicker the natural selection of the "passive hero" endowed with magical powers. Thus were myths spawned as the fairy tale's vital ingredient, as a constituent part of Marxism. It is noteworthy, also, that during perestroika people watched the televised parliamentary proceedings and endless political debates deep into the night. Having rested during the working hours, the folk was ready to get on with its most riveting and emotionally charged labors.

Five-year economic plans accomplished in four years and the obsessive desire to catch up with and overtake America were but instances of the accelerated mythological time, when magical stallions and charmed wolves covered a thousand miles in split seconds, while children grew up into epic heroes in a matter of hours. Hence, the proverb: "The children of others grow faster." These must be children fathered by "the father of all nations," by Baba Yaga, by assorted fairy monsters and their ideological offsprings. The uncertain time frame combined with the preference for exact dates (one day, three months, or twenty years allotted to accomplish the task, be this erecting a castle or building communism) signaled the intention to deceive. The magical, surreal sense of time infused leaders with enthusiasm and made them sing: "Centuries' tasks are accomplished in years." In just one night the fabulous hero was expected to weave a carpet, bake bread, plow the land, sow and harvest the wheat, grow the garden, erect the palace, put up a bridge. And why not? "We have no fear of icebergs and storm-clouds." Which only proves that "In our darings we are always right."

The fairy tale rewards the hero for being passive. "By the will of the pike I do as I like," intones the fool, and without lifting a finger his wish is instantly granted. The song, on the other hand, praises the will, the endeavor:

> And if we have to, we will move mountains . . .
> Jacks of all trades, we'll make our dreams come true. . . .
> You and I—sure we're worth something
> If even the mountain tops bow to us.

In real life, though, being active or passive would make no difference to us. The fabled fool was worthless, yet he got whatever he wished because from the start he eschewed effort. The hero extolled by the song, the one who "moved mountains," sooner or later lost everything he had: "The elevation of the fool over the great warrior, the substitution of magical help for personal effort, the weakness of heroic elements in general—such are the most painfully evident features of the Russian fairy tale. In this enchanting poetic dream the Russian seeks peace and rest; the fairy tale lends wings to the dream and at the same time dissipates its energy."[22] The Soviet song corrected this shortcoming. Lucky fools gave way to heroes brimming with energy. They no longer counted on heaven-sent miracles; they were demiurges, creating the world with the supernatural help rendered by songs, with the help of the magical word.

The fool in Russian tales might not be smart, but he is wise and cunning. Fools are unencumbered by the romanticism that besets the bright ones. Down-to-earth creatures, fools are happy with what they have. It is the smart ones who turn out to be quite ordinary, even naive. Fools defy the norm, and not just because they are lazy. The smart ones lead boring lives, go to work, look for bargains, and are afraid of being taken advantage of. By contrast, fools are idle, carefree, and happy-go-lucky and frequently break the rules. The fool is a contemplative, self-sufficient philosopher—the most intimate folk hero. Whereas the fairy tale "enlists as its heroes the most unremarkable, unattractive, unenviable characters,"[23] the song resolves this enigmatic contradiction by promoting heroes who are the cream of the crop:

> If I've dreamed you up, be just as I imagine . . .
> The brightest, strongest, kindest, sweetest one of all. . . .

Clearly, you need a comparative offset to be able to tell who is the best. The best are those who defeat the worst. Which is why, singing their popular songs, the folk not only savored their aesthetic qualities and enjoyed erotic relief but also forged weapons against their enemies, enlisting the song for its future struggles. And "struggle" with us has always been a predominantly aesthetic category tinged with erotic pleasure.

* * *

The song praised the epic heroes, those "free slaves" who used to be just slaves, scholars who once were illiterates, generous gift-givers who knew poverty at first hand. But most importantly, it elevated active romantics over passive fools. Somewhere along the line, the singer mutated into a magician, and an archaic myth was transfused into a contemporary art style glorifying the legendary present:

> Why? Well, it's really simple, my dear.
> I didn't learn what life is from the textbook.
> Magic is my real trade. And if you want me to,
> I can make you as beautiful as Cinderella.

That is right: the promise is to turn the girl not into a princess but into a beautiful Cinderella, the hard-working heroine for whom "workdays are holidays."

Mark Berness, a star Russian entertainer with magnetic appeal, especially for women, sang this song about the magician, and his listeners seemed to believe every promise he whispered in their ear. He must have believed the words himself. "Our songs carry our ideas into life," insisted

Berness, "and therefore the aesthetic evolution of our song is for us an ideological issue."[24] Berness is talking about lyrical songs, songs about love and friendship, and not just about fighting songs. Indeed, "the poet in Russia is more than just a poet." According to this ideology, the true Soviet man must have an acute aesthetic sensitivity. The only puzzle confronting fairyland heroes is how to "sing to the end the song we have dreamed up." As long as the song is being sung, active fools can enjoy life to its fullest. Once you are through, however, you have to start from the beginning, and the very song that turned mundane folks into happy heroes loses its magic. Suddenly, you are back to square one, returned to the unhappy time before the singing commenced. But "that's the way we were born—never to give up anywhere."

We know from the song that "everyone becomes a hero when the motherland commands." At the same time, we are told "that's the way we were born." From this it follows that the Soviet man is genetically endowed with mythological capabilities directly linked to his mass-messianic origins. Some auxiliary qualities that the song instilled in the "masters of the land" included the ability to see the invisible, hear the unspoken, and understand the language of birds:

> Sing to us of the wild mountains, you free-wheeling wind,
> Of the mysteries hidden at the bottom of the seas,
> Of the birds' talk, . . . of the virgin forest,
> Of the wild beasts' trails, . . . of iron muscles . . .
> Set our souls on fire, make everyone desire
> To catch up with and overtake our fathers!

The song fuels our "heart's fiery engine," tempers our "iron muscles," compels one to confide, "My heart is racing like an engine."

Surpassing time, space, and one's parents is the implacable necessity. Failure to sever the umbilical cord with the motherland suggests the unsurpassing infantilism in the little masters, trailblazer-fools whose dreams are as childish as their valor. No matter how fervently mothers desired to see their children doing well, how selflessly they nurtured them to maturity, the fathers, whose accomplishments children were called upon to overshadow, would catch up with them and cut short their adventurous offsprings' lives:

> To become an American one must commit a crime, which is known as the Orestes complex. One has to commit matricide. In Western Europe, where the Oedipus complex prevails, the son kills the father and marries mother nature. In the East, we find the Rustam complex, when the

father kills the son, for the father represents tradition. The same is true in Russia: fathers are stronger than sons. Ivan the Terrible and Peter the Great both killed their sons. Literature furnishes similar examples: Taras Bulba in Gogol's epic story, the hero of Gorky's *Artamonov Brothers*. The Oedipus story is turned on its head: the father kills the son and marries his daughter-in-law. Much like Gorky himself, who had an affair with the wife of his son, Maksim. Thus, the Rustam complex prevails in Russia; the Orestes complex in America.[25]

Young Eagles of the Fleet,
They come into their own to relieve the old guard.

With time, the young eagles will turn into "Stalin's falcons" and follow an imperative "to remain young at heart," to stay young forever, to labor valiantly and then cease to exist. Young masters are eaglets, their airplanes are big eagles, and Father Stalin is the "wings of the eagle":

Bidding farewell to her son, Mother said with pride:
You're not a coward, You're the son of the eagle,
So go, son, great deeds await you.

The son of the eagle must have been fathered by the eagle:

The eagle power counts eaglets by the millions
And the nation is proud of them.

The eaglet is the son of the father eagle and mother earth. Remember the girl Katyusha from the popular song who "came out on the steep riverbank"? She was in love with "the blue eagle of the steppe," and that could only mean that she loved both father and son. "We love our Motherland like a young bride," sang the young eagles, but they were scared away by the father, who cut short their lives, who took pride in them but also hated them for their excessive attachment to their mother, for the threat they posed to his power, for their immodest desire "to climb the highest heights."

If fairy tales capture the nation's collective unconscious, songs continue and expand this mythological cosmogony—national in its form and socialist in its content—in the new historical era. The traditional predilection for folklore-inspired imagery has not lost its primary aesthetic (and not just ideological) significance in our time, although the transformation of the fairy tale into song called for sacrifices on the part of the singers:

> Oh, my city, . . . I call you "my beloved,"
> Give your soul to it, and it will make you happy.

Sounds like a bargain with the devil: Give me your soul, I will make you happy:

> Throughout the land, from the mountain tops,
> Where the eagle flies so freely,
> The nation makes a beautiful song
> About great and beloved Stalin.

More about Stalin:

> He embodies the virtues of the great leader
> With the gentle compassion of the father.

And here is an expert's opinion on the folkloric bond between insemination and death:

> Folk songs still glorify the falcon. . . . The favorite and most important incarnations of the Thunderer were eagle and falcon. . . . This identification of God, responsible for thunder and rain, with the eagle is clearly conveyed in this ancient charm: "The eagle was flying from behind the Khvalyn Sea (the sea-sky), throwing stones and flints about the shores. He sent an arrow of lightning into the wet earth, striking spark and fire from the flint. And the cloud poured rain." . . . In more recent times, when arrows were replaced by rifles, lightning was likened to gun shot. This is evident from the following riddle: "The eagle flies, exhaling flames, carrying the man's death on his tail."[26]

Or, as Gogol's immortal hero Taras Bulba yells to his son, "I begot you, and so I'll kill you.":
"Pagans often saw their gods as a cross between a man and a bird."[27] The eagle-father calls on his eaglets to rise above the vast land and then sends them back to their mother's womb, out of which the newfangled birds—and new songs—will fly in due course.

* * *

"Difficult assignments" are common in fairy tales as well as reality that aspires to become a fairyland. But then, "We are not looking for easy trails." The central and barely articulated task given to the fairy-tale hero is ... to perish. It is very important that "difficult assignments" seem impossible (it is impossible to build socialism, for no one knows what it is, nonetheless it has been built). "The assignment takes a particular form—putting the fiancé to the test. When 'power' is invoked here, it is anything but physical strength. What is truly being tested here is the magic power embodied in the hero's helper."[28] Magic is baffling, but so is the refrain from the popular revolutionary song:

> Fearless, we shall battle for Soviet power,
> And perish one and all in this struggle.

"The assignments and requisite perils the princess sets before her suitor reflect not so much her desire to choose the best groom as the secret hope that there will be no groom at all."[29] This observation by Propp is most perceptive, and it goes to the heart of the matter. The bride is not against the idea of marriage as such. It is the particular groom she is not happy about, and she goes out of her way to put off what seems to be a happy ending because it would mean the end to "difficult assignments" and the beginning of an easy—and therefore meaningless—life. The faraway and uncertain future is more precious than the present, and the more effort is spent to bring about the future, the longer the road leading to it. Remember: "Fearless, we shall battle for Soviet power, and perish one and all in this struggle." In the end, the power will still be there, but we will not. So, as long as one lives, the battle continues, as does the song:

> For as long as my feet can walk,
> As long as my eyes can see,
> As long as my lungs can breathe,
> I shall be moving onward ...
> Propelled by my heartbeat toward the disquieting future.

These sentiments trace their roots to the most mysterious of all Russian fairy tales, on which generations of Russian and Soviet people were raised:

> A hen hatched a golden egg. The old man tried to break it, but he couldn't. The old woman tried to break it, but she couldn't. A mouse ran along, wagged her tail, the egg fell and broke by itself. The old man cried, the old woman cried, and the hen said: "Don't cry, folks. I'll hatch you another egg. Not golden but an ordinary one."

Why are the old man and the old woman crying over the broken egg? Didn't they both want the egg to break? Why not rejoice now that they have gotten their way? This family is remarkable because it labors so hard to avoid achieving its stated goal. Its members try to break the egg, but they do not really want it broken. Keeping busy means daydreaming or singing along. A dream come true ruins your life. That is why the old man with the old woman is crying: there is nothing left to do. That is why the mere thought of the song coming to an end is so terrifying.

Fairy tales teach us that wealth is perilous and poverty profitable. This solves the dilemma—"to have or have not." All one has to do is pay close attention to . . . words. Both fairy tale and Kafkaesque reality are permeated with mystic attitudes toward words, which are an analog of or substitute for actions. The word could land you in jail, the word could save your life, and the word that was sung guaranteed you sublime, liberating, nay, sensual pleasure. Our song ascends to the sun like the "troika-bird," soothing our burning hearts each time it rises from the ashes like a phoenix.

The mysterious logic that reverses the natural sequence of cause and effect stems either from faith in the word or intuition about its inherent falsehood. But the law of the "identity and struggle of the opposites," or of the antinomic character of "alcoholic consciousness," still holds. In the Russian fairy tale, as in life, it is the poor who are oppressed, but it is the poor, the meek and the weak, who defeat the mighty (like the rooster who fools the fox). Ivan reaches the crossroads, where he chooses the road "leading to your doomsday," but manages to survive and defeat his enemies. Then we are invited to a feast, where we are wined and dined but leave with an empty stomach. It is good to be wealthy, but it is only a matter of time before the poor will take your possessions: "Once in the gutter, now a knight," says the proverb, but another one warns of the reverse transformation, "from knight to the gutter." "Once nothing, now everything." By will of the pike, the peasant Emelya became a king. By the commandment of the golden fish, the old fisherman's wife became a queen. To be sure, in the end she lost everything the golden fish granted her, but that was because she wanted even more. The cardinal alternative—all or nothing—appears to harbor two incompatible things, but beneath this superficial antagonism there is a fundamental unity of opposites. Thus, "alcoholic," that is, dual, consciousness is based on the law of the "identity and struggle of opposites."

"Working days are holidays for us" means that there are neither workdays nor holidays. There is only total—totalitarian—uniformity; all heterogeneity is suppressed and distinctions are obliterated. In songs, much like in fairy tales, "vast distances contract" and "nights resemble days." Extremes tend to exaggerate a specific, low-key event, blowing it into something global: revolution is always "world revolution," success means that "we are ahead of the whole world," struggle proves that "nothing can stop us," empowering the Soviets means that "all power goes to the Soviets," and if we are to perish, "we shall perish one and all." In the fabled reality, idea serves as metaphor, reality as fairy tale, song as magic:

> In bitter cold the song will warm you
> In blistering heat, refresh you like cool water.

And of course, the living appear as dead and the dead as living:

> As if alive, speaks Lenin to the living. . . .
> Lenin—more alive today than anybody living.

*　*　*

"Where does the Motherland begin?" From a picture in the textbook, from a bench in your backyard, from a song your mother sang to you, but most importantly, "From the oath you gave Her in your heart of hearts." Hence,

> Our concern is very simple,
> What we care about is this,
> May our Motherland live forever,
> Nothing else matters to us . . .

Our sole (all or nothing) concern is to assure our motherland's well-being, even if that means that all of us perish. The motherland's life is always imperiled by her enemies, who never sleep. And so, "my heart is always nudging me toward a disquieting future." This maniacal drive, "higher and higher," turned the wayfarer into a perpetuum mobile with "a fiery engine for a heart" for whom freedom and labor are the same thing, workdays are holidays, and writers are engineers of human souls. In the end, the wayfarer turns into a vagabond, a refugee, and a freedom fighter:

> Where does the Motherland begin?
> Perhaps, in the train wheels' rumbling.

Thus went the famous song. But these train wheels ultimately ran over the people, who convinced themselves that they were a divinely chosen people:

> Come with me . . . Let's climb to the very top —
> Beyond the clouds, . . . Across the seas and forests

But: "Across the seas and forests, the sorcerer takes the knight."

The song's hero is akin to the knight-sorcerer, half-man, half-God. This metamorphosis has been captured in folk songs:

> To make his work easier, a wise Englishman invents a steam engine,
> Tired by his labor, our Russian muzhik bursts into a song, "Dubinushka."

"Dubinushka" (cudgel) is the title of a popular song that warns us that sooner or later the muzhik will "find an even bigger cudgel to do away with the gentry, the tsar, and the priests."

This instrument of retribution, born out of song and often transformed beyond recognition, is handed down from one generation to another. But the song itself is also a tool that aids the Russian laborer, just as the steam engine aids the English worker. This mighty weapon-cum-tool left an indelible imprint on man, Soviet man, who belongs to the antimachine civilization:

> You are the master, you are the Lord of the universe,
> Oh, mighty working man.
> In the palm of your hand,
> You can hold mountains and forests.

Or consider this line:

> We are happier than many,
> We may be stronger than gods.
> For gods created the earth,
> But we are creating cities on it.

The master of cities holds god's creation in the palm of his hand. Is it any wonder that "I, he, you, she—our whole nation" are more powerful than all the gods and would think nothing of dispensing with those fabulous gifts:

Today, I've given her the sky,
Tomorrow, I'll present her with the earth.

"Happiness for eternity" so firmly ensconced itself in our songs that very little of it was left for mundane life. Heaven and hell became indistinguishable, a nearly perfect equilibrium was established between poetry and truth, the warrior and the fool, the long road and dead ends, superliminal time and time that stands still: "Were underground palaces built to serve as bomb shelters or were bomb shelters originally conceived as palaces? . . . Is a graveyard the trapdoor to paradise, or is paradise a stopover on the way to the graveyard? Paradise is at the graveyard's side, the graveyard is the foundation for paradise."[30]

The song pulled down the wall that once separated the real and imagined worlds, eliminated the distinction between top and bottom (says the hero of *In the Gutter*, a play written by the engineer of human souls, Maksim Gorky: "Man! That word has a proud ring to it!"), and between victory and defeat, which, it is said, a true poet "should not be too quick to tell apart." Surely, the same applies to our entire creative folk, who have spun off those fairy tales, songs, and anecdotes.

In the fairy tales we find clues to the mystery of the lucky fools, the princesses toiling at night like exemplary workers, the kings who seek council from drunkards, the "lie" that is always "well-heeled," the Russian man who feels out of place everywhere. The fairy tale goads us to find an answer to this puzzle in sorrow; the song points us in the opposite direction.

When the dream has finally come true and paradise has been built on the graveyard, there is nothing much left to do except die (the death wish, the yearning for "the other life," is stronger in the Russian than the will to live), or keep on chasing the bluebird of happiness to ever loftier heights. The ultimate happiness is in seeing to it that the Motherland lives forever. Craving life is not enough; one ought to strive to make it better. Eternal perfection lures us on, giving no respite. "Oh, my heart, you never let me rest." Workdays merging with holidays fill the heart with frenzied joy:

The train wheels are repeating . . .
My addresses, phone numbers,
And these are scattered across so many cities . . .
There is no street, no city in my address —
My address is the Soviet Union!

When the Soviet Union finally collapsed, Mother Earth quavered, erasing familiar street names, obliterating the addresses we used to know. All the

Soviet man had left was song. We are living through extraordinary times today, when all the myths are dying. Witness all the sorcerers, astrologists, and witch doctors invading our TV screens. They have precise names and addresses, and their drivel doesn't seem to perturb us. Myths lend stability to the public mind; fairy-tale miracles happen suddenly, "all by themselves." At first we rejoiced when the myths began to fall by the wayside. Now that the floodgates of truth are open, we are desperately trying to stave off its tide, which threatens to engulf us. Even when we see through its deception, we do not want to see the myth explode and recoil from the sight of the mythological ruins. People still believe that "truth is good, but happiness is dearer." As Gogol sarcastically wrote in his poem in prose, *Dead Souls* (Mertvye Dushi):

> "Do you really think we are oblivious to our life's inanities? Surely we can see that many things around here are distressing. Why don't you show us something beautiful and exciting, instead, so that we can lose ourselves in a sweet dream!"
>
> "Now, now, my dear fellow, don't bother me with the tales about my wretched estate and its many woes," the landlord tells his bailiff. "I know it myself. Don't you have better things to tell me? Help me forget this sad world, and you'll make my day."[31]

The total disarray that pervades our existence today testifies to the fact that our romantic sensibilities are waning, that the myth has lost its magical poetic power. The only myth that continues to fire the imagination is the one about Russia's mysterious, messianic destiny. Alas, even this most seductive of our myths has shown cracks.

The rest is silence . . .

* * *

Realizing the difficulties that this text must pose for the non-Russian reader, I wish to accentuate a few central points discussed above (the way a bilingual publication marks the proper stress in foreign words to avoid mispronunciation).

First, the problem formulated in this chapter has a wide range of references, associations, and interpretations that resonate through the writings of Russian philosophers, historians, and classical Russian and Soviet writers. Space constraints have forced me to omit certain substantive details and condense the text to a concise and metaphorical exposition. This work should provoke the reader to read or reread the original sources, be these Russian fairy tales or Dostoevsky's novels, song anthologies, or scholarly works by Lev Karsavin or Nikolai Lossky, recorded anecdotes or Mikhail Zoshchenko's short stories. The three central themes of this study—fairy tales, songs, and anecdotes—are dealt with separately and at greater length in my other publications.[32]

Second, the demythologized reality encountered by post-Soviet man destroyed the very foundation on which he stood. The old proverb, "Truth is good but happiness is better," faithfully captures the protective role of folklore, especially because in Russia, whatever the political climate, there were always several "truths," which could not be grasped without the explanatory world view that ideology/mythology furnishes to the common man. Which is why folklore, in the broadest possible sense, provides a key to understanding any sociocultural processes that unfolded and are still unfolding on the territories of the former Soviet Union.

For nothing has really changed in spite of all the grandiose transformations.

Thus, rebuilding the Church of Christ the Savior (on the very spot where the Palace of Soviets was supposed to have been built but never was, remaining a paper palace and a symbol, an "underwater place" of the otherworldly communist kingdom) is bound to become a monument to the current postcommunist leaders. Yet another edition of the "project of the century."

Third, we can marvel at the extraordinary social role that the anecdote played for decades, as it whittled away at the tragic and at the same time comic foundations of official ideology/mythology and bred in ironic Soviet man the pride of slaves who feel victorious when they recount their anecdotes. To be sure, these victors also fall prey to their own wit, to their very ability to see from without the reality they embody. And I mean "victims" quite literally: many people in Russia have already forgotten the time when you could get a prison sentence for telling a joke.

Many arguments, examples, and quotations could be adduced to illustrate this point. For instance, recall Tolstoi's *Anna Karenina:* "We Russians are always that way. Perhaps this is our strength that we can see our shortcomings, but we are prone to overdo it, to find solace in irony, which is always on the tip of our tongue. I'll tell you this: Give the same rights and institutions of self-governance to another European people, say, to Germans or Englishmen, and they would use it to fortify freedom, whereas we only know how to laugh."[33]

That man's fate could depend on his right to anecdote is the discovery of Soviet civilization. This discovery transcends politics; it brings you to the realm of pure existence and ethnography and touches upon the problem of national character. The above-mentioned anecdote—"'Why is living so expensive these days?' 'Because life has become a luxury'"—tells us more about the current situation, say, in Chechnia, than endless stories about organized crime or arm sales to Russia's enemies, whom Russian boy soldiers now have to face on the battlefields. . . . This two-liner (it is no metaphor!) cuts to the very core of phantasmagoric and barbaric events—past and present.

Finally, to be sure, old myths guaranteed the sometimes dissonant yet still undeniable intactness of the simple Soviet man. The consoling mythologeme about the passive, contemplative Ivan the Fool inheriting the earth achieved its appointed task brilliantly, as did the life-asserting mythologeme that pictured the indomitable hero of Soviet songs as master of the universe. Our song was akin to a magic wand helping a fairy-tale hero to achieve his task. After all, the Soviet people did believe that "Anyone who cannot sing and hear those songs, will never know how to be happy." Again, this is hardly a metaphor.

Noted by Nikolai Berdiaev and highlighted in Russian and Soviet folklore, maximalism, the longing for all or nothing, remains the principal option facing the Russians, whatever the real or imaginary "pluralism" and "freedom of choice" available to them today. It is this alternative—all or nothing—that marginalizes the great masses of people who have worked their whole lives and still earned nothing. The problem is not just the "capitalist stage" of development and its inevitable by-products, for this "stage" is but a metaphor, a "figure of speech."

Forrest Gump, the dim-witted hero of Robert Zemeckis's movie that has enjoyed such success in the United States and that is closely woven into American history, only superficially resembles Ivan the Fool of Russian fairy tales. The mentally challenged Gump overcomes his handicaps, his social and personal marginality. Ivan the Fool, by contrast, never wishes to be like everybody else. He gets ahead precisely because he stands apart. As foolish and lazy as he might be, he is chosen by God. Pure, unselfish, utterly devoid of greed, Forrest Gump is the hero "normal" American society needs so badly today. But this new wrinkle in the traditional Hollywood mythology brings to mind the hero that was once celebrated in the movies and songs of Stalin's era. By contrast, the simpleton Lenya Golubkov—a contemporary Russian Forrest Gump who speaks to us in popular TV commercials—could no longer become a Russian national hero. The project of fusing the "American dream" with Russia's Ivan the Fool, of turning the fool loose and making him succeed in the new reality, has failed miserably. Devoid of illusions, shorn of ideological props, our reality and mass culture can no longer support these myths.

I wish to conclude with the dignified and I believe indubitable words of Pushkin: "Of course, I loathe my homeland from head to toe, though I feel annoyed when a foreigner shares this feeling."[34]

Notes

This article was translated from the Russian by Sergei Volynets and Dmitri N. Shalin. The author wishes to express her gratitude to the George Soros Foundation for its support.

1. This chapter relies heavily on Russian and Soviet folklore material that is likely to be unfamiliar to a foreign reader. Some of this material (for example, jokes and anecdotes) remains uncollected, appears in rare sources, or exists in several versions, none more authentic than the other. I shall not try to document every single folk saying, fairy tale, or anecdote cited here. Instead, I shall mention a few general sources that the reader familiar with the Russian language might wish to consult: *Poslovitsy russkogo naroda: Sbornik V. Dalia v dvukh tomakh* (Moscow: Khudozhestvennaia Literatura, 1984); *Byliny* (Leningrad: Sovetskii Pisatel, 1986); *Pesni katorgi i ssylki* (Moscow: Politkatorzhan, 1930); *Pesni borby i protesta* (Moscow: Znanie, 1977); *Pesni v soldatskikh shineliakh* (Moscow: DOSAAF, 1970); *Pesni i chastushki* (Saratov, 1956); *Pesni 50-kh godov* (Moscow, 1986); *Pesni razluk i vstrech* (Moscow: Khudozhestvennaia literatura, 1968); *Pesni sovetskikh kompozitorov* (Moscow: Sovetskii kompozitor, 1987). For further information about the sources on Soviet anecdotes, see Zara Abdullaeva, "Vse my vyshli iz anekdota," *Znanie—Sila*, no. 2 (1993): 113–20.

2. V. Y. Propp, *Folklor i deistvitelnost* (Moscow, 1976), p. 85.

3. "Dialog miezhdu S. Mironenko i Mironenko S.," *Dekorativnoe iskusstvo v SSSR*, no. 1 (January 1991): 17.

4. A. Zinoviev, *Gomo Sovetikus* (Moscow, 1991), p. 6.

5. Quoted in A. Pan, *I. Dunaevsky* (Moscow: Sovetskaia muzyka, 1956), p. 6.

6. Ibid., p. 70.

7. I. Dunaevsky, *Articles. Memoirs.*

8. V. Orlov, "Letnie nochi v Moskve poslednego generalnogo sekretaria," *Moskovskie novosti*, no. 7 (1993).

9. E. Shvarts, *The Shadow*, in *Pesy* (Leningrad: Iskusstvo, 1972), p. 207.

10. Quoted in Pan, *I. Dunaevsky*, p. 22.

11. Ibid., p. 32.

12. Marquis de Custine, *Zapiski o Rossii* (Moscow: SP Interprint, 1990), p. 93.

13. V. Paperny, *Culture-2* (Ann Arbor, Mich.: Ardis, 1985), p. 234.

14. P. Y. Chaadaev, *Stati i pisma* (Moscow: Sovremennik, 1989), p. 190.

15. M. Petrovsky, "Chto otkryvaetsia zolotym kliuchikom," in *Knigi nashego detstva* (Moscow: Khudozhestvennaia literatura, 1986), pp. 170–71.

16. Ibid., p. 171.

17. V. Y. Propp, *Istoricheskie korni volshebnoi skazki* (Leningrad: Nauka, 1986), p. 57.

18. Ibid., p. 331.

19. Ibid., p. 357.

20. Propp, *Folklor i deistvitelnost*, p. 88.

21. Quoted in Paperny, *Culture-2*, p. 237.

22. Quoted in A. Sinyavsky, *Ivan durak* (Paris: Sintaksis, 1991), p. 37.

23. Ibid., p. 25.

24. Quoted in L. Rybak, *Mark Berness* (Moscow: Iskusstvo, 1976), p. 77.

25. Quoted in *Tsennosti amerikanizma i russkii vybor* (Moscow: Soiuz kinematografistov Rossii, 1992), pp. 4–5.

26. A. N. Afanasiev, *Drevo zhizni* (Moscow: Sovremennik, 1983), pp. 120–23.

27. Ibid., p. 132.

28. Propp, *Istoricheskie korni*, p. 305.

29. Ibid.

30. Paperny, *Culture-2*, p. 244.

31. N. Gogol, *Mertvye dushi* (Moscow: Khudozhestvennaia literatura, 1969), p. 288.

32. See Zara Abdullaeva, "Skazkobyl," *Iskusstvo kino*, no. 1 (1992): 88–102; "Vse my vyshli iz anekdota"; "Tolko pesnia ostaetsia s chelovekom," *Iskusstvo kino*, no. 8 (1993): 79–86.

33. L. N. Tolstoi, *Sobranie sochinenii v dvenadtsati tomakh* (Moscow: Khudozhestvennaia Literatura, 1958), VIII: 35.

34. L. N. Tolstoi to P. A. Vyazemsky, May 27, 1826, in ibid., X: 208.

8

Literary Culture

MAURICE FRIEDBERG

What role should literature play in society? Since the late eighteenth century, Russian men of letters have heatedly debated this question. Nikolai Novikov and Denis Fonvizin, Aleksandr Pushkin and Vasily Zhukovsky, Nikolai Gogol and Mikhail Saltykov-Shchedrin, Vissarion Belinsky and Nikolai Chernyshevsky, Lev Tolstoi and Fyodor Dostoevsky, Marina Tsvetaeva and Osip Mandelshtam, Vladimir Nabokov and Aleksandr Solzhenitsyn, Yevgeny Yevtushenko and Joseph Brodsky—every generation of Russian writers would tackle the problem and stake out a position on the proper relationship between literature and society. The proponents in this ongoing debate disagreed on many substantive points, but they all agreed that literature's mission is vital to society, that it is a national resource that must be tapped if society is to live up to its true potential.

Conservative Dostoevsky and radical Chernyshevsky stood at opposite ends of the political spectrum of their time, yet they saw eye to eye on the ennobling, transformative role that literature was called upon to play in Russian society. Dostoevsky's famous maxim, "Beauty will save the world" is but one example of the great hopes that Russian thinkers pinned on literature and art in society. Even when some writers rebelled against the politicization of art and dedicated themselves to art for art's sake, as did the poet Afanasy Fet, they were seen by many contemporaries as taking a political stance. For better or for worse, Russian writers assumed, and acted upon the assumption, that literature matters, that the fate of Russian literature and the fate of Russian society are intertwined. Vasily Rozanov's ruminations on literature and the Russian revolution— "There could be no doubt that literature killed Russia"[1]—fall squarely within the traditional, exalted Russian vision of literature as a social force waiting to be harnessed for the good of society.

The Bolsheviks' conscious efforts to turn literature into a tool of social engineering should be seen in this context. Socialist realism, around which the Soviet Writers' Union coalesced, was as much a literary doctrine as it was a political practice radically linking literature and politics.

This doctrine ostensibly elevated the status of writers in society, but it also subordinated their craft to political imperatives and subjected creative writing to state control. This might not have been exactly what nineteenth-century Russian writers had in mind, but the radical merging of literature and politics that marked the Soviet era can be seen as an (over)extension of some of their most cherished precepts and hopes.

In this chapter, we shall explore the transformation of Russian literary culture in the Soviet era and post-Soviet years. I begin with the historical roots of socialist realism, examine its theory and practice, then turn to the relaxation of literary controls after Stalin's death, discuss the process of erosion of the doctrine and practice of socialist realism during perestroika, and finally, review the emerging literary trends in post-Soviet Russia.

The Origins and Formative Stages of Socialist Realism

The roots of Soviet literary culture extend beyond the establishment of the Soviet state itself. Maksim Gorky's Mother was written, ironically, some years before the Bolshevik revolution, while the author resided in the United States (the country, it might be noted, that also contributed to the cause of the tradition of May Day observances) and is one hallmark of that culture's avant la lettre. Nikolai Chernyshevsky's What Is to Be Done, a novel often cited in communist hagiographies as the inspiration for generations of nineteenth-century Russian revolutionaries (including, significantly, the founder of the Soviet state himself, as well as his martyred brother) is another. And yet, we submit, Soviet literary culture, properly speaking, came into being only in 1932, with the formation of the single Union of Soviet Writers and the proclamation of socialist realism as its sole literary creed. It is not only that during the 1920s noncommunist writers' organizations and their journals continued to function (their members and contributors were, indeed, the decade's most prominent authors) and independently operated publishing houses attempted to supply the public with books for which there was genuine demand. Other considerations argue for this periodization as well. Prior to 1932, the party refused to endorse even those literary groupings that enthusiastically and sincerely tried to advance the communist cause, such as the Proletkult and the Russian Association of Proletarian Writers (RAPP). They attempted to accomplish this by painstaking extrapolation, from the zigzags of party dogma and shifting policy priorities, of implications for writers of prose, dramatists, and poets. The party's reluctance to recognize any of the eagerly Bolshevik literary organizations as its authorized spokesmen was simply an expression of distrust. As enunciated before the revolution by such theoreticians as Georgy Plekhanov (particularly in Art and Society, 1912–13) and Lenin himself (in his essay "On Party Organization and Party Literature," 1905), Russian Marxists, themselves strongly influenced by such native strains of the radical tradition as the so-called revolutionary democrats, attached great importance to literature's political potential. (That this view reflected conditions peculiar to Russia, a country where, in the absence of freedom of the press, parliamentary institutions, or even a socially activist church, literature served as a sublimation for all of these, is another matter.) Not unexpectedly, therefore, the decision was made that the issue was far too vital to be delegated to poets and novelists, however well intentioned. It was the Communist party itself, and the party alone, that was to decide on the ways and means to implement its objectives and tactics in literature. Not that the party failed to appreciate the usefulness of Soviet writing that was created prior to the establishment of the Writers' Union. Dmitry Furmanov's Chapaev (1923), a semidocumentary account of the taming of an undisciplined civil war hero by a sober Bolshevik commissar, was one such novel; Fyodor Gladkov's Cement (1925), the first important fictional portrayal of industrialization and of the formation of the new Soviet woman, was another; Aleksandr Fadeev's The Rout (1927), a Tolstoian tale of a band of Red guerrillas in the Far East, was a third. Together with Vladimir Mayakovsky's impassioned modernistic verse and Mikhail Sholokhov's two novels, The Quiet Don (1928–31), an epic canvas of the bloody fratricidal war that preceded the establishment of Soviet rule in the Cossack region, and his Virgin Soil Upturned (1932, 1960), which recounted the brutal collectivization of agriculture in the same area, all were to be retroactively—if anachronistically—claimed for socialist realism. Indeed, like the poetry of Mayakovsky and the novels of Furmanov, Gladkov, and Fadeev, they were to be listed matter-of-factly among the masterpieces that Socialist Realism begot, notwithstanding the fact that Quiet Don violates a number of the doctrine's central tenets, as do Mayakovsky's drama and verse. But then, inconsistency and compromises mark many features of Soviet literary culture, which over the years was often forced to adjust its rigidly enunciated theoretical principles and their enforcement to realities imposed by the book market. An old American saying comes to mind, "You can lead a horse to water but you cannot make him drink." Try as they may, Soviet librarians ultimately could not force the public to actually read the books they offered. It was this reader's veto power that accounts over the years for Soviet literary culture's many retreats from its cherished ideological goals. More often than not, however, under the conditions that were established in 1932, individual authors intent on seeing their works in print would fashion their writings to what they perceived (or were actually told) were the desires of editors of literary journals or publishing houses. One such incident is recounted in a 1933 satirical story by Ilya Ilf and Evgeny Petrov. "How the Soviet Robinson Crusoe Was Created" describes the process whereby a close replica of the children's classic was transformed into a run-of-the-mill socialist realist potboiler. The unstated import of the story is that the circumstances created by the monopolistic nature of Soviet publishing deprived the hapless writer of an alternative available to writers elsewhere. Submitting his manuscript to another journal offered little hope because the original editor's demands were a reflection not of his subjective tastes but of political directives from above that left him with little latitude, as the remarkable degree of ideological, thematic, and even artistic uniformity of the bulk of Soviet writing beginning with the early 1930s attests.

Early in that decade it became apparent that the Communist party placed very high hopes on the arts. Literary culture—writers and poets above all, but also theatrical directors, filmmakers, composers, painters, and even circus performers—was to be the party's closest helper in the more than ambitious task of creating the New Soviet Man who would be free of old "bourgeois" vices and values and embody communist virtues. The New Soviet Man would unquestioningly place collective welfare over personal desires, work over pleasure, future goals over present difficulties. He would be implacable with foes of the Soviet cause and ever ready to serve it in any way that might be required. Last but not least, he would blindly accept the Communist party's authority in defining the elucidation of all of the above categories in practice.

In literature (and to some extent the arts as well) the method chosen to advance this goal was the creation of inspirational writing that would present the reader with models for emulation, in other words, a continuation of the prerevolutionary tradition of Chernyshevsky's *What Is to Be Done* and Gorky's *Mother*. The unintended irony of the decision was that both of these novels, and Gorky's in particular, were closely modeled on the hagiography of the Russian Orthodox Church, and these saints' lives (*zhitiya*) had in turn been intended to inspire the faithful to the imitation of Christ. Idealized models for emulation may also be found in neoclassical comedies and tragedies, even though, as a rule, they are far less interesting than the villains and rogues they oppose. Starodum, the spokesman for old virtues and moral rectitude in Denis Fonvizin's *Minor*, the only eighteenth-century play still often performed on the Russian stage, is a good example of such a model. Yet there is no arguing the fact that it is his brutish antagonists, the Prostakovs and Skotinins, that delight modern theatergoers. At the same time, placing the positive hero at the center of the attributes of Soviet writing signified a break with the traditions of the nineteenth-century Russian classics that socialist realism claimed to continue.[2] For the fact of the matter is that truly positive heroes who can serve as models for impressionable readers are relatively scarce in classical Russian writing, which is rarely overtly didactic. Evgeny Onegin is no paragon of virtue (nor, for that matter, is Tatyana), and Anna Karenina is no ideal for emulation. Nor are Raskolnikov, Uncle Vanya, Oblomov's friend Stoltz, any of the male protagonists in Turgenev, or, for that matter any of Gogol's characters of either sex. Of the three whales on which the universe of socialist realism was to rest, only one, *ideinost*, the requirement that a literary work (or, as the case may be, a canvas, a musical composition, a sculpture, and so on) embody a significant idea, bore any resemblance to nineteenth-century Russian artistic traditions. (It is this particular trait more than any other that imparts to much of the classic literary legacy qualities associated with the concept of "high seriousness.") That requirement, however, was largely vitiated by the commandment of *partiinost*, which obligated the writer to eschew all pretense of objectivity and openly register his sympathies with positive values and hostility toward, say, bourgeois survivals in the consciousness of his characters. With the exception, characteristically, of such novels as Gorky's *Mother*, *partiinost* has few pre-Soviet antecedents. Mikhail Lermontov clearly disapproved of Pechorin but did not portray him simply as a repugnant villain. The same is true of Tolstoi's Vronsky and Karenin, Hélène Bezouhoff, and even Napoleon Bonaparte; Dostoevsky's Fyodor Karamazov, his intellectual son Ivan, and his half-wit natural son Smerdyakov, and so on. The third requirement, *narodnost*, or popular accessibility, could be (and was) interpreted in a variety of ways, although in practice it was used to banish overly difficult and experimental art. Its ultimate result was the disappearance of modernist tendencies from Soviet writing, ultratraditional academic painting, and a theater and ballet that showed little change from Stanislavsky's stage and the *Swan Lake* of imperial Russia. Most unique (and ultimately most damaging) was the ideologically inspired requirement of *tipichnost*. Reality, the high priests of socialist realism decreed, was to be depicted "in its revolutionary development," it was to be future-oriented: the typical was not that which was, admittedly, typical of *today*, but that which was to become typical *tomorrow*. As Andrei Sinyavsky pointed out in his 1959 essay "On Socialist Realism," this "visionary" portrayal of reality, while compatible enough with religious or phantasmagoric art, clashed with the trappings of the traditional realistic prose that was obligatory in conventional Soviet writing. It resulted in hundreds of literary works in which familiar surroundings and realia of daily life were incongruously combined with the contrived "future-oriented" psychology of Stalinist Positive Heroes. Such potboilers became particularly common during the last decade of the dictator's life. Not surprisingly, a great many of them, although published with high press runs and acclaimed by obedient communist reviewers, met with little enthusiasm on the part of the reading public and millions of copies had to be pulped.

Socialist Realism: Theory and Practice

Occasionally, the "permanent" commandments of socialist realism were temporarily augmented by supplementary strictures. Although these were, in essence, clearly derived from the core articles of faith, they sometimes represented their *reductio ad absurdum*. Thus, for example, the theory of the so-called conflictless drama that flared up briefly in the wake of World War II was rooted in the belief that with the steady progress of the Soviet cause (especially when viewed in its future-oriented "revolutionary development") there would, properly speaking, be no conflict on the stage between the harmful and the useful, the deformed and the beautiful, and so on, but only *between the good and the better*, the adequate and the exceptional, the competent and the brilliant. The new theory, needless to say, was discredited before long because, by depriving plays of their traditional moving force, it threatened to permanently destroy the Soviet theater.[3] Other than that, during the two decades between the official proclamation of socialist realism as the Soviet Union's sole literary and artistic creed and Stalin's death in 1953, the condition of the country's literary culture at a specific point in time accurately reflected the stringency with which its articles of faith were being enforced. Most oppressive were the years 1946–53, the period of Zhdanov's witch hunts, which included the expulsion from the Writers' Union of the poet Anna Akhmatova and the humorist Mikhail Zoshchenko, as well as the orgy of "anticosmopolitan" purges of Jews and other admirers of Western culture. (Curiously, neither Akhmatova nor Zoshchenko were charged with any anti-Soviet activity; their crime was the more elusive quality of *bezydeinost*, the lack of *ideinost*.)

Somewhat paradoxically, the years 1934–41 were relatively more relaxed, even though they included the period of mass terror, show trials of "enemies of the people," and the deportation and murder of scores of prominent authors, such as Isaak Babel and Osip Mandelshtam. Most unexpectedly, however, the period of greatest permissiveness in literature coincided with the years of the nation's life-and-death struggle with German Nazi invaders. One obvious reason for this was the relaxation of the party's grip on the arts: the war was certainly no time for doctrinal communist quibbles. Thus, hitherto proscribed motifs of religious faith and

Russian, as distinct from Soviet, patriotism were not merely tolerated but often openly encouraged. In wartime conditions, *ideinost, partiinost, narodnost*, and *tipichnost* translated in literature into portrayal of hatred for the foreign invader and the willingness to endure the ordeal in order to save Mother Russia. Authentic, nonpoliticized human feelings of sorrow, longing, camaraderie forged in battle, and dreams of meeting one's beloved again were readmitted to Soviet poetry. Imperial Russian military traditions could once again be extolled in Russian drama and prose. Silenced noncommunist poets, such as Akhmatova and Boris Pasternak, reappeared in print, while such party hacks as Aleksei Surkov demonstrated that they, too, were capable of depicting honest emotions in their verse. The war's grim truths found expression in such novels as Viktor Nekrasov's *In the Trenches of Stalingrad*, and even to a degree in the writings of such socialist realist functionaries as Aleksandr Korneichuk (*The Front*, a play), Konstantin Simonov (the novel *Days and Nights*), and, most significantly, Aleksandr Fadeev. Long the head of the Writers' Union, Fadeev had in his time in effect signed many a death sentence of fellow authors. After Khrushchev's denunciation of Stalin's crimes in 1956, Fadeev committed suicide. The story of Fadeev's *Young Guard* is instructive. First published toward the end of the war, it gained immediate popularity. As William E. Harkins notes, Fadeev's book became "one of the most popular novels on the Second World War. It deals with the partisan resistance of young people living under the German occupation and is based in part on actual events. In spite of the somewhat conventional conception of patriotism which the book embodies, the characterizations are striking."[4]

Looking back at the literary legacy of these three decades of socialist realism, we detect a distinctive pattern of artistic successes and failures. Intentionally or not, a number of Soviet authors succeeded in producing works of lasting merit by contriving to restrict themselves to genres immune, as it were, to the constraints of doctrinaire socialist realism. Foremost among these, of course, was the pseudo-genre of silence, or writing "for the drawer" to which Isaak Babel referred only half-ironically in the mid-1930s. It was this "genre" that produced the discovery, in the 1960s, of several brilliant satirical novels by Mikhail Bulgakov. First printed two decades after the author's death, these were important enough to warrant the reevaluation not only of Bulgakov's place in twentieth-century Russian literature but of the broader field of Russian social and political satire during the 1920s and 1930s. Much of this unpublished writing was verse by the country's leading poets, including Akhmatova, Mandelshtam, and Pasternak. Although some of it had earlier been printed abroad, the bulk was not allowed to appear in the Soviet Union until long after Stalin's death.

Individual authors succeeded in navigating the stormy seas of socialist realism in a manner that allowed them to avoid the perilous reefs of *ideinost, partiinost, narodnost,* and *tipichnost.* Clearly, none of the four criteria appear remotely relevant to Mikhail Prishvin's tales of forests and animals or to historical novels set in the distant past, such as Vasily Yan's trilogy about the Mongol invasion in the thirteenth century. (Nor, for that matter, do they seem apposite to Aleksei Tolstoi's *Peter the Great,* even though the novel was but a thinly veiled paean of praise to Stalin.) Logically, the strictures of socialist realism also seem inapplicable to writing that ostensibly satirized "bourgeois" mentality, such as the immensely popular short stories of Mikhail Zoshchenko and the widely read novels of Ilf and Petrov, *The Twelve Chairs* and *The Golden Calf.*

This, incidentally, helps explain much of Zoshchenko's and Ilf and Petrov's reader appeal. Ordinary men and women identified with Zoshchenko's hapless protagonists and their endless tragicomic struggle with the hardships and absurdities of daily life in the Soviet state. They laughed at the unseemly reality that grandiloquent slogans could not conceal. They nodded at the unheroic city folk whose speech betrayed their dutiful reading of *Pravda* and attendance at indoctrination meetings but whose actions continued to be shaped by such traditional emotions as greed, fear, and vanity. Those readers identified also with Ostap Bender, the picaresque hero of *The Twelve Chairs* and *The Golden Calf,* who was no "bourgeois survivor" but an honest-to-goodness Soviet crook, born of Soviet conditions, which afforded ample opportunity for his shenanigans.

There was yet another reason for the great allure of these authors. Not one of these books is marred by the ubiquitous Soviet literary figure of the Positive Hero, that repository of communist virtues whose annoyingly didactic pieties would place Ostap Bender and Zoshchenko's protagonists in a "correct" perspective. As for the possible usefulness of these books to the Bolshevik authorities, one can assume with confidence that the millions of Soviet readers of these books (and they were often, quite literally, read to shreds) gave little thought to the problem of whether Zoshchenko or Ilf and Petrov had, in fact, intended to satirize "bourgeois" mentality.[5] Be that as it may, the fact remains that during periods of heightened ideological vigilance (such as, for instance, 1946–53), writings that merely appeared to avoid open affirmation of communist militancy were, at best, not reprinted (this was the fate of Ilf and Petrov) or were openly denounced, as were Zoshchenko and Akhmatova. There was also a third category of Soviet writing that ignored the strictures of socialist realism with impunity. It consisted of a relatively small number of literary works (Sholokhov's *Quiet Don,* referred to earlier, is the best-known single example) that the authorities found useful for one reason or another and therefore turned a blind eye to their ideological defects. Most of the writings in this category appeared during World War II. Their obvious contributions to the war effort were apparently accepted as compensation for their shortcomings as communist sermons. Nekrasov's *In the Trenches of Stalingrad* was one such celebrated novel; Simonov's *Days and Nights* was equally famous in its day.

What of the bulk of conventional Soviet writing? Much of it, as suggested above, remained unread. But thousands of such books, including scores of Stalin prize-winning novels, were avidly read for rather curious reasons.

Soviet sociologists of literature define a "Columbus complex" as the desire to distill from fictional works a measure of purely factual information about the physical settings, customs, and values that are portrayed in such books. Paradoxically, it was this curiosity, this quest for information, that attracted tens of millions of Soviet readers to some of the worst Stalinist potboilers.

Aware of the artistic limitations of featuring ordinary workers and collective farmers as Positive Heroes and models for emulation (too many readers would find them quite unbelievable), Soviet literary artisans often preferred to portray in that role middle-level party functionaries, factory directors, scientists, and artists. All of these were members of what Milovan Djilas called the New Class, and rank-and-file readers had never known any such people personally. They had never seen the insides of their apartments or, for that matter, of their rest homes, shopping facilities, or even hospitals. All of these were concealed from ordinary mortals. Countless Soviet readers wanted to find out what these exalted beings—those, as Orwell put it, more equal than the others—ate for dinner, how their wives dressed, and how they socialized and with whom. As Vera S. Dunham pointed out, this New Class was a Soviet variant of the prerevolutionary Russian *meshchanstvo:*

> It represents today, as it did before, a middle-class mentality that is vulgar, imitative, greedy and ridden with prejudice. . . . In the Soviet world, meshchanstvo appears at every rung of the social scale. In one aspect it refers to the social climbing and careerism of the newly rich; in another to complacent vegetation. A vice admiral of the Soviet navy may be a meshchanin, and a professor may easily be seen as wallowing in meshchanstvo as a post-office clerk or party official, to say nothing of their wives. In many ways, in fact, meshchanstvo is a familial and feminine affair, and its pretentiousness expresses itself in the number and size of material acquisitions, with which the newly arrived aim to impress. Fervor for positions is a key trait.[6]

Significantly, a similar curiosity about the life of the upper classes had contributed, before the revolution, to the great demand among newly literate Russian urban readers (and also, to some degree, peasant readers) for popular fiction that described the comings and goings of the rich and famous. In the Romanov empire, educated Russians (both conservatives and radicals) were alarmed by this trend:

> Critics of popular literature were often animated by mutually exclusive visions of the Russia of the future, yet they shared the belief that the popular commercial literature of the marketplace was harmful and should be supplanted by a more wholesome alternative . . . many critics expressed a common concern about what they called the "cynicism" of the commercial literature. By cynicism they meant the popular author's appeals to worldly desires and materialistic daydreams, and the presentation of the attainment of earthly delights by fair means and foul. Criticism from clerics, state bureaucrats, Westernizers, the populists, liberal enlighteners, and Marxists varied in intensity and with time, but most were united in the view that the lower class reader and the market could not be left alone to determine the literary fare of "the reader from the people."[7]

Literature in Post-Stalinist Russia

Although the exact degree of its success cannot, of course, be gauged with any degree of accuracy, it appears in retrospect that of the values socialist realist writing strove to foster over the years, none gained general acceptance—not selfless labor enthusiasm and not concern for collective will over individual desires. The Communist party and Comrade Stalin were feared, not loved. At the most, Soviet literature may have made a modest contribution to the strengthening of wartime Russian patriotism and hatred of the German invader. It would, indeed, have been ironic if communist pulp fiction, like its prerevolutionary variety, contributed to greater awareness of social inequality and economic injustice, if it fostered a sense of resentment on the part of the impoverished Soviet workers and peasants of the privileges enjoyed by the New Class in a society ostensibly dedicated to the abolition of inequality.

But then, resentment of social inequality and economic injustice was also reinforced by the two other components of Soviet literary culture, the prerevolutionary Russian classics and translated Western European and American writing. Indeed, as I argue at length elsewhere,[8] the selection and dissemination of both kinds of non-Soviet writing in the Soviet Union heavily favored those books that supported the Soviet thesis that economic deprivation of ordinary people and unfair privileges of the ruling classes are endemic *to capitalism*. Textbooks and teachers in classrooms explained to the young that Turgenev and Tolstoi and Chekhov portrayed conditions that, fortunately, no longer obtain in Russia, whereas Honoré de Balzac and Emile Zola, Heinrich Heine and Charles Dickens, and Theodore Dreiser describe life that has changed but little in the capitalist West. Whether Soviet students at the time found such reasoning convincing is, of course, debatable. Be that as it may, reading Russian classics and translated Western literature certainly contributed to the further sensitizing of Soviet students to social injustice.

The four components of Soviet literary culture prior to Stalin's death occasionally reinforced each other's message. It may be argued, for instance, that such values as courage and self-denial are contained in the Russian classics and in scores of early Soviet novels (particularly those with civil war and World War II settings), as well as such perennial favorites of Russia's young as Ethel Voynich's *The Gadfly* or the writings of Jack London. Indeed, several Soviet novels in this category, such as Nikolai Ostrovsky's *How the Steel Was Tempered* and *Born of the Storm*, as well as Arkady Gaidar's *Timur and His Team*, achieved instantaneous renown. But there were also those revolutionary books that clashed head-on with modern Soviet values. As I wrote thirty years ago:

> Will he [the Soviet reader], perhaps think twice after reading Lermontov's lines about blue uniforms and obedient people? . . . Will he remain certain that Saltykov-Shchedrin's Pompadours and Pompadouresses all disappeared from Russia on November 7, 1917? That [Shchedrin's] Judas Golovlyov can quote only *religious* scriptures and drive people to insanity? . . . Will the reading of Pushkin and Turgenev leave him unshaken in the belief that peasants are unhappy only when exploited by *individual* masters? . . . Will any contemporary Soviet readers repeat the question posed many years ago by Nekrasov: "Who can be happy and free in Russia?" More important—are not some of the moral values found in the Russian classics in flagrant contradiction to those preached by the Soviet state? Is not the spirit of moderation and compromise that permeates the works of Turgenev the opposite of Communist intransigence? Does not Dostoevsky belie the assertion that religion is merely an opiate for the people and that addicts to this narcotic are simple and backward men? Do not his writings suggest that faith may aid reason rather than clash with it? How is the reader to reconcile Pushkin's glorification of the permanence of human friendship with the Soviet practice of renouncing old comrades on the slightest hint "from above? . . . " What about the contrast between the irreverent attitude toward political authority in the classics and Soviet reality? . . . What of the millions of copies of the fables of Krylov, some of which must be memorized by every Soviet schoolboy—fables that preach such

traditional virtues as truthfulness, honesty, goodness, charity, modesty, prudence, justice? Do not these help to unmask pretense and hypocrisy? Do they not help to discover that even the Soviet Emperor may, after all, be naked?[9]

The disintegration of socialist realism, which began almost immediately after Stalin's death in 1953, greatly intensified after Nikita Khrushchev's 1956 speech, which exposed many of the dictator's crimes. Much of Soviet writing quickly jettisoned a number of its hallowed attributes, including its "inspirational" quality and Positive Heroes as carriers of communist virtues that readers would wish to emulate. Under-standably, the relaxation of ideological pressures resulted in the hurried writing and publication of such muckraking novels as Ilya Erenburg's *The Thaw* (after which the first post-Stalin years were named), Vladimir Dudintsev's *Not by Bread Alone*, and also catapulted to fame Yevgeny Yevtushenko, a young poet of modest gifts. The values that this new Soviet writing championed were, to a non-Soviet observer, unexciting: honesty, truthfulness, sincerity. To millions of Soviet readers, however, their open articulation was of momentous significance. It implied a break with the Stalinist past and an attempt to reclaim the ethical legacy of pre-Soviet culture. Before long, another ethical category was rediscovered in published new fiction. Compassion, a concept with strongly religious overtones, emerged as a leitmotif of Aleksandr Solzhenitsyn's writings published in the Soviet Union prior to the novelist's expulsion from the country. It is particularly prominent in *One Day in the Life of Ivan Denisovich*, one of the first literary works to portray the universe of Soviet concentration camps, and in the parable-like story *Matryona's Home*. Solzhenitsyn's Ivan Denisovich, an ordinary uneducated Russian trying merely to survive in the arctic hell of a Soviet camp, is the first of a new species of literary heroes, the System's Victim. Solzhenitsyn's other novels, which achieved fame in the West and which feature similar protagonists, such as *The First Circle* and *Cancer Ward*, could not be printed in the Soviet Union until shortly before the dissolution of the Soviet Union in 1991. Nor was his monumental study of the Soviet penal camps, *Gulag Archipelago*.

Solzhenitsyn was neither the first nor the only author to deal with this explosive subject. Scores of books had appeared in the West (ultimately, they were all published in Russia as well) that described Stalin's jails, torture, and subarctic camps, ranging from Evgeniia Ginzburg's *Journey into the Whirlwind* to Varlam Shalamov's *Kolyma Tales* with the author's deliberately understated tones, to Anatoly Pristavkin's *A Golden Cloud Settled for the Night*, an artistically impressive account of Stalin's deportations of entire ethnic groups from the Caucasus. Others were more ambitious, as was Anatoly Rybakov's massive novel *Children of the Arbat*, with its pseudo-Tolstoian canvas of Soviet society gradually destroyed by Stalinist terror. Still others, such as Mikhail Shatrov's series of historical plays, attempted to pinpoint the precise time when Lenin's "idealistic" revolutionary party was seized by Stalin's criminal clique.

All these generally probed individual manifestations of Stalinism, however. A broader panorama of Soviet society after a half century of communist rule emerges from a substantial number of novels that appeared in the 1960s and 1970s. They are particularly noteworthy for their depiction of three social groups: the younger members of the privileged New Class; educated urban women; and the peasantry. The first are depicted with clear authorial disapproval in several works of Yury Trifonov, particularly *The Exchange, The Long Goodbye, The House on the Embankment,* and *The Old Man.* The sons and daughters (and grandsons and granddaughters) of civil war heroes and the hard-working builders of Soviet industry are nothing but ordinary greedy philistines, or worse. Natalya Baranskaya's *A Week Like Any Other* and I. Grekova's *Ladies' Hairdresser* and *The Hotel Manager* portray the unenviable lot of Soviet women driven to desperation by the demands of their jobs and families that are aggravated by perpetual shortages, waiting in lines, and overcrowded apartments. Baranskaya and especially Grekova describe their heroines with a profound concern that is occasionally tempered with gentle satire. By contrast, understatement is rare in works of authors identified with the so-called village prose school, and with good reason: conditions they depict really call for indignation and pity, a posture, it might be added, more traditional in Russian writing. Victor Terras defines village prose as

> a genre of post-Thaw literature which deals in a sympathetic way with
> rural life and with people who are not in the mainstream of organized,
> Party-controlled, production-oriented life. The two mainsprings of this
> genre are, on the one hand, compassion with the social misfit or under-
> dog and his alienated view of modern society, and on the other, a feeling
> that the very backwardness of a peasant unaffected by Party ideology
> and modern ways may have allowed him to retain certain values
> (Christian, or even pre-Christian, universally human) to which modern
> man is insensitive.[10]

Wolfgang Kasack, too, emphasizes that such works of country prose as Solzhenitsyn's *Matryona's House* did much to focus attention "on the human and especially the Christian religious values preserved in the central Russian village despite the conditions of poverty." He singles out for praise the novels of Valentin Rasputin, which "convincingly defend the religious and universal human norms of tradition," as well as the writings of Vladimir Soloukhin which champion not only Russian villages but also the nation's cultural treasures such as "churches, monasteries, icons and noblemen's residences."[11] It should be noted, however, that side by side with their championship of the downtrodden Russian peasants, of Russian nationalism, and of Christian values, some writers of country prose also display a darker side of that ideology. Not a few, such as Soloukhin and Viktor Astafiev, are prone to jingoistic nationalism and xenophobia: the latter gained notoriety for his "Fishing for Gudgeon in Georgia," with its blatantly racist overtones, and for his virulently anti-Semitic letters to Natan Edelman, the late literary historian. And it was Vasily Belov, a leading author of country prose, who in 1986 published *Everything Lies Ahead*, an unabashedly anti-Semitic novel.

Russian Literature in the Post-Soviet Era

Can one speak of a *Soviet* literary culture in post-Soviet Russia? Yes, although with some obvious reservations reflecting the demise of socialist realism. Gone are production novels, and Positive Heroes are no more. Instead, one finds such new subjects as religion, or more precisely, the life of the clergy and the faithful, much in the manner of Nikolai Leskov. Sergei Kaledin's *Humble Cemetery* broke that taboo some years ago, and much of his later work deals with similar subjects. Another innovation is reading matter (the Russian term, *chtivo*, is openly contemptuous) that hardly aspires to the lofty status of literature. The book market has been flooded of late with translations of Western thrillers, romances, and soft porn. Some of these are venerable classics, such as Margaret Mitchell's *Gone With the Wind*. Inevitably, there are Russian imitations, for example, the "sequels" to the Mitchell novel, innumerable detective stories, and somewhat clumsy erotic novels, of which Viktor Erofeev's *Russian Beauty* is a good example (an updated nineteenth-century bawdy novel in verse, *Luka Mudishchev*, is another). It goes without saying that recent Russian writing in general is infinitely more relaxed in its treatment of human sexuality than it ever was in Soviet times.[12]

An important group of younger authors, freed from the constraints of socialist realism, is experimenting with nonrealistic fiction. As Deming Brown observes:

> In recent works of [Anatoly] Kim, [Ruslan] Kireev, [Vladimir] Orlov, and [Anatoly] Kurchatkin, the real and the unreal are made to co-exist in a mixture of the ordinary, the fantastic and the supernatural. Kim's mysticism and his increased interest in metaphysical matters, in fact, make him seem more a romantic than a realist; Orlov joins him in combining

the romantic with the everyday. Orlov's use of phantasmagoria and Kurchatkin's depiction of dark powers at work in the otherwise ordinary world represent other kinds of departure from realism. Similarly, the use of parable by several of these authors seems at variance with realism. While Kurchatkin's anti-utopia [*Notes of an Extremist*] is realistic in its narrative manner, the story manifestly exceeds the bounds of the possible.[13]

All of the nonrealistic works enumerated above were printed in established literary journals that have been hospitable of late to unconventional writing, the latter seen as a way to bolster the literary journals' sagging circulations (*Novy mir* now has a press run of 29,000 and *Moskva*, 20,000; just a few years ago, during perestroika, many journals printed *millions* of copies). Nevertheless, a milestone in the recognition of the legitimacy of avant-garde writing was the launching in 1990, only months before the dissolution of the Soviet Union, of the "thick" journal *Vestnik novoi literatury*. With a press run of 2,000 (a respectable enough figure nowadays in Russia), the St. Petersburg journal's editorial board includes some leading avant-garde authors: Viktor Erofeev, Viktor Krivulin, Evgeny Popov, Dmitry Prigov, Aleksandr Sidorov, and Elena Shvarts. The seventh issue (1994) features verse by some of the leading modernist poets, including Lev Rubinshtein, Oleg Okhapkin, Sergei Ryzhenkov, and the late Mikhail Dikovnin, as well as prose by Boris Kudryakov, Svetlana Vasilieva, and Naum Brod. There is also a translation of a complex Hebrew novella by the late Shmuel Agnon.

The avant-garde authors, though no longer hounded by the establishment, are obviously destined to remain on the fringes of literary life. The mainstream remains resolutely committed to Soviet-style realism and to concerns that characterized its undoctrinaire and undogmatic practitioners, such as Yury Trifonov. Vladimir Tendryakov was, strictly speaking, Trifonov's contemporary, and he died a year before the advent of glasnost and perestroika. Many of Tendryakov's works, however, were published posthumously and thus constitute a bridge to the older Soviet literary culture. Novels in this category include *An Assassination Attempt on Mirages* (written in 1977–80, published in 1987), which speculates on historical events as they might have developed in the absence of Jesus Christ—or, in an analogy that suggests itself, of Lenin and Stalin. The novella *The Clear Waters of Kitezh* (written in 1977–80, published in 1986) also belongs in that group. It relates the story of a lethargic provincial town that suddenly awakens to an impending geological disaster but immediately reverts to its passive state when a forged "letter to the editor" suggests that higher authorities are not amused by the spontaneous outburst of initiative. The memoir *The Hunt* (written in 1971, published in

1988) similarly is óne such "bridge." It recalls the year 1948, the height of the anti-Semitic, "anti-cosmopolitan" purges, the criminal behavior of the novelist and literary bureaucrat Fadeev as well as the shameful silence of others, including Tendryakov himself, then only a student.

Andrei Bitov's *Pushkin House* was also a "bridge": published abroad in 1978, it was first printed in Russian in 1987. Filled with literary and historical allusions, it is a novel written to delight the educated elite. But then, most of Bitov's strongly introspective work, like that of Trifonov, describes intellectuals and conflicts and aspirations that are characteristic of that milieu.

One other author should be mentioned among the literary "bridges." He is Fazil Iskander, whose mock epic, *Sandro of Chegem*, an account of the misadventures of a picaresque ne'er-do-well, had been published in the 1970s and 1980s—always in censored form—but was allowed to appear uncensored only in 1988. Irreverent and playful, offering the Russian reader an enticing picture of an exotic Caucasus inhabited by wise fools and incurable skeptics, *Sandro of Chegem* is, indeed, a "bridge" that defies completion: Iskander continues to spin off from it a variety of yarns.

A vastly popular subject of the first post-Soviet years (although its appeal seems now to be gradually waning) was Russian history. The country's past was regarded as a way of explaining Russia's idiosyncratic national destiny (particularly the riddle of the establishment in 1917 of the Bolshevik state, the years of Stalin's bloody dictatorship, and—if only by implication—the roots of its eventual downfall) and also what is perceived as the Russian national character. Events leading to the collapse of the Romanov empire and the eventual proclamation of communist rule are described in Aleksandr Solzhenitsyn's monumental novel, *The Red Wheel*, whose sheer bulk, as I had opportunity to observe in the late summer of 1994 in Moscow and Siberia, scares off many potential readers. Anatoly Rybakov's *Children of the Arbat*, a "bridge" novel in several parts, launched when the Soviet Union was still in place, concluded in 1994 with the publication of *Dust and Ashes*. The time span of the novel is vast, from the early postrevolutionary years to World War II. Approximately the same period provides the setting for Vasily Aksyonov's *Generations of Winter*. Both Aksyonov and Rybakov offer intelligent analyses of Stalin's terror and convincing portraits of many historical personages, including, of course, the dictator himself. Georgy Vladimov (like Aksyonov, an emigré, although in recent years the designation has been losing much of its meaning) published an impressive novel about World War II, *The General and His Army*, in the Moscow journal *Znamia*.[14]

But then there were historical novels covering a wide spectrum of periods and issues, ranging from Yury Buida's *Athalie*, which describes a dissolute Russian princess from the times of Catherine the Great,[15] and the historically even more remote *Clearch and Heraclea*, Yuliia Latynina's novel set in ancient Greece,[16] to Yury Maslov's novella *Colonel Vysheslavtsev's Choice*, which portrays the chaos of the civil war, and Vasily Belov's novel in progress, *The Year of the Great Turnaround*. Belov, a leading exponent of country prose in the 1960s and 1970s, published his novel about the destruction of the traditional peasant way of life by Stalin's forced collectivization in *Nash sovremennik*, the leading journal of right-wing, nationalistically minded authors. Understandably, the problem of Russia's unique historical mission and the riddle of the Russian soul agitates these authors more than it does their more liberal and cosmopolitan colleagues. Indeed, the subject is discussed in nearly every issue of *Nash sovremennik*. This is not to say that the nonnationalists shun the subject altogether. Moderates (Vyacheslav Pyetsukh, for example) deal with it too, as do liberals and even emigrés, such as Fridrikh Gorenshtein and Feliks Svetov. However, as already mentioned, interest in historical topics is on the decline. Years ago, the Marxist Russian historian Mikhail Pokrovsky observed that history is politics projected into the past. A growing number of authors appear to eschew this indirect path in favor of head-on ideological fiction not unlike that of the Soviet era. Thus, Ivan Shevtsov (the reactionary Stalinist author of *The Ends of the Earth* [1961], in which villains read the then liberal *Novy mir* and translated Western fiction, bear suspiciously non-Russian names, and have hooked noses) surfaced in the neo-Bolshevik journal *Molodaia gvardiia*[17] with a novel entitled *The Blue Diamond*. Shevtsov's new opus reveals the true forces behind the Bolsheviks in 1917 (which are the same as those that oppress Russia at present) and features also a general who believes in the resurrection of a Soviet Russia.

More disquieting is the appearance in the staunchly nationalistic and religious *Moskva* (the journal's tendency is faithfully reflected on its cover, which depicts Saint George slaying a dragon) of three tales by Valentin Rasputin.[18] A leading writer of prose in the 1960s and 1970s and the foremost representative of country prose, Rasputin gradually shifted his political allegiances from moderate opposition to the Soviet regime to open enmity to post-Soviet Russia. For some years he wrote little fiction, devoting himself instead to environmentalist causes and journalism. The three tales in *Moskva* may signal his return to literary pursuits, albeit, in contrast to his earlier work that brought him international renown, highly politicized. The first story, *Senya Is on His Way*, relates the story of an elderly farmer whose ire is aroused by the smut that inundates post-Soviet television. He writes to the Moscow television authorities, who reply politely that they can understand the concerns of an aging man whose values differ from modern ones, "implying that elderly people are fools." The farmer is agitated when television shows unarmed people marching to occupy Ostankino television during the abortive putsch of 1993. They were mowed down by professional soldiers, and after that the "radio in the kitchen kept shouting about the enemies of the people, Fascists and stormtroopers, while Senya had visions of twelve-year-old mothers plucked out of school for the purpose. . . ." The implication here is that they were lured into prostitution, pornographic films, and smutty television shows. Rasputin ends his story thusly: "Senya is on his way. He'll get there." In a similar vein, "Young Russia" portrays young men and women corrupted by the new culture of easy money, casual sex, and contempt for work, while "In a Siberian City" demonstrates that the new "democratically elected" authorities are arbitrary and cruel. The following exchange is worth noting. An upright opponent of the new democrats calls a representative of the new authorities "an American bastard," to which the "American" replies, "and you are a Russian bastard." The Russian answers, "I am Russian, but not a bastard," and, significantly, the "American" democrat offers this rejoinder, "You mean there are Russians who are not bastards?" Rasputin's message to his readers is simple: The democrats, that is Yeltsin and company, are simply American agents who hold the Russian nation in contempt.

During the closing decades of the Soviet regime, right-wing literary journals frequently charged liberal Russian authors with slandering their country. The accusation was unfounded. What the liberals were intent on doing was continuing the venerable literary tradition of exposing social pathology and injustice. That tradition survives in post-Soviet Russia as well. Significantly, a large number of victims of social injustice portrayed in post-Soviet Russian writing are women. Their plight is described with much compassion by Tatiana Tolstaya, Viktoriia Tokareva, and especially Lyudmila Petrushevskaya. Petrushevskaya's frightening portrait of a middle-aged woman trying to care simultaneously for a daughter and her illegitimate child and for a senile mother is certainly memorable.[19] It is also, one may add, more timely than the oftentimes shrill writings of her nationalistic colleagues and more in keeping with the legacy of the great classics. As Pushkin expressed it in his "Monument," his claim to the affection of the Russian nation is rooted in his celebration of freedom in a cruel age, as well as in his appeals for compassion toward the fallen.

Notes

1. Vasily Rozanov, "Apokalipsis nashego vremeni," in *Izbrannoe* (Munich: A. Neimanis, 1970), p. 492.

2. For an excellent treatment of the subject, see Rufus W. Mathewson, Jr., *The Positive Hero in Russian Literature*, 2d ed. (Stanford: Stanford University Press,

1975). Many thoughtful observations may also be found in Regine Robin, *Socialist Realism: An Impossible Aesthetic* (Stanford: Stanford University Press, 1992).

3. For a discussion of this episode in the history of Soviet theater, see this writer's "Russia's Conflictless Drama," *Nucleus: A Little Magazine* 1, no. 3 (Winter 1954): 100–102.

4. William E. Harkins, *Dictionary of Russian Literature* (New York: Philosophical Library, 1956), p. 113.

5. Curiously, however, the issue continues to be debated in post-Soviet Russia. Thus, in 1992 Lyudmila Saraskina argued, much as the late Arkady Belinkov did in his 1976 book on Olesha, that Ilf and Petrov were sincerely helping the Communist party to discredit the old Russian intelligentsia and its non-Soviet values. Benedikt Sarnov disagreed, claiming that in reality *The Twelve Chairs* and *The Golden Calf* ridicule Soviet values. See *Oktiabr*, nos. 3, 6 (1992).

6. Vera S. Dunham, *In Stalin's Time: Middle-class Values in Soviet Fiction* (London: Cambridge University Press, 1976), pp. 19–20. There is, of course, much irony in the fact that the philistine qualities of old Russia's *meshchanstvo* were routinely denounced before the revolution by the liberal intelligentsia and, with special vehemence, by the Marxists and their allies.

7. Jeffrey Brooks, *When Russia Learned to Read: Literary and Popular Literature, 1861–1917* (Princeton: Princeton University Press, 1985), p. 298.

8. Maurice Friedberg, *Russian Classics in Soviet Jackets* (New York: Columbia University Press, 1962), and *A Decade of Euphoria: Western Literature in Post-Stalin Russia* (Bloomington: Indiana University Press, 1977).

9. Friedberg, *Russian Classics in Soviet Jackets*, pp. 170–72.

10. Victor Terras, ed., *Handbook of Russian Literature* (New Haven: Yale University Press, 1985), p. 91.

11. Wolfgang Kasack, *Dictionary of Russian Literature Since 1917* (New York: Columbia University Press, 1988), p. 447.

12. A good recent example is Marina Palei's novella "Gde zarozhdaetsia veter" (*Novy mir*, no. 12 [1994]), which describes one patient's conversations with a psychiatrist.

13. Deming Brown, *The Last Years of Soviet Russian Literature* (New York: Cambridge University Press, 1993), p. 123.

14. *Znamia* (May and June 1994).

15. *Volga*, no. 11 (1993).

16. *Druzhba narodov*, no. 1 (1994).

17. *Molodaia gvardiia*, no. 11–12 (1993) and no. 1–2 (1994).

18. *Moskva*, no. 7 (1994).

19. Lyudmila Petrushevskaya, "Vremia noch" (The Time Is Night), *Novy mir*, no. 2 (1992). Petrushevskaya continues here, as it were, her earlier work, which exposed the physical and moral squalor of the intelligentsia's milieu, such as "Nash krug" (Our Circle of Friends).

9

Artistic Culture

DANIIL B. DONDUREI

Official Blueprints and Unofficial Realities of Soviet Artistic Culture

"The poet in Russia is more than just a poet." This line from Yevgeny Yevtushenko's verse hints at the unique place that artistic culture has occupied in Russia's tragic history. From Aleksandr Radishchev and Lev Tolstoi to Aleksandr Solzhenitsyn and Arseny Tarkovsky, writers, painters, filmmakers—cultural producers of every kind—have undertaken to explain Russian society to itself. The common view that depicts Soviet art as subservient to ideology is well grounded in fact, but it tends to conceal as much as it reveals. Soviet artists served the state and thus could not help but be influenced by the nation's poisonous political climate. But they also thrived in the pungent native soil, soared high in their struggle against the system, and carved out an inner space where they could experiment with their craft and turn their humiliation into inspired works of art. Soviet artistic culture is a paradoxical tangle of forces, impulses, and relations generated by the nation's spiritual and social currents, which defy attempts to dispose of them in one fell swoop.

Take, for instance, the ideological pressure under which Soviet artists had to labor for some seventy years. It weighed heavily on artistic creativity, but it also inspired an unofficial art that flourished on the Soviet Union's cultural reservations. The same goes for popular or mass culture, which shaped a multilayered mythological consciousness steeped in official values and beliefs; at the same time, it fulfilled a certain therapeutic and compensatory function by fostering an ideal of closely knit human relations based on love, friendship, and ethical concerns. Filmmakers Grigory Aleksandrov and Ivan Pyriev, painters Aleksandr Deineka and Pyotr Konchalovsky, and composers Aram Khachaturian and Isaak Dunaevsky did sell themselves to the authorities, but in the process they managed not only to save their lives but also to produce some genuinely innovative art.

Russian Marxists did not create tension between the state and the artist—this tension predated the October revolution—but they exacerbated the situation by insisting that the artist subordinate his creative impulses to the noble goal of improving people's lives. Pushing the idea to its logical extreme, Bolsheviks proclaimed that serving the common good was the mark of genuine art and that failure to subordinate one's artistry to the revolutionary cause could be taken as proof that one did not belong to the profession. In 1918, People's Commissar Anatoly Lunacharsky promised that Soviet power would "mercilessly purge the temple of art from all those who are out to sell it and poison people's minds." Soviet art had to be dedicated exclusively to the propaganda and education of "the widest masses of working people." According to this ideologeme, all unaffiliated, nonpartisan, and foreign artistic experience was judged to be suspect, alien, or bourgeois and consequently incompatible with the building of a new socialist culture and personality.[1]

"The taming of art," as Yury Elagin aptly called this process, required that all cultural institutions be nationalized, governed from one center, subjected to censorship, and used to promote uniformity among artists. Agitprop, or the Department of Agitation and Propaganda, was set up in 1920 at the party Central Committee and charged with the task of "guiding the political education in the RSFSR [the Russian Federation] in its entirety." Alongside this overarching agency and under its watchful eyes flourished other state and public organizations responsible for what Soviet ideologists liked to call "cultural building." The most important among these organizations were the "creative unions," which, beginning in the 1930s, moved to enlist all writers, painters, composers, theater artists, filmmakers, and architects. Creative unions helped the party monitor the artistic process in the country, and their leaders did whatever was necessary to ensure that their rank-and-file members followed the doctrine of socialist realism.

The official artistic culture was distinguished by its totality. The heroes brought to life by Soviet artists had to be universally admired, be this Dmitry Furmanov's Chapaev, Arkady Gaidar's Timur, or Sergei Mikhalkov's Uncle Stepa, a noble representative of the ruthless Soviet militia. This does not mean that the aesthetic doctrine remained unchanged throughout the Soviet era. Periodically, new campaigns would be instigated to promote naturalism, everdayism, academism, documentalism, or some other artistic fad deemed to be the order of the day. Somewhere along the line, Ilya Erenburg even dared to attack photographic realism, which "sells itself as a reflection of real life." Still, each innovation had to be sanctioned from above, and it remained in vogue as long as it had the official seal of approval, which could be revoked at any time.

The keen interest that the party took in Soviet art comes across in lengthy broadsides published in *Pravda*, the Communist party's official newspaper. In 1936, a series of articles appeared in this authoritative source, bearing such eloquent titles as "Chaos Instead of Music," "Falsehood in the Ballet," "Cacophony in Architecture," and "About the Defiling Painters." During the Great Terror systematically carried out by Stalin, an artist's aesthetic convictions were literally a matter of life and death. Every poetic word, paintbrush, or dance step was closely scrutinized to ensure that it adhered to an ideologically sound pattern. Whenever the latest campaign would break out, be this the struggle against rootless cosmopolitans or the celebration of multi-ethnic Soviet art, artists had to show their enthusiasm. Emphases on the Soviet classics, the nation's economic achievements, or the people's victory in World War II were periodically decreed as the most important artistic themes, which then became more or less mandatory for all art practitioners. In the same fashion, the Communist party's Central Committee or the KGB departments responsible for art could instigate a national debate about the latest theater premier or painting exhibit, as was the case with the 1973 premier of *Master and Margarita*, a play directed by Yury Lyubimov, or with the (in)famous art exhibit staged in 1975 at the Palace of Economic Achievements. The public's real interest and opinion did not count in such carefully orchestrated discussions, which were planned ahead by the party bosses, who used their power to settle scores with the nonconformist intellectuals and to reward the politically correct ones. The latter learned to navigate between official values and the shifting political currents. Even when the audience clearly favored one artistic product over another, the outcome did not mean much, for honorariums and praise lavished on artists had little to do with the proceeds from a show. The law of supply and demand was inoperative under the monopoly conditions prevailing in Soviet art. The masses might crave Hollywood movies, but the authorities refused to order more than ten Hollywood films a year. About as many films were imported annually from India. Box office considerations could never override ideological imperatives. Any film, record, or book was deemed to be a priori "unprofitable" if it did not conform to correct political standards. While the Communist party tirelessly monitored artistic products for signs of ideological infractions, it strenuously avoided examining the economic consequences of its harebrained schemes. Artistic production in the Soviet Union had to submit to the same principles of centralized planning and cope with the same shortages and distribution gaps as the rest of the Soviet economy. Thus, the State Cinema Committee determined which movie theater would show a certain film on a given day, with every single movie showing in every single movie theater following, at least in theory, a centrally approved plan. This absurd supercentralization persisted for decades and survived into the early perestroika years.

According to Osip Mandelshtam, works created by Soviet artists could be broken down into two categories: those created with permission and those created without. "I want to spit on those writers who write what is permitted," wrote Mandelshtam in his *Fourth Prose*. "I want to hit them over the head with a stick. . . . I would forbid such writers to marry and have children."[2] Few authors dared to explore the realm of unpermitted subjects and ideas during the Soviet reign. Most dutifully followed the ideologically proven path. Some remained ambivalent, alternatively trying to march in lock step with the masses and strike on their own, to obey the party line and express their uncensored feelings. Very few shunned the requisite conformism altogether and dared to challenge the monolithic value system decreed by the regime.

It goes without saying that artistic life in such a complex modern society as the Soviet Union could never be fully controlled from one center. Things had to go awry, as orders were passed down the chain of command. There were also internal policy divisions within the Communist party itself, which Soviet artists learned to exploit. During the Khrushchev-inspired debate over Stalin's crimes, for instance, a number of works were published, including Solzhenitsyn's *One Day in the Life of Ivan Denisovich*, which would not have had a ghost of a chance at other junctures in Soviet history. The official blueprint for Soviet artistic culture failed to suppress the unofficial reality, which remained far more diverse than the taboo-laden party guidelines would have it. Various unofficial strands of artistic life sprang to life after Stalin's death and even prospered in the relatively liberal times unleashed by Nikita Khrushchev. In addition to the quasi-official ranking system that arranged all Soviet artists according to their contribution to building a socialist society, there was an unofficial hierarchy that assigned prestige to artists according to their skills, talents, and personal courage. An artistic event frowned upon by ideological watchdogs could be hailed by the nonconformist intelligentsia, the information about it swiftly spread by word of mouth. Similarly, independent artists could boycott a highly touted art exhibit by a state-decorated painter.

It would be wrong, therefore, to judge Soviet artistic culture by official pronouncements, formal reviews, and award ceremonies, which consistently glossed over the complex realities of artistic life in the Soviet Union. Hidden behind the "iron curtain" was a complicated process that absorbed within its bounds bizarre, utterly incongruous elements: the un-limited power of ancient warlords, feudal corporate guilds, predatory capitalist practices, and a centralized system of aesthetic education. When the Communist party finally yielded its monopoly on power, it left be-hind a murky legacy that included, along with the ecological and spiri-tual Chernobyls, diverse cultural achievements with a continuous appeal to the cultural elite and mass consumers alike. After all, official Soviet cul-ture was produced not just by witless political opportunists but also by highly talented artists. Hence, mistaken are those progressive liberals who dismiss Soviet artistic culture in toto and treat its products exclu-sively as ideological ciphers devoid of artistic merit.

Soviet Artistic Culture Under Perestroika

The Gorbachev era was marked by the erosion of ideological taboos and the dismantling of socialist realism. Censorship was rapidly losing its grip on the artistic spirit. The party line that used to separate right from wrong, the aesthetically meritorious from the aesthetically worthless, was now open to second-guessing. By the late 1980s, most artists had dis-carded their ingrained habits of self-censorship; some dug out evidence of their nonconformist past and proudly paraded it before the public. Spearheading the revolt in the arts, at their fifth national congress, mem-bers of the Cinema Union refused to reelect officially approved candi-dates for the organization's top offices—an act of breathtaking courage by 1986 standards. Long humiliated and repressed, the artistic intelligentsia savored its revenge against the "art critics in civilian clothes" who had done the party's and KGB's bidding among artists in the past. Previously suppressed art works by Soviet and foreign authors were exhumed and made public for the first time. In 1986 the Stanislavsky Theater staged Beckett's play *The Chairs*, and in 1987 the Ermolaeva Theater produced his *Waiting for Godot*. In the 1980s, *Novy mir* published Solzhenitsyn's *Gulag Archipelago*. The same year, an immensely popular countercultural film, *Little Vera*, was released in Soviet movie theaters. Next year, the Sovremennik Theater staged a play by Soviet dissident writer Vladimir Voinovich. Meanwhile, nonconformist works by Soviet artists began reaching audiences abroad, some earning top honors at international competitions. All these innovations made it abundantly clear that Soviet artistic culture was undergoing a major, perhaps revolutionary, change.

"In my view, Russia is the only country today where there is artistic freedom. It is hard to say how long this situation will last. Freedom al-ways faces challenges. One of its enemies is the market, the other censor-ship."[3] This remarkable testimony belongs to Andrei Konchalovsky, a

Soviet filmmaker who knew firsthand the artistic scene in both Soviet Russia and the capitalist West. Indeed, perestroika offered Soviet artists golden opportunities for free self-expression. Political constraints no longer stifled artistic creativity. At the same time, the paternalistic socialist state continued to take care of artists' needs, effectively relieving them from any economic responsibility. Every third film produced during the heyday of perestroika failed to recoup a tenth of its production cost. Hundreds of millions of rubles were lost, but since these were "nobody's rubles" generated by the still socialist economy, nobody complained. The question of the place that art should occupy in a postcommunist society did not hit Russian artists until after perestroika was nearly over. When Eric Weisman, former vice chairman of Warner Brothers, told a Moscow audience during his lecture about American cinema that "the movie director is worth as much as the proceeds from his last movie," Russian filmmakers were visibly upset. Such crass materialism seemed incompatible with the artists' lofty aspirations.[4] The Russian artistic intelligentsia always believed that "money could only ruin art," that the artist "has to choose between commercial success and his talent." In the land of dying socialism, commercial success still appears to be a random event, the luck of the draw. It might bring the artist a fortune, but it is in no way indicative of his work's artistic merit. If anything, success at the box office bodes ill for the development of a true artist, whose calling is to create timeless spiritual values, not to please the public.

Still, many artists took notice that the changed political climate might bring one spectacular financial success. In July 1988, at a major auction organized by a Western company, four paintings produced by a practically unknown artist, Grigory Bruskin, fetched $700,000, the largest personal profit ever made in the history of Russian art.[5] That Russian artists could spark interest in the West and have some real market value became clear from numerous art exhibits, film festivals, and musicians' contests that showcased Russian art abroad. Anyone who had incurred the wrath of the communist authorities in the past could now expect a sympathetic hearing abroad. The popularity that Mikhail Gorbachev and his reforms enjoyed in the West must have rubbed off on Soviet artists. True or not, former dissident artists were perceived in the West as Gorbachev's soulmates, active carriers of liberal culture who helped bring the end of the cold war. "Sotsart," an artistic current that mocked socialist values by hyperextending socialist symbols and images, gained special favor in the West. Works by its representatives were prominently featured not only in elite art magazines but also in mass consumption publications, such as *Reader's Digest.* One by one, all barriers to art exports from Russia fell.

Just as Soviet art found a niche in Western markets, Russian emigré art made its way back home. Joseph Brodsky, Eduard Limonov, Willy

Tokarev—no border patrol could keep ex-Soviet artists from regaining a mass audience, entering the local markets in Russia, affecting the fortunes of publishers and art entrepreneurs. Art production in Russia increasingly came under the sway of market mechanisms. Indicative in this respect is the fate of the publishing industry in postcommunist Russia.

It is well known that the word—written and spoken—has always had an extraordinary significance in Russia. As the saying goes, "In Russia, word *is* deed." This old saw is literally true: a word could land someone in jail or deliver someone from bondage. Strict control over words uttered and printed had been a high priority for Russia's rulers, communist and noncommunist. As soon as the Communist party began to lose its monopoly on power, Russia saw an explosion of free speech. The floodgates were flung open in 1989, when party apparatchiks made a last-ditch effort to stem the tide of glasnost by limiting circulation of the most popular publications. This clumsy attempt failed miserably. Thousands of new magazines and periodicals hit the newsstands, catering to the public's insatiable appetite for free information. At the same time, the publishing industry experienced an unprecedented boom. Artistic books, astrological treatises, sex manuals, self-help guides—whatever the Soviet reader wanted to know about anything and everything was now printed and made available in regular bookstores or makeshift stands set up by private book vendors.

Just as the centuries-old civilization of *unfreedom of speech* expired, however, "the most reading nation on earth" turned a deaf ear to the free word. Within a few years of total glasnost, the public lost its interest in reading literature and listening to speeches. The "thick" literary journals that once boasted circulations in the millions now print fewer than 5 percent of the copies they circulated during the height of perestroika. Once immensely popular newspapers could not sell enough copies to support themselves and had to beg for government subsidies to stay in business. Book prices have skyrocketed, making the most sought after volumes unaffordable for the average buyer. Even when prices are within reach, consumers often choose to spend their money elsewhere. Ex-Soviet citizens have grown tired of the orgy of glasnost. Igor Klyamkin, Nikolai Shmelev, Gavriil Popov, and dozens of other prominent opinion makers who once captivated the entire nation with their fiery oratory and inspired essays have all but disappeared from the political center stage. The establishments that made headway during perestroika are being revamped under pressure from the market. Well-established bookstores are forced to sublet space to other businesses. In the fall of 1992, the passer-by could spot brand-new Cadillacs, Pontiacs, and Chevrolets prominently displayed among the bookshelves waiting to be taken out from the well-known bookstore nestled on the first floor of the newspaper *Trud*. Store administrators had to curtail their declining business to make room for the glamour business of the future. In a striking metaphor, shiny cars symbolizing capitalism assumed the honorary place inside the building, while the books epitomizing Russia's precapitalist past were ready to be thrown out onto the streets.

Similar metamorphoses marked the transition to postcommunist realities in other cultural domains. The first Russian film market dates back to 1988, when movie distributors wrestled the right to buy films with an eye to their profit potential rather than ideological purity. This revolt spelled the end of the old communist bondage system that mandated which pictures were to be filmed, which shown to the public, and which indefinitely shelved. Foreign products inundated Russian television and movie theaters, their share jumping from 35 percent in 1986 to 85 percent in 1989.[6] At about the same time, pirated video tapes poured into the country. The growth in cultural imports was accompanied by an explosion of domestic artistic production. Hundreds of new art galleries, movie studios, theater groups, and musical collectives sprouted in urban centers. Giant companies, like Roskontsert and Mosfilm, managed to rid themselves of state control and made tentative moves toward financial independence.

Given this explosion of artistic activity, one would expect public interest in art to soar as well. But as with the publishing industry, the reality turned out to be less palatable. As soon as creative endeavor was freed from all ideological fetters, Russian artists confronted a formidable challenge: a sharp decline of public interest in art. In 1986, the film industry lost money. Movie theater attendance dropped from nearly 2 billion tickets sold in 1986 to 950 million sold in 1988. Concert halls and theaters could not attract enough people to fill one third of their seats.[7] Ironically, interest in cultural events evaporated as soon as every Russian (and not just the well-connected members of the cultural elite) were allowed to watch once forbidden movies by Pier Paolo Pasolini and listen to the much vilified music of Arnold Schonberg. Even the pornographic films that flooded the Russian market during the late 1980s failed to arrest the steep decline in the nation's cultural consumption. The chronic shortages of cultural goods endemic to socialist society finally came to an end, and so did the Russian public's yen for art.

This does not mean, of course, that Russians have no more interest in cultural and artistic products. What happened was that artistic consumption shifted from the public arena to private homes, which by the end of the 1980s had become the locus of cultural life in the country. According to sociological data gathered in this period, Russian citizens spent five to six times more time and eight to ten times more money on home entertainment and private cultural consumption than on attendance in theaters, concerts, art exhibits, and other public cultural venues. Something strange also happened to the quality of cultural consumption.[8] The Russian intelligentsia in particular used to pride itself on its highly selective approach to what its members read or viewed; new findings indicated that intellectuals and nonintellectuals alike were watching television programs across the board, as though fearing that life itself would grind to a halt if the tube went blind. Twenty-seven percent of viewers reported that their television sets were turned on even when nobody was watching. "I don't like what I see, but I enjoy watching it anyhow," wrote an avid television viewer in his letter to the editor. Another one angrily denounced a television station because "I had to stay up until midnight to watch the garbage you put on the screen, as if I didn't have anything better to do."

Changing public attitudes took their toll on artists. Some prominent film directors (Gleb Panfilov, Elen Klimov, Aleksei German, Andrei Smirnov) stopped making movies. Well-known stage directors (Anatoly Vasiliev, Lev Dodin, Kama Ginkas) do more work abroad than at home. The same is true of Russia's leading musicians (Vladimir Spivakov, Yury Kitaenko, Alfred Shnitke) and painters (Ilya Kabakov, Leonid Purygin, Igor Ganikovsky). Still others went the commercial route, consciously catering to mass market tastes, however distasteful the final product. Emigration, the bulk of which was comprised by the intelligentsia, had reached 200,000 people annually by the late 1980s.

The Art, the Artist, and the Quasi-Market

Let us now examine more closely the muddled relationship between art and market in the post-Soviet era, as exemplified by the Russian film industry. From 1988 on, the Russian artistic intelligentsia, including filmmakers, had most of their dreams come true. There were virtually no limits to what intellectuals could say about their society, government, or political system. Virtually all sexual taboos were abandoned. The state underwrote artistic work with little or no regard for its financial viability, giving artists the incentive to take up ambitious projects. The Russian cinema industry worked overtime. Producers, screenwriters, actors, stage hands—everybody had as much work as they could handle. Financiers aggressively invested in risky movie projects, seemingly without concern for economic realities.[9] Artists did not stand to make much money from their undertakings, but they did not have to worry about starving either, even though the ultimate product might be a financial flop. The socialist system continued to subsidize creative activity, never mind that the artists lampooned socialism and its by-products. There were still nomenklatura bureaucrats with close ties to the party who had to okay the project, but sensing the changing of the guards, they did not miss a chance to show their benevolent support for perestroika art.

This situation, which lasted for about three years, produced disastrous results. After the path-breaking picture *Little Vera*, only one home-grown movie made the top-twenty list of the country's most popular films. No amount of sex and violence inundating the screen could change the general trend: movie theater attendance dropped fourfold between 1988 and 1992. Even when the Russian economy reached the breaking point and made it impossible to continue generous state subsidies of art, movies continued to be made in the face of this economically absurd situation.

One reason why the movie industry did not go bankrupt under these trying circumstances was the shadow economy, which targeted the movie business for its money-laundering schemes. There is a lot that Russian artists could learn from Russian entrepreneurs when it comes to imagination and creativity.[10] Say, there is a film produced by a company for 2 million rubles (prices are still in line with Gorbachev-era inflation rates). It is purchased by a phantom company that has no relationship to the movie industry whatsoever. The studio where the film was shot had all of its expenses reimbursed, plus an arbitrary established profit of a million and a half rubles was paid to the producers by the shady company that now owns the movie. The company that purchased distribution rights doctors the documents that attest to the fabulous proceeds of 10 million rubles from movie runs in the nation's movie theaters. From that point on, the illegal money made from unrelated shady deals is legitimized. You can bet that the principals in this game were paid off with hefty bribes that made them rich by Russian standards. Meanwhile, the film in question has not been shown to the public once.

Another scheme would have the producer get the money from a bank to pay for equipment, studio space, and actors' fees, spend a whole lot less for actual shooting, and in the end present the resultant film as an experimental product of such extraordinary aesthetic quality that it could not possibly be understood by the moviegoing public. Nobody ever sees the film, the investors are bought out (remember, the money is nobody's!), and auditors are still such a rarity that there is no point worrying about them. In the end, the lost money is written off as a bad investment by the state.

Or else the studio director might strike a deal with a foreign company that wants to use local facilities, show a fictitious price tag in the official documents, and then split the difference with its foreign partners. The studio director's personal profit could be deposited in a bank account abroad. All this in spite of the fact that the studio facilities are not privately owned, that they still belong to the state, or which is the same thing, they are collectively owned by the Russian people.[11] Add to this a chance to speculate on the changing conversion rates when you do transactions in both hard currency and soft (in Russia they are called "wooden") rubles, and you can see that the movie business provided many fresh opportunities in the post-Soviet period.

We should keep in mind, however, that local cinema had something to gain from all this wheeling and dealing. Hollywood paid Mosfilm, the preeminent Russian movie company, in dollars for Andrei Konchalovsky's picture *The Inner Circle*, and the proceeds more than made up for the losses that Mosfilm incurred by producing two dozen Russian films. Similar stories come from Lenfilm and other leading movie companies that have their own production base and offer foreign companies their facilities. In those heady years, studio administrators did not look too closely at the projects undertaken by local directors, as long as the latter showed an overall profit. As to Russian filmmakers, they never cared that much about box office success. High-brow pictures, the ones that win prizes at the international movie festivals, rarely attract much attention from the general public anyhow. As long as the artists are allowed to exercise their artistic freedom, they are more than willing to shoot pictures for each other.

Thanks to this inane political economy of artistic production, films were shot that could not be sold, or sold without being copied, or copied without being distributed to theaters. "The new Russians," those entrepreneurs who sponsored many films in the perestroika and postperestroika years, did not care much about quality. The cult of hopelessness, or *chernukha*, permeated the movies of this period. Under the pretense of being truthful to reality, financial mentors encouraged artists to use one color, one emotional tonality, one cruel method to elicit the viewer's response.

Even after the Soviet Union collapsed, its economy continued to churn out products that were not meant for consumption, that were not designed to make profit, that were produced for some mysterious purposes that had nothing to do with art. For all the talk about profit, marketing, cost accounting, and so on, Russia still has no market in place. At best we can talk about a quasi-market that imitates its external forms. This is not to deny that revolutionary changes have taken place in the last few years in the financing, production, and distribution of art in Russia. But the central relationship for a market economy between the producer and the consumer remains profoundly distorted. The Russian market is still largely immune to the law of supply and demand. Nor is there any credible system of accounting that would allow a bona fide investor or economist to make an informed judgment about industry conditions. There is no national statistical agency to track the data and report on federal and local trends. You cannot be sure how many studios are open for business at any given point, how many viewers saw a particular picture, what the production cost was, and so on. All this is a commercial secret. Credible information is a luxury in a country that, defying Marx, is moving from mature socialism via eternal feudalism toward primitive capitalism. Or could it be that reliable information is a barrier to relentless wheeling and dealing? Here the words of the Marquise de Custine, the nineteenth-century Frenchman who traveled to Russia and observed her inimitable mores come to mind: "In theory, everything seems so overregulated that one can hardly live under this regime. But in practice, exceptions abound, so much so that the resultant chaos and contradictions make you wonder how on earth one could govern the country under these circumstances."[12]

Russian artists are struggling to shake loose their old shackles and adjust to the new economic conditions, but in the process they are discovering that the old artistic culture—cliché-ridden, politically stifling, full of envy and petty rivalries—was not without its graces. For all its absurdities, it bred a sense of belonging and solidarity that comes from being a member of an exclusive guild. Like a centaur, Soviet artistic culture spliced together and made possible the coexistence of diverse interests and groups. It fed a mythology that was familiar to all, that united under one umbrella all those exposed to the same principles, even though some of these principles were experienced as hated official stereotypes. At least there was a feeling of collective injustice, of shared fate, of a common dead end where any artist could be hounded by ideological watchdogs. Now this cozy feeling of negative and positive togetherness is gone, the artistic space is being totally revamped, and those who inhabit it find themselves competing for the same resources, divided by market forces more than they ever were by ideological differences. The aesthetics of socialist surrealism has fallen by the wayside; the artist has been thrown on his own devices; at last, he is free. But the creative boom promised by vulgar sociology has failed to materialize. "I am not sure why," confides Aleksei German, "but we made our best movies when stagnation reigned supreme and everything was prohibited."[13]

Russia as an Artistic Colony of the West

Now that we have examined the shady transactions between the quasi-market and Russian artistic culture, we can turn to the relationship between the state, the artist, and local and international markets. Specifically, we shall try to understand the impact of the international art market on Russian art and the policies through which the Russian state is trying to regulate artistic activity.

The fine arts have always been among the most conservative domains of Russian artistic culture. It is all the more astounding how quickly the practitioners in this field have adjusted themselves to postsocialist realities. Within a few years, Soviet painters and craftsmen were attending international art auctions, forming joint ventures with Western customers, selling their ware for hard currency, and opening bank accounts abroad. The explanation is rather simple: painting is a labor-intensive art that does not require sophisticated technology and equipment—or, for that matter, a mass audience. In the old Soviet Union, it was practiced by individuals who might have quarreled with the socialist state but who managed to carve out a niche for themselves and, in relative obscurity, perfected their skills and developed innovative ideas. Painters, animation artists, craftsmen, and other fine art practitioners did not have to do as much catching up with the West as artists in some other fields. When liberal reforms rolled in, they were ready to come out of the closet fully equipped for the new deal. However, the state saw the field's considerable potential as a source of hard currency and geared its tax policy accordingly. More than half of the profits made by the artists have to be returned to the state in the form of taxes. If a transaction between a Russian artist and Western customer involves hard currency, the state prefers to keep the dollars, deutsche marks, or franks and pay the artist the after-tax portion of his profit in rubles. But the economic strength of the ruble does not compare with that of freely convertible currencies. Nor are Russian art collectors in a position to pay top prices for national art (an art work that could be sold abroad for thousands of dollars would not fetch a fraction of that amount at home). As a result, the artist is placed in a situation where he is either going to cheat a state that tries to rob him and his dealer or to resettle in the West. Russian artists keep $50 million to $60 million in foreign banks, according to some conservative estimates. All the participants in this charade—the dealers, gallery administrators, collectors, and of course artists—are convinced that they are being cheated, that somebody is out to deprive them of their fair share of profit. The pressure is mounting for all those involved in fine arts to make a killing, evade taxes, and then bid goodbye to this monstrous, inefficient, corrupt system.

Our very best artists, in both the fine and performing arts, are leaving the country in droves in hopes of escaping the clutches of the sputtering economy. Painters, craftsmen, composers, musicians—entire orchestras and ballet schools—are saying goodbye to their homeland and settling in the West. The best Russian composers are now permanently residing in Germany. Even more ominously, second string musicians, dancers, singers, philologists, and architects are straining to land a contract abroad as teachers, coaches, chorus line performers—whatever can get them out of the sinking country. Most of them have no wish to leave their country permanently, but they believe they have to bide their time abroad until things back home settle enough to afford them a half-decent living.

A related problem is the tendency to gear all artistic output to export needs. Consciously and unconsciously, Russian artists today strive to adjust their priorities and criteria to Western standards. They are trying hard to please potential customers abroad and along the way neglect their own creative impulses. The dictate of the Western markets could be no less stifling than the standards laid out by Mikhail Suslov's Politburo. Whether the artist follows socialist realism or places himself in the service of his new employer, he has to do somebody else's bidding. For some Russian artists, it was easier to submit to the hated ideological strictures of the past when there seemed to be no other choice than it is to subordinate their artistic impulses to the free market's demands.

If Russia ever was an artistic superpower, it does not seem to be one any longer. There is an uneasy feeling in the air that the country has turned into an artistic colony of the West, a feeling reinforced by scores of art dealers and entrepreneurs rummaging Moscow for artistic bargains, like Victorian Englishmen in Africa or India. Nonetheless, superpower habits and pretenses are dying hard, even in the face of mounting evidence that the nation's standards of living are on par with, if not Lesotho then certainly Thailand. Meanwhile, unofficial art, this fountain of creativity in the past, has virtually disappeared.[14] The spiritual opposition that fed this uncensored artistic endeavor has been sapped. It was easier for the artist to assume a defiant stance when Andrei Zhdanov, Mikhail Suslov, and Yegor Ligachev wagged their fingers and threatened to put artists in jail.[15] With double-think and the multilayered aesthetic sensibilities it engendered becoming a thing of the past, the artistic intelligentsia has little to nourish its nonconformist impulses.

The New Aesthetics and Mass Culture

Official Soviet ideology prided itself on creating a state with "mass aesthetic literacy," "the highest prestige of art," and "genuinely free artistic activity." None of these clichés withstood the test of time. We can size up the situation by taking a closer look at current television programming and examining the manner in which mass media shape popular culture.

If you watch Russian television today for any length of time, you are likely to conclude that the Russian viewer must know English to watch the news, appreciate a movie, or understand the advertising. A synchronized Russian translation could be provided, depending on the program and its sponsors' agenda. Nothing new here: English may well become a universal language for the global media-market civilization of the future, but the pace of change is staggering.

Take the children's program *Rock Lesson*, which first aired in 1992. The program hosts are a sixteen-year-old girl, symbolically named "Barbie" after the internationally acclaimed doll, and a young boy, Vanya, apparently born after the death of Leonid Brezhnev. Vanya asks his counterpart all sorts of questions that might interest members of his generation, like how to dance rap and hip-hop, how to dress up in order to resemble the dance machine M.C. Hammer, what love is and how to make out. The national children's audience, which includes kids from provincial towns like Syzran and Vologda, are instructed how to look like Americans and act like the average European. One might think that Russian children had already emigrated and cannot waste a day without learning the hippest dance step, tuning in on the top-ten show, or finding out the latest development in the sensational rape trial of American heavyweight boxer Mike Tyson. The pirated Hollywood movies and Hollywood-style programming that jam Russian TV do a far better job of changing the country's centuries-old mind set than all Yeltsin decrees put together. We can judge this from a survey conducted in 1991 among six-year-old Muscovites. When researchers asked Moscow kindergarten graduates, "Who do you love the most?" the answer was: mother, father, Chip and Dale, Captain Power, and only then . . . grandma.

Do not rush to conclude, however, that American values dominate Russian mass culture. Russians may be dreaming about a trip to Disneyland and the taste of a burger at McDonalds, but when it comes to loftier matters, they crave the Mexican soap opera *The Rich Also Cry*. Very few viewers completely missed this sensational series, which Russian TV programmers aired a few years ago. It broke all the rating records, easily outstripping American blockbusters in popularity and tying the nation to their screens for months on end. I do not know whether the guns fell silent in Nagorno-Karabakh, where Armenians and Azeris were fighting, but it is a fact that viewers in Moldova and Lithuania thwarted their governments' decision to boycott Moscow TV because they could not bear the thought of missing the end of this melodrama.[16] Veronica Castro, the Mexican actress who played the soap opera's main character, emerged as one of the country's most popular personalities in the 1992 polls, placing right behind the country's president, head of government, and vice-president.

There are several reasons why this run of the mill soap opera had such a hypnotic effect on the audience in the former Soviet Union. Perhaps the most compelling one is the full rehabilitation of lowly—mass—culture in postindustrial societies, where it invariably supplants folklore as the archetypical mode of construction for social reality. Among the main features distinguishing mass culture are the nonambiguity of moral judgments, consistency of values, accepted wisdom of common sense, inescapability of suffering, and abiding optimism. Over 60 percent of television viewers in the former Soviet Union who saw this soap opera (twice as many as any other television program, including the news) gratefully clung to the helping hand extended to them by the Mexican producer. Disoriented, neglected, and scorned, the millions of Russian-speaking viewers found in this unpretentious television series the certainty they missed in their everyday life. The program allayed their fears before the menacing English-speaking civilization that threatens their life experience with words like "voucher," "digest," "broker," "impeachment," and "rating." It relieved their inferiority complex before high modernist culture and strengthened their heart in the face of an uncertain future. After watching this soap opera, many ex-Soviets could summon enough courage to say no to the violence and sex that invaded their screens, to resist aggressive advertising and ruthless politicians. The Russians took Latin American culture to heart because it appeared to them devoid of ethnic, economic, and generational differences. They felt more attuned to the problems facing the Salvators' family with its colorful array of dons and señoritas, than with their own reality being shoved down their throats by familiar political and artistic personages competing with each other for the dubious honor of painting the most dire scenario for the future. The simple folk who survived the Soviet regime know the difference between fiction and reality, yet they prefer to trust fiction, which tells them that evil will be punished and loyalty rewarded, that in spite of its endless confusions and challenges, life is really simple and all people can be divided into two classes: angels and demons. The only problem is how to tell them apart.

Trial by Freedom:
Prospects for the Russian Artistic Market

Soviet artistic culture has been often pictured in black and white: official art approved by the Communist party, on the one hand; and unofficial, experimental art that flourished on the fringes of society, on the other. Looked at from the vantage of the present, the reality seems more complex than common judgment allows. Compared to the market-imposed uniformities, the art produced during the Soviet era now appears to be complex, nuanced, pluralistic, daring, and often inspired. It may be premature to talk about the decline of artistic culture in today's Russia, but we can attest to the precipitously declining public demand for art. When a book salesman can earn twenty times as much as a writer and a professor's salary is typically lower than his student's income, the public turns away from art and looks for other venues of personal growth.

The drop in art's prestige is inevitable in a country where art served as a political club, research laboratory, and psychological therapy and performed numerous other functions not central to its mission. With the public redeploying its interests and resources toward material comfort, a slogan once issued by a nineteenth-century aesthetic realist, Dmitry Pisarev—"boots are above Pushkin"—seems to have come true. The status of art as an aesthetic force binding the nation together has been compromised, and along with it, the need to cultivate aesthetic sensibilities. Art has lost its power to confer prestige on its practitioners and connoisseurs. Your place in the group hierarchy depends on your ability to tell the difference between a Toyota and Nissan more than on your ability to distinguish between Jean-Paul Sartre and Albert Camus. It has more to do with your awareness of Baskin Robbins ice cream flavors than with the fact that you have attended an exhibit featuring paintings from the Prado. The "new Russians," who resemble yuppies in their fondness for expensive suits and glitzy cars, are yearning not for tickets to attend a Tarkovsky retrospective but for a vacation in the Bahamas. They cannot stand the intelligentsia's interminable kitchen debates about the country's future that used to absorb the country's cultural elite. Now, consumer culture has supplanted artistic culture, imported culture has pushed aside domestic culture, and mass culture has stamped out elite culture. The Russian artist can no longer hope to earn a living by selling his art to local consumers. To survive, he has to appeal to the state, shady businessmen, and foreign buyers. What would Russian filmmakers do without a money-laundering sponsor, given galloping inflation, dwindling ticket sales, the flood of pirated videos, and a virtual guarantee that any locally produced movie will not earn more than a quarter of its cost?[17] If current trends continue, Russian filmmakers will lose the last outlet for their artistic production—national television.

Private capital pushes aside government in mass culture–oriented industries like television and show business. Our television industry, including state-owned channels, survive chiefly on profits from advertisement. In December 1994, one minute of prime-time television advertisement in Russia cost $30,000 to $40,000. Meanwhile, the number of nongovernment television studios in Moscow, St. Petersburg, and virtually all provincial Russian cities continues to grow, with roughly 3,000 private and cable television stations officially registered in the country by mid-1995.

In less lucrative cultural production areas (museums, concerts, theater, and movies), the state continues to be the major presence. Since 1992, when the state relinquished strict price control, the price tag of producing one movie jumped from between $50,000 and $100,000 to $1 million at the end of 1994. At best, one fourth of movie production costs can be recovered through regular ticket and television rights sales. But then what else could one expect when millions of Russian viewers only watch pirated American films on cable television?

The movie industry in Russia shrank but hardly disappeared, thanks to the underground economy and clever financial machinations. There were 300 full-feature films produced in 1991 in Russia, compared to 100 films in 1994. By early 1995, over 4 million families (one out of nine families in the country) had a videotape machine. The sales of blank videocassettes is currently about 20 million a year; 80 million videocassettes are available for rent. According to experts, hundreds of millions of dollars are recycled through this industry every year, most of it successfully evading taxation. The Russian public now has a chance to watch Western hit movies about the same time they are shown in European and American capitals (laser discs are stolen straight from Hollywood!).

It will not be long before Russian-made movies made in recent years will lose their last refuge—national television. The only type of movies that continue to enjoy high ratings among Russian television audiences are old communist hits of a bygone era. Nothing produced during the perestroika and post-Soviet years has an audience in today's Russia. Just a few years ago, the fate of Russian mass culture in general and the movie industry in particular depended on the fate of the underground economy. Now the key question for the future of artistic culture in Russia is how the shadow economy can integrate itself with its legitimate counterpart.

We are witnessing a great historical experiment: the titanic struggle between Russian economic theory and practice, on the one hand, and a Western-style market economy, on the other.[18] If capitalist market laws prevail in Russia, we should see the Russian film industry coming to the brink of extinction. Already most of the 500 movie studios in the country are without business. The result will be massive unemployment among artists, perhaps mitigated by the arrival of advertising agencies and other start-up businesses that use artistic skills.[19] If matters are allowed to drag on, Russia's voodoo economics will avoid forging a bond between the art industry and mass consumers.

As always, our best minds are tirelessly pondering the question of how to build the market in postcommunist Russia, how to make the state serve its citizens instead of sacrificing individual interests to the state. Some point to precedents from the prerevolutionary era, when Russia made considerable strides toward the market under the able stewardship of Counts Witte and Stolypin. As Gogol once lamented, Russia's privileged fate is to skip the present and dream its way into the future. The fantastic blend of old and new structures in today's Russia, legal and black markets, reflects the inertia of a centuries-old cultural tradition that stubbornly resists radical reforms.[20] But there is always hope. Unlike gas and oil, the nation's supply of renewable artistic talent is vast. Perhaps one day, the country will manage to put it to good use. Perhaps it will even find a place within its own borders for both mass and high culture, consumer and elite art. Meanwhile, the question persists of when, if not whether, the country will develop a viable economics, and at what price. As a student of culture put it: "I know that the market has many advantages, but we should remember the inhospitable native soil where it is struggling to sink roots, our fabled capacity to make a mockery of the most wonderful ideas that we seek to adopt. How many times in the past were we made to feel foolish and idiotic after sowing one thing and harvesting something altogether different?"[21]

The fate of art in Russia, both socialist and nonsocialist, tells us something important about the society as a whole. We simply need to figure out what it might possibly be.

Notes

This article was translated from the Russian by Dmitri N. Shalin. The author wishes to thank the George Soros Foundation and the International Research and Exchanges Board for their support.

1. K. Aiermakher, "Sovetskaia literaturnaia politika mezhdu 1917 i 1932," 3–62, in *V tiskakh ideologii. Antologiia literaturno-politicheskikh dokumentov. 1917–1927 gg.* (Moscow: Knizhnaia Palata, 1992).

2. Osip Mandelshtam, *Sochineniia v dvukh tomakh* (Moscow: Khudozhestvennaia Literatura, 1990), II: 92.

3. "Interviu s Andreem Konchalovskim," *Iskusstvo kino*, no. 8 (1989): 89.

4. "Ne v dengakh schastie," *Iskusstvo kino*, no. 10 (1989): 3–5.

5. D. Dondurei, "Zhenitba iskusstva na dengakh," *Smena*, no. 6 (1991): 140–52.

6. D. Dondurei, "Kvartira: novyi tip uchrezhdeniia kultury," in *Gorodskaia kultura: Problemy kinovatsii* (Moscow: NII Kultury, 1987), p. 58.

7. *Natsionalnoe kino: Strategiia vyzhivaniia* (Moscow: NII Kinoiskusstva, 1991), p. 10.

8. "Sovetskaia ruletka," *Ogonek*, no. 28 (1991): 22.

9. S. Kordonsky, "Sotsialnaia struktura i mekhanizm tormozheniia," in *Postizhenie* (Moscow: Progress, 1989), pp. 36–51.

10. I. Reig, "Nelegalnaia ekonomicheskaia deiatelnost," in *Postizhenie*, pp. 203–16.

11. *Tenevaia ekonomika* (Moscow: Ekonomika, 1991), p. 17.

12. *Zapiski o Rossii Markiza de Kustina* (Moscow: SP Interprint, 1990), p. 109. The translations here and elsewhere in this chapter are by Dmitri Shalin.

13. "Interviu s A. Germanom," *Sovetskaia kultura* (October 17, 1989).

14. Valery Podoroga, "Elena Dolgikh: Nonstop interviu," *Artograph*, no. 1 (1993): 39.

15. V. Fomin, "Polka," pp. 3–15, in *Dokumenty, svidetelstva, komentarii* (Moscow: NII Kinoiskusstva, 1992).

16. D. Dondurei, "Marianna Zastupnitsa," *Nezavisimaia gazeta* (November 18, 1992).

17. *Otechestvennoe kino: Strategiia vyzhivaniia* (Moscow: NII Kinoiskusstva, 1991), pp. 28–51.

18. A. Bunich, "Tenevye opukhali legalnoi ekonomiki," in *Tenevaia ekonomika* (Moscow: Ekonomika, 1990), p. 14.

19. *Proryv k realnosti: Sotsialnoe proektirovanie v sfere kultury* (Moscow: NII Kultury, 1990), pp. 3–63.

20. K. Razlogov, *Kommertsiia i tvorchestvo: Vragi ili soiuzniki?* (Moscow: Iskusstvo, 1990), pp. 3–63.

21. L. Nevler, "Pravila dlia iskliuchenii," *Znanie-Sila*, no. 9 (1988): 37.

10

Labor Culture

VLADIMIR S. MAGUN

Labor Morality Under Socialism

Soviet leaders always took a keen interest in workers' behavior and sought to keep work ethics under strict state control. A complex network of values and regulations was developed for this purpose after the October 1917 revolution. They were best articulated in the "political economy of socialism," which purported to present a scientific picture of the country's economic life. Textbooks on socialist economy were widely circulated in the Soviet Union and appropriate courses included in a core curriculum for all higher education institutions in the country. Basic tenets of socialist political economy were taught in introductory social science classes in high schools. Leading educators helped popularize the subject, major research centers in the nation continued to perfect the science of socialist economics. A prominent place in socialist political economy was given to work ethics, labor motives, employment opportunities, reward structure, and other characteristics of socialist labor culture. In this chapter, I shall examine socialist labor morality, the relationship between official Soviet blueprints and unofficial realities, the changes that socialist labor culture has undergone in recent years, and the emerging trends in labor morality and work ethics in post-Soviet society.

Work and Employment
in Socialist Ideology

To begin with, all things connected with labor had a special significance in the state ideology that evolved in Russia after the communists came to power. The revolution itself was justified by the need to put an end to the exploitation of labor, to eliminate capitalists who misappropriated the "surplus value" produced by the proletariat, and to level social and economic differences separating various classes in society. These tasks were to be accomplished by rooting out private property, socializing the means of production, eliminating the class of private entrepreneurs, and radically restructuring the institution of labor.

The political slogans that propelled the Bolsheviks to power sidestepped the production and labor process proper and focused instead on the distribution and redistribution of the wealth produced in prerevolutionary Russia. However, as the new social order began to stabilize, communist leaders' attention shifted to production and the need to motivate workers in their daily labors. Gradually, the Soviet Union transformed itself into what Hannah Arendt called "work society," where "work and labour activity are not only a natural precondition for human existence, but where work also has a central cultural value and where work institutions assume a central role in the entire societal structure."[1] In effect, Soviet ideology surrounded labor with a sacred halo and pronounced hard work on behalf of the state to be each citizen's sacred duty. This ideology was inspired by orthodox Marxism, and specifically by its emphasis on activity, labor-created value, the toiling proletariat as an embodiment of social progress, and the central role that tool-aided behavior was supposed to have played in human evolution.[2]

According to Soviet ideology, every able-bodied individual had to be inducted into the labor force: dodging employment and living on unearned income were condemned. The Soviet constitution faithfully reflected this precept. Thus the last version of the constitution adopted by the former Soviet Union read: "It is a duty, as well as an honor, for every able-bodied citizen in the USSR to work conscientiously in his chosen, socially useful activity, and strictly to observe labor discipline. Evading socially useful work is incompatible with the principles of socialist society."[3] The Supreme Soviet passed several legal acts based on this principle that criminalized "social parasites" or job shirkers. Among the more sensational cases stemming from these laws was the conviction of the poet Joseph Brodsky for parasitism. Brodsky, who would later be awarded the Nobel prize for literature, was exiled to the northern Arkhangelsk region, where he was to submit to "forced employment." As the basis for his ruling, the judge cited the May 4, 1961, resolution passed by the Presidium of the Russian Federation Supreme Soviet calling for additional measures against those evading public labor. Labor-centrism came to the fore during the official campaign against "unearned incomes," which was triggered by the special decree on "Combatting Unearned Incomes" issued by the Supreme Soviet in 1986. This decree put a criminal spin on even those limited forms of independent economic activity that were hitherto available to Soviet citizens, such as selling produce from the puny plots owned by members of collective farms. The decree also cast a shadow over inheritance practices, lottery winnings, gifts from relatives, and other earnings unrelated to a person's work.[4]

Another economic tenet that circumscribed the labor process in Soviet society concerned ownership of the means of production: land, raw materials, machinery, labor tools, and so forth. The socialist political economy sanctioned two basic forms of ownership: national and cooperative/collective. In both cases, workers were cast as co-owners with equal stakes in production means and products. As to private ownership of production means and the private entrepreneurship it engendered, these were pronounced alien to socialism. Engaging in private enterprise became a criminal activity. As a result, both *evading work (failure to be gainfully employed in an official enterprise) and the most active form of employment (engaging in a private enterprise) appeared to be outlawed.* The only recognized form of employment was hired labor for the state, which stood behind every industrial and service enterprise in the nation, or for the collective farm in agriculture, which legally constituted a separate form of ownership but in practice did not differ much from state-owned enterprises.

A closer look at this form of employment suggests that it did not live up to its official billing. Socialist ideology touted employees as public property co-owners who worked for nobody but themselves. Usually invoked was an appropriate quotation from Lenin, which said that "for the first time after centuries of work for others, coercive toil for the exploiters, the possibility of work for oneself has become a reality."[5] In fact, socialist workers did not have any say in important economic decisions—the functions that normally come with ownership rights—and thus could hardly be construed as co-owners.[6]

Still, the co-ownership ruse accomplished an important goal: under the premises of socialist political economy, the labor force could no longer be seen as a salable commodity. This, in turn, allowed Communist party ideologists to claim that there was no labor market under socialism. Indeed, how could citizens, who own all property, sell their labor to themselves? References to "selling" and "purchasing" labor, the "price of labor," and "wage labor" were discarded as inapplicable to the socialist system. Wherever the words "hire" and "wage labor" cropped up, they usually appeared in quotation marks and were used with reservations.[7] Here is a sample of the rationalizations designed by the socialist political economists to buttress this point:

> Those who own the means of production cannot purchase their ability to work from themselves.[8]
>
> The working class cannot sell its labor power to itself, since it owns the means of production. Consequently, only the outward appearance of

hire survives when it comes to the employees' relation to society through which they exercise their right to work.[9]

Normative Motives and Workers' Attitudes

The ideological constructs presented above go to the heart of socialist ideology and define in the broadest terms the place this ideology accorded to labor in society. In addition to these general principles, socialist political economy articulated more specific normative guidelines pertaining to the goals and motivations of socialist labor. Two instructive distinctions could be singled out in regard to socialist labor motives and goals. The first involved the distinction between the personal and public interests that motivate labor activity. Personal interests included the worker's own needs, as well as those of his family. Public interests referred to the well-being of the collective and community as a whole. The second relevant distinction juxtaposed two types of worker's interests: "spiritual" and "material." Spiritual needs were linked to the labor process itself and were defined as the satisfaction the worker derives from work well done, from finding an outlet for one's creativity, from the respect that a hard-working person earns from one's co-workers. Material needs had to do with remuneration for one's contribution to public production, be this in the form of salary or nonmonetary benefits. This normative distinction partly coincides with what students of labor call "intrinsic" and "extrinsic" labor motives,[10] or work as a "value in itself" and as an "instrumental" activity.[11]

Up until the late 1980s, official Soviet ideology clearly favored public over private interests and spiritual over material labor motives. The priority given to public motives perfectly fitted the totalitarian mold of Soviet society, which subordinated the individual to the state. Disdain for the worker's personal interests was camouflaged by the notion that public ownership over the means of production gave everybody the same stake in the production process and assured that personal or private interests were in the end identical with the interests of the community as a whole. After all, don't all socialist workers toil for themselves, even if they are technically state employees? Don't they own the product of their labor, even if they cannot dispose of it personally? And wouldn't they therefore naturally be inclined to value the manager's directives as their own?

Such were the normative expectations that Soviet ideologists harbored about the socialist work ethic. Actual labor morality among Soviet workers was another story. Indicative in this respect was workers' reaction in the late 1920s to the campaign promoting exemplary labor by individual workers and work teams. This officially approved initiative aimed at lowering general pay rates, raising production quotas, accelerating work processes, introducing penalties for substandard performance, and the like. The campaign did not sit well with workers who, as researchers would later point out, resisted pressures to intensify the labor process.[12] Clearly, workers were unwilling to sacrifice personal interests to the "public good." Even so-called *udarniki*—exemplary workers who routinely overfulfilled their production quotas—did not surrender their own and their families' interests. But when *udarniki* complained about low pay rates, they risked being branded greedy profiteers (*shkurniki*) by trade union bosses, who threatened to disband their work teams. Nor were Soviet peasants thrilled by the prospect of being herded into collective farms and working for anybody but themselves and their families.

Numerous developments attest to the fact that official labor morality and everyday Soviet reality did not coincide. This would become more evident in post-Stalinist Russia, when workers would sometimes be driven to direct actions protesting official indifference to their basic needs. One of the most dramatic events of this kind happened in 1962, in Novocherkassk, where the authorities called in troops to stamp out a demonstration by workers protesting hikes in food prices.[13]

Data from sociological surveys point in the same direction. Thus, an important study of workers from twelve industrial enterprises in Leningrad conducted in 1976 by Dr. Vladimir Yadov and his associates revealed that 63–73 percent of those polled listed good earnings as the most valuable quality they are looking for in a job. No more than 6 percent of respondents mentioned the opportunity to participate in management decisions as an important job specification, and only 18 percent singled out a job's "creative content."

Study of Russian immigrants further corroborates these findings.[14] Among the factors negatively affecting the Soviet economy, Russian immigrants, who were polled in the 1970s, listed low earnings, poor working conditions, the shortage of consumer goods, and bad housing accommodations—all factors pertaining to the workers' personal and family well-being. Thus, we can argue that *material interests, rather than ideologically inspired spiritual needs predominated in Soviet workers' values since at least the mid-1970s.*[15]

Realizing the gap between normative expectations and everyday labor morality, Soviet ideologists emphasized the transitional nature of socialist society, which was conceived in Marxism as the initial phase of communist socioeconomic formation. It is only with the onset of communism— the ultimate stage of social evolution—that spiritual labor motives would fully inform labor morality. Lenin described this historically new type of labor ethics:

> Communist labor, in the narrower and stricter sense of the term, is free labor for society's sake; labor done not as duty, not to win the right to certain products, not according to preset legalized quotas, but voluntary labor without quotas and without expectations of remuneration; labor as the custom of working for the common good and as a conscious (and habitual) realization of the necessity to labor for the common good; labor as a need of a healthy body.[16]

One could trace this stance to the well-known passage in Marx's "Critique of the Gotha Program," which stated that "at the highest stage of communist society, ... labor will cease to be solely a means of living and become in itself a primary necessity of life."[17] Lenin's words were, in some cases, even stronger.[18]

But this distinction between the two phases of communism—socialism as the initial stage of the communist production mode and the ultimate stage of fully developed communism—gave socialist ideologists an inferiority complex clearly evident in the apologetic tone with which they described the motivational dynamics actually observed under socialism.

Protestant and Socialist
Labor Ethics

A comparison between the socialist and Protestant (capitalist) work ethics is clearly in order here. Both the Protestant work ethic as analyzed by Max Weber in his classic study[19] and Soviet models of labor morality are distinguished by their emphasis on labor as a vital sphere of human activity. Both tend to underplay personal and family consumption motives as a primary basis for labor activity. The elevation of spiritual over material needs in Soviet ideology offers an instructive parallel to the religious motives that propelled early capitalists in their economic undertakings. In the Soviet case, we also have tangible evidence that real personal consumption was kept at a minimum. This can be gleaned from a comparison between the public consumption and industrial accumulation funds in the Soviet era. During the early stages of rapid industrialization in the Soviet Union, the relative weight of consumption funds dwindled, while that of accumulation funds grew from 10–15 to 40–45 percent. In later years, capital accumulation funds sometimes accounted for more than 60 percent of national income in the Soviet Union.[20]

Early capitalist growth in the West revealed some similar cultural trends, including attempts to curb consumer motivation in Calvinist ideology, which denounced the most conspicuous forms of consumption as sinful. According to this ideology, it was one's success in practical activity that should be displayed, not personal wealth that accrued to the individual as a result of his labor. Whatever resources were left unused in personal consumption were to be reinvested in production, thereby maximizing the divine grace that devolved on the successful entrepreneur.[21] Some similarities between Protestant and socialist ethics may have to do with the fact that both were instrumental in speeding up the modernization process, which, as Peter Berger showed, has had two different paths—capitalist and socialist.

Besides these parallels, there were fundamental differences between the labor ethics championed by socialist and Protestant ideologies: The former renounced private ownership; the latter appealed to personal initiative firmly rooted in private property. Another point that formally divided the two models concerned the manner in which the individual was to be fully rewarded for his efforts: Socialist ideology promised a state of bliss in this world as soon as full-blown communism came into its own; Protestant teaching saw salvation fully attainable only in the world to come. Given the somewhat uncertain time frame within which full-blown communism was to be expected, the socialist promise tended to recede into an indefinite future and thus was to be redeemed only for the "generations to come."

As we can see, the Protestant ethic and socialist labor morality helped motivate labor during the early stages of capital accumulation, with the Protestant model accentuating personal efforts on the basis of private property and the socialist model stressing individual efforts on the basis of state ownership as the surest path toward rapid industrialization in the Soviet Union. However, if the Protestant work ethic gave rise to the "spirit of capitalism" and spurred economic growth in the West, secular socialist ideology failed to generate the "spirit of communism" or to furnish the foundation for sustained economic growth in the socialist East.

Beyond Socialist Labor Morality

The fundamental cultural and economic changes that shook Soviet society in the late 1980s and that continue to unfold at present could not but affect labor morality. Let us now turn to new developments in Russian labor culture. In addition to the normative and ideological blueprints for labor ethics that preoccupied us in the previous section, we shall also focus on current trends in everyday labor culture as revealed in recent sociological inquiries into labor motives and work ethics. We begin with changing employment patterns.

Diversification of Normative
Employment Patterns

Perhaps the most dramatic evidence that the dogmas of socialist economics have lost their magic power was the legalization of private enterprise. Suppressed and persecuted for many decades, private entrepreneurial activity was not reinstated overnight. The first movement in this direction was the official blessing that Mikhail Gorbachev bestowed on cooperative enterprises. Private enterprise was further strengthened by the law on "Enterprises and Entrepreneurship" passed by the Russian Parliament, which among other things spelled out entrepreneurial rights.[22] The constitution adopted by the Russian Federation during the December 1993 national referendum stipulated that "every person has the right to use freely his abilities and property to engage in entrepreneurial and other economic activities unrestricted by law."[23]

As to public opinion, its growing acceptance of entrepreneurship is reflected in the polls, which point to an increasing number of individuals wishing to start their own businesses. The figures are impressive, even if it is clear that some respondents are unprepared to follow through on their expressed wishes. For example, an October 1990 opinion survey probed the Soviet urban population's interest in various kinds of businesses and the means of production they would like to obtain. The poll listed common businesses like shops, restaurants, and service outlets. The results pointed to a significant number of individuals who wanted to open their own business, even though no opportunity might exist for this at present: a third of Russian citizens living in urban areas expressed an interest in starting their own business. And this was *before* the massive push toward privatization in post-Gorbachev Russia. The numbers were even more impressive in other republics of the former Soviet Union: 43 percent in Ukraine, and over 50 percent in Armenia, Moldova, Georgia, and Lithuania.[24] A poll conducted a year later showed that fully 20 percent of Moscow high school graduates would like to start a private business.[25]

Entrepreneurial activity was even less threatening and unheard of to farmers. Since the early 1930s, Soviet agriculture had entailed two sectors: the public/collective sector, which absorbed most of the arable lands in the nation, and the private sector, comprising the small plots assigned to farmers and their families for private use. Although the private sector included a fraction of the nation's lands used in agriculture, it accounted for half of all potatoes and one third of the eggs and meat sold in the Soviet Union during recent decades. Clearly, we are dealing here with private business based on the labor of farmers and their family members, a rudimentary capitalist sector that, despite adverse conditions, existed throughout the Soviet era and continues to flourish today.[26]

Private enterprise needs both an entrepreneur and hired labor. During the early perestroika years, Socialist ideologists sneered at free enterprise because it would restore the "exploitation" of hired labor allegedly absent under socialism, a system supposedly incompatible with work for hire. Contrary to such sentiments, the urban majority in Russia and other Soviet republics supported hired labor. By the end of 1990, the opportunity to work for a private owner was endorsed by most people in the Soviet Union, except for respondents in Turkmenia, Kirghizia, and Kazakhstan. The three Baltic republics, along with Armenia and Ukraine, registered the biggest majorities favoring this type of employment.[27] Moreover, as recent studies show, employment in a private enterprise is now a more attractive option than a job in a state-owned outlet.[28]

All these changes in the legal environment and public opinion led to the rapid growth of new employment patterns. The statistical data show that by early 1993, 16 million people in the Russian Federation were employed in new enterprises, almost all of these privately owned.[29] Judged by self-reports, 30 percent of those employed claimed that they were engaged in profit-oriented activities, including 8 percent who considered themselves enterprise co-owners with a voice in the decision-making process and 3 percent who were sole enterprise owners.[30] Together, these findings clearly suggest that public opinion in Russia has endorsed employment at nonstate enterprises.

Another interesting feature pertaining to the employment situation in Russia is the proliferation of secondary employment, which allows the individual to supplement income from a primary job. As we saw above, this phenomenon was widely spread in the rural areas, where work on one's private plot constituted secondary employment. Now the multiple employment pattern, once denounced by the Soviet authorities, is beginning to spread in the cities, especially the big ones. In November 1993, 40 percent of the adult male population in big cities had two or more jobs.[31] To be sure, many people are forced to seek secondary employment to supplement their meager incomes, which are eaten up by relentless inflation. At the same time, a person is more independent from any single employer when he holds several jobs and for the first time feels that he indeed owns his labor power, skills, and abilities. Thus a genuine mobilization of labor resources is taking place in Russia, and this is not just a matter of drawing new workers into the economic process but the more intensive involvement of the well-established and most active part of the labor force.

We have examined some of the new employment opportunities sanctioned by the Russian state and generally endorsed by public opinion. Alongside these changes have come the official recognition of *un*employment, which for a long time was decried as incompatible with socialism.

The Employment Act adopted by the Russian Parliament on April 19, 1991, explicitly defined the status of the unemployed, spelled out the procedures covering unemployment registration, and outlined benefits that the unemployed could receive from the state.[32]

Naturally, most Russian citizens are not thrilled by the prospect of losing their jobs and would like to see full employment guaranteed by the state. However, if we are to judge from the polls, a substantial part of the Russian population is growing accustomed to the grim reality of joblessness and is beginning to adapt to such a possibility.[33] Several million Russian workers have already had firsthand experience of unemployment. Just a decade ago, such a situation would have seemed preposterous, as the experts unanimously predicted a labor shortage. This judgment, based on the extrapolation of past socioeconomic trends, runs afoul of the radical changes that have swept the country in the last few years.[34]

These employment trends have had their impact on labor discipline. A survey of personnel managers at several large Moscow enterprises conducted in summer 1992 revealed that workers were reportedly growing more disciplined and responsible, a shift that personnel managers greeted with approval and that could be attributed largely to the uncertain labor market and the increased likelihood of layoffs.[35] We can expect the transition to a market economy and the sobering effect that unemployment exerts on labor discipline to have a continuous impact on labor ethics.

In addition to involuntary unemployment, we should mention an important cultural change in public attitudes toward individuals who do not wish to be involved in the labor process. Before perestroika, every able-bodied Soviet citizen of working age was obligated to seek public employment. But the Russian Federation Employment Act, adopted on April 19, 1991, stipulates that "citizens possess the exclusive right to dispose of their capacity for productive and creative labor. Coercive employment is inadmissible, with the exception of cases expressly stipulated by law. Nonemployment should not give grounds for administrative or any other liability."[36] This change is duly reflected in the current Russian Constitution, which no longer mentions employment as a duty, even though it still stipulates the right to dispose freely of one's labor power, to choose one's occupation, to obtain remuneration for one's work without discrimination, and to be protected from unemployment.

One can hardly overestimate the importance of all these transformations in the Russian labor law and labor morality. Labor is losing the halo of sacredness it wears in a socialist society. It is no longer seen as an obligation rooted in the individual's responsibility to the state and is increasingly conceived of as a matter of personal choice. At the same time, the new labor morality has enriched employment patterns in the country and encouraged entrepreneurial initiative. As a result, individuals have begun to feel like the true owners of their labor force. They act less as state employees and more like sellers of their labor. This newly acquired taste for freedom, however, has confronted the Russian work force with fresh problems and serious responsibilities that the market economy has brought in its wake.

Current Trends in Labor Attitudes and Values

As we noted above, Soviet society could never overcome the gap between official labor ethics, which touted public good along with job content as normative labor motives, and the real motivation that propelled Soviet workers, most of whom saw their labor as a means of furthering their personal and family well-being. The breakdown of totalitarianism effectively eliminated this contradiction. In the late 1980s and early 1990s, a fundamental cultural shift took place that legitimized personal interests and private life. Also fully rehabilitated were material, bodily needs, which used to be denigrated as secondary and base compared to higher spiritual needs. "Base" bodily functions have grown in importance and become culturally at least as legitimate as the "lofty" spiritual ones.[37] We should judge the parallel cultural rehabilitation of personal wealth and private property, as well as the vastly expanded access to real goods now legally available to individuals and families, in the same perspective.

Hence it should come as no surprise that today, as in the 1970s, private, material interests dominate in job motivation. Two surveys, one conducted in 1989 and the other in 1990, polled factory workers about jobs they would have liked to perform.[38] Respondents were asked to choose any number of required job characteristics from among seventeen possible job features presented by the researchers. The responses indicate that the majority of the individuals polled marked the items directly bearing on their personal interests and their family's well-being. The opportunity for good earnings topped the list, while the possibility to improve housing conditions with the employer's help, to operate in a comfortable working environment, to use reliable and safe industrial equipment, and to deal with agreeable and likable co-workers followed closely. "Good earnings" were singled out as important by 70 percent of all respondents, as compared to 43–44 percent of those polled who gave a high rating to an "interesting job." This list of leading personal motives combines the desire to maximize job "rewards" and reduce to a minimum personal "costs" associated with poor working conditions, faulty tools, and tension in the workplace. This finding is remarkably consistent with worldwide trends detected in the World Values Survey of more than twenty countries, including Russia. The Russian survey, conducted in early

1991,[39] showed that 80 percent of respondents marked "good earnings" as an important job characteristic. If we compare these results to the 1976 study, we can see that Russian employees' values have remained stable for at least two decades. The desire to earn more—not to labor for work's sake as a primary human need—motivated Russian employees during this entire period.

Very tangible are the changes in the range and quality of goods and services that workers aspire to purchase with their money. With the barrier to the free flow of information coming down, the Russian population has developed consumption expectations that are not dissimilar in principle from those commonly found in the West. This increase in consumption (and consequently in salary) expectations could be gleaned from the comparison between expectations of high school graduates in 1985 and the early 1990s regarding such indicators as the desire to own a car, a private summer cottage, and so on.[40] Noteworthy also is the fact that the growth in salary and consumption aspirations goes hand in hand with a diminished willingness on the part of employees to expend a given amount of their labor power in order to satisfy their aspirations. Thus the above-mentioned comparative study of adolescents revealed that in the last few years there has been a noticeable drop in the willingness of young people to face labor hardships (such as working in cold climates, away from their families, in especially labor-intensive and monotonous job settings, and so on). Yury Levada reports similar results. The two surveys, one conducted in 1989 and the other in 1992, asked Russian citizens the same question: "What do you think is important to be successful in life?" During the four years that elapsed between the first and second poll, the proportion of the respondents who answered that the requirement for success was "hard and deliberate work" dropped from 45 percent to 32 percent.[41] In light of these findings, it is easier to understand why the desire to increase personal earnings shares top billing with the desire to minimize personal cost in the hierarchy of job values of contemporary Russian employees.

It is common to interpret the revolution in consumption expectations and the decline in the willingness to face work hardships as a sign of a breakdown in moral values. But I think it would be more appropriate to criticize past labor ethics, which demanded hard work in exchange for few tangible goods or for a mere reprieve from punishment. It is to mask the absurdity of such a demand that the socialist labor morality goaded employees to enjoy the labor process itself and derive satisfaction from the fact that they were participating in the great adventure of building a communist society. Given this history of labor morality in the Soviet Union, the current aversion to hard work and sacrifices can be seen as an understandable reaction to traditional Soviet labor culture.

However, the unwillingness to expend personal effort should not be overinterpreted but rather judged against the backdrop of growing multiple or secondary employment which shows that Russian employees want not so much to curtail their *gross* labor efforts and expenditures as to decrease the *relative* weight of the personal labor efforts needed to produce one item of output for a unit of pay. Current trends might be described as the *shift from a lower to higher cost-benefit ratio of the individual's rewards to his or her costs*. Hardly justified, therefore, are those commentators who believe that "it is hard to lure a nation like Russia into the pursuit of more money; a more sublime goal is needed to get it going."[42] Personal and family prosperity is rapidly becoming a sublime goal that beckons the Russian labor force toward a better future.

Labor-Management Relations

As official lies about employees owning the means of production have been exposed, hard-edged truths about wage labor for the state have become more and more evident to Russian workers. These truths might be painful, but they also have had a positive effect on labor, which is taking stock of its shared interests and setting out to defend them through their own labor organizations—independent trade unions, strike committees, workers' councils, and the like.[43] The turning point was the mass strikes by Soviet miners in 1989, which exploded communist myths about labor as a spiritual need and about the natural harmony prevailing in labor–management relations under socialism. After decades of submission, Russian state employees moved to assert their group interests.[44]

The dynamics of attitudes toward ownership and industrial management yield ample evidence that the labor force in Russia is not only conscious of its group interests but also willing to act on them. We have mentioned earlier the research on values that demonstrated the salaried labor force's central concern with good earnings and personal/family well-being. The same study attempted to gauge wage earners' interest in co-managing their enterprises. The respondents were presented with several options, ranging from readiness to cede to outside owners all operational control over a given enterprise to an arrangement where the employees owned their enterprise and elected their own managers. More than half of Russian respondents preferred an option where they could own their enterprise collectively and appoint their managers. Among the countries that participated in this international survey, this was by far the highest figure.[45]

Closer analysis yields some further insight into wage earners' preference for participation in enterprise management. Among the countries involved in this survey, the exsocialist entities (Poland, Russia, Belarus,

Latvia) were the most committed to the scheme that involves employees in property ownership and management at their enterprises. As we can see, even the cardinal change in the outlook on ownership and property relations that has occurred in Russia in recent years has not altered the salaried work force's preference for collective forms of privatizing the nation's means of production.

Another sign that hired labor is individualistically biased can be gleaned from the answer to the following question: "Some say that one should follow instructions of one's superior even when one does not fully agree with them. Others say that one should follow one's superior's instructions only when one is convinced that they are right. With which of these two options do you agree?" The answers included the following options:

"Should follow instructions" (one point).

"First see whether they are correct" (three points).

"It depends" (two points).

The "insubordination index" compiled on the basis of these answers shows that the Russian population scored the highest on their readiness to second-guess and defy managers' decisions.[46] Other exsocialist countries took second place in their labor force's readiness to interfere with management decisions.

The high score that Russian respondents showed on the insubordination scale supports David Stark and Michael Burawoy's studies in which the authors examined the management patterns in socialist countries. According to Stark, who studied Hungarian enterprises, the socialist economy combines centralized planning at the national economic level with market-style haggling between workers and managers at the shop-floor level.[47] Burawoy, who worked in a Russian factory for several months, was amazed at the extent to which the actual labor process under socialism had diverged from official prescriptions: "From a capitalist perspective it is difficult to understand how such anarchy in production could lead to an enterprise as successful as Polar Furniture. The secret of the capitalist enterprise lies in the managerial control over production, a control entirely absent at Polar [the Russian factory's name]."[48]

After the decades of neglect suffered from their communist bosses, members of the exsocialist labor force want to assert their dignity and human rights. They resent the political and trade union leaders who misrepresented their interests in the past, they are fed up with being extolled to work hard for token remuneration, and they are contemptuous of their incompetent bosses. Given these longstanding grievances, one can understand why workers might be trying to carry their newly found democratic freedoms into the economic sphere. Yet, like workers in capitalist countries, they may have to learn to live with democratic institutions in the political sphere and the autocratic management practices prevalent in a capitalist economy.[49]

Conclusion:
Toward a Post-Soviet Labor Ethic

In this chapter, I have tried to show that socialism created its own labor culture, which included specific labor values and labor morality. This labor morality successfully functioned as a mobilizing device during the period of forced industrialization but gradually lost its legitimacy and yielded to unofficial norms that markedly differed from the orthodox doctrine. These changes laid a motivational groundwork for a market economy, some elements of which appeared on the micro level way before the macro-social framework for a market economy was in place. What this means, among other things, is that the transformation of the socialist system into a market economy has deep roots in the consciousness of Russian people and is not something artificially imposed from without.

The antitotalitarian revolution brought in its wake a new labor culture based on private property for production assets and, even more importantly, on the individual's real ownership of his or her labor force, including the freedom to dispose of it as he or she sees fit. At the head of the new labor culture are the consumer interests of the worker and the worker's family. Its other relevant component is the close attention that salaried workers pay to the cost-benefit ratio of their work. This norm, which is now being extended to other economic resources besides labor, is akin to the personal thriftiness that played such a central role at the dawn of Western capitalism as an element of the Protestant ethic.

The new labor morality requires proper ideology to back it up. Fully legitimized labor norms, in turn, could help mobilize labor in the post-Soviet marketplace. Whether Russia can pull out of its present economic crisis and evolve into a prosperous society depends in large measure on the success of this process.

Notes

This chapter was translated from the Russian by Tatiana L. Butkova and Dmitri N. Shalin. The study was supported in part by grants from the International Research and Exchanges Board and the George Soros Foundation. The author is very grateful to Professor Dmitri N. Shalin for his encouragement and editorial help with this chapter.

1. A. Kasvio, "Work Society in Crisis? Institutional Changes in Working Life and the New Challenges to the Sociology of Work," Working Paper no. 9, Department of Sociology and Social Psychology, University of Tampere, Finland, 1984, p. 2.

2. See G. S. Batishchev, "Deiatelnostnaia sushchnost cheloveka kak filosofskii printsip," in *Problema cheloveka v sovremennoi filosofii* (Moscow: Nauka, 1969); Vs. Vilchek, *Proshchanie s Marksom (algoritmy istorii)* (Moscow: Progress, 1993).

3. *Konstitutsiia (Osnovnoi Zakon) Soiuza Sovetskikh Sotsialisticheskikh Respublik* (Moscow: Izvestiia, 1978), article 60, p. 20. This article was repeated verbatim in the former Constitution of the RSFSR (Moscow: Sovetskaia Rossiia, 1979), pp. 19–20.

4. "Ukaz Prezidiuma Verkhovnogo Soveta SSSR ob usilenii borby s izvlecheniem netrudovykh dokhodov, 23-ogo maia 1986 g." in *Vedomosti Verkhovnogo Soveta SSSR*, May 28, 1986, no. 22.

5. V. I. Lenin, "Kak nam organizovat sorevnovanie?" in *Sobranie sochinenii*, 5th ed., vol. 35 (Moscow: Politizdat, 1962), p. 196.

6. For more details, see V. E. Gimpelson and A. K. Nazimova, "'Master na proizvodstve: Dogma I realnost," *Sotsiologicheskie issledovaniia*, no. 8 (August 1991): 22–31.

7. The socialist ideology's aversion to the notion of "hire," whatever its stated rationale, reflects a key difference between socialist and capitalist culture. The latter has no misgivings about the notion of the contract and treats it as a central element in relations between individuals, groups and organizations, people and the state, and so on (see Peter L. Berger, *The Capitalist Revolution. Fifty Propositions about Prosperity, Equality, and Liberty* [New York: Basic Books, 1991]). We can surmise that this difference has to do with the Soviet authorities' reluctance to spell out their contractual relations with rank-and-file Soviet citizens. The lack of a formal contract, the preference for the "informal understanding," made control over Soviet leaders' performance by their subjects more difficult.

8. M. I. Volkov, ed., *Politekonomika: Uchebnik dlia ekonomicheskikh vuzov I fakultetov*, 5th ed., vol. 2 (Moscow: Politizdat, 1982), p. 175.

9. G. A. Kozlov, ed., *Politicheskaia ekonomika*, vol. 3 (Moscow: Mysl, 1977), p. 277.

10. D. E. Berlyne, "Motivational Problems Raised by Exploratory and Epistemic Behavior," in S. Koch. *Psychology: A Study of a Science*, vol. 5 (New York: McGraw-Hill, 1963); E. L. Deci, *Intrinsic Motivation* (New York: Plenum, 1975).

11. V. A. Yadov, "Otnoshenie k trudu: Teoriticheskaia model i realnye tendentsii," *Sotsiologicheskie issledovaniia*, no. 3 (May 1983).

12. See B. A. Kozlov, G. A. Bordiugov, E. Y. Zubkova, and O. V. Khlevniuk, *Istoricheskii opyt i perestroika. Chelovecheskii faktor v sotsialno ekonomicheskom razvitii SSSR* (Moscow: Mysl, 1989), pp. 83–84.

13. See V. Ponomarev, *Obshchestvennye volnenia v SSSR: ot XX sezda KPSS do smerti Brezhneva* (Moscow: Aziia, Levyi Povorot, 1990), pp. 4–5; V. Konovalov, Iu. Bespalov, "Postavlena tochka v rassledovanii novocherkasskikh sobytii 1962 goda," *Izvestiia*, June 4, 1994.

14. Paul R. Gregory, "Productivity, Slack, and Time Theft in Soviet Economy," in James R. Millar, ed., *Politics, Work, and Daily Life in the USSR: A Survey of Former Soviet Citizens* (Cambridge: Cambridge University Press, 1987), pp. 255–60, 273–74.

15. This conclusion runs contrary to the findings of the sociological study *Chelovek i ego rabota*, conducted under the leadership of Dr. Vladimir Yadov (A. G. Zdravomyslov, V. P. Rozhin, and V. A. Yadov, eds., *Chelovek i ego rabota. Sotsiologicheskoe issledovanie* [Moscow: Mysl, 1967]; in English: A. G. Zrdavomyslov, V. P. Rozhin, and V. A. Yadov, eds. *Man and His Work: Sociological Study*, translated by S. P. Dunn [New York: 1970]). According to this classic study, it was job content and not salary that mattered most to young workers. One is tempted to attribute this contrast to the difference between the romantic 1960s and the pragmatic 1970s. However, I think this would be a misinterpretation. The results reported by the above-mentioned authors can be more plausibly attributed to the methods they used to measure job values. To measure the subjective value the worker attached to a particular work facet, the authors calculated the coefficient of covariation between the respondent's overall job satisfaction and his or her satisfaction with a given work facet. Yet in Russian, the very semantics of the word "satisfaction" suggests more immediate, direct rewards (in contrast to more instrumental, indirect ones), which is why intrinsic job facets are apt to produce higher coefficients than extrinsic ones. For more detail, see V. S. Magun, *Potrebnosti i psikhologiia sotsialnoi deiatelnosti lichnosti* (Leningrad: Nauka, 1983), pp. 104–37.

16. V. I. Lenin, "Ot razrusheniia tvorcheskogo uklada k tvorchestvu novogo," in *Sobranie sochinenii*, vol. 40 (Moscow: Politizdat, 1963), p. 315.

17. K. Marx, "Kritika gotskoi programmy," in K. Marx and F. Engels, *Sobranie sochinenii*, 2nd ed., vol. 19 (Moscow: Politizdat, 1961), p. 20.

18. V. I. Lenin, "Podgotovitelnye materialy k knige 'Gosudarstvo i revoliutsiia,'" *Sobranie sochinenii*, vol. 33 (Moscow: Politizdat, 1962), p. 187. The hope of turning labor into a self-propelling activity is akin to the search for a perpetuum mobile. It is characteristic in this respect that communist utopianism included physical utopianism as a vital component.

19. M. Weber. "Protestantskaia etika i dukh kapitalizma," in M. Weber, *Izbrannye proizvedeniia* (Moscow: Progress, 1990).

20. L. A. Gordon and A. K. Nazimova, *Rabochii klass SSSR: Tendentsii i perspektivy sotsialno-ekonomicheskogo razvitiia* (Moscow: Nauka, 1985); L. A. Gordon, "Sotsialnaia politika v sfere oplaty truda," *Sotsiologicheskie issledovaniia*, no. 4 (July 1987).

21. R. M. Stark, *Sociology* (Belmont, Ca.: Wadsworth, 1989), pp. 504–5.

22. "Zakon RSFSR 'O predpriiatiiakh i predprinimatelskoi deiatelnosti,'" in *Vedomosti Sezda Narodnykh Deputatov RSFSR i Verkhovnogo Soveta RSFSR*, no. 30, Moscow, 1990.

23. *Konstitutsiia Rossiiskoi Federatsii* (Moscow: Iuridicheskaia Literatura, 1993), p. 14.

24. For further details, see D. Slider, V. Magun, and V. Gimpelson, "Public Opinion on Privatization: Republic Differences," *Soviet Economy* 7, no. 3 (1991): 256–75.

25. V. S. Magun and A. Z. Litvintseva, *Zhiznennye pritiazaniia rannei iunosti i strategii ikh realizatsii: 90-e i 80-e gody* (Moscow: Institute of Sociology, Russian Academy of Sciences, 1993).

26. See Lev Timofeev, "Tekhnologiia chernogo rynka, ili krestianskoe iskusstvo

golodat," in Lev Timofeev, *Chernyi rynok kak politicheskaia sistema. Publitsisticheskoe issledovanie* (Vilnus–Moscow: VIMO, 1993), and "Apparat protiv kapitala. Iskhod etoi bitvy opredelit budushchee derevni" *Izvestiia*, June 16, 1993.

27. Slider, Magun, and Gimpelson, "Public Opinion on Privatization." This position was endorsed by the democratic press. Such materials as the front-page table in the weekly *Argumenty i fakty*, no. 22 (1991), which had a circulation in excess of 20 million, had an impact on the public mentality. This table indicated that in 1989 the leading capitalist countries allotted 55 percent of their GNP to labor remuneration, as against 36 percent in the Soviet Union, whose employees were allegedly working for themselves.

28. Magun and Litvintseva, *Zhiznennye pritiazaniia*, p. 48.

29. *Ekonomika i zhizn*, no. 7 (1993).

30. *Zerkalo mnenii. Rezultaty sotsiologicheskogo oprosa naseleniia Rossii za noiabr 1993 g.* (Moscow: Institut Sotsiologii Rossiiskoi Akademii Nauk, Tsenter Sotsioekspress, 1993), p. 35.

31. Calculated on the basis of data gathered by V. A. Mansurov and his associates at the Sotsioekspress Center, Institute of Sociology, Russian Academy of Sciences.

32. "Zakon RSFSR o zaniatosti naseleniia v RSFSR," in *Vedomosti Sezda Narodnykh Deputatov RSFSR i Verkhovnogo Soveta RSFSR*, no. 18, Moscow, 1991, pp. 516–53.

33. V. L. Kosmarsky, "Bezrabotitsa," in *Ekonomicheskie i sotsialnye peremeny: monitoring obshchestvennogo mneniia*, no. 2 (1993): 26–29. See also V. Magun and V. Gimpelson, "Russian Workers' Strategies in Adjustment to Unfavorable Changes in Employment," *Economic and Industrial Democracy: An International Journal* 14 (supplement) (November 1993): 95–117.

34. See, for example, V. I. Perevedentsev, "Vosproizvodstvo naseleniia i semia," *Sotsiologicheskie issledovaniia*, no. 2 (1982): 80–88.

35. V. E. Gimpelson and O. Y. Kiseleva, "Dykhanie bezrabotitsy: Pochemu ne sbylis katastroficheskie prognozy," *Vek*, no. 10 (March 18, 1993): 7.

36. "Zakon RSFSR o zaniatosti naseleniia v RSFSR," para. 1, p. 516.

37. The impact of this trend on youth psychology is discussed in M. Zhamkochian and A. Magun, "Put k sebe," *Znanie—sila*, no. 12 (1992): 10–17.

38. This study was undertaken in 1989 by V. S. Magun and V. E. Gimpelson at a state factory in Taganrog (489 respondents), with a followup in 1990 at a cooperative factory in Moscow (289 respondents).

39. The Moscow Region portion of this study was conducted by E. I. Bashkirova and V. S. Magun. V. G. Andreenkov supervised the all-Russia segment of the same study. The questionnaire used in the Moscow Region and Belarus was translated from English by E. I. Bashkirova, V. S. Magun, A. P. Vardomatsky, and V. A. Yadov. The World Values Survey was conducted under the general guidance of Dr. Ronald Inglehart. For a more detailed picture of job values and attitudes among Russians, see Vladimir S. Magun, ed., *Trudovye tsennosti russkogo naseleniia* (forthcoming).

40. Magun and Litvintseva, *Zhiznennye pritiazariia*.

41. Y. A. Levada, "Vektory peremen: Sotsiokulturnye koordinaty izmenenii," *Ekonomicheskie i sotsialnye peremeny: Monitoring obshchestvennogo mneniia*, no. 3 (1993): 5–9.

42. M. Antonov, "Chto s nami proiskhodit?" *Oktiabr*, no. 8 (1987).

43. To be sure, trade unions existed under the old regime as well, but they did not defend workers' interests against the administration and the state. Trade union leaders were appointed by the party and carried out the policies decreed by the administrations. While their names and rhetoric might have changed, the old trade unions have retained their influence and organizational networks. On the new trade unions in Russia, see L. A. Gordon, *Ocherki rabochego dvizheniia v poslesotsialisticheskoi Rossii. Subektivnye nabliudeniia, soedinennye s popytkoi obektivnogo analiza promezhutochnykh rezultatov issledovaniia* (Moscow: Solidarnost, 1993).

44. In a series of studies of Soviet industrial enterprises in the 1970s and 1980s, we examined the relationship between employee satisfaction and performance. Our data show that, for the most part, the two go hand in hand, which suggests that the interests of employees and the management coincide. However, in all samples we discovered a fair number of cases where high labor efficiency coexisted with low job satisfaction on the part of the salaried worker, and vice versa—which signaled a gap between labor–management interests. For further detail, see V. S. Magun, "Dva tipa sootnosheniia mezhdu produktivnostiu truda i udovletvorennostiu rabotoi," *Sotsiologicheskie issledovaniia*, no. 4 (1983); "Metod rasshirennykh faktorov," *Sotsiologicheskie issledovaniia*, no. 1 (1985); "Two Types of Correlations between Labor Productivity and Job Satisfaction," *Soviet Sociology* 23, no. 4 (1985); "Work Performance and Job Satisfaction: A Coexistence of Positive and Negative Correlations," in *Research in Soviet Social Psychology* (Berlin: Springer, 1986); "The Relationships between Job Performance and Work Satisfaction in Soviet and American Organizations," *Sociological Research: Translations from Russian*, no. 3 (May–June 1993).

45. Here is the distribution of answers to this question for Russia and the Moscow Region: "The owners should rule their business or appoint the managers"—10 and 13 percent respectively; "The state should be the owner and appoint the managers"—11 and 7 percent; "The owners and the employees should participate in the selection of managers"—16 and 22 percent; "The employees should own the business and should elect the managers"—53 and 54 percent; "Don't know"—10 and 4 percent. The impact that such attitudes have on the privatization process is discussed in P. Sutela. Insider Privatization in Russia: Speculations on Systemic Change. A paper presented at the 25th Annual Meeting of the AAASS, Honolulu (1993), pp. 19–22.

46. The following is the distribution of all answers for Russia and the Moscow Region: "Should follow instructions," 18 and 18 percent, respectively; "Must be convinced first," 54 and 53 percent; "Depends," 24 and 28 percent; "Don't know," 3 and 1 percent.

47. D. Stark, "Insights on Internal Labor Markets," *American Sociological Review* 51, no. 4 (1986).

48. M. Burawoy and P. Krotov, "The Soviet Transition from Socialism to Capitalism: Worker Control and Economic Bargaining in the Wood Industry," *American Sociological Review*, no. 1 (1992): 28. See also M. Leontiev and V. Naishul, "Sushchestvuet ogromnyi spros na poriadok," *Segodnia*, no. 75 (November 6, 1993).

49. Robert A. Dahl, *Vvedenie v ekonomicheskuiu demokratiiu* (Moscow: Nauka–ICPA, 1991).

11

Civic Culture

YURI A. LEVADA

There has hardly been a stretch in Russian history more saturated with sweeping changes than the period between 1988 and 1995. Packed into this exceedingly brief historical era were the rise of "perestroika" and the fall of its illustrious leader, Mikhail Gorbachev; the collapse of the Soviet Union and the emergence in its place of fifteen independent states; the August 1991 communist putsch and the democrats' triumphant ascension to power; the proliferation of virulent ethnic conflicts and the recognition of the abiding need for cooperation; the bloody October 1993 confrontation between the executive and legislative powers and the surprising strength that the nationalist and communist forces showed in the first multiparty parliamentary elections in postcommunist Russia. Then, of course, there was the war in Chechnia. As people watched their political elites reshuffled and familiar institutions crumble, they could not help feeling alternatively elated, confused, and disillusioned. No sooner were hopes for a democratic renewal raised than they were dashed by unexpected hardships, which made some feel nostalgic for the lost security of the communist system.

As we try to take stock of these changes and assess their impact on Russian political culture, we should realize that the institutional transformations tell us only half the story. Hidden behind the visible structural dislocations are less apparent and often confusing trends in public consciousness. To appraise the state of public mind in today's Russia, we need to draw on public opinion surveys. In particular, we shall draw on the data collected by the National Center for Public Opinion Research, which has been tracking political developments in the former Soviet Union since the early years of perestroika.[1]

Among the changes that have shaken Soviet society in recent years, none is more important than the breakdown of the Communist party's monopoly on power. The one-party state might be history now, but the political tradition in which it was rooted is not. This tradition predates the Soviet Union and extends much further into Russian history. Thus, today's reformers have to grapple not only with the totalitarian institutions built in the communist era but also with the authoritarian practices that have existed in Russia for centuries. Far from being destroyed, the old totalitarian structures and authoritarian mentalities have demonstrated a remarkable capacity for social mimicry and adaptability. Undemocratic political sensibilities are manifest in the institutions of mass communications, and old stereotypes continue to dominate public opinion. Reasons for the persistence of the old attitudes should be sought in the Russian political tradition, in the nation's civic culture, which was retained and amplified by the Soviet regime. Authoritarianism sustained by both violence and pervasive paternalism, a nearly universal disregard for legal norms and procedures, and an intolerance toward dissent are among the most salient features of Russian civic culture. On the one hand, this culture breeds widespread fear, obedience, and sycophancy; on the other, it encourages rebellion and contempt for any authorities or law among the Russians. We must bear in mind this political heritage when we contemplate the most recent upheavals in Russian history. At the same time, we should not gloss over real, if contradictory and painful, changes that Russian civic culture has undergone in recent years.

"Political participation," "political support," and "public trust," worn-out clichés though they are, have acquired decidedly new meaning since democratic reforms began to transform Russia. Just a few years ago, "participation" and "support" were arbitrarily invoked by the Communist party whenever it wished to turn on the mechanisms of "double-think" and "unanimity." Now people in Russia have an opportunity to stake out their own political position and develop a conscious attitude toward politicians, parties, and social events, including the option of withdrawing their trust altogether. The traditional preference for unanimity remains strong and the choices practically available to the individual are quite limited, but the very fact that there *is* a choice in political matters is undeniable.

We can isolate three stages in the nation's political development since 1985. The first stage coincides with Gorbachev's perestroika and is distinguished by the half-hearted efforts to reform the Soviet system from above and from within by using the leverages provided by the system itself. Systematic opinion surveys that began in earnest in this period point to the growing prestige of Gorbachev and his politics, the expansion of glasnost in the public domain, and the rising hopes (especially among the intelligentsia) for liberal reform. The key question that roused the public at this point was: Who is to blame? This is a question familiar to several generations of Russian reformist intellectuals who have searched for ways to apportion blame for the nation's sorry state. The list of suspects submitted in the late 1980s included communist political leaders charged with distorting the "true" socialist model. All critics—from the top party brass to extreme Russian nationalists to liberal dissidents—singled out Stalin as the major culprit. This was a neat way to exonerate oneself from responsibility and to spare the system's fundamental political institutions from serious criticism. Research findings from this period support this view. In 1988, 13 percent of Soviet citizens named Stalin and his legacy as the main cause of the country's problems. This figure grew to 35 percent in 1989. Similarly, Gorbachev's popularity among his countrymen peaked in 1988 at 51 percent, and interest and trust in the mass media crested in 1989. After that, perestroika ran out of steam, the Soviet leader's popularity plummeted, and radical reform ideas gained in prominence.

The second stage in Russia's political transformation raised another question: Who can you trust? In 1990, Boris Yeltsin took center stage as the new man of the year, first as a proponent of a more radical approach to perestroika and later as a radical democratic reformer. Political forces shaping public opinion underwent significant transformation in this period. The reform alliance that gave perestroika its initial thrust and helped to legitimize it faded from the public scene. The public lost interest in the critical press and its endless exposés of past abuses. Faced with a rising tide of militant nationalism, looming prospects of authoritarianism, and the imminent breakdown of the Soviet Union, reform intellectuals retreated in disarray. The high point of this second stage was the August 1991 putsch, when Communist party apparatchiks made a desperate attempt to reclaim power, and the following radical counterputsch engineered by Yeltsin and his democratic supporters. The Soviet period of Russian history officially ended here, but some of its key institutions and mentalities have persisted. Our polls show that Yeltsin's popularity peaked in July 1990, when he was elected to chair the Russian Parliament. This finding suggests that Yeltsin appealed to the people first and foremost as a radical opposition leader.

As the public began to lose interest in political debunking and stories of Stalinist excesses, the new stage of Russia's political transformation commenced. This third stage, which dated back to early 1992, raised another question well known to reform-minded Russian intellectuals: What is to be done? The answer was sought not so much in unearthing new enemies and plotting new revolutions as in freeing prices from state control, encouraging private enterprise, and granting more autonomy to regional authorities. The liberal policies pursued at this stage tended to be idealistic, impractical, and sometimes downright irrational. Liberalism and state reforms clearly parted company. Meanwhile, the populace shunned ideology and gave the sacramental formula, "What is to be done," a pragmatic reading, doing what it could to muddle through everyday life.

Such a turn of events was particularly painful for the authoritarian society. Ever since Russia embarked on the course of modernization some 150 years ago, it had relied exclusively on authoritarian means to move the country forward. Perestroika and postperestroika reformers acted in the same tradition, seeking to impose reforms from above. By the end of 1992, support for political institutions and leaders had hit a new low. Spurred by the exliberal scandal-mongering oppositional press, public consciousness turned against all politicians and reforms. Perestroika intellectuals grew increasingly angry, aggressive, and divisive. No national leader or political group seemed capable of commanding authority and providing moral guidance. But then again, state resources for ramming social reforms down society's throat were exhausted—a fact that political leaders had a hard time digesting.

This is not to say that the people deserted their reform leaders altogether. They still could lend their support to Yeltsin at a critical juncture, as they did during the April 1993 national referendum and once again—for a short period only—during the October 1993 showdown between the president and the Parliament. But their skepticism about Yeltsin's program remained palpable; they resented the high inflation and unemployment fostered by reform policies. Public consciousness became thoroughly deideologized, and the absence of credible political programs or leaders did not seem to alarm Russian citizens.

Like most societies trying to shake their totalitarian legacy, today's Russia is propelled forward not by a coherent reform program but by the confluence of events, circumstances, and unexpected crises necessitating ad hoc solutions and improvisations. Throughout this seemingly haphazard development, however, one can detect a trend toward the structuralization of society—a trend especially important in a country that suppressed independent interest groups in the past. In the *political sphere*, new parties began to emerge, which formed a nucleus for future pluralistic politics. *Economic interest groups* grew conscious of their particular agenda and sought to consolidate their influence through various organizational outlets. In the *area of norms and values*, society emancipated itself from the patronage of the state, which had mandated values for its citizens.[2] Universal human values and negotiated norms of everyday life emerged as alternative sources of legitimation in society. Opinion surveys from this period give further substance to this generalization. Let us take a closer look at the process of political differentiation as captured in our findings.

The National Center for Public Opinion Research has tracked public attitudes toward political life in Russia for several years. As Table 11.1 shows, the participatory spirit essential to democracy has been slow to emerge. There has been a marked drop in the number of "veterans" as well as "newcomers" to politics. The percentage of those who are disappointed with or have lost interest in politics is increasing. At the same time, fewer individuals find the political process closed to them. It is not

TABLE 11.1 The Dynamics of Public Opinion 1 (percentage of total answers)

	1988	1989	1990	1991	1992
I have always participated in public life	10	13	7	4	3
Now I have a real opportunity to participate	11	1	1	1	0.5
There is still no real opportunity to participate	33	22	21	17	19
Lately, I have lost interest in public life	–	12	14	16	16
I have no interest in politics	7	12	11	21	26
The most important question today is the fate of our nation	34	32	26	28	26

Source: Vsesoiuznyi Tsentr po Izucheniiu Obshchestvennogo Mneniia.

so much the inaccessibility of politics that presents a challenge to Russian democracy as the lack of sustained interest in political matters. Further details can be gleaned from the age distribution of the respondents. At the early stages of political reforms in Russia, those reporting a high level of political participation were primarily individuals aged forty to fifty. Toward the end of the period in question, politically active individuals were primarily those fifty-five years and older. That is to say, respondents reporting high political participation tended to be older. By contrast, individuals who had lost their interest in or were disappointed with politics were often young, followed by the middle-aged group. Those who felt that they exerted no influence on politics were also likely to be young and, toward the end of the period, middle-aged.

A few words on such terms as "politics," "public life," and "political participation," as well as "the fate of your nation" are in order here. The meaning of these terms underwent considerable change between 1988 and 1992. During the Soviet era, "politics" meant something official and imposed from above on the common citizen. It included obligatory meetings and officially sanctioned demonstrations declaring unanimous support for the government, plus the Young Communist League's pseudo-popular initiatives. In the early glasnost era, between 1987 and 1988, public consciousness was agitated and politicized. This was especially apparent among the young people and the "generation of the sixties"—dissident intellectuals whose formative years coincided with Khrushchev's thaw. Political clubs and seminars sprang up throughout the country, with participants making daring speeches and proposing novel political schemes. The circle of people united in these groups was fairly narrow, but their influence grew rapidly, spurred in part by the liberal press. This liberal "club culture" operated with the approval of Communist party reformers, who tried to steer the debate into "constructive channels" and keep reforms within the basic framework of the Soviet system of government. Later on, mass political movements would begin to gather force, bringing in their wake semi-open elections and ethnic conflicts. The political process could no longer be controlled from one center, yet it did not acquire the stable features of a multiparty system. With the Communist party exiting center stage after August 1991, a political vacuum ensued and has not been filled since. After all, the Communist party was not a political structure but a state monopoly structure; the absence of viable political institutions and organizations simply became more apparent after the Communist party's sudden collapse.

Totalitarian societies tend to confer "political" status on each and every problem facing the nation, yet they remain profoundly apolitical, not just because the masses of people are politically disenfranchised but because no real political interests are allowed to crystalize and acquire stable organizational form. Where everything is declared to be political, especially every initiative undertaken by the extant powers, nothing qualifies as a genuinely political event. Politics, the state, the constitution, elections—all these phenomena are robbed of their political content, while public and private life, as well as ideology and economics, are radically conflated.

To be sure, a purely totalitarian society has hardly ever existed. Any concrete historical polity has to compromise its principles for the sake of efficiency, and Soviet society was no exception to this rule. The "period of stagnation" in Soviet history was filled with such compromises and inconsistencies and can be seen as the practical limit of adaptability that a totalitarian society could reach in its efforts to appear normal and civilized (hence the ironic label: "Stalinism with a human face"). The dissolution of totalitarian structures spurs the differentiation of public and private spheres, of political, economic, social, cultural, and other institutions that hitherto had merged. To judge from the available data, this process of differentiation is now under way, albeit moving sluggishly, and it is marred by many contradictions.

Perestroika stimulated the politicization of Russian society, but it failed to create a viable political structure. We can see this era as the period of primary *politicization* or political *agitation*. (I deliberately avoid talking about any "awakening" or "renaissance" because these terms imply that some dormant political structures were waiting to be reignited—a wrong assumption in the case of post-Soviet society.) During this stage, the party-state apparatus continued to hold the monopoly on power and to impede the formation of independent political parties and groups. The pyramid of power had the Communist party at the top, and free elections were not possible.

The first sign of change was a shift in public attitudes toward the traditional power structures, which was accompanied by a weakening of the totalitarian monolith. Soviet citizens might have laughed at their leaders in the privacy of their homes, but they obeyed the authorities in public. In the post-Soviet era, the powers no longer had to be taken seriously, and as more and more people effectively ignored government orders, the powers lost their effectiveness. The attitude toward politics was now composed of two elements: passive identification with certain leaders (which did not differ much from the old Soviet attitude) and political agitation (or mobilization) whipped up by perestroika reforms. Both elements were doomed to disappear once real political structures began to take shape. Mass politicization inevitably led to disappointment in the quasi-politics that marked the transitional period between totalitarianism and democracy. All the changes that perestroika brought about in the political domain—elections, parties, demonstrations—bore the mark of their origins and remained essentially quasi-political and unstable. Sooner or later, the primary politicization of society would have to give way to the formation of a civic culture and genuine political structures that reflected diverse political interests and made a multiparty, pluralistic polity possible. There were signs that such structures had begun to form after 1989, but these were very early and distressingly weak portents.

If stable and working political structures are so hard to come by in Russian politics today, it is because the political interests that these structures are supposed to represent are still largely nascent and inchoate. Nor is there a viable political milieu—a middle class—where such interests would have a chance to crystalize. Not only are coherent political platforms missing from Russia's political scene; the political slogans, concepts, and ideas around which stable political groupings could form remain barely audible. There is no dearth of new political headings and noisy statements, but what exactly they stand for in terms of specific policies is very hard to fathom. When a political party or group declared itself in the old Parliament, it was usually a by-product of the latest schism in parliamentary politics and not an indication that the party expressed the interests of a certain constituency and intended to press for electoral victory.

Current public opinion surveys show that the political divisions do not so much reflect the political differentiation in the country as they reveal the latest swing in the popularity of a particular leader or group. As long as society remains organized around the structures of power—popular or not—it will not know genuine pluralism and political consolidation.

The current difficulties with building a viable political culture in Russia have one unsettling consequence: disenchantment with democracy and a paucity of legitimate political structures. The bridge that was supposed to link old and new Russia stretches only half way, not reaching the other side. Politics in the transitional period has bred discontent, provoked frequent crises, and obscured the criteria by which one could judge the progress toward democracy. Especially distraught and disappointed are those circles that succumbed to the initial euphoria and developed unrealistic hopes for imminent reforms. I am talking about the country's reform-minded political elites and liberal postdissident intellectuals, including emigré circles, which exerted a certain influence on politics in the transitional period. If you look at rank-and-file individuals, those normally reached by pollsters, you find a far greater stability in mood over the period under study. One could even speak about certain sociopsychological types of responses to the political turmoil, which seem quite independent of the nature of events. Instructive in this respect are the answers to the following survey question: Which mood was most common last year among the people you know? (see Table 11.2).

Why did the leaders who came to prominence on the wave of perestroika fail to retain power? Quite apart from their personal dispositions, they were selected for a deconstructive role. They helped tear down the old political institutions, but they proved inept when it came to the constructive task of building up new political structures. This deconstructive thrust of the early perestroika reformers reflected the gap between the "can-do" self-image they communicated to their followers and their far more limited practical skills and personal abilities. These leaders were sold on the idea that Soviet socialism could be rejuvenated, that they were the movers and shakers behind the reforms, that they could cleanse "true Leninism" of Stalinist distortions and return the country to the pristine sources of communist ideology. All innovations that sprang to life during the Gorbachev era—the opening up of the mass media, elections featuring alternative candidates, campaigns against corruption and bureaucratic excesses—were animated by the idea of reclaiming the revolutionary past, with the party apparatus posing as the prime engine for this renewal. The 1989–90 national election campaign was dominated by leaders who were brought to power with the Communist party's tacit or open approval and who were looking to the past rather than the future for their programmatic statements. When the totalitarian structures crumbled, however, they were entirely unprepared to offer constructive policies and assume the mantle of leadership. Not even dissident intellectuals, with a

TABLE 11.2 The dynamics of Public Opinion 2 (percentage of total answers)

	1990	1991	1992
Hope	13	20	17
Confusion	23	27	24
Despair	28	27	18
Confidence	6	6	5

Source: Vsesoiuznyi Tsentr po Izucheniiu Obshchestvennogo Mneniia.

few notable exceptions, were free from the liberal Soviet mentality of renewal and restoration. All reforms were to be imposed from above by wise leaders drawn from the educated stratum of intellectuals.

Meanwhile, the foundations of Soviet socialism and the international empire it fostered collapsed much faster than anybody thought possible. As soon as it became clear that hopes for a smooth transition to freedom and prosperity were widely exaggerated, the old-style leaders and their institutions came under attack. Very quickly they turned from facilitators into stumbling blocks impeding reforms. The reformist alliance, which included party reformers, the liberal democratic intelligentsia, and nationalistic forces, fell apart. Each group formed its own power center, however poorly organized, and each was distinguished by vociferous attacks on the state and the executive power. The key divide between political forces at the time was the line between the radical pragmatic reformers who gathered around the executive power and various oppositional currents. Among the most salient manifestations of this division was the confrontation between the presidential and parliamentary branches of power that came to a head in 1993.

Those leaders who failed to transcend their perestroika-from-above illusions disappeared from the political scene. Such was the fate of party reformers and intellectuals gathered around Gorbachev. Others joined newly founded factions and groups. Gorbachev's demise could be attributed to the rise of Yeltsin, who presented himself to the nation as a more radical reformer. But the drop in popularity that Yeltsin's government suffered in 1993 suggested that the country was ready for a new form of leadership and political organization.

The Soviet Union has always been a "mobilized society," that is, a society based on political activism organized from above and controlled by the hierarchy of state power. The political regimes that governed Russia throughout much of its history relied on force, propaganda, and centralized control to keep the country moving. Unorganized and undifferentiated masses of people were to be brought into action and compelled toward the goal set forth by the higher authorities. Intellectual and moral resources were mobilized in the same way as any other, with the intelligentsia enlisted to do the authorities' bidding. Mobilization is the only form in which a totalitarian society can exist. By contrast, civil society is possible only when interest groups and autonomous civic structures are allowed to flourish and individual interests have a chance to be articulated and communicated to others. To be sure, mobilized and civil societies are but ideal types that approximate reality in all its richness and possibilities. Yet, these are useful models that help us to understand the nature of political processes in the transitional period.

Both the theory and practice of a mobilized society implied that the political masses are passive and pliable, that power mechanisms must be employed to push them in the right direction. Characteristically, Bolsheviks favored such terms as "levers," "transmission belts," and "cogs," which underscored their philosophical commitment to the mobilizational ethics of government. The despotism and coercion endemic to the Russian political tradition might account for the ruthlessness with which the Bolsheviks set out to realize their mechanical model of mobilizational politics. This model had three principal components: omnipotent authority; subservient people; and since the middle of the nineteenth century, the intelligentsia. In recent years, the role of direct coercion and fear-fostering propaganda has diminished. The "transmission belts," to use Lenin's favorite expression, have been loosened. But the Russian polity has not fully shaken the mobilizational structures and certainly not the old mobilizational mentality. This is evident in the fact that agitation and apathy—the two states most common in a mobilizational society—are characteristic of post-Soviet society, where emotional excitement and moral tension are typically followed by periods of depression and asthenic apathy.

The mobilizational thrust of recent Russian reforms was apparent in the Gorbachev era, and it was especially evident in the propaganda technology used by the elites. Mobilizational mechanisms weakened afterward, but they were still working during the August 1991 putsch and the April 1993 national referendum. In both cases, society was mobilized in the face of attempts to restore the old regime, even though most people had lost their early enthusiasm for reforms. Still, this was mobilizational activism and not the kind of steady participatory practice that undergirds democratic politics. Except for the nationalistic and ethnic movements that unite the constituency around the idea of the opposition to the center and local sovereignty, alternative forms of political participation remain in a rudimentary stage. The path from a mobilizational political culture to a participatory civil society is yet to be charted in the post-Soviet era.

If we take a closer look at Russian political elites, we can see that their evolution mirrors the problems facing the society that seeks to shed the old and build a new civic culture. Soviet society had two kinds of elites: a power elite and a cultural elite (the intelligentsia). Both suffered a serious setback in the current political crisis. Following the tradition of the Russian intelligentsia, Soviet intellectuals sought to modernize the state and its citizens. They provided intellectual and moral legitimation to the authorities and at the same time served, albeit to a lesser degree, as the critics of the system. The Soviet intelligentsia owed the state its ideological, political, and economic autonomy, which is why it aimed primarily at the liberal rationalization of the regime. Perestroika spurred the intelligentsia's illusions that a wise reformer, drawing expert advice, could revamp Russian society. Glasnost encouraged intellectuals to believe that they would be the experts called upon to provide the high-brow theoretical rationale for the reforms. Yet, intellectuals hardly qualified for this role, since few of them possessed expert knowledge adequate to the task at hand. That is not to gainsay the key, indeed crucial, role that the intelligentsia played in stirring public opinion and mobilizing society in the early perestroika years. But that was the intelligentsia's swan song. The crisis of perestroika in 1990–91 led to disillusionment among intellectuals, who, along with other national elites, were given to profound pessimism about the country's future. The triangular structure of power that had carried the Russian polity through more than a century—power–people–intelligentsia—had collapsed.

Highly instructive in this respect is the fate of glasnost. Perestroika's major and most enduring accomplishment, glasnost lost its luster in the post-perestroika period. The freedom of speech, the freedom to publish and assemble, is still in place, but its role as a central factor in public life is diminishing. The uncensored word has lost its capacity to rouse the imagination and spur the public on to action. The public takes glasnost for granted, or else views it with suspicion. This is probably the way it should be in a normal democratic society, where glasnost serves informational, aesthetic, and other functions. But Russian society today is hardly a functional democracy, and the indifference to free speech is a symptom of the underlying crisis.

As the democratic process continues, the Russian intelligentsia is likely to lose its traditional mobilizing role and turn into an educated cultural and technical elite. Intellectuals are bound to become specialists, that is, if Russian society evolves into a participatory democracy. If it follows a different type of development, the intelligentsia will continue to vacillate between despair and patriotic messianism. In any event, there is no return to the traditional triangular power structure.

For the first time in Soviet history, perestroika transformed Russian politicians from larger-than-life figures exemplifying a particular cause into flesh and blood individuals with clearly visible strengths and all too apparent weaknesses. Mikhail Gorbachev, Dmitry Ligachev, Andrei Sakharov, Boris Yeltsin (and, I should add, Ronald Reagan, Margaret Thatcher, and several other Western politicians) were concrete individuals who could not hide behind carefully polished images, who thrust themselves into the public eye by virtue of their willingness to take a stand, to venture a personal and sometimes unpopular opinion. The negative side of this development was the personalization of politics. Political divisions were defined as personal confrontations between Gorbachev and Ligachev, Sakharov and Gorbachev, Gorbachev and

Yeltsin, and so forth. However, in the postperestroika years, all politicians suffered in public opinion, their popularity taking a dramatic plunge. Here are the ratings that the two most prominent Russian politicians were given in a series of polls identifying the man of the year (see Table 11.3). The 1992 figures show that barely one-sixth of all those polled gave their vote to the man of the year. Three times as many votes went to Yeltsin during the April 1993 referendum, but this figure reflected the mobilizational agitation that preceded this referendum. Once the political strain subsided, the leaders lost their appeal in the pubic eye. Now we have clear signs that politics are getting more and more depersonalized, that leadership structure and legitimation patterns are undergoing systemic change.

Soviet society produced not so much political leaders as party bosses whose legitimacy derived from their allegiance to the party cause and personal connections to the higher strata of power. A popular image was important to the party bosses, who cultivated it assiduously through propaganda and mass media (Stalin's cult of personality is most revealing in this respect). But their "personal charisma" did not precede their ascent to power; rather, it devolved on them after they entrenched themselves in the power structure.

Gorbachev and Yeltsin are the last two Soviet-style leaders in contemporary Russian politics, although their ascents to power followed different paths. Gorbachev received his leadership mantle from the Communist party. He tried to legitimize his power as the president elected by the Parliament, but his efforts proved a failure. Yeltsin came to national prominence as a party maverick and an opposition leader. Later on, he was chosen by popular vote to be the president of the Russian Federation. He assumed real power after the August 1991 putsch and the dissolution of the Soviet Union. Along with the mantle of leadership, he inherited the "secondary charisma" that belonged to and protected anyone who controlled the state machinery. In 1993, with the state machinery sputtering, Yeltsin's popularity ratings began to slide.

The crisis of power that unfolded in late 1993 dramatized the crisis of the old political culture and all its peculiar modes of legitimation, support mobilization, and political leadership. To grasp the meaning of the bloody confrontation between the president and the Parliament we need

TABLE 11.3 The Dynamcs of Public Opinion 3 (percentage of total vote)

	1988	1989	1990	1991	1992
Mikhail Gorbachev	51	44	16	14	1
Boris Yeltsin	5	19	44	38	17

Source: Vsesoiuznyi Tsentr po Izucheniiu Obshchestvennogo Mneniia.

to go back to earlier sociopolitical developments, beginning with the collapse of party-state hegemony. These tragic events are but a stage in the ongoing political and constitutional crisis that will, in all likelihood, continue for months and years. The 1993 summer opinion surveys show the public clamoring for law and order as a counterbalance to the mounting chaos and anarchy. To a society that never lived under a genuine constitution and frequently spurned the rule of law, dictatorial means seemed a fair price to pay for instituting an order. When confronted with a choice between authoritarian rule by President Yeltsin and a military dictatorship by excommunists, the first choice—government by presidential dictate—was given a clear preference. The populace still saw Yeltsin as the best hope for political and economic reforms. Yeltsin's decision to dissolve and later to storm Parliament should be seen against the backdrop of this popular support for strong actions designed to restore order without turning back the wheel of history. Our data show that in the beginning of October, the majority (52 percent) of the Russian population generally supported Yeltsin's decision to do away with the old Parliament, while 24 percent of the respondents opposed his action. Yeltsin's decision drew particularly strong approval from college-educated people (61 percent supported and 20 percent disapproved of the action), whereas less well-educated respondents, those without a high school diploma, showed the least enthusiasm for the radical course of action (44 percent approved and 28 percent disapproved of Yeltsin's decision). Nobody anticipated that the confrontation between the president and the Parliament would take a bloody turn, and most likely nobody wanted the showdown to go that far, but the configuration of political forces and public opinion in the nation directed the course of events. Public opinion in Russia took the side of the president and generally approved his use of force, in part because it followed the bloodbath provoked by the militant supporters of Parliament. According to the findings gathered in mid-October 1993 by the National Center for Public Opinion Research, 20 percent of the respondents stated that Yeltsin's recourse to force was timely and 35 percent believed that he waited too long to clamp down on his opponents. The majority of those polled declared that Yeltsin had the right to dissolve Parliament. This judgment, which was not entirely consistent with the constitution, showed that the population was willing to disregard the legal niceties in the face of a severe political crisis. However, the mood in the country soon changed once again. Yeltsin's ratings slipped in November 1993, which led to the defeat of his allies in the December 12 parliamentary election.

Subsequent events—the December 1993 parliamentary elections—showed that Yeltsin might have been too hasty suspending the constitution. Disillusionment with the democratic process, pervasive economic hardship, and reformers' failure to coordinate their efforts translated into a surprising show of strength by the ultranationalists led by Vladimir Zhirinovsky. As our findings show, Zhirinovsky, the head of the mislabeled Liberal Democratic party, drew his support chiefly from the lower middle class. Those who voted for him were people with a below-average education, employed in sectors of the economy vulnerable to unemployment, concerned about the crime situation, and humiliated by Russia's loss of superpower status. The traditional Soviet working class voted for radical nationalists, but older and retired people were most prominent among Communist party supporters. Nearly a third of those who gave their voice to Zhirinovsky waited until election day to make up their mind. Few voters knew much about Zhirinovsky and his party; most chose this venue as a way to dramatize their displeasure with the reforms and their negative impact on standards of living. The vote for Zhirinovsky was mainly a vote against the establishment. Some of his supporters indicated that they regretted their vote, so he might be a temporary phenomenon on the Russian political scene. It is certainly too early to tell. What seems perfectly clear now is that dismantling the old Russian and Soviet political tradition and replacing it with a viable democratic civic culture will be a long and arduous process.

Notes

This chapter was translated from Russian by Dmitri N. Shalin. The author wishes to acknowledge the George Soros Foundation and the International Research and Exchanges Board for their support.

1. See *Social and Economic Changes: Public Opinion Monitoring* no. 1–8 (Moscow: VCIOM, 1993), and ibid., no. 1–4 (1994).

2. Yuri Levada, ed., *Sovetskii prostoi chelovek* (Moscow: VCIOM, 1993).

Conclusion: Toward a Post-Soviet Society

FREDERICK STARR

Is it too early to speak of "postcommunist consciousness" in Russia? Little time has passed since the fall of communism, and the cultural outlook of a people changes only slowly. At the same time, over the scant half-decade since the emergence of a new state called Russia the defining issues of that country have already passed through several distinct phases, according to Yuri Levada.

For these reasons, the authors represented in this volume have shown a commendable tentativeness and caution in identifying the consciousness of postcommunist Russia. The implied conclusion is itself important, namely, that the deeper values informing Russian culture today are by no means clear. Lacking a crystal ball, several of the authors have confined themselves to identifying the "objective" circumstances affecting culture that are bound to prevail for a while.

Thus, Daniil Dondurei is surely right to indicate that patronage of the arts has already undergone a transformation, with the state's dominance having been replaced by more diverse and market-based sources of support. Something similar has occurred in intellectual life as a whole, where, as Dmitri Shalin shows, the very concept of a generalized intellectual is giving way to a more function-based notion that leaves the highly educated part of the population more focused on specific sets of modern skills and the highly diverse settings in which they are employed, as opposed to their membership in a guild of "mental workers."

Using a term that gained wide currency in Eastern Europe beginning with Poland in the early 1980s and Russia by 1988, Yuri Levada speaks of an emerging "civic culture." This refers to a condition in which the state is reduced to the status of one important organization among many in society, in which a plethora of other organizational forms buffer and mediate individuals' relations to government, and in which rights against the state protect equally individuals, voluntary associations, and their prop-

313

erty. The emergence of the concept of "civic culture" in Russia and neighboring states says as much about the past as about the present. Even the most ardent champion of civil society has to admit that in Eastern Europe and the former Soviet Union its core definition is negative, a condition of "noncommunism."

What both sides of this debate have in common is the assumption that postcommunist consciousness in Russia will gain its identity, both positively and negatively, from the communist order it seeks to replace. In other words, to understand Russia's new cultural values, one must gain a fresh perspective on the culture of communism.

The boldness of recent reinterpretations of the culture of communism is a striking example of Hegel's quip that "the owl of Minerva flies at night." Until recently, leading trends in the analysis of Soviet culture all stressed the importance of periodization within the Soviet era, as if to underscore the capacity of Soviet civilization to evolve and change over time. With the waning of Soviet rule, however, it is the continuities that stand out and provide the background against which a postcommunist mentality will emerge. None of the authors in this volume undervalue the extent of change that occurred after Stalin's death, but all indicate how such change took place alongside the continuation of official ideals dating from the pioneer Bolsheviks, and amid the perpetuation of ownership and control over nearly all property by the heirs of Stalin and Lenin. Stated differently, our authors set the present situation not against a constantly shifting Soviet cultural scene but against a recent past that is at best bifurcated, with parts of the public having found their way to new values but with many others remaining true to values left over from the era of Soviet rule.

As Alexander Etkind argues in his brilliant essay, Marxism-Leninism was at its core transformational and utopian. The Soviet "experiment" has as its goal the creation of a "New Soviet Man" who would be governed by a psychology differing radically from anything that existed before. Taking Nietzsche's notion of the *Übermensch* to its logical conclusion, Kremlin leaders set forth the objective of fulfillment through work, the worship of power, and the repression not only of carnal pleasures and the satisfactions of daily life (*byt*) but also the very consciousness of mortality and finitude in human existence.

It goes without saying that all this implied both a Rousseauian rejection of original sin and a Darwinian belief in the infinite malleability of human consciousness. While antecedents for both views can be found in the writings of Marx, the more direct forebearers of the Soviet cultural ideal are the boldest radicals of Russian thought on the eve of the revolution, including the soft-spoken librarian of the old Rumiantsev Museum and *arch-provocateur* of consciousness, Nikolai Fyodorov. With Fyodorov, the early Bolshevik sought to achieve transcendence in the here and now by overcoming all humankind's limitations, including death. Soviet culture, then, was at war not merely with the ideals of bourgeois society but with human nature itself. Its eventual failure, our authors imply, can be traced to this brute fact.

The clear implication of this line of reasoning is that the fall of communism should bring to the fore once more those deeper Russian values that communism had submerged. Indeed, Professor Pankhurst develops this idea in his chapter on the Russian Orthodox Church, while Professor Boym takes a similar approach in her enjoyable paean to everyday life and the homely ficus plant. For all its merits, this approach runs the danger of producing a picture of the pre-Soviet past that is a rather narrow caricature. In one of the most remarkable essays in this collection, Professor Paramonov broadens the stage by offering a reinterpretation of Russia's deeper cultural legacy that, in its paradoxes and contradictions, suggests the breathtaking range of possibilities that may exist in the present. Paramonov begins by accepting the "patrimonial" interpretation of Russian development, according to which the entire society and state were once considered the tsar's personal property, to be disposed of at his will. At the same time, Paramonov acknowledges a contrary current of pluralism, privacy, and independence from the state, which he traces to Prince Andrei Bogolyubsky's refusal to move his court to Kiev in the twelfth century. Following a line of argument pioneered in the late nineteenth century by Moscow jurist Boris Chicherin, Paramonov then suggests how this alternative tradition of pluralism, privacy, and localism gained strength.

Against this background, we must ask again the question posed by Dmitri Shalin, namely, whether Stalin was an aberration or an expression of Russia's destiny. If the former, then one might expect that Russians would gradually but, in the end, successfully pick up some of the "lost threads" of their deeper culture and weave them into a new cultural consciousness for the dawning century. If the latter, then one might reasonably expect the legacy of Stalin or, more accurately, of Soviet culture as a whole, to persist for a long time.

It is to their credit that our authors failed to reach a consensus on this important question. On balance, however, they seem to argue that what they variously call Stalinism, Leninism, or simply the Soviet cultural consciousness has deep roots in Russian culture and is bound to outlive the specific socioeconomic environment that protected and nourished it during the Soviet era. The key to this thesis lies in Professor Paramonov's assertions regarding Lenin's paradoxical appropriation of the Slavophile heritage of communitarian thought and his wedding of that heritage to Westernizers' statism.

It is not necessary to recite again the dialectical argument that has been employed since Nikolai Berdiaev's day to uphold this interpretation. Suffice it to say that it begins with the Westernizers' thesis, follows with the Slavophiles' antithesis, and culminates in various late nineteenth- and early twentieth-century syntheses, among which Bolshevism proved to be the most potent. In longer perspective, this argument suggests that the dualism inherent in Russian culture from the time of Tsar Aleksei Mikhailovich in the seventeenth century down to the great debates of the nineteenth century was overcome in a perverse and dangerous way with the paradoxical marriages of communal peasant and proletariat, on the one hand, and communal proletariat and state, on the other.

Professor Kon traces the process by which this synthesis prevailed down to the end of Soviet rule, even as the intelligentsia and parts of the broader population underwent a "long moral emancipation." Eventually, both the individual personality and private life reemerged from the shadows, albeit surreptitiously and without confronting directly the official orthodoxies. The price of this incomplete emancipation was the maintenance of a hypocritical silence in public, which in turn nourished various forms of self-hatred, particularly on the part of the intelligentsia. It might be added that the "emancipated" intelligentsia's continued dependence upon the state for its support and very existence as a class must have further contributed to such self-loathing. Professor Abdullaeva's references to the widespread dark humor (*anekdoty*) of the Brezhnev years hints at the pathology created by this situation.

This, in broadest outline, is the picture of a single and coherent paradigm of Soviet culture put forward by the very talented contributors to this volume. This culture was all-embracing in its aspirations and was undergirded by a set of institutions created explicitly to embody a genuinely "Soviet" consciousness. Professor Boym's account of life in a communal apartment (*kommunalka*) might have been paralleled by similar accounts of life in everything from professional unions to the media of communications. Above all, this system was crystalized in myths that continued to dominate every aspect of public discourse even after they had long since begun to erode in the privacy of kitchen table conversations.

Over the past thirty years, Western observers have faithfully documented every step in the process of decay of the myths that formerly had defined the mobilized Soviet society. In retrospect, it is clear that those Western observers failed adequately to appreciate the extent to which the endless droning of those same myths in the public sphere continued to define the values of official life long after they had ceased to be taken seriously by millions of ordinary people in their private realms. Still less did most Western observers, in their eagerness to document the emergence of a civic consciousness independent of the state, adequately acknowledge the enduring impact of the hundreds of Soviet institutions created to uphold the myths. Focused mainly on the steady emergence of individualistic, pluralistic, and privatized values, they were unprepared to appreciate the partial vacuum created by Gorbachev's attack on the old consciousness.

Gorbachev himself was caught unawares by the appearance of this vacuum. His goal may have been to lay the basis of a new Soviet system freed of what he called "Stalinism," but the very language he employed—direct, blunt, and stripped of cant—helped rip apart the entire edifice of official Soviet values. The breakup after 1989 of the organizational structures created to serve the New Soviet Man further deepened the cultural crisis that accompanied the establishment of the new Republic of Russia. No wonder that Professor Kon speaks of "complete anomie, lawlessness, and normlessness" and that Yury Levada's surveys of public opinion down to 1994 revealed widespread disorientation and confusion.

Enter paradox. At the very moment when one is tempted to seize upon the notion of cultural vacuum as the key to post-Soviet consciousness, it turns out that the attitudes and practices of the Soviet era are not as dead as they may have seemed. Professor Friedberg notes areas of continuity between Soviet and post-Soviet literature, as if to suggest that many writers found it convenient simply to pour new wine into old bottles. In the same vein, Professor Kon refers to the continuity of preindustrial "zero-sum" thinking in the Soviet and post-Soviet eras. This habit of mind, which holds that one person's gain must necessarily be another's loss, is like a brake on change. "Envy, disguised as social justice," Kon writes, "is the most powerful enemy of social and economic progress." Especially among the older generation, this attitude links past and present.

It is Professor Paramonov who details the most striking paradox of all, namely, the miraculous transformation of the most outspoken enemies of Soviet rule into its last champions. At first glance, Russia's ruralist "country prose" writers of the 1970s and 1980s appeared as resolute opponents of Soviet statism who successfully thwarted the most grandomanic Soviet project of all, the diversion of Siberian rivers southward to Central Asia. The fall of communism completely disoriented these patriotic ruralists, who discovered that they had in fact been psychologically dependent upon a powerful state after all and that their identity derived from the act of opposing it. In quick order they rediscovered the "Eurasian" movement of the 1920s and transformed themselves into champions of state power (*derzhavniki*), as opposed to the rights of individuals and voluntary associations. This metamorphosis was like Lenin's assimilation of the Slavophile tradition, but in reverse. Even though it involved only a few people, this shift cannot be lightly dismissed, for it affirms once more the dialectical and organic wholeness of Russian cultural consciousness, with all its attendant paradoxes.

In the end, however, the new statism may prove to be only a minor episode in a larger evolution toward a civic culture. The authors represented in this volume depict with great clarity the process by which the old Soviet cultural consciousness has broken apart. Gone is the ideal of labor as the highest fulfillment, and also the discursive quality that made much Soviet writing inaccessible to outsiders. Indeed, the entire organizational structure of Soviet high culture has collapsed, and with it the public's interest in "serious" books, music, and art. Surging in to fill their place is a new affirmation of ordinary life and genuine popular culture that wells up "from below" rather than being disseminated to a passive public "from above." The young have largely abandoned the old identities, and have moved quickly to emancipate themselves from the tutelage of the state and to accept individual entrepreneurship as a social norm.

Yuri Levada has characterized the old Soviet order as a "mobilized society," in which cultural values derived from the edicts of party and state functionaries. The present evolution may be slow and painful, yet millions of Russians, especially the young, seem to be groping toward a very different ideal, namely, a "self-mobilized" society and culture. This implies a degree of individuation and pluralism that would have been inconceivable a mere decade ago. As if to give this new cultural ideal permanence, a host of new organizational structures embracing nearly every field of culture and the arts has gradually come into being. Even if the pace is slow, the radicalism of this transformation can scarcely be denied, for it brings forth the dialectical opposite of virtually every key feature of the old Soviet cosmology.

One may be tempted to dismiss this new "civic culture" as merely the latest in a long series of short-lived and ultimately frustrating bursts of enthusiasm for private and volunteerist initiatives that dates back to the Decembrist era in the early nineteenth century. Notwithstanding the impressive contemporary data cited by Levada, a cynic may well argue that "civic culture" represents more an ideal than reality, especially at a time when thoughtful writers like Richard Sennett (in *The Fall of Public Man*) question the vitality of civic culture even in Western Europe and America. Thus, if Tolstoi's Pierre Bezukhov was a naive dreamer, why should we think any better of his heirs in the world today? For all the radicalism of the revolution in consciousness in Russia today, this question remains on one's lips.

At this point we must stress once more the tentativeness that hangs over the entire post-Soviet cultural enterprise. Since the new economic and political structures have yet to take definitive form, it is simply premature to declare victory for the "civic culture" that Professor Levada finds evidence for as he begins to sift the evidence gathered in his nationwide surveys. Yet, it cannot be denied that the very language and mode of expression in virtually every field of endeavor have changed since the fall of communism. No less important, history itself is undergoing a transformation. The reemergence of the twelfth-century Prince Andrei Bogolyubsky as a progenitor of the new pluralism has already been noted. In the same vein, the eighteenth-century agronomist and champion of local life, Andrei Bolotov, has recently emerged from the shadows as a kind of ideal of the new civic culture.

This process of rediscovering a usable past has only begun. As it progresses, remarkable individuals and whole cultural movements that have for a century been relegated to the footnotes will come to the fore once again. History's winners will become its losers, and its losers will stand forth as winners. Depending on how thoroughgoing this process is, Russia will experience the most paradoxical of all the shifts considered in this volume, namely, the emergence of a vital civic consciousness that is found to have surprisingly deep roots in Russian culture.

Afterword

BRUCE MAZLISH

The seventy-five-year Soviet "experiment" is over. It came to an end without war, invasion, or violent revolution, which is unusual. In this sense, it was largely an internal collapse. As several scholars have pointed out, the Soviet system failed because its bureaucratic and totalitarian institutions were unable to move from the old Fordism to the new computer-inspired technology. Thus, the system's very successes undermined its ability to make a transition to the second stage of modernization.

It is important to see the Soviet demise in a global context, for the competition that Soviet society faced was on this level. The "socialism in one country" proclaimed by Soviet leaders implied an isolation that could hardly be maintained in the century that has seen the unprecedented explosion of global communications. As Charles Maier has written, "The Communist collapse was a reaction to forces for transformation that have gripped West and East alike, but which Western Europeans (and North Americans) had responded to earlier and thus with less cataclysmic an upheaval."[1]

Rooted in both internal and external factors, the communist collapse has had reverberations the world over. It has reshaped the international arena, leaving its mark even on such distant and/or limited areas such as East Central Europe, the Middle East, and Africa. It has left Russia largely shorn of its empire but still immensely powerful and important. One consequence is that Russia's future will affect the future of all other societies; and Russia's future, in turn, will be shaped by its own heritage from a pre-Soviet, as well as a Soviet, historical past and culture.

The present book is an informed study of the Russian past and present that lets us glean this country's, and indirectly our own, possible future. A reader learns about broad areas of Russian culture in the context of certain large questions.

I should make it clear that I myself am not a specialist in either Soviet or Russian history. My training has been in European intellectual and cultural history, to which I have added an interest in conceptualizing global history. However, an outsider's perspective may serve to raise comparative issues, as well as some questions central to social science in general.

Russian Culture at the Crossroads, in my view, raises fundamental questions concerning continuity and change, as well as value change, social transformation, and the possibilities of modifying human nature. Although its main focus is Russian culture proper, the book's appeal transcends its stated topic. In this postscript, I shall address Russian aspirations insofar as they shed important light on interactions between the local and the global.

* * *

The word "culture" is used throughout this volume in the most diffuse sense. Most generally, it refers to the values, morals, and actions of a people, the Russians, rather than to their institutions. It is about "spiritual" qualities more than material ones, although the two are obviously interconnected. In fact, the book can be seen as a counterpart to Max Weber's *Protestant Ethic and the Spirit of Capitalism,* in that it asks essentially the same question: What are the features in Russian culture that may foster or hinder its transformation into a democratic and market-oriented society?

There are different ways one could approach Russian culture with such a question in mind. The authors of this study examine, among other sources, high and low culture, folklore and fairy tales, the iconography of everyday life, the culture of work, and the findings of public opinion polls. The result is a new insight into a Russian culture that is both wide and deep, rooted in the past, and flowering, noxiously or otherwise, in the present.

Such an undertaking makes sense only if we recognize and accept that cultures are wholes, disjointed and contradictory though they might be. This inquiry also implies that the pre-Soviet and Soviet experience embody both good and bad features. We must ask why so many gifted thinkers, writers, and artists flocked to the revolutionary cause. How did Blok, Mayakovsky, and others manage to produce lasting works of art, their ideological blinders notwithstanding? What was there in the totalitarian environment that nourished friendship and creativity? And which are that era's unexpected, perverted, yet tangible gains that will have to be surrendered in a freer, democratic, market-oriented society of the future?

To ask such questions is not to be a "fellow traveler" and condone past abuses but to look realistically at the actual historical landscape through which we have been passing. Fellow travelers overrated Soviet achievements; we would do well to recognize that, amid the terrible evil, there were some accomplishments. If we reject such acknowledgment, then we will not understand Russian culture and its tormented effort to come to terms with itself.

* * *

Alexis de Tocqueville, writing about the *ancien régime* and the French revolution, insisted on the continuity between the two and, in the French case, on the way that the centralizing tendencies of the absolutist monarchy persisted into the revolutionary regime. Similarly, we need to be aware of continuities between tsarist Russia and its Soviet successor, and now between the Soviet Union and its Russian heir. Such continuities will include both desirable and undesirable features. It is one of the chief merits of the present book that it describes in great detail this two-faced inheritance.

The fact is that Soviet totalitarianism was not total; unofficial life, including political dissent, underground art, and a black market, went on in communist Russia. The regime's pretensions to total control were utopian; it was never a monolith, and the system's downfall underscored this point. Nevertheless, its pretensions must be taken seriously, for some of Russia's "best and brightest" took the Soviet promise quite seriously, especially in the early years after the Bolshevik revolution. Like some religious idealists before them, the Bolsheviks sought to form a "New Man"—the "New Soviet Man," that is. Tacitly taking a page from the Bible and explicitly drawing from nineteenth-century literature, the leaders of Soviet society promised that its members would be free from the sorrier aspects of human nature as it had been known hitherto. Such a new man, and new woman, would be entirely without personal interest, existing solely for the good of other humans and society as a whole.

As the present volume documents, the entire culture was to be devoted to this ambitious project. Literature, in the form of socialist realism, set the correct models, as did academic art. Psychology and pedagogy were called upon to supply "scientific methods" for nurturing the socialist psyche. Work was defined accordingly as a universally important activity designed to shape the New Soviet Man's personality. Thus was set in motion one of the greatest experiments in reshaping human nature and transforming society. Not only did it fail, but it also caused immense suffering to those caught in its juggernaut.

It might be tempting to explain away this whole undertaking and its unraveling as reflecting unique Russian experience. There is much in Russian history that points in this direction. Yet, we must understand Soviet experience in global terms, as a historical experiment deeply rooted in Western and Christian thought and ideals. Millennial aspirations have been a constant in the West, exploding especially in the seventeenth century and leading to the secular utopianism of the eighteenth-century Enlightenment. We might recall that the American revolution sought to create its own "New Man" inhabiting a "New World" and establishing a "New Order." Just look at the back of a U.S. dollar bill for the evidence. J. Hector St. John de Crevecoeur, in his fundamental statement, "What is an American?" (1792), declared that "The American is a new man, who acts upon new principles."

Similarly, with the industrial revolution as his inspiration, Robert Owen, in his "A New View of Society," declared, "Any character, from the best to the worst, from the most ignorant to the most enlightened, may be given to any community, even to the world at large, by applying certain means; which are to a great extent at the command and under the control, or easily made so, of those who possess the government of nations." Later on, behavioral psychology would try to give scientific form to the "certain means." Marx, of course, listed Owen among his utopian precursors and shared with him the utopian desire to mold a new man.

Although it failed in its execution, the Soviet Union's efforts to realize its version of the New Man fed on fundamental aspirations of Western thought. Russian culture, naturally, gave specific features to this Pygmalion-like attempt, but it was itself part and parcel of a larger Christian and Western culture.

* * *

The Bolsheviks endeavored to transform tsarist Russia, with all its cultural traditions, into a Soviet system producing *and* produced by a "New Man." The tremendous moral and cultural change promised by the Bolsheviks has failed to materialize. Yet, major elements of this project, along with large chunks of tsarist heritage smuggled into Soviet society, are still evident in the present effort to transform Russia into a democratic and market-oriented system.

Will current attempts to reinvent Russia be any more successful than previous ones? In both tsarist times and today, the campaign for a new Russia goes forward (or backward) under the banners of Westernizers and Slavophiles. The Russian religious heritage bears witness to this struggle, and the Russian Church remains an active participant in it. A product of the split into Eastern and Western Christianity, the Russian Orthodox Church fuels the debate about Russia's place in the East–West rivalry. The question is whether Russia is part of the West, part of the East, or a unique Eurasian culture unto itself.

The dispute between the Westernizers and Slavophiles frames many of the essays collected in this book. What can be added here is that this question itself should be placed in a larger frame. From the very beginning of the modernizing process in the West, a struggle has ensued between those who wish to press ahead toward a "modern" society and those who are opposed to it in the name of tradition and/or community. In England, home of the first industrial revolution, William Cobbett, William Wordsworth, and Thomas Carlyle, for example, sound the alarm about the price of modernization and modernism. In Germany, by the second half of the nineteenth century, the clash is given classical form in Ferdinand Tönnies' famous dichotomy of *Gemeinschaft* (community) and *Gesellschaft* (society). Thus, Russia is not unique in its historical pulls and pushes but only in the specific cultural form under which the struggle takes place.

In many respects, Russia under the Bolsheviks experienced modernization, and thus "Westernization," but it has never attained full modernity or savored all its fruits. That is to say, Russian society was industrialized, but its culture was not officially problematized; it escaped the widespread fragmentation, thoroughgoing pluralism, and inventive excitement endemic to Western modernism. In reflecting on the longstanding division between Slavophiles and Westernizers, it is important to note that Russian and Soviet intellectuals failed sufficiently to confront the issues of modernism and its consequences—the failure especially conspicuous in the case of the so-called Westernizers. It is only in the post-Soviet years that, for example, postmodernism has emerged as a topic of lively discussion among Russian intellectuals.

* * *

Civil society has emerged as a major concern of Western historiography. Historians such as Reinhard Koselleck and philosophers such as Jürgen Habermas have written major treatises on the subject, seeking to highlight civic culture and its role in the emergence of modern, democratic societies. Civil society, usually contrasted to the state, is linked to the middle class, to effective public opinion, and to individualist values, and it occupies a space between the self-interested individual and the formal institutions of the state.

How does civil society figure in Russia? Recent historians of the French revolution have connected the topic to private life and everyday existence, and many of the Russian scholars in this book follow that lead. Can we say, then, that Russia will emulate the West in creating the civil society that is vital to the rise of democracy and a market economy? In seeking an answer to this question, one must ask whether a real middle class exists, or is emerging, in Russia. Was the opposition to the decaying Soviet state actually led by voluntary associations such as ecological groups, rock bands, and soccer clubs? In short, the term "civil society" must itself be deconstructed.

* * *

One last topic needs to be singled out: the intelligentsia and its role in Russian culture. If I correctly read the authors who have contributed to this book, they appear to be announcing the end of the intelligentsia. The striking fact is that many of those who are forecasting the intelligentsia's demise themselves belong to this doomed class. There is a terrible poignancy to their analysis.

The Russian intelligentsia appears to be unique, set off from what elsewhere are mere intellectuals, as, say, in France. Both groups, Russian and French, have had enormous moral power in their societies (in sharp contrast to the role played by intellectuals in the United States). The difference seems to be that the Russian intelligentsia, denied proper parliamentary and political outlets, historically defined itself either in opposition to or support of the state. Intellectuals in France, by contrast, have defined themselves primarily in opposition to the middle class and its "philistine" culture, conveniently accepting the fact that the bourgeois culture and state tolerate their criticism. This is not to gainsay that Russian intellectuals remained critical of capitalist culture, but this critique was directed primarily at the West. Philistinism in Russia proper was supposed to be short-lived, yielding to a new culture, shorn of the narrow concerns of a full-blown capitalist economy and society.

In any case, the Russian intelligentsia shared with both tsarist and Soviet hierarchies the belief that policy and guidance were to be handed down from on high. In a new "democratizing" Russia, the intelligentsia's position has become shaky as the market-based economy increasingly has undermined its members' primary source of livelihood. It seems that the new "moral economy" has rendered the intelligentsia's role dispensable. Not all-purpose intellectuals but experts and professionals are needed to reform state and society. The thinking in abstract philosophical or Aesopian-metaphoric terms that once distinguished a Russian intellectual is no longer necessary or sufficient. "Double-think" is out of style, but then so is the moral and intellectual schizophrenia that it bred.

Many observers have commented on the fact that the breakdown of communist systems in Russia and Eastern Europe failed to rekindle any idealistic dreams. At best, there is a belief in a Friedman-like Chicago

School economy and the pursuit of private gain. Otherwise, there is a vacuum of faith, now increasingly filled with ethnic and national sentiments. It is a mistake, I believe, for Westerners to view former communists who turn to nationalism as solely engaged in a cynical act. They may also be obeying nature's injunction against vacuums; in this case, the vacuum is a spiritual one.

Meanwhile, new voices have been making themselves heard in post-Soviet society. Television and soap operas have been competing successfully with serious newspapers and literary works in promoting a new morality. Are we observing a new Russian culture in the making or is it simply that the old wine is being poured into new bottles? How will so-called mass culture and the high culture of the fading intelligentsia mesh, or clash? Only time will tell, although time seems to be running out for the intelligentsia.

The intelligentsia as a social group may be in its death throes, but its individual members are very much alive. Many of them, including some writing in this volume, tormented by their own ambivalence about their past involvement in Russia's culture, are able to give us extraordinary glimpses into the struggle for the Russian spirit that has gone on in the pre-Soviet, Soviet, and post-Soviet eras. These individuals are our guides in the journey that the former Soviet Union is taking into a contested future, where democracy and a new form of capitalism may be more a hope than a reality. *Russian Culture at the Crossroads* is admirable in its authors' valiant attempts to convey a sense of a lived reality and to offer a panoramic view of the Russian cultural past, present, and future.

Notes

1. Charles Maier, "Why Did Communism Collapse in 1989?" *History Workshop* (Spring 1991).

About the Book
and Editor

During the waning years of Soviet power, glasnost laid bare the distress of people trapped in a system they despised but felt powerless to change. The reexamination of values that began then continues today in the search for a new Russian culture, one rooted in the pre-Soviet past but dynamic and evolving, enabling Russians to meet the challenges they face in the contemporary world.

Multi-textual, polyphonic, and contradictory, the current Russian cultural discourse is richly reflected in these essays by a diverse group of authors from Russian and American academic and cultural circles. Each chapter focuses on a particular cultural domain, surveying the historical origins of Russian beliefs and behaviors, exploring their Soviet and post-Soviet permutations, and highlighting the range of choices that Russians are facing at this critical juncture. The decisions they make will shape their society and culture for generations to come.

Illuminating the universal significance of the Soviet experience, this volume raises provocative questions about the social, political, and economic sources of cultural change.

Dmitri N. Shalin is associate professor of sociology and head of the program in Russian and East-Central European studies at University of Nevada–Las Vegas. He is editor of *Self in Crises: The Self and Postmodern Condition* and of *Habermas, Pragmatism and Critical Theory*.

About the Contributors

Zara Abdullaeva is an editor and commentator for various publications on the Russian cinema. She is the author of *Vne igry: Oleg Yankovsky v teatre ikino* [Out of Play: Oleg Yankovsky in theatre and Cinema]. She lives and works in Moscow.

Svetlana Boym is professor of Slavic and comparative literatures at Harvard University. She is the author of two books, *Common Places: Mythologies of Everyday Life in Russia* and *Death in Quotation Marks: Cultural Myths of the Modern Poet*, and of the play *The Woman Who Shot Lenin*.

Daniil B. Dondurei is a research fellow at the National Institute for Cinema Art in Moscow. He has published more than one hundred articles on cinema, fine art, and culture in Russia.

Alexander M. Etkind is a professor at the Institute of Psychoanalysis in St. Petersburg and senior researcher at the Institute of Sociology, Russian Academy of Sciences. He is the author of *Eros nevozmozhnogo: Istoriia psikhoanaliza v Rossii* [Eros of the Impossible: The Story of Psychoanalysis in Russia] (English edition forthcoming from Westview).

Maurice Friedberg is professor of Slavic languages and literatures in the Center for Advanced Study at the University of Illinois–Urbana-Champaign. He is the author of *Russian Classics in Soviet Jackets; A Decade of Euphoria: Western Literature in Post-Stalin Russia; Russian Culture in the 1980s;* and, most recently, *How Things Were Done in Odessa: Cultural and Intellectual Pursuits in a Soviet City* (Westview, 1991).

Igor S. Kon is a senior fellow at the Institute of Ethnography, Russian Academy of Sciences. He is the author of over twenty books, most recently *The Sexual Revolution in Russia: From the Age of the Czars to Today*.

Yuri A. Levada is professor of sociology and head of the National Center for Public Opinion Research in Moscow. He is the author most recently of *Sovetsky prostoi chelovek: Opyt sotsialnogo portreta na rubezhe 90x*.

Vladimir S. Magun is senior research associate at the Institute of Sociology, Russian Academy of Sciences. He is the author of *Potrebnosti lichnosti i psikhologiia sotsialnoi deiatelnosti* [Personality Needs and Psychology of Social Activity].

Bruce Mazlish is professor of history at Massachusetts Institute of Technology and the editor, with Ralph Buultjens, of *Conceptualizing Global History* (Westview, 1993). He is the author of several books.

Jerry G. Pankhurst is associate professor and chair of sociology at Wittenberg University. He is editor, with Michael Paul Sacks, of *Understanding Soviet Society* and of *Contemporary Soviet Society: Sociological Perspectives*.

Boris M. Paramonov is a professor of philosophy and a senior commentator for Radio Free Europe/Radio Liberty. He is the author of hundreds of articles, a member of the *Zvezda* editorial board, and author of *A Portrait of a Jew*.

Frederick Starr is president of the Aspen Institute and author of *Red and Hot: The Fate of Jazz in the Soviet Union, 1917–1991* and *The Legacy of History in Russia and the New States of Eurasia*.

Index